Fourth Edition

Sentence Skills
with Readings

Fourth Edition

Sentence Skills
with Readings

John Langan
Atlantic Cape Community College

Paul Langan

 Higher Education

Boston   Burr Ridge, IL   Dubuque, IA   New York   San Francisco   St. Louis
Bangkok   Bogotá   Caracas   Kuala Lumpur   Lisbon   London   Madrid   Mexico City
Milan   Montreal   New Delhi   Santiago   Seoul   Singapore   Sydney   Taipei   Toronto

 **Higher Education**

Published by McGraw-Hill, an imprint of The McGraw-Hill Companies, Inc., 1221 Avenue of the Americas, New York, NY 10020. Copyright © 2010, 2005, 2001, 1997. All rights reserved. No part of this publication may be reproduced or distributed in any form or by any means, or stored in a database or retrieval system, without the prior written consent of The McGraw-Hill Companies, Inc., including, but not limited to, in any network or other electronic storage or transmission, or broadcast for distance learning.

This book is printed on acid-free paper.

3 4 5 6 7 8 9 0 DOC/DOC 0 9

Student Edition
ISBN: 978-0-07-353326-1
MHID: 0-07-353326-2

Instructor's Edition
ISBN: 978-0-07-723740-0
MHID: 0-07-723740-4

Editor in Chief: *Michael Ryan*
Publisher: *David Patterson*
Sponsoring Editor: *John Kindler*
Marketing Manager: *Allison Jones*
Developmental Editor: *Jesse Hassenger*
Project Manager: *Lori Hazzard,*
    Macmillan Publishing Solutions

Cover Designer: *Preston Thomas*
Production Supervisor: *Tandra Jorgensen*
Media Project Manager: *Ronald Nelms, Jr.*
Composition: *11/13 Times Roman*
    by Macmillan Publishing Solutions
Printing: *45# New Era Matte by R. R. Donnelley*

Credits appear on page 678 and constitute an extension of the copyright page.

Library of Congress Cataloging-in-Publication Data

Langan, John, 1942–
  Sentence skills with readings / John Langan. -- 4th ed.
     p. cm.
  Includes bibliographical references and index.
  ISBN-13: 978-0-07-353326-1 (alk. paper)
  ISBN-10: 0-07-353326-2 (alk. paper)
  1. English language--Sentences--Problems, exercises, etc. 2. English language--Rhetoric--Problems, exercises, etc. 3. English language--Grammar--Problems, exercises, etc. 4. Report writing--Problems, exercises, etc. 5. College readers. I. Title.
  PE1441.L356 2009
  808'.0427--dc22

                                             2008049421

The Internet addresses listed in the text were accurate at the time of publication. The inclusion of a Web site does not indicate an endorsement by the authors or McGraw-Hill, and McGraw-Hill does not guarantee the accuracy of the information presented at these sites.

www.mhhe.com

Praise for *Sentence Skills*

"I would describe the text as very useful, adaptable and current. It can meet a number of needs within today's classrooms. The descriptive language works for audio-visual generations that continue to fill our classrooms. I like the tone, style and level of the text."
—Terry Clark, Kennedy-King College

"A well-defined, viable resource for teaching and learning the basic fundamentals of grammar and writing in any mode of instruction."
—Judy Covington, Trident Technical College

"Three major strengths are the clear writing style, excellent organization, and number and variety of activities and assignments."
—Pamela Hudson, Hawaii Community College

"Sentence Skills with Readings is a comprehensive, approachable text. The book successfully reminds readers that clear, effective sentences lead to clear, effective writing and that the ability to achieve such a level of sentence skills is critical to success in college, at work, and in everyday life."
—Lisa Schultz, Moraine Valley Community College

"I come back to Langan's work because of his easy-going, accessible, student-friendly, clear style and tone. His breakdown of writing into the four bases is the clearest I have found anywhere."
—Syd Bartman, Mt. San Antonio College

"Because it is so complete, Sentence Skills with Readings is perfect for the new teacher, or one who has just been assigned to a class. The seasoned teacher will enjoy the many features of the text and still have room to customize his or her class."
—G. Jack Pond, Leeward Community College

About the Authors

John Langan has taught and authored books on writing and reading skills for over thirty years. Before teaching, he earned advanced degrees in writing at Rutgers University and in reading at Rowan University. John now lives with his wife, Judith Nadell, near Philadelphia. In addition to his wife and Philly sports teams, his passions include reading and turning nonreaders on to the pleasure and power of books. Through Townsend Press, his educational publishing company, he has developed the nonprofit "Townsend Library"—a collection of more than seventy new and classic stories with wide appeal to readers of all ages.

Paul Langan has tutored adult students in basic reading and writing skills since he was a college undergraduate. Beginning as a community college student, he went on to graduate with honors from La Salle University and later earned a Master's Degree in reading, writing, and literacy from the University of Pennsylvania. In addition to editing and authoring a popular series of young adult novels, Paul has taught composition at Camden County College. A husband and father, he lives "a stone's throw" from Philadelphia and recently had a long-term hope fulfilled when the Phillies finally won the World Series.

Contents

PART 3: Reinforcement of the Skills   454

PART 4: Readings for Writing   522

APPENDIXES   614

To the Instructor

Key Features of the Book

Sentence Skills with Readings will help students learn to write effectively. It is an all-in-one text that includes basic rhetoric and gives full attention to grammar, punctuation, mechanics, and usage.

The book contains ten distinctive features to aid instructors and their students:

1. **Coverage of basic writing skills is exceptionally thorough.**

   The book pays special attention to fragments, run-ons, verbs, and other areas where students have serious problems. At the same time, a glance at the table of contents shows that the book treats skills (such as dictionary use and spelling improvement) not found in most other texts. In addition, parts of the book are devoted to the basics of effective writing, to practice in editing and proofreading, and to strategies for achieving variety in sentences.

2. **The book has a clear and flexible format.**

   It is organized in three easy-to-use parts. Part One is a guide to the goals of effective writing followed by a series of activities to help students practice and master those goals. Part Two is a comprehensive treatment of the rules of grammar, mechanics, punctuation, and usage needed for clear writing. Part Three provides a series of combined mastery, editing, and proofreading tests to reinforce the sentence skills presented in Part Two.

   Since parts, sections, and chapters are self-contained, instructors can move easily from, for instance, a rhetorical principle in Part One to a grammar rule in Part Two to a combined mastery test in Part Three.

3. **Opening chapters deal with the writer's attitude, writing as a process, and the importance of specific details in writing.**

   In its opening pages, the book helps students recognize and deal with their attitude toward writing—an important part of learning to write well. In the pages that follow, students are encouraged to see writing as a multistage process that moves from prewriting to proofreading. Later, a series of activities helps students understand the nature of specific details and how to generate and use those

- *The Merriam-Webster Dictionary* **(0-07-310057-9)**: Based on the best-selling *Merriam-Webster's Collegiate Dictionary,* it contains over 70,000 definitions.
- *The Merriam-Webster's Thesaurus* **(0-07-310067-6)**: This handy paperback thesaurus contains over 157,000 synonyms, antonyms, related and contrasted words, and idioms.
- *Merriam-Webster's Vocabulary Builder* **(0-07-310069-2)**: Introduces 3,000 words and includes quizzes to test progress.
- *Merriam-Webster's Notebook Dictionary* **(0-07-299091-0)**: This popular dictionary provides an extremely concise reference to the words that form the core of the English vocabulary and is conveniently designed for three-ring binders; it provides words and information at students' fingertips.
- *Merriam-Webster's Notebook Thesaurus* **(0-07-310068-4)**: Designed for three-ring binders and helps students search for words they might need today. It provides concise, clear guidance for over 157,000 word choices.
- *Merriam-Webster's Collegiate Dictionary and Thesaurus, Electronic Edition* **(0-07-310070-6)**: Available on CD-ROM, this online dictionary contains thousands of new words and meanings from all areas of human endeavor, including electronic technology, the sciences, and popular culture.

Contact your local McGraw-Hill representative or consult McGraw-Hill's Web site at **www.mhhe.com/english** for more information on the supplements that accompany *Sentence Skills with Readings 4th Edition.* You may also send an e-mail to **langan@mcgraw-hill.com**.

Acknowledgments

Reviewers who have contributed to this edition through their helpful comments include

Lindy Atoms, *Sierra College*

Sydney Bartman, *Mt. San Antonio College*

Craig Barto, *Charleston Southern University*

David Rask Behling, *Waldorf College*

E. Ferol Benavides, *Anne Arundel Community College*

Milton Bentley, *Central Georgia Technical College*

Andrew Cavanaugh, *University of Maryland University College*

Terry Clark, *Kennedy-King College*

Judy Covington, *Trident Technical College*

Stephanie Bechtel Gooding, *University of Maryland University College - Europe*

Pamela Hudson, *Hawaii Community College*

Valere Hull, *Oklahoma State University*

Julie Kissel, *Washtenaw Community College*

Daniel Lanelle, *Georgia Highlands College*

Jaque Lyman, *Anne Arundel Community College*

Jamie Moore, *Maricopa Community College*

Lisa Moreno, *Los Angeles Trade Technical College*

Debbie Naquin, *Northern Virginia Community College*

Lisa Schultz, *Moraine Valley Community College*

Dennis Tettelbach, *University of Maryland University College*

Dennielle True, *Manatee Community College*

Maria Villar-Smith, *Miami Dade College*

Arnold Wood Jr., *Florida Community College at Jacksonville*

I owe thanks as well for the support provided by John Kindler and Aaron Zook at McGraw-Hill. My gratitude also goes to Paul Langan, who has helped this book become even more student-friendly than it was before.

Joyce Stern, Assistant Professor at Nassau Community College, contributed the ESL Tips to the Annotated Instructor's Edition. Professor Stern is also Assistant to the Chair in the department of Reading and Basic Education. An educator for over thirty years, she holds an advanced degree in TESOL from Hunter College, as well as a New York State Teaching Certificate in TESOL. She is currently coordinating the design, implementation, and recruitment of learning communities for both ESL and developmental students at Nassau Community College and has been recognized by the college's Center for Students with Disabilities for her dedication to student learning.

Donna T. Matsumoto, Assistant Professor of English and the Writing Discipline Coordinator at Leeward Community College in Hawaii (Pear City), wrote the Teaching Tips for the Annotated Instructor's Edition. Professor Matsumoto has taught writing, women's studies, and American studies for a number of years throughout the University of Hawaii system, at Hawaii Pacific University, and in community schools for adults. She received a 2005 WebCT Exemplary Course Project award for her online writing course and is the author of McGraw-Hill's *The Virtual Workbook,* an online workbook featuring interactive activities and exercises.

John Langan

Fourth Edition

Sentence Skills
with Readings

PART 1

Effective Writing

Introduction

Part One is a guide to the goals of effective writing and includes a series of activities to help you practice and master these goals. Begin with the introductory chapter, which makes clear the reasons for learning sentence skills. Then move on to Chapter 2, which presents all the essentials you need to know to become an effective writer. You will be introduced to the four goals of effective writing and will work through a series of activities designed to strengthen your understanding of these goals. Finally, walk through the steps of the writing process—from prewriting to proofreading—in Chapter 3. Examples and activities are provided to illustrate each step, and after completing the activities, you'll be ready to take on the paragraph writing assignments at the end of the chapter.

At the same time that you are writing papers, start working through the sentence skills in Parts Two and Three of the book. Practicing the sentence skills in the context of actual writing assignments is the surest way to master the rules of grammar, mechanics, punctuation, and usage.

Can you think of other careers, besides the one pictured here, in which good written communication skills are required? Why do you think writing is important to so many different types of careers?

Learning Sentence Skills

1

Why Learn Sentence Skills?

Why should someone planning a career as a nurse have to learn sentence skills? Why should an accounting major have to pass a competency test in grammar as part of a college education? Why should a potential physical therapist or graphic artist or computer programmer have to spend hours on the rules of English? Perhaps you are asking questions like these after finding yourself in a class with this book. On the other hand, perhaps you *know* you need to strengthen basic writing skills, even though you may be unclear about the specific ways the skills will be of use to you. Whatever your views, you should understand why sentence skills—all the rules that make up standard English—are so important.

Clear Communication

Standard English, or "language by the book," is needed to communicate your thoughts to others with a minimal amount of distortion and misinterpretation. Knowing the traditional rules of grammar, punctuation, and usage will help you write clear sentences when communicating with others. You may have heard of the party game in which one person whispers a message to the next person; the message is passed, in turn, along a line of several other people. By the time the last person in line is asked to give the message aloud, it is usually so garbled and inaccurate that it barely resembles the original. Written communication in some form of English other than standard English carries the same potential for disaster.

To see how important standard English is to written communication, examine the pairs of sentences on the following pages and answer the questions in each case.

1. Which sentence indicates that there might be a plot against Ted?
   a. We should leave Ted. These fumes might be poisonous.
   b. We should leave, Ted. These fumes might be poisonous.

2. Which sentence encourages self-mutilation?
   a. Leave your paper and hand in the dissecting kit.
   b. Leave your paper, and hand in the dissecting kit.

3. Which sentence indicates that the writer has a weak grasp of geography?
   a. As a child, I lived in Lake Worth, which is close to Palm Beach and Alaska.
   b. As a child, I lived in Lake Worth, which is close to Palm Beach, and Alaska.

4. In which sentence does the dog warden seem dangerous?
   a. Foaming at the mouth, the dog warden picked up the stray.
   b. Foaming at the mouth, the stray was picked up by the dog warden.

5. Which announcer was probably fired from the job?
   a. Outside the Academy Awards theater, the announcer called the guests names as they arrived.
   b. Outside the Academy Awards theater, the announcer called the guests' names as they arrived.

6. Below are the opening lines of two students' exam essays. Which student seems likely to earn a higher grade?
   a. Defense mechanisms is the way people hides their inner feelings and deals with stress. There is several types that we use to be protecting our true feelings.
   b. Defense mechanisms are the methods people use to cope with stress. Using a defense mechanism allows a person to hide his or her real desires and goals.

7. The following lines are taken from two English papers. Which student seems likely to earn a higher grade?
   a. A big problem on this campus is apathy, students don't participate in college activities. Such as clubs, student government, and plays.
   b. The most pressing problem on campus is the disgraceful state of the student lounge area. The floor is dirty, the chairs are torn, and the ceiling leaks.

continued

8. The following sentences are taken from reports by two employees. Which worker is more likely to be promoted?
    a. The spring line failed by 20 percent in the meeting of projected profit expectations. Which were issued in January of this year.
    b. Profits from our spring line were disappointing. They fell 20 percent short of January's predictions.

9. The following paragraphs are taken from two job application letters. Which applicant would you favor?
    a. Let me say in closing that their are an array of personal qualities I have presented in this letter, together, these make me hopeful of being interviewed for this attraktive position.

        sincerely yours'

        Brian Davis
    b. I feel I have the qualifications needed to do an excellent job as assistant manager of the jewelry department at Horton's. I look forward to discussing the position further at a personal interview.

        Sincerely yours,

        Richard O'Keeney

In each case, the first choice (*a*) contains sentence-skills mistakes. These mistakes include missing or misplaced commas, misspellings, and wordy or pretentious language. As a result of such mistakes, clear communication cannot occur—and misunderstandings, lower grades, and missed job opportunities are probable results. The point, then, is that all the rules that make up standard written English should be a priority if you want your writing to be clear and effective.

Success in College

Standard English is essential if you want to succeed in college. Any report, paper, review, essay exam, or assignment you are responsible for should be written in the best standard English you can produce. If you don't do this, it won't matter how fine your ideas are or how hard you worked—most likely, you will receive a lower grade than you would otherwise deserve. In addition, because standard English requires you to express your thoughts in precise, clear sentences, training yourself to follow the rules can help you think more logically. The basic logic you learn to practice at the sentence level will help as you work to produce well-reasoned papers in all your subjects.

Success at Work

Knowing standard English will also help you achieve success on the job. Studies have found repeatedly that skillful communication, more than any other factor, is the key to job satisfaction and steady progress in a career. A solid understanding of standard English is a basic part of this vital ability to communicate. Moreover, most experts agree that we are now living in an "age of information"—a time when people who use language skillfully have a great advantage over those who do not. Fewer of us will be working in factories or at other types of manual labor. Many more of us will be working with information in various forms—accumulating it, processing it, analyzing it. No matter what kind of job you are preparing yourself for, technical or not, you will need to know standard English to keep pace with this new age. Otherwise, you are likely to be left behind, limited to low-paying jobs that offer few challenges or financial rewards.

"First off, there's no 'y' in resume . . ."

Success in Everyday Life

Standard English will help you succeed not just at school and work but in everyday life as well. It will help you feel more comfortable, for example, in writing letters to friends and relatives. It will enable you to write effective notes to your children's schools. It will help you get action when you write a letter of complaint to a company about a product. It will allow you to write letters inquiring about bills—hospital, medical, utility, or legal—or about any kind of service. To put it simply, in our daily lives, those who can use and write standard English have more power than those who cannot.

Your Attitude toward Writing

Your attitude toward writing is an important part of learning to write well. To get a sense of just how you feel about writing, read the following statements. Put a check beside those statements with which you agree. (This activity is not a test, so try to be as honest as possible.)

_____ 1. A good writer should be able to sit down and write a paper straight through without stopping.

_____ 2. Writing is a skill that anyone can learn with practice.

——————   3. I'll never be good at writing because I make too many mistakes in spelling, grammar, and punctuation.

——————   4. Because I dislike writing, I always start a paper at the last possible minute.

——————   5. I've always done poorly in English, and I don't expect that to change now.

Now read the following comments about these five statements. The comments will help you see if your attitude is hurting or helping your efforts to become a better writer.

1. **A good writer should be able to sit down and write a paper straight through without stopping.**

   The statement is *false*. Writing is, in fact, a process. It is done not in one easy step but in a series of steps, and seldom at one sitting. If you cannot do a paper all at once, you are like most of the other people on the planet. It is harmful to carry around the false idea that writing should be an easy matter.

2. **Writing is a skill that anyone can learn with practice.**

   This statement is *absolutely true*. Writing is a skill, like driving or cooking, that you can master with hard work. If you want to learn to write, you can. It is as simple as that. If you believe this, you are ready to learn how to become a competent writer.

   Some people hold the false belief that writing is a natural gift that some have and others do not. Because of this belief, they never make a truly honest effort to learn to write—and so they never learn.

3. **I'll never be good at writing, because I make too many mistakes in spelling, grammar, and punctuation.**

   The first concern in good writing should be *content*—what you have to say. Your ideas and feelings are what matter most. You should not worry about spelling, grammar, and punctuation while working on content.

   Unfortunately, some people are so self-conscious about making mistakes that they do not focus on what they want to say. They need to realize that a paper is best done in stages and that the rules can and should wait until a later stage in the writing process. Through review and practice, you will eventually learn how to follow the rules with confidence.

4. **Because I dislike writing, I always start a paper at the last possible minute.**

   This practice is all too common. You feel you are *going to* do poorly, and then your behavior ensures that you *will* do poorly! Your attitude is so negative that you defeat yourself—not even allowing enough time to really try.

Again, what you need to realize is that writing is a process. Because it is done in steps, you don't have to get it right all at once. Just get started well in advance. If you allow yourself enough time, you'll find a way to make a paper come together.

5. **I've always done poorly in English, and I don't expect that to change now.**

How you may have performed in the *past* does not control how you can perform in the *present*. Even if you did poorly in English in high school, it is in your power to make this one of your best subjects in college. If you believe writing can be learned, and if you work hard at it, you *will* become a better writer.

In brief, your attitude is crucial. If you believe you are a poor writer and always will be, chances are you will not improve. If you realize you can become a better writer, chances are you will improve. Depending on how you allow yourself to think, you can be your own best friend or your own worst enemy.

How This Book Is Organized

- A good way to get a quick sense of any book is to turn to the table of contents. By referring to the Contents pages, you will see that the book is organized into three basic parts. What are they?

  Part One: Effective Writing

  Part Two: Sentence Skills

  Part Three: Reinforcement of the Skills

- In Part One, the final section of Chapter 3 includes activities in *the writing process*.

- Part Two deals with sentence skills. The first section is "Sentences." How many sections (skills areas) are covered in all? *five*

- Part Three reinforces the skills presented in Part Two. What are the three kinds of reinforcement activities in Part Three?

  Combined Mastery Tests

  Editing and Proofreading Tests

  Combined Editing Tests

- Helpful charts in the book include the *checklist of sentence skills* on the inside back cover.

- Finally, the six appendixes at the end of the book are:

  (A) How a Computer Can Help, (B) Parts of Speech,

  (C) ESL Pointers, (D) Sentence-Skills Diagnostic Test,

  (E) Sentence-Skills Achievement Test,

  (F) Answers to Introductory Activities and Practice Exercises.

How to Use This Book

First, read and work through Part One, Effective Writing—a guide to the goals of effective writing followed by a series of activities to help you practice and master these goals. Your instructor may direct you to certain activities, depending on your needs.

Second, take the diagnostic test on pages 647–653. By analyzing which sections of the test give you trouble, you will discover which skills you need to concentrate on. When you turn to an individual skill in Part Two, begin by reading and thinking about the introductory activity. Often, you will be pleasantly surprised to find that you know more about this area of English than you thought you did. After all, you have probably been speaking English with fluency and ease for many years; you have an instinctive knowledge of how the language works. This knowledge gives you a solid base for refining your skills.

Your third step is to work on the skills in Part Two by reading the explanations and completing the practices. You can check your answers to each practice activity in this part by turning to the answer key at the back of the book (Appendix F). Try to figure out *why* you got some answers wrong—you want to uncover any weak spots in your understanding.

Your next step is to use the review tests and mastery tests at the end of each chapter in Part Two to evaluate your understanding of a skill in its entirety. Your instructor may also ask you to take the other reinforcement tests in Part Three of the book. To help ensure that you take the time needed to learn each skill thoroughly, the answers to these tests are *not* in the answer key.

The emphasis in this book is on writing clear, error-free sentences. The heart of the book is practice material that helps reinforce the sentence skills you learn. A great deal of effort has been taken to make the practices lively and engaging and to avoid the dull, repetitive skills work that has given grammar books such a bad reputation. This text will help you stay interested as you work on the rules of English that you need to learn. The rest is a matter of your personal determination and hard work. If you decide—and only you can decide—that effective writing is important to your school and career goals and that you want to learn the basic skills needed to write clearly and effectively, this book will help you reach those goals.

A Brief Guide to Effective Writing

2

This chapter and Chapter 3 will show you how to write effective paragraphs. The following questions will be answered in turn:

1. What is a paragraph?

2. What are the goals of effective writing?

3. How do you reach the goals of effective writing?

What Is a Paragraph?

A *paragraph* is a series of sentences about one main idea, or *point*. A paragraph typically starts with a point, and the rest of the paragraph provides specific details to support and develop that point.

Consider the following paragraph, written by a student named Gary Callahan.

www.mhhe.com/langan

Returning to School

Starting college at age twenty-nine was difficult. For one thing, I did not have much support from my parents and friends. My father asked, "Didn't you get dumped on enough in high school? Why go back for more?" My mother worried about where the money would come from. My friends seemed threatened. "Hey, there's the college man," they would say when they saw me. Another reason that starting college was hard was that I had bad memories of school. I had spent years of my life sitting in classrooms completely bored, watching clocks tick ever so slowly toward the final bell. When I was not bored, I was afraid of being embarrassed. Once a teacher called on me and then said, "Ah,

---

continued

forget it, Callahan," when he realized I did not know the answer. Finally, I soon learned that college would give me little time with my family. After work every day, I have just an hour and ten minutes to eat and spend time with my wife and daughter before going off to class. When I get back, my daughter is in bed, and my wife and I have only a little time together. Then the weekends go by quickly, with all the homework I have to do. But I am going to persist because I believe a better life awaits me with a college degree.

The preceding paragraph, like many effective paragraphs, starts by stating a main idea, or point. A *point* is a general idea that contains an opinion. In this case, the point is that starting college at age twenty-nine was not easy.

In our everyday lives, we constantly make points about all kinds of matters. We express all kinds of opinions: "That was a terrible movie." "My psychology instructor is the best teacher I have ever had." "My sister is a generous person." "Eating at that restaurant was a mistake." "That team should win the playoff game." "Waitressing is the worst job I ever had." "Our state should allow the death penalty." "Cigarette smoking should be banned everywhere." In *talking* to people, we don't always give the reasons for our opinions. But in *writing,* we *must* provide reasons to support our ideas. Only by supplying solid evidence for any point that we make can we communicate effectively with readers.

An effective paragraph, then, must not only make a point but also support it with *specific evidence*—reasons, examples, and other details. Such specifics help prove to readers that the point is reasonable. Even if readers do not agree with the writer, at least they have in front of them the evidence on which the writer has based his or her opinion. Readers are like juries; they want to see the evidence so that they can make their own judgments.

Take a moment now to examine the evidence that Gary has provided to back up his point about starting college at twenty-nine. Complete the following outline of Gary's paragraph by summarizing in a few words his reasons and the details that develop them. The first reason and its supporting details are summarized for you as an example.

POINT: Starting college at age twenty-nine was difficult.

REASON 1: *Little support from parents and friends*

DETAILS THAT DEVELOP REASON 1: *Father asked why I wanted to be dumped on again, mother worried about tuition money, friends seemed threatened*

REASON **2:** _____

DETAILS THAT DEVELOP REASON **2:** _____

REASON **3:** _____

DETAILS THAT DEVELOP REASON **3:** _____

_____

_____

As the outline makes clear, Gary provides three reasons to support his point about starting college at twenty-nine: (1) he had little support from his friends or parents, (2) he had bad memories of school, and (3) college left him little time with his family. Gary also provides vivid details to back up each of his three reasons. His reasons and descriptive details enable readers to see why he feels that starting college at twenty-nine was difficult.

To write an effective paragraph, then, aim to do what Gary has done: begin by making a point, and then go on to support that point with specific evidence. Finally, like Gary, end your paper with a sentence that rounds off the paragraph and provides a sense of completion.

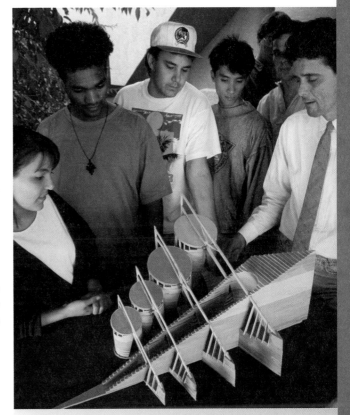

If you were to write a paragraph about the reasons why you are in college, what point would you begin your paper with and what three reasons would you provide to support that point?

The Goals of Effective Writing

Now that you have considered an effective student paragraph, it is time to look at four goals of effective writing.

Goal 1: Make a Point

It is often best to state your point in the first sentence of your paper, just as Gary does in his paragraph about returning to school. The sentence that expresses the main idea, or point, of a paragraph is called the *topic sentence.* Your paper will be unified if you make sure that all the details support the point in your topic sentence. Activities on pages 15–18 will help you learn how to write a topic sentence.

Goal 2: Support the Point

To support your point, you need to provide specific reasons, examples, and other details that explain and develop it. The more precise and particular your supporting details are, the better your readers can "see," "hear," and "feel" them. The activities on pages 18–35 will help you learn how to be specific in your writing.

Goal 3: Organize the Support

You will find it helpful to learn two common ways of organizing support in a paragraph—*listing order* and *time order.* You should also learn the signal words, known as *transitions,* that increase the effectiveness of each method. The activities on pages 39–42 will give you practice in the use of listing order and time order, as well as transitions, to organize the supporting details of a paragraph.

Goal 4: Write Error-Free Sentences

If you use correct spelling and follow the rules of grammar, punctuation, and usage, your sentences will be clear and well written. But by no means must you have all that information in your head. Even the best of writers need to use reference materials to be sure their writing is correct. So when you write your papers, keep a good dictionary and grammar handbook nearby (you can use Part Two of this book).

In general, however, save them for after you've gotten your ideas firmly down in writing. You'll see in the next part of this guide that Gary made a number of sentence errors as he worked on his paragraph. But he simply ignored them until he got to a later draft of his paper, when there would be time enough to make the needed corrections.

Activities in the Goals of Effective Writing

The following series of activities will strengthen your understanding of the four goals of effective writing and how to reach those goals. The practice will also help you prepare for the demands of your college classes.

Your instructor may ask you to do the entire series of activities or may select those activities most suited to your particular needs.

www.mhhe.com/langan

Activities in Goal 1: Make a Point

Effective writing advances a point, or main idea, in a general statement known as the *topic sentence*. Other sentences in the paragraph provide specific support for the topic sentence.

The activities in this section will give you practice in the following:

- Identifying the Point
- Understanding the Topic Sentence
- Identifying Topics, Topic Sentences, and Support

Identifying the Point

Each group of sentences below could be written as a short paragraph. Circle the letter of the topic sentence in each case. To find the topic sentence, ask yourself, "Which is a general statement supported by the specific details in the other three statements?"

Begin by trying the example below. First circle the letter of the sentence you think expresses the main idea. Then read the explanation.

Activity

1

EXAMPLE

 a. Newspapers are a good source of local, national, and world news.

 b. The cartoons and crossword puzzles in newspapers are entertaining.

 c. Newspapers have a lot to offer.

 d. Newspapers often include coupons worth far more than the cost of the paper.

> **EXPLANATION**   Sentence *a* explains one important benefit of newspapers. Sentences *b* and *d* provide other specific advantages of newspapers. In sentence *c,* however, no one specific benefit is explained. Instead, the words "a lot to offer" refer only generally to such benefits. Therefore sentence *c* is the topic sentence; it expresses the main idea. The other sentences support that idea by providing examples.

1. a. Even when Food City is crowded, there are only two cash registers open.
    b. The frozen foods are often partially thawed.
    c. I will never shop at Food City again.
    d. The market is usually out of sale items within a few hours.

2. a. Buy only clothes that will match what's already in your closet.
    b. To be sure you're getting the best price, shop in a number of stores before buying.
    c. Avoid trendy clothes; buy basic pieces that never go out of style.
    d. By following a few simple rules, you can have nice clothes without spending a fortune.

3. a. Once my son said a vase jumped off the shelf by itself.
    b. When my son breaks something, he always has an excuse.
    c. He claimed that my three-month-old daughter climbed out of her crib and knocked a glass over.
    d. Another time, he said an earthquake must have caused a mirror to crack.

4. a. Mars should be the first planet explored by astronauts.
    b. Astronauts could mine Mars for aluminum, magnesium, and iron.
    c. The huge volcano on Mars would be fascinating to study.
    d. Since Mars is close to Earth, we might want to have colonies there one day.

5. a. Instead of talking on the telephone, we send text messages.
    b. People rarely talk to one another these days.
    c. Rather than talking with family members, we sit silently in front of our TV sets all evening.
    d. In cars, we ignore our traveling companions to listen to the radio.

Understanding the Topic Sentence

As already explained, most paragraphs center on a main idea, which is often expressed in a topic sentence. An effective topic sentence does two things. First, it presents the topic of the paragraph. Second, it expresses the writer's attitude or opinion or idea about the topic. For example, look at the following topic sentence:

> *Professional athletes are overpaid.*

In the topic sentence, the topic is *professional athletes;* the writer's idea about the topic is that professional athletes *are overpaid.*

For each topic sentence that follows, underline the topic and double-underline the point of view that the writer takes toward the topic.

EXAMPLES

<u>Living in a small town</u> <u>has many advantages.</u>

<u>Talking on a cell phone while driving</u> <u>should be banned in every state.</u>

1. College textbooks are very expensive.

2. Cat owners and dog owners are two different types of people.

3. Public speaking is terrifying to many people.

4. The best things in life are free.

5. Disasters often bring out the best in people.

6. Serving on a jury can be an educational experience.

7. Our landlord is a strange man.

8. Loud car stereos should be made illegal.

9. The food in the cafeteria is unfit for humans to eat.

10. Divorce is not always the right answer to marriage problems.

Identifying Topics, Topic Sentences, and Support

The following activity will sharpen your sense of the differences between topics, topic sentences, and supporting sentences. Each group of items below includes one topic, one main idea (expressed in a topic sentence), and two supporting details for that idea. In the space provided, label each item with one of the following:

> *T* — topic
> *MI* — main idea
> *SD* — supporting details

1. _____ a. Supermarkets.

   _____ b. Supermarkets make food shopping very convenient.

   _____ c. It saves time to buy most or all of your food in one store.

   _____ d. Most supermarkets provide plenty of parking.

2. _____ a. Children whose mothers smoke are more likely to have behavioral disorders.

_____ b. Children of smoking mothers suffer harmful effects.

_____ c. Research shows that secondhand smoke increases children's chances of getting lung diseases.

_____ d. Mothers who smoke cigarettes.

3. _____ a. Beethoven's deafness did not prevent him from composing magnificent music.

_____ b. His Ninth Symphony was written when he was totally deaf.

_____ c. Beethoven's deafness.

_____ d. He wrote the famous Third Symphony, one of his most popular works, after his hearing had begun to fail.

4. _____ a. Many refuges and parks have walkways where people in wheelchairs can pass through various bird environments.

_____ b. Bird watching can be enjoyed even by people with physical disabilities.

_____ c. Many birding hotspots feature an auto tour, allowing birds to be viewed from a vehicle.

_____ d. Bird watching.

5. _____ a. Vocational school graduates often become some of the best-paid professionals in the United States.

_____ b. Vocational training can have significant benefits in life.

_____ c. Vocational education.

_____ d. Many vocational school graduates eventually start their own successful businesses.

Activities in Goal 2: Support the Point

Effective writing gives support—reasons, facts, examples, and other evidence—for each main point. While main points are general (see page 15), support is *specific;* it provides the details that explain the main point.

To write well, you must know the difference between general and specific ideas. It is helpful to realize that you use general and specific ideas all the time in your everyday life. For example, in choosing a DVD to rent, you may think, "Which should I rent: an action movie, a comedy, or a romance?" In such a case, *DVD* is the general idea, and *action movie, comedy,* and *romance* are the specific ideas.

Instead of a vague statement that tickets were "sold out extremely quickly," we get exact and vivid details: "The ticket window opened at 10:00 A.M., and the tickets for the good seats—those in front of the stage—were sold out an hour later."

Specific details are often like a movie script. They provide us with such clear pictures that we could make a film of them if we wanted to. You would know just how to film the information given in the second set of sentences. You would show the fans in line under a hot sun and, later, sleeping on the concrete. The first person in line would be shown sleeping without a pillow under her head. You would show tickets finally going on sale, and after an hour you could show the ticket seller explaining that all the seats in front of the stage were sold out.

In contrast, the writer of the first set of sentences (*a*) fails to provide the specific information needed. If you were asked to make a film based on set *a,* you would have to figure out on your own just what particulars to show.

When you are working to provide specific supporting information in a paper, it might help to ask yourself, "Could someone easily film this information?" If the answer is yes, your supporting details are specific enough for your readers to visualize.

Each topic sentence below is followed by two sets of supporting details. Write *S* (for *specific*) in the space next to the set that provides specific support for the point. Write *G* (for *general*) next to the set that offers only vague, general support.

Activity

8

> HINT Which set of supporting details could you more readily use in a film?

1. *Topic sentence:* Watching a rented movie at home is cheaper and more convenient than going to a movie theater.

    _____ a. Going to a first-run movie with the whole family costs us much more than it would to enjoy some pretty good movies at home. Also, food of all kinds at the theater is certainly more expensive than food we can easily make at home or even have delivered. It's not crowded at home, either. And if we have to leave our seats at the theater for some reason or other, we end up missing several minutes of the movie. But at home, we don't have that problem at all.

    _____ b. For the $44 it cost to take the family to a movie last night, we could have rented five recent movies. Instead of waiting in line for ten minutes to spend $3 per soda and $4.50 per box of pop-corn, we could have had pizza delivered. And at the theater, when we left to take our son to the restroom, it took us five minutes to figure out what was happening on the screen when we got back. At home, we could have paused the movie for a few minutes.

2. *Topic sentence:* Young children can be difficult travel partners.

   _____ a. First, they constantly ask, "Are we there yet?" even minutes after you have left your driveway. Then they always forget things—such as going to the bathroom or bringing their favorite toy—so that you have to stop or go back home. Worst of all is their constant arguing over such things as who is "making noises" or "looking at me in a funny way" and their pestering an adult to make the other child stop.

   _____ b. First, just a short time after you roll out of your driveway, they begin to ask about the trip. Then, they always want to stop for something that they need or something they have forgotten to do. Finally, the most annoying thing they do is get mad at each other for unimportant things. When this happens they often drag whichever adult is present into their arguments, pestering him or her over and over.

3. *Topic sentence:* I find life much easier in summer than in winter.

   _____ a. In the summer, I don't have to spend half an hour putting on sweaters, heavy socks, boots, coat, hat, and gloves. When I'm driving, I don't have to crawl at 10 miles per hour to avoid slipping off icy roads. And when I'm walking outside, I don't have to climb over snowbanks or wade through slush.

   _____ b. For one thing, I save a great deal of time in the summer every day because I don't have to put on heavy clothing to keep from freezing to death. The summer weather is very comfortable. In summer, also, it is much easier to get from place to place, whether I'm driving my car or going somewhere on foot.

4. *Topic sentence:* Eating chocolate is not as unhealthy as most people think.

   _____ a. As chocolate lovers know, eating chocolate in any form can make you feel better at certain times. It is a wonderful treat. Of course, snacking on too much of any food, especially sweets, can be bad for you. We all know that. But eating chocolate doesn't seem to have any lasting effect on your health. And that's definitely good news.

8. *The weather has been dreadful* all weekend.

_____

_____

9. My dog can *do a wonderful trick.*

_____

_____

10. The children *acted up* when ordered to come in the house.

_____

_____

Selecting Details That Fit

The details in your paper must all clearly relate to and support your opening point. If a detail does not support your point, leave it out. Otherwise, your paper will lack unity. For example, circle the letter of the two sentences that do *not* support the topic sentence below.

Topic sentence: Mario is a very talented person.
   a. Mario is always courteous to his professors.
   b. He has created beautiful paintings in his art course.
   c. Mario is the lead singer in a local band.
   d. He won an award in a photography contest.
   e. He is hoping to become a professional photographer.

EXPLANATION   Being courteous may be a virtue, but it is not a talent, so sentence *a* does not support the topic sentence. Also, Mario's desire to become a professional photographer tells us nothing about his talent; thus sentence *e* does not support the topic sentence either. The other three statements all clearly back up the topic sentence. Each in some way supports the idea that Mario is talented—as an artist, a singer, or a photographer.

Activity

11

In each group below, circle the two items that do *not* support the topic sentence.

1. *Topic sentence:* Leaving car windows open during a rainstorm can damage a car.

   a. Any books or newspapers sitting on the car seats can be ruined.

   b. Wet carpets have a tendency to get moldy and eventually rot.

   c. Sitting on a wet seat can soak a passenger's clothing.

   d. Getting an instrument panel wet can cause short circuits.

   e. Water can permanently stain leather seats and dashboards.

2. *Topic sentence:* Rosa is a perfect employee.

   a. She always arrives at work on time.

   b. She saves most of her paycheck for bills.

   c. Rosa never misses a day of work.

   d. She is very polite to co-workers.

   e. She often tries to persuade her friends to get a job.

3. *Topic sentence:* Popcorn popped and served without fat is a healthy choice for a snack.

   a. Popcorn itself is very low in fat and in calories.

   b. It's high in complex carbohydrates, which are better for many people than the simple carbohydrates in sugary snacks.

   c. Many people love popcorn as much as other snacks that aren't as good for them.

   d. Unlike many snacks, popcorn helps digestion because it is a good source of fiber.

   e. Popcorn tastes best freshly made.

4. *Topic sentence:* It's hard being the little brother of an award-winning student and athlete.

   a. When you were both in grade school, your brother always managed to protect you from the school bullies.

   b. At the start of each school year, teachers and coaches exclaim, "We expect you to live up to your brother's standards!"

   c. When you get less than perfect grades, all you hear is, "It's a shame you can't be more like your brother."

   d. Your brother leaves for college next year, but promises to help you with your homework over the phone whenever you want.

   e. At family reunions, everyone crowds around your big brother to hear all the details of his latest accomplishments.

5. *Topic sentence:* In recent years, several factors have caused people to move out of large cities and into nearby suburbs.

   a. A loss of jobs within cities has forced people to seek work outside of the city.

   b. High city taxes have driven people out of the cities in search of cheaper living.

   c. Improved pollution-control methods have lowered air pollution in many cities.

   d. Big cities have more cultural and artistic resources than smaller cities and suburbs.

   e. The wish for open space and less-crowded neighborhoods has drawn many people to the suburbs.

Providing Details That Fit

Each topic sentence below is followed by one supporting detail. Add a second detail in each case. Make sure your detail supports the topic sentence.

Activity

12

1. *Topic sentence:* There are good reasons why the movie rental store is losing so many customers.

   a. The store stocks only one copy of every movie, even the most popular titles.

   b. _____

2. *Topic sentence:* The little boy did some dangerous stunts on his bicycle.

   a. He rode down a flight of steps at top speed.

   b. _____

3. *Topic sentence:* Craig has awful table manners.

   a. He stuffs his mouth with food and then begins a conversation.

   b. _____

4. *Topic sentence:* There are many advantages to living in the city.

   a. One can meet many new people with interesting backgrounds.

   b. _____

5. *Topic sentence:* All high school students should have summer jobs.

   a. Summer jobs help teens learn to handle a budget.

   b. _____

Add two supporting details for each of the topic sentences below.

1. *Topic sentence:* The managers of this apartment building don't care about their tenants.

   a. Mrs. Harris has been asking them to fix her leaky faucet for two months.

   b. _____

   c. _____

2. *Topic sentence:* None of the shirts for sale were satisfactory.

   a. Some were attractive but too expensive.

   b. _____

   c. _____

3. *Topic sentence:* After being married for forty years, Mr. and Mrs. Lambert have grown similar in odd ways.

   a. They both love to have a cup of warm apple juice just before bed.

   b. _____

   c. _____

4. *Topic sentence:* It is a special time for me when my brother is in town.

   a. We always go bowling together and then stop for pizza.

   b. _____

   c. _____

5. *Topic sentence:* Our neighbor's daughter is very spoiled.

   a. When anyone else in the family has a birthday, she gets several presents too.

   b. _____

   c. _____

Providing Details in a Paragraph

The following paragraph needs specific details to back up its three supporting points. In the spaces provided on the next page, write two or three sentences of convincing details for each supporting point.

A Disappointing Concert

Although I had looked forward to seeing my favorite musical group in concert, the experience was disappointing. For one thing, our seats were terrible.

_____

_____

_____

_____

_____

_____

In addition, the crowd made it hard to enjoy the music. _____

_____

_____

_____

_____

_____

Finally, the band members acted as if they didn't want to be there. _____

_____

_____

_____

_____

Activities in Goal 3: Organize the Support

Effective writing includes clearly organized support. In a paragraph, details are often arranged in a *listing order* or *time order* so readers can make sense of them. In addition, *transitions* or signal words help make the support easy to read and understand.

The activities in this section will give you practice in the following:

www.mhhe.com/langan

- Understanding Listing and Time Order
- Understanding Transitions
- Using Transitions
- Organizing Details in a Paragraph

Understanding Listing and Time Order

Listing Order The writer can organize supporting evidence in a paper by providing a list of two or more reasons, examples, or details. Often the most important or interesting item is saved for last because the reader is most likely to remember the last thing read.

Transition words that indicate listing order include the following:

one	second	also	next	last of all
for one thing	third	another	moreover	finally
first of all	next	in addition	furthermore	

The paragraph on page 11 about starting college uses a listing order: it lists three reasons why starting college at twenty-nine is not easy, and each of those three reasons is introduced by one of the transitions in the box above. In the spaces below, write in the three transitions:

<u>   *For one thing*   </u>   <u>   *Another*   </u>   <u>   *Finally*   </u>

The first reason in the paragraph about starting college is introduced with *for one thing,* the second reason by *another,* and the third reason by *finally.*

Time Order When a writer uses time order, supporting details are presented in the order in which they occurred. *First* this happened; *next* this; *after* that, this; and so on. Many paragraphs, especially paragraphs that tell a story or give a series of directions, are organized in time order.

Transition words that show time relationships include the following:

first	before	after	when	then
next	during	now	while	until
as	soon	later	often	finally

Read the paragraph below, which is organized in time order. Underline the six transition words that show the time relationships.

Della had a sad experience while driving home last night. She traveled along the dark, winding road that led toward her home. She was only two miles from her house when she noticed a glimmer of light in the road. The next thing she knew, she heard a sickening thud and realized she had struck an animal. The light, she realized, had been its eyes reflected in her car's headlights. Della stopped the car and ran back to see what she had hit. It was a handsome cocker spaniel with blond fur and long ears. As she bent over the still form, she realized there was nothing to be done.

The dog was dead. Della searched the dog for a collar and tags. There was nothing. Before leaving, she walked to several nearby houses, asking if anyone knew who owned the dog. No one did. Finally Della gave up and drove on. She was sad to leave someone's pet lying there alone.

The main point of the paragraph is stated in its first sentence: "Della had a sad experience while driving home last night." The support for this point is all the details of Della's experience. Those details are presented in the order in which they occurred. The time relationships are highlighted by these transitions: *while, when, next, as, before,* and *finally.*

Understanding Transitions

Transitions are words and phrases that indicate relationships between ideas. They are like signposts that guide travelers, showing them how to move smoothly from one spot to the next. Be sure to take advantage of transitions. They will help organize and connect your ideas, and they will help your readers follow the direction of your thoughts.

To see how transitions help, put a check mark beside the item in each pair that is easier to read and understand.

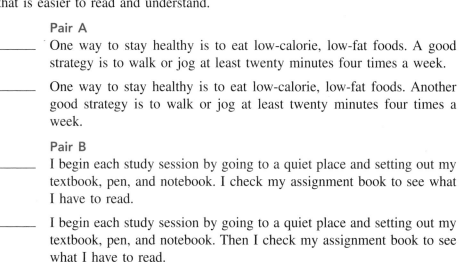

Pair A

_____ One way to stay healthy is to eat low-calorie, low-fat foods. A good strategy is to walk or jog at least twenty minutes four times a week.

_____ One way to stay healthy is to eat low-calorie, low-fat foods. Another good strategy is to walk or jog at least twenty minutes four times a week.

Pair B

_____ I begin each study session by going to a quiet place and setting out my textbook, pen, and notebook. I check my assignment book to see what I have to read.

_____ I begin each study session by going to a quiet place and setting out my textbook, pen, and notebook. Then I check my assignment book to see what I have to read.

EXPLANATION   In each pair, the second item is easier to read and understand. In pair A, the listing word *another* makes it clear that the writer is going on to a second way to stay in shape. In pair B, the time word *then* makes the relationship between the sentences clear. The writer first sets out the textbook and a pen and notebook and *then* checks an assignment book to see what to do.

Using Transitions

As already stated, transitions are signal words that help readers follow the direction of the writer's thought. To see the value of transitions, look at the two versions of the short paragraph below. Check the version that is easier to read and understand.

_____ a. Where will you get the material for your writing assignments? There are several good sources. Your own experience is a major resource. For an assignment about childhood, for instance, you can draw on your own numerous memories of childhood. Other people's experience is extremely useful. You may have heard people you know or even people on TV or radio talking about their childhood. Or you can interview people with a specific writing assignment in mind. Books and magazines are a good source of material for assignments. Many experts, for example, have written about various aspects of childhood.

_____ b. Where will you get the material for your writing assignments? There are several good sources. First of all, your own experience is a major resource. For an assignment about childhood, for instance, you can draw on your own numerous memories of childhood. In addition, other people's experiences are extremely useful. You may have heard people you know or even people on TV or radio talking about their childhood. Or you can interview people with a specific writing assignment in mind. Finally, books and magazines are a good source of material for assignments. Many experts, for example, have written about various aspects of childhood.

> **EXPLANATION** You no doubt chose the second version, *b*. The listing transitions—*first of all, in addition,* and *finally*—make it clear when the author is introducing a new supporting point. The reader of paragraph *b* is better able to follow the author's line of thinking and to note that three main sources of material for assignments are being listed: your own experience, other people's experience, and books and magazines.

The following paragraphs use listing order or time order. In each case, fill in the blanks with appropriate transitions from the box preceding the paragraph. Use each transition once.

Activity

15

1. | **after   before   later   then   when** |

On those miserable days when everything goes wrong, I like to fantasize about a day when everything would go right. On my fantasy day, I'd wake up early, a few minutes _____ the alarm would have gone off, and outside my window I'd see sparkling sunshine and blue sky. _____ dressing unhurriedly, I'd stroll to the bus stop, arriving just as the bus pulled up. I'd get a nice window seat, and _____ the bus would roll into town with no traffic tie-ups. When I arrived at work, my boss would greet me with a big smile and tell me he was giving me a raise. _____, at lunch time, he'd take me to a posh restaurant to celebrate. And _____ I arrived home that evening, my neighbor would be waiting for me with tickets to the ball game.

2. | **third   finally   for one thing   second   in addition** |

Though not all migraine headaches are alike, they tend to have typical features. _____, migraines are unpredictable—they may come every few days or weeks, or months may go by without an attack. A _____ feature is that while a migraine can be set off by stress, it usually doesn't develop until after the stressful event is over. _____, a migraine is one-sided: the pain is on the left or right side of the face or head, and for any individual it's usually on the same side. _____, the pain is throbbing and may be accompanied by nausea. _____, a coming attack is often signaled by an "aura": a period during which the individual may feel tired or depressed or may have difficulties with vision, such as seeing flashes of light or being unable to read.

3. | **when   later   during** |

_____ the winter of 1928, a terrible flu epidemic raged across the United States. Many employees of Miles Laboratories, a pharmaceutical company in Elkhart, Indiana, were home sick. But _____ the president of Miles Labs visited the office of the Elkhart newspaper, he found every employee healthy and at work. The paper's editor explained that at the first hint of a cold symptom, he dosed staff members with a combination of aspirin and baking soda. The president was impressed with the idea. He _____ asked his company chemists to come up with a tablet that combined the two ingredients. In 1931 the resulting product, Alka-Seltzer, was put on the market.

4. | **another   last   first of all   also** |

Date rape has become a serious issue for high school and college students. There are some basic strategies for protecting yourself from date rape and its consequences. _____, double-date or group-date, especially if you are going out with someone you don't know very well. _____ thing to remember is not to drink alcoholic beverages. Alcohol can cloud your judgment and harm your memory. _____, avoid parties that are not chaperoned. At a party, stay with the crowd. Never allow anyone to lure you or force you into an empty room or hidden area. _____, if all of the precautions fail and you fall victim to date rape, go immediately to a hospital or rape crisis center and seek medical help and counseling.

Organizing Details in a Paragraph

The supporting details in a paragraph must be organized in a meaningful way. The two most common methods of organizing details are listing order and time order. The activities that follow will give you practice in both methods of organization.

Use *listing order* to arrange the scrambled list of sentences that follow. Number each supporting sentence 1, 2, 3, . . . so that you go from the least important item to what is presented as the most important item.

Note that transitions will help by making clear the relationships between some of the sentences.

Topic sentence: You can protect yourself and your valuables while traveling by keeping a few guidelines in mind.

_____ Keep an immediate store of cash in your purse or wallet, but hide the rest of your money and your credit cards in a money belt.

_____ Second, be aware of your surroundings and of the people around you.

_____ The first rule is plain common sense: Pack light.

_____ The less you have to carry, the less you'll have to lose, and the less vulnerable you'll look to a would-be thief.

_____ But the biggest favor you can do yourself is not to keep all your valuables in one place.

_____ Don't discuss where you are staying, where you are going, or other personal details so that strangers can overhear you.

_____ That way, if your purse or wallet is stolen, you won't lose everything.

_____ In addition, make photocopies of your driver's license, credit cards, and other important documents, so you have all that information on hand in case the originals are stolen.

Use *time order* to arrange the scrambled sentences below. Number the supporting sentences in the order in which they occur in time (1, 2, 3, . . .).

Note that transitions will help by making clear the relationships between sentences.

Topic sentence: If you're interviewing for a job, following these steps will help you make a good impression.

_____ One way to make sure you're on time is to do a "practice run" to figure out exactly how long it takes you to get to the office and find a parking spot or to walk from the bus or subway stop.

_____ After the interview, be sure to send a thank-you note that says again how much you are interested in the job.

_____ You can find out the company "look" by going by the office at quitting time and seeing what employees are wearing.

_____ As soon as you've scheduled the interview, decide what outfit you will wear.

_____ On the big day, do whatever is necessary to arrive for the appointment on time—even a few minutes early.

_____ For example, if you are interviewing for a sales job, say, "As a psychology major, I've learned a lot about what makes people want to buy."

_____ Choose an outfit that makes you look as though you already work for the company.

_____ During the interview itself, make it clear how your abilities make you a good choice for the position.

The Writing Process

3

Steps in the Writing Process

Even professional writers do not sit down and write a paper automatically, in one draft. Instead, they have to work on it a step at a time. Writing a paper is a process that can be divided into the following steps:

- *Step 1:* Getting Started through Prewriting
- *Step 2:* Preparing a Scratch Outline
- *Step 3:* Writing the First Draft
- *Step 4:* Revising
- *Step 5:* Editing and Proofreading

These steps are described on the following pages.

Step 1: Getting Started through Prewriting

What you need to learn first are strategies for working on a paper. These strategies will help you do the thinking needed to figure out both the point you want to make and the support you have for that point.

There are several *prewriting strategies*—strategies you can use before writing the first draft of your paper:

- Freewriting
- Questioning
- Clustering
- Making a list

Freewriting

Freewriting is just sitting down and writing whatever comes into your mind about a topic. Do this for ten minutes or so. Write without stopping and without worrying at all about spelling, grammar, or the like. Simply get down on paper all the information about the topic that occurs to you.

Here is the freewriting Gary did on his problems with returning to school. Gary had been given the assignment "Write about a problem you are facing at the present time." Gary felt right away that he could write about his college situation. He began prewriting as a way to explore and generate details on his topic.

EXAMPLE OF FREEWRITING

One thing I want to write about is going back to school. At age twenty-nine. A lot to deal with. I sometimes wonder if Im nuts to try to do this or just stupid. I had to deal with my folks when I decided. My dad hated school. He knew when to quit, I'll say that for him. But he doesn't understand Im different. I have a right to my own life. And I want to better myself. He teases me alot. Says things like didnt you get dumped on enough in high school, why go back for more. My mom doesnt understand either. Just keeps worring about where the money was coming from. Then my friends. They make fun of me. Also my wife has to do more of the heavy house stuff because I'm out so much. Getting back to my friends, they say dumb things to get my goat. Like calling me the college man or saying ooh, we'd better watch our grammer. Sometimes I think my dads right, school was no fun for me. Spent years just sitting in class waiting for final bell so I could escape. Teachers didnt help me or take an intrest, some of them made me feel like a real loser. Now things are different and I like most of my teachers. I can talk to the teacher after class or to ask questions if I'm confused. But I really need more time to spend with family, I hardly see them any more. What I am doing is hard all round for them and me.

Look at this photo and freewrite for several minutes about a task you find difficult or challenging.

Notice that there are problems with spelling, grammar, and punctuation in Gary's freewriting. Gary is not worried about such matters, nor should he be. He is just concentrating on getting ideas and details down on paper. He knows that it is best to focus on one thing at a time. At this stage, he just wants to write out thoughts as they come to him, to do some thinking on paper.

You should take the same approach when freewriting: explore your topic without worrying at all about being "correct." At this early stage of the writing process, focus on figuring out what you want to say.

Questioning

Questioning means that you think about your topic by writing down a series of questions and answers about it. Your questions can start with words like *what, when, where, why,* and *how.*

Here are some questions that Gary might have asked while developing his paper, as well as some answers to those questions.

www.mhhe.com/langan

EXAMPLE OF QUESTIONING

Why do I have a problem with returning to school?	My parents and friends don't support me.
How do they not support me?	Dad asks why I want to be dumped on more. Mom is upset because college costs lots of money. Friends tease me about being a college man.
When do they not support me?	When I go to my parents' home for Friday night visits, when my friends see me walking toward them.
Where do I have this problem?	At home, where I barely see my wife and daughter, and where I have to let my wife do house things on weekends while I'm studying.
Why else do I have this problem?	High school was bad experience.
What details back up the idea that high school was bad experience?	Sat in class bored, couldn't wait to get out, teachers didn't help me. One embarrassed me when I didn't know the answer.

Clustering

Clustering is another prewriting strategy that can be used to generate material for a paper. It is helpful for people who like to do their thinking in a visual way.

In clustering, you begin by stating your subject in a few words in the center of a blank sheet of paper. Then as ideas come to you, put them in ovals, boxes, or circles around the subject, and draw lines to connect them to the subject. Put minor ideas or details in smaller boxes or circles, and also use connecting lines to show how they relate.

Keep in mind that there is no right or wrong way of clustering. It is a way to think on paper about how various ideas and details relate to one another. The following is an example of clustering that Gary might have done to develop his idea.

EXAMPLE OF CLUSTERING

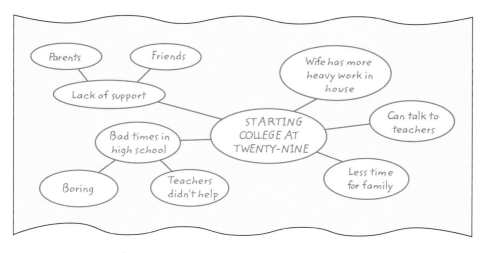

Making a List

In *making a list*—a prewriting strategy also known as *listing, list making,* and *brainstorming*—you make a list of ideas and details that could go into your paper. Simply pile these items up, one after another, without worrying about putting them in any special order. Try to accumulate as many details as you can think of.

After Gary did his freewriting about returning to school, he made up the list of details shown below.

EXAMPLE OF LISTING

> parents give me hard time when they see me
> Dad hated school
> Dad quit school after eighth grade
> Dad says I was dumped on enough in high school
> Dad asks why I want to go back for more

continued

Mom also doesnt understand

keeps asking how Ill pay for it

friends give me a hard time too

friends call me college man

say they have to watch their grammar

my wife has more heavy work around the house

also high school was no fun for me

just sat in class after class

couldnt wait for final bell to ring

wanted to escape

teachers didnt help me

teachers didnt take an interest in me

one called on me, then told me to forget it

I felt like a real loser

I didnt want to go back to his class

now I'm more sure of myself

OK not to know an answer

talk to teachers after class

job plus schoolwork take all my time

get home late, then rush through dinner

then spend evening studying

even have to do homework on weekends

One detail led to another as Gary expanded his list. Slowly but surely, more supporting material emerged that he could use in developing his paper. By the time he had finished his list, he was ready to plan an outline of his paragraph and to write his first draft.

Notice that in making a list, as in freewriting, details are included that will not actually end up in the final paragraph. Gary decided later not to develop the idea that his wife now has more heavy work to do in the house. And he realized that several of his details were about why school is easier in college ("now I'm more sure of myself," "OK not to know an answer," and "talk to instructors after class"); such details were not relevant to his point.

It is natural for a number of such extra or unrelated details to appear as part of the prewriting process. The goal of prewriting is to get a lot of information down on paper. You can then add to, shape, and subtract from your raw material as you take your paper through the series of writing drafts.

Important Points about Prewriting Strategies

Some writers may use only one of the prewriting strategies described here. Others may use bits and pieces of all four strategies. Any one strategy can lead to another. Freewriting may lead to questioning or clustering, which may then lead to a list. Or a writer may start with a list and then use freewriting or questioning to develop items on the list. During this early stage of the writing process, as you do your thinking on paper, anything goes. You should not expect a straight-line progression from the beginning to the end of your paper. Instead, there probably will be a constant moving back and forth as you work to discover your point and decide just how you will develop it.

Keep in mind that prewriting can also help you choose from among several topics. Gary might not yet have decided which problem to write about. Then he could have made a list of possible topics—areas in his life in which he has had problems. After selecting two or three topics from the list, he could have done some prewriting on each to see which seemed most promising. After finding a likely topic, Gary would have continued with his prewriting activities until he had a solid main point and plenty of support.

Finally, remember that you are not ready to begin writing a paper until you know your main point and many of the details to support it. Don't rush through prewriting. It's better to spend more time on this stage than to waste time writing a paragraph for which you have no solid point and not enough interesting support.

Step 2: Preparing a Scratch Outline

A *scratch outline* is a brief plan for a paragraph. It shows at a glance the point of the paragraph and the main support for that point. It is the logical backbone on which the paper is built.

www.mhhe.com/langan

This rough outline often follows freewriting, questioning, clustering, or listing—or all four. Or it may gradually emerge in the midst of these strategies. In fact, trying to outline is a good way to see if you need to do more prewriting. If a solid outline does not emerge, then you know you need to do more prewriting to clarify your main point or its support. Once you have a workable outline, you may realize, for instance, that you want to do more listing to develop one of the supporting details in the outline.

In Gary's case, as he was working on his list of details, he suddenly discovered what the plan of his paragraph could be. He went back to the list, crossed out items that he now realized did not fit, and added the following comments.

EXAMPLE OF LIST WITH COMMENTS

Starting college at twenty-nine isn't easy—three reasons

parents give me hard time when they see me

Dad hated school

Dad quit school after eighth grade

Dad says I was dumped on enough in high school

Dad asks why I want to go back for more   *Parents and friends don't*
                                               support me

Mom also doesnt understand

keeps asking how Ill pay for it

friends give me a hard time too

friends call me college man

say they have to watch their grammar

~~my wife has more heavy work around the house~~

also high school was no fun for me

just sat in class after class

couldnt wait for final bell to ring

wanted to escape   *Bad memories of*
                                               school
teachers didnt help me

teachers didnt take an interest in me

one called on me, then told me to forget it

I felt like a real loser

I didnt want to go back to his class

~~now I'm more sure of myself~~

~~OK not to know an answer~~

~~talk to teachers after class~~

job and schoolwork take all my time

get home late, then rush through dinner   *Not enough*
                                               time with
then spend evening studying   *family*

even have to do homework on weekends

Step 5: Editing and Proofreading

The next-to-last major stage in the writing process is *editing*—checking a paper for mistakes in grammar, punctuation, usage, and spelling. Students often find it hard to edit a paper carefully. They have put so much work into their writing, or so little, that it's almost painful for them to look at the paper one more time. You may simply have to *will* yourself to carry out this important closing step in the writing process. Remember that eliminating sentence-skills mistakes will improve an average paper and help ensure a strong grade on a good paper. Further, as you get into the habit of checking your papers, you will also get into the habit of using sentence skills consistently. They are an integral part of clear, effective writing.

The checklist of sentence skills on the inside back cover of the book will serve as a guide while you are editing your paper.

Here are hints that can help you edit the next-to-final draft of a paper for sentence-skills mistakes.

EDITING HINTS

1. Have at hand two essential tools: a good dictionary (see page 89) and a grammar handbook (you can use Part Two of this book).

2. Use a sheet of paper to cover your essay so that you expose only one sentence at a time. Look for errors in grammar, spelling, and typing. It may help to read each sentence out loud. If the sentence does not read clearly and smoothly, chances are something is wrong.

3. Pay special attention to the kinds of errors you tend to make. For example, if you tend to write run-ons or fragments, be especially on the lookout for these errors.

4. Try to work on a typewritten or word-processed draft, where you'll be able to see your writing more objectively than you can on a handwritten page; use a pen with colored ink so that your corrections will stand out.

Shown below are some of the corrections in spelling, grammar, and punctuation that Gary made when editing his paper.

Part of Gary's Edited Draft

Starting college at age twenty-nine was difficult. For one thing, I did not have much support from my parents and friends. My father asked, "Didn't you get dumped on enough in high school? Why go back for more?" My mother ~~woried~~ *worried* about where the money ~~were~~ *was* coming from. Friends would make fun of me. "Hey, there's the college man," they would say as soon as they saw me. . . .

All that remained for Gary to do was to enter in his corrections, print out the final draft of the paper, and proofread it (see hints on proofreading on the next page) for any typos or other careless errors. He was then ready to hand the paper in to his instructor.

Proofreading, the final stage in the writing process, means checking a paper carefully for errors in spelling, grammar, punctuation, and so on. You are ready for this stage when you are satisfied with your choice of supporting details, the order in which they are presented, and the way they and your topic sentence are worded. You will already have attempted to correct all grammar, spelling, and punctuation errors.

At this point in his work, Gary used his dictionary to do final checks on his spelling. He used a grammar handbook (such as the one in Part Two of this text) to be sure about grammar, punctuation, and usage. Gary also read through his paper carefully, looking for typing errors, omitted words, and any other errors he may have missed before. Proofreading is often hard to do—again, students have spent so much time with their work, or so little, that they want to avoid it. But if it is done carefully, this important final step will ensure that your paper looks as good as possible.

PROOFREADING HINTS

1. One helpful trick at this stage is to read your paper out loud. You will probably hear awkward wordings and become aware of places where the punctuation needs to be improved. Make the changes needed for your sentences to read smoothly and clearly.

2. Another helpful technique is to take a sheet of paper and cover your paragraph so that you expose just one line at a time and check it carefully.

3. A third strategy is to read your paper backward, from the last sentence to the first. This helps keep you from getting caught up in the flow of the paper and missing small mistakes—which is easy to do, since you're so familiar with what you mean to say.

Activities in the Writing Process

These activities will give you practice in some of the prewriting strategies you can use to generate material for a paper. Try to do two or more of these prewriting activities.

Freewriting

On a sheet of paper, freewrite for several minutes about the best or most disappointing friend you ever had. Don't worry about grammar, punctuation, or spelling. Try to write, without stopping, about whatever comes into your head concerning your best or most disappointing friend.

Activity 1

Questioning

On another sheet of paper, answer the following questions about the friend you've started to write about.

Activity 2

1. When did this friendship begin and how long did it last?
2. Where did you meet your friend?
3. What is one reason you think highly or disapprovingly of this friend? Give one quality, action, comment, etc. Also, give some details to illustrate this quality.

4. What is another reason for your opinion of your friend? What are some details that support the second reason?

5. Can you think of a third reason? What are some details that support the third reason?

Activity 3

Clustering

In the center of a blank sheet of paper, write and circle the words *best friend* or *most disappointing friend*. Then, around the circle, add reasons and details about the friend. Use a series of boxes, circles, or other shapes, along with connecting lines, to set off the reasons and details. In other words, try to think about and explore your topic in a very visual way.

Activity 4

Making a List

On separate paper, make a list of details about the friend. Don't worry about putting them in a certain order. Just get down as many details about the friend as occur to you. The list can include specific reasons for your opinion of the person and specific details supporting those reasons.

Activity 5

Scratch Outline

On the basis of your prewriting, prepare a scratch outline made up of your main idea and the three main reasons for your opinion of your friend. Use the form below:

_____ was my best *or* most disappointing friend.

Reason 1: _____

Reason 2: _____

Reason 3: _____

Activity 6

First Draft

Now write a first draft of your paper. Begin with your topic sentence, stating that a certain friend was the best or most disappointing one you ever had. Then state the first reason to support your main idea, followed by specific details supporting that reason. Next, state the second reason, followed by specific details supporting that reason. Finally, state the third reason, followed by support.

Don't worry about grammar, punctuation, or spelling. Just concentrate on getting down on paper the details about your friend.

Revising the Draft

Activity

7

Ideally, you will have a chance to put your paper aside for a while before writing the second draft. In your second draft, try to do all of the following:

1. Add transition words such as *first of all, another,* and *finally* to introduce each of the three reasons for your opinion of the friend you're writing about.

2. Omit any details that do not truly support your topic sentence.

3. Add more details as needed, making sure you have plenty of support for each of your three reasons.

4. Check to see that your details are vivid and specific. Can you make a supporting detail more concrete? Are there any persuasive, colorful specifics you can add?

5. Try to eliminate wordiness (see page 445) and clichés (see page 442).

6. In general, improve the flow of your writing.

7. Include a final sentence that rounds off the paper, bringing it to a close.

Editing and Proofreading

Activity

8

When you have your almost-final draft of the paper, proofread it as follows:

1. Using your dictionary, check any words that you think might be misspelled. Though the spell-checking features on most word-processing programs are useful tools, they often do not detect commonly misused words (see pages 412–434) such as *there, their,* and *they're.* Make sure you proofread your draft manually to avoid such errors.

2. Using Part Two of this book, check your paper for mistakes in grammar, punctuation, and usage.

3. Read the paper aloud, listening for awkward or unclear spots. Make the changes needed for the paragraph to read smoothly and clearly. Even better, see if you can get another person to read the draft aloud to you. The spots that this person has trouble reading are spots where you may have to do some rewriting.

4. Take a sheet of paper and cover your writing so that you can expose and carefully check one line at a time. Or read your writing backward, from the end of the paragraph to the beginning. Look for typing errors, omitted words, and other remaining errors.

Don't fail to edit and proofread carefully. You may be tired of working on your paper at this point, but you want to give the extra effort needed to make it as good as possible. A final push can mean the difference between a higher and a lower grade.

Ten Writing Assignments

Your instructor may ask you to do one or more of the following paragraph writing assignments. Be sure to check the rules for paper format on page 289.

Writing Assignment

1 Providing Examples

Listed below are three topic sentences, followed by specific examples, the supporting details. On a piece of paper, invent two additional examples to support each point. Try to make your examples as specific and as realistic as the ones shown.

Point: My friend Mac has several dangerous driving habits.

1. For one thing, he never signals when he's going to make a left-hand turn. The only warning a car behind Mac has is when he slows down suddenly.

2. . . .

3. . . .

Point: My apartment is in need of repairs.

1. When it rains, water runs down through the ceiling light fixture in the bedroom. The ceiling is always damp and soggy, and there is a musty odor that grows stronger every day.

2. . . .

3. . . .

Point: There are three kinds of everyday happenings that really annoy me.

1. First of all, I hate waiting in long lines at a store, especially when several employees are standing around nearby when they could be opening up another register.

2. . . .

3. . . .

A Great Snack

2

Everyone has a favorite snack. What is yours? Maybe it is a huge plate of tortilla chips coated with cheese, a bowl of vanilla ice cream sprinkled with semi-sweet chocolate chips, or a stack of chocolate graham crackers to dip in hot cocoa with marshmallows floating on top. Write a paragraph about preparing and eating your perfect snack, including any special way, place, or time you prefer to eat the snack.

Begin your paragraph with a statement that summarizes the details you plan to write about, such as this: "One of my favorite snacks is a ham and cheese sandwich with pickle chips, which must be made and eaten in just the right ways." Then go on to explain in detail just how you prepare your snack. For the example above, you would include what kind of bread you use, how many slices of ham and cheese you put on, and where exactly you position the pickle chips. You would then go on to write about how you like to eat your creation. For instance, perhaps the best way to eat your favorite snack is late at night while sitting on your living room couch with a good book in your hand and the TV turned on with the sound turned down.

Your paragraph will be organized in time order, describing the different steps that are involved in your enjoyment of the snack. Help your reader follow your supporting details by using time transition words, such as *first, next, then,* and *finally.*

A Special Photograph

3

Pictures have a magical power. They freeze moments in time forever, allowing us to look back to events that happened long ago. Find a photograph that has special meaning for you. Perhaps it is a photo of a family member who has passed away or a childhood picture of you and a close friend. Write a paragraph describing the picture and explaining its significance. Begin with your topic sentence, perhaps similar to one of the following:

> A photo I have of me with my first girlfriend, Dana, is very special for two reasons.

> A photograph of a funny scene during my tenth birthday party reminds me of the most fun—and the funniest—birthday party I ever had.

Since your readers will not actually see the picture, it is up to you to provide descriptive details so that they will know just what the picture looks like. You might use that description as a starting point for the specific details needed to support your topic sentence.

After describing the photo referred to in the first topic sentence above, for example, you would go on to explain the two reasons mentioned. One reason might be that the photo was taken on a particularly wonderful date. A colorful description of that date will help readers see just how terrific it was. Your second reason might be that Dana is the person you ended up marrying, and that photo is the earliest one of you two together. A few more details about the photo—how you two posed, the expressions on your faces—may tell how the photo shows you suspected even then you would end up together. (You may wish to attach a copy of the photo to the draft of the paper that you hand in.)

Writing Assignment

4 | Your Position in the Family

Psychologists have concluded that there are significant differences in being an only, oldest, middle, or youngest child. Which of these are you, and how did it influence the way you were brought up? Did you have more responsibilities than your brothers and sisters? If you were an only child, did you spend a lot of time with adults? Were you a spoiled youngest child? Jot down the advantages and disadvantages that come to mind.

Use the most important ideas on your list to develop a paragraph on how you think your position in your family affected you. Begin with your topic sentence, a statement such as this: "As the second of three children, I received less attention, was given more independence, and was pushed less to achieve than my brother and sister." Use specific examples to illustrate each part of your topic sentence. Try to make your examples interesting and colorful by including very specific relevant details, such as how things looked and what was said.

Writing Assignment

5 | An Embarrassing Moment

Each of us has been embarrassed at some time or other. Thankfully, we often look back at our embarrassing moments years later and smile. Write a paragraph about an embarrassing incident that happened to you which you can smile about today. The paragraph should provide lots of specific detail so that readers can feel and understand your embarrassment.

Begin your paragraph with a topic sentence that tells readers the general situation in which you were embarrassed, such as any of the following.

My first day on the job as a waiter ended with an embarrassing accident that still makes me cringe a little today.

When I met my girlfriend's parents, something happened that was so embarrassing it took me many months to be able to smile about it.

One of the most embarrassing moments in my life happened in high school when I was walking in the cafeteria with a platter of meat loaf on my tray.

You might find freewriting to be a useful way of quickly getting down on paper the story you want to tell. Then you can use that freewriting as a starting point by adding, subtracting, and refining. As you tell events in the order in which they happened, help your readers follow your narrative by using time transitions like *first, next, then,* and *finally.*

Writing Assignment

Leaving Home   6

Sooner or later most young people leave the home they have grown up in to begin life on their own. While the feeling of independence may be thrilling, flying the coop also involves numerous problems. Write about one problem that many people are likely to meet when they live away from home for the first time. Your thesis statement should be similar to either of these:

When young adults move out on their own for the first time, they are

likely to experience a problem with _____.

When I moved out of my parents' home to live on my own for the first

time, one problem I experienced was _____.

Before beginning this paragraph, you may want to make a list of problems that young people on their own for the first time are likely to experience or problems that you experienced when you were first on your own. Select one of those problems to write about. Make sure you use adequate and relevant support to back up your point.

Writing Assignment

7   Life on the Job

At some point or other, each of us has had a job that we have strong feelings about. Write a paragraph about the best or worst job you have ever had. You might begin with a general description of your job, explaining what it was and what you were supposed to do.

Here are some thesis statements that may help you think about your own paper.

> I hated my government office job because the building was in bad condition, the rules were ridiculous, and many of the workers were unhappy.

> I love my job as a waiter because my boss is friendly, the schedule is flexible, and the pay is good.

Writing Assignment

8   A Letter of Praise or Criticism

Most of us watch some television, listen to the radio, or read the newspaper. We have each seen, heard, or read things that we have found enjoyable or offensive. Write a letter to a television network, radio station, or newspaper in which you compliment or criticize something that you saw, listened to, or read. Don't just say you liked or disliked your topic. Instead give two or three detailed reasons that support your feelings either way.

Writing Assignment

9   The Most Important Qualities in a Person

TV ads, music videos, and many popular TV shows suggest that our culture values physical beauty, strength, and wealth. But are these the most important qualities a person can have? Can you think of others that are more important? For example, which is better: for a teenager to learn how to be cool or how to be kind? Think about the most important qualities a person can have and choose one that you think is very important. Write a paragraph in which you show why the trait you chose is so crucial.

A good prewriting strategy is to write a list of personal qualities that are important to you. Then choose the one that you feel most strongly about. Freewrite on some of these potential topics to see if they make strong subjects. In this way, you'll be able to determine whether a particular quality will work for this assignment.

Alternatively, write a paragraph titled "The Most Unpleasant Quality in People."

Writing Assignment

An Analysis of Spending Habits

10

Like many people, you probably would be happy if you could put more of your money aside for future needs, perhaps next year's tuition, another car, or even a new home. But—also like many people—you may find that by the end of each month, there is nothing much left of your paycheck. Often, a careful analysis of spending habits turns up several ways a person can find some cash to squirrel away. To prepare for this assignment, do a careful analysis of your own spending and shopping patterns. Then write a paragraph about one way you feel that you can change your spending habits in order to feed your bank account. Use at least three specific details.

Here's a sample scratch outline for this assignment:

Topic sentence: I now see that I can spend much less at the supermarket by being more disciplined.

(1) I can be more careful about using coupons.

(2) I can take better advantage of sales.

(3) I can buy less junk food.

If after analyzing your spending habits you feel that you have been doing a good job of making the most of your paycheck, write a paragraph instead about your success. A thesis statement for that paragraph might go like this: "An analysis of my spending habits shows that I have been doing a pretty good job of keeping down my food expenses."

PART 2

Sentence Skills

Introduction

Part Two explains the basic skills needed to write clear, error-free sentences. While the skills are presented within five traditional categories (sentences; verbs, pronouns, and agreement; modifiers and parallelism; punctuation and mechanics; word use), each section is self-contained so that you can go directly to the skills you need to work on. Note, however, that you may find it helpful to cover Chapter 4, "Subjects and Verbs," before turning to other skills. Typically, the main features of a skill are presented on the first pages of a section; secondary points are developed later. Numerous activities are provided so that you can practice skills enough to make them habits. The activities are varied and range from underlining answers to writing complete sentences involving the skill in question. One or more review tests at the end of each section offer additional practice activities. Mastery tests conclude each chapter, allowing you to immediately test your understanding of each skill.

Look at the photo here and imagine you have been asked to write a paper about your ideal college experience. What kinds of people do you hope to meet? What classes will you take? What would you like to accomplish? Using any of the prewriting techniques (freewriting, questioning, clustering, making a list), spend time prewriting for a paper on this topic.

4

Subjects and Verbs

Introductory Activity

Understanding subjects and verbs is a big step toward mastering many sentence skills. As a speaker of English, you already have an instinctive feel for these basic building blocks of English sentences. See if you can insert an appropriate word in each space below. The answer will be a subject.

1. The _____ will soon be over.

2. _____ cannot be trusted.

3. A strange _____ appeared in my backyard.

4. _____ is one of my favorite activities.

Now insert an appropriate word in the following spaces. Each answer will be a verb.

5. The prisoner _____ at the judge.

6. My sister _____ much harder than I do.

7. The players _____ in the locker room.

8. Rob and Marilyn _____ with the teacher.

Finally, insert appropriate words in the following spaces. Each answer will be a subject in the first space and a verb in the second.

9. The _____ almost _____ out of the tree.

10. Many _____ today _____ sex and violence.

11. The _____ carefully _____ the patient.

12. A _____ quickly _____ the ball.

Answers are on page 660.

The basic building blocks of English sentences are subjects and verbs. Understanding them is an important first step toward mastering a number of sentence skills.

Every sentence has a subject and a verb. Who or what the sentence speaks about is called the *subject;* what the sentence says about the subject is called the *verb.* In the following sentences, the subject is underlined once and the verb twice:

People gossip.

The truck belched fumes.

He waved at me.

Alaska contains the largest wilderness area in the United States.

That woman is a millionaire.

The pants feel itchy.

A Simple Way to Find a Subject

To find a subject, ask *who* or *what* the sentence is about. As shown below, your answer is the subject.

Who is the first sentence about? People

What is the second sentence about? The truck

Who is the third sentence about? He

What is the fourth sentence about? Alaska

Who is the fifth sentence about? That woman

What is the sixth sentence about? The pants

It helps to remember that the subject of a sentence is always a *noun* (any person, place, or thing) or a pronoun. A *pronoun* is simply a word like *he, she, it, you,* or *they* used in place of a noun. In the preceding sentences, the subjects are persons (*People, He, woman*), a place (*Alaska*), and things (*truck, pants*). Note that one pronoun (*He*) is used as a subject.

A Simple Way to Find a Verb

To find a verb, ask what the sentence *says about* the subject. As shown below, your answer is the verb.

What does the first sentence *say about* people? They <u>gossip</u>.

What does the second sentence *say about* the truck? It <u>belched</u> (fumes).

What does the third sentence *say about* him? He <u>waved</u> (at me).

What does the fourth sentence *say about* Alaska? It <u>contains</u> (the largest wilderness area in the United States).

What does the fifth sentence *say about* that woman? She <u>is</u> (a millionaire).

What does the sixth sentence *say about* the pants? They <u>feel</u> (itchy).

A second way to find the verb is to put *I, you, he, she, it,* or *they* in front of the word you think is a verb. If the result makes sense, you have a verb. For example, you could put *they* in front of *gossip* in the first sentence above, with the result, *they gossip,* making sense. Therefore, you know that *gossip* is a verb. You could use the same test with the other verbs as well.

Finally, it helps to remember that most verbs show action. In "People gossip," the action is gossiping. In "The truck belched fumes," the action is belching. In "He waved at me," the action is waving. In "Alaska contains the largest wilderness area in the United States," the action is containing.

Certain other verbs, known as *linking verbs,* do not show action. They do, however, give information about the subject of the sentence. In "That woman is a millionaire," the linking verb *is* tells us that the woman is a millionaire. In "The pants feel itchy," the linking verb *feel* gives us the information that the pants are itchy.

Practice

1

In each of the following sentences, underline the subject and double-underline the verb.

> **HINT** To find the subject, ask *who* or *what* the sentence is about. Then, to find the verb, ask what the sentence *says about* the subject.

1. Rachel poured extra virgin olive oil into the skillet.

2. The company offered a fifty-dollar rebate on every energy-efficient refrigerator bought during the month of June.

3. The talk show host introduced ten-year-old Drake as a future *American Idol* star.

4. Taryn adjusted the volume on her iPod as she entered the library.

5. The discarded cigarette butt burned a hole in the upholstery.

6. The bathroom upstairs is infested with cockroaches.

7. Royden tripped over the tangled cables behind my office desk.

8. The sports drink quenched my thirst.

9. The lawn trimmer tossed small rocks and other debris into the air.

10. Volunteers collected canned meats, beans, and peanut butter for the food bank.

Follow the directions given for Practice 1. Note that all of the verbs here are linking verbs.

Practice 2

1. The best shows on television this week were the ads.

2. In some countries, an after-dinner burp is a compliment to the cook.

3. Mirror sunglasses always look eerie, like a robot's eyes.

4. My voice sounds terrible in the morning.

5. Tamika became engaged to Hassan after just three dates.

6. Harold's new after-shave lotion smells like cleaning fluid.

7. Visitors often appear fearful at my German shepherd's bark of greeting.

8. To a female fly, a male's wing vibrations are a love song.

9. My head cold feels like a combination of fatal headache and torture by sneezing.

10. In some ways, the change from tadpole to frog seems as much of a miracle as the change from frog to prince.

Follow the directions given for Practice 1.

1. One lonely neon light glowed in the distance.

2. The kite soared into the sky at the end of a taut, vibrating string.

3. Manuel caught a foul ball at the game.

4. The skaters shadowed each other's movements perfectly.

5. Fluorescent lights emphasized the lines in the tired man's face.

6. Tracy reads to her bedridden grandmother every night.

7. Marsha's oversized glasses slipped down her nose twenty times a day.

8. Carelessly, Jane gave the children too much candy.

9. The squirrel jumped from one tree branch to another.

10. Carpenters constructed a wooden wheelchair ramp next to the stone steps of the church.

More about Subjects and Verbs

Distinguishing Subjects from Prepositional Phrases

The subject of a sentence never appears within a prepositional phrase. A *prepositional phrase* is simply a group of words beginning with a preposition and ending with the answer to the question *what, when,* or *where.* Here is a list of common prepositions.

Common Prepositions

about	before	by	inside	over
above	behind	during	into	through
across	below	except	of	to
among	beneath	for	off	toward
around	beside	from	on	under
at	between	in	onto	with

When you are looking for the subject of a sentence, it is helpful to cross out prepositional phrases.

~~In the middle of the night~~, we heard footsteps ~~on the roof~~.

The magazines ~~on the table~~ belong ~~in the garage~~.

~~Before the opening kickoff~~, a brass band marched ~~onto the field~~.

The hardware store ~~across the street~~ went ~~out of business~~.

~~In spite of our advice~~, Sally quit her job ~~at Burger King~~.

Cross out prepositional phrases. Then underline subjects and double-underline verbs.

Practice

4

 1. Stripes of sunlight glowed on the kitchen floor.

 2. The black panther draped its powerful body along the thick tree branch.

 3. A line of impatient people snaked from the box office to the street.

 4. At noon, every siren in town wails for fifteen minutes.

 5. The tops of my Bic pens always disappear after a day or two.

 6. Joanne removed the lint from her black socks with Scotch tape.

 7. The mirrored walls of the skyscraper reflected the passing clouds.

 8. Debris from the accident littered the intersection.

 9. Above the heads of the crowd, a woman swayed on a narrow ledge.

10. The squashed grapes in the bottom of the vegetable bin oozed sticky purple juice.

Verbs of More Than One Word

Many verbs consist of more than one word. Here, for example, are some of the many forms of the verb *help:*

Some Forms of the Verb *Help*

helps	should have been helping	will have helped
helping	can help	would have been helped
is helping	would have been helping	has been helped
was helping	will be helping	had been helped
may help	had been helping	must have helped
should help	helped	having helped
will help	have helped	should have been helped
does help	has helped	had helped

The following sentences contain verbs of more than one word:

Yolanda is working overtime this week.

Another book has been written about the Kennedy family.

We should have stopped for gas at the last station.

The game has just been canceled.

TIPS

1. Words like *not, just, never, only,* and *always* are not part of the verb, although they may appear within the verb.

   Yolanda is not working overtime next week.

   The boys should just not have stayed out so late.

   The game has always been played regardless of the weather.

2. No verb preceded by *to* is ever the verb of a sentence.

   Sue wants to go with us.

   The newly married couple decided to rent a house for a year.

   The store needs extra people to help out at Christmas.

3. No *-ing* word by itself is ever the verb of a sentence. (It may be part of the verb, but it must have a helping verb in front of it.)

   We planning the trip for months. (This is not a sentence, because the verb is not complete.)

   We were planning the trip for months. (This is a complete sentence.)

Underline subjects and double-underline verbs. Be sure to include all parts of the verb.

Practice

5

1. Only Einstein could have passed that math test.

2. She could have been killed by that falling rock.

3. The children did not recognize their father in his Halloween costume.

4. The hunger strikers have been fasting for four days.

5. I could not see the tiny letters on the last row of the eye doctor's chart.

6. People may be wearing paper clothing by the year 2050.

7. He should have studied longer for the final.

8. Rosa has been soaking in the bathtub for an hour.

9. Long lines of southbound geese were flying overhead.

10. My little brother can ask the same stupid question five times in a row.

Compound Subjects and Verbs

A sentence may have more than one verb:

The dancer stumbled and fell.

Lola washed her hair, blew it dry, and parted it in the middle.

A sentence may have more than one subject:

Cats and dogs are sometimes the best of friends.

The striking workers and their bosses could not come to an agreement.

A sentence may have several subjects and several verbs:

Holly and I read the book and reported on it to the class.

Pete, Nick, and Eric caught the fish in the morning, cleaned them in the afternoon, and ate them that night.

Underline subjects and double-underline verbs. Be sure to mark *all* the subjects and verbs.

Practice

6

1. The trees creaked and shuddered in the powerful wind.

2. The little girl fell off the jungle gym and landed in the dirt.

3. On Sunday, I will vacuum the upstairs rooms and change the linens.

4. The late afternoon sun shone on the leaves and turned them to gold.

5. Sam and Billy greased their chapped lips with Vaseline.

6. The tall, masked man and his Native American friend rode off into the sunset.

7. My sister and I always race each other to the bathroom in the morning.

8. Nia breathed deeply and then began her karate exercises.

9. At the party, Phil draped a tablecloth around his shoulders and pretended to be Dracula.

10. The professional wrestler and his opponent strutted around the ring and pounded on their chests.

Review Test 1

www.mhhe.com/langan

Underline the subjects and double-underline the verbs. As necessary, cross out prepositional phrases to help find subjects. Underline all the parts of a verb, and remember that you may find more than one subject and more than one verb in a sentence.

1. The endings of most movies are happy.

2. I should have filled the car with gas before work.

3. The female of many animals is larger than the male.

4. Three buildings on our block are for sale.

5. Dozens of ants gathered around a scoop of pink ice cream on the sidewalk.

6. Many shoppers saw the pennies on the floor but would not pick them up.

7. Squirrels can collect thousands of nuts in one season.

8. Genetically modified fruits and vegetables should be banned in this country.

9. An extra key was placed under the big empty planter by the front door.

10. Ved dieted for a year, lost a hundred pounds, and lowered his high blood pressure.

Review Test 2

Follow the directions given for Review Test 1.

1. A collection of watercolor paintings was damaged in the flood.

2. Everything in that linen store is on sale at 40 percent off.

3. My son is looking for dinosaur bones in the backyard.

4. According to surveys, most people talk to their dogs.

5. Jay and Elise were married two years ago and are divorced already.

6. At dinnertime, my cat meows and rubs against my leg.

7. The huge tree outside our kitchen window throws lovely shadows on the kitchen wall in the afternoon.

8. My parents and the Greens played bridge for hours and argued constantly.

9. Deanna chose a chocolate from the box, took one bite, and put the piece back.

10. Mona removed Ed's arm from her shoulders and ran from the theater with tears in her eyes.

NAME: _____

DATE: _____

Subject and Verbs

Underline subjects and double-underline verbs. Cross out prepositional phrases as necessary to help find subjects. (Be sure to underline all the parts of a verb. Also, remember that you may find more than one subject and one verb in a sentence.)

1. My cat sleeps on the radiator.

2. An opened bag of lemon cookies hung over the edge of the shelf.

3. Margie and Paul walked hand in hand into the haunted house.

4. Those early Beatles records have become collectors' items.

5. Twenty people crammed themselves into the tiny elevator.

6. The truck driver got out his jumper cables and attached them to the battery of my ear.

7. The man in the gorilla suit is my brother.

8. Vince always watches football on television but almost never goes to a game.

9. Unable to find his parents in the supermarket, Billy sat down and cried.

10. She opened the book, placed her finger at the top of the page, and began to speed-read.

Subject and Verbs MASTERY TEST 2

Underline subjects and double-underline verbs. Cross out prepositional phrases as necessary to help find subjects. (Be sure to underline all the parts of a verb. Also, remember that you may find more than one subject and one verb in a sentence.)

1. Nancy burned her arm on the charcoal grill.

2. I always keep a first-aid kit in the trunk of my car.

3. He has been looking for that book for at least a week.

4. The new office manager was hired on Tuesday and fired on Wednesday.

5. My grandfather is often troubled by arthritis.

6. Cheryl and her sister found a ten-dollar bill in the wastebasket.

7. Fred ran across the porch and tripped on a loose board.

8. Those violent cartoons on Saturday morning television are too scary for small children.

9. All of the leftover Christmas decorations just went on sale at half price.

10. Bonnie and Clyde strode into the bank, waved their guns, and told everyone to lie down on the floor.

NAME: _____

DATE: _____

Subject and Verbs

Underline subjects and double-underline verbs. Cross out prepositional phrases as necessary to help find subjects. (Be sure to underline all the parts of a verb. Also, remember that you may find more than one subject and one verb in a sentence.)

1. Tom reads the sports pages every morning.

2. The name of that woman just flew out of my head.

3. Our dog whined pitifully during the violent thunderstorm.

4. That screen has at least twenty holes and needs to be replaced.

5. Her problems are starting to sound like TV reruns.

6. Three copies of that book have been stolen from the library.

7. The little girl with pigtails did graceful cartwheels in the yard.

8. My sixth-grade teacher never could understand my questions.

9. We bought a broken floor lamp at our neighbor's garage sale and then could not decide what to do with it.

10. The mud slides, flooded roads, and washed-out bridges were caused by last week's heavy rains.

Subject and Verbs   MASTERY TEST 4

Underline subjects and double-underline verbs. Cross out prepositional phrases as necessary to help find subjects. (Be sure to underline all the parts of a verb. Also, remember that you may find more than one subject and one verb in a sentence.)

1. A low whistle suddenly pierced the silence.

2. Liz had spread her beach towel over the hot sand.

3. At the health food bar, Bob was sipping a strawberry-coconut milk shake.

4. Our old car has been repaired only three times in the last four years.

5. Annabelle's skin turned bright orange from the indoor tanning lotion.

6. Marsha and Ann begged their parents for permission to go to the concert.

7. The officer dismounted from his motorcycle, walked over to me, and asked for my license and registration.

8. Bananas, skim milk, and bran buds were the ingredients in the breakfast drink.

9. I listened to all the candidate's promises but did not believe a single one.

10. A doctor and nurse walked into the room, pulled down Mike's covers, and ordered him to roll over.

Fragments

Introductory Activity

Every sentence must have a subject and a verb and must express a complete thought. A word group that lacks a subject or a verb and that does not express a complete thought is a *fragment*.

Listed below are a number of fragments and sentences. Complete the statement that explains each fragment.

1. Children. *Fragment*

   Children cry. *Sentence*

   "Children" is a fragment because, while it has a subject *(Children)*, it lacks a _____ *(cry)* and so does not express a complete thought.

2. Dances. *Fragment*

   Lola dances. *Sentence*

   "Dances" is a fragment because, while it has a verb *(Dances)*, it lacks a _____ *(Lola)* and so does not express a complete thought.

3. Staring through the window. *Fragment*

   Bigfoot was staring through the window. *Sentence*

   "Staring through the window" is a fragment because it lacks a _____ *(Bigfoot)* and also part of the _____ *(was)* and because it does not express a complete thought.

4. When the dentist began drilling.   *Fragment*

   When the dentist began drilling, I closed my eyes.   *Sentence*

   "When the dentist began drilling" is a fragment because we want to
   know what happened when the dentist began drilling. The word group
   does not follow through and _____.

   Answers are on page 661.

What Fragments Are

Every sentence must have a subject and a verb and must express a complete
thought. A word group that lacks a subject or a verb and does not express a
complete thought is a *fragment*. Following are the most common types of fragments that people write:

1. Dependent-word fragments
2. *-ing* and *to* fragments
3. Added-detail fragments
4. Missing-subject fragments

Once you understand the specific kind or kinds of fragments that you might
write, you should be able to eliminate them from your writing. The following
pages explain all four types of fragments.

Dependent-Word Fragments

Some word groups that begin with a dependent word are fragments. Here is a
list of common dependent words:

Common Dependent Words

after	if, even if	when, whenever
although, though	in order that	where, wherever
as	since	whether
because	that, so that	which, whichever
before	unless	while
even though	until	who
how	what, whatever	whose

Whenever you start a sentence with one of these dependent words, you must be careful that a dependent-word fragment does not result. The word group beginning with the dependent word *after* in the selection below is a fragment.

<u>After I stopped drinking coffee.</u> I began sleeping better at night.

A *dependent statement*—one starting with a dependent word like *after*—cannot stand alone. It depends on another statement to complete the thought. "After I stopped drinking coffee" is a dependent statement. It leaves us hanging. We expect in the same sentence to find out *what happened after* the writer stopped drinking coffee. When a writer does not follow through and complete a thought, a fragment results.

To correct the fragment, simply follow through and complete the thought:

After I stopped drinking coffee, I began sleeping better at night.

Remember, then, that *dependent statements by themselves* are fragments. They must be attached to a statement that makes sense standing alone.*

Here are two other examples of dependent-word fragments.

Brian sat nervously in the dental clinic. <u>While waiting to have his wisdom tooth pulled.</u>

Maria decided to throw away the boxes. <u>That had accumulated for years in the basement.</u>

"While waiting to have his wisdom tooth pulled" is a fragment; it does not make sense standing by itself. We want to know in the same statement *what Brian did* while waiting to have his tooth pulled. The writer must complete the thought. Likewise, "That had accumulated for years in the basement" is not in itself a complete thought. We want to know in the same statement what *that* refers to.

> ## How to │ Correct Dependent-Word Fragments
>
> In most cases, you can correct a dependent-word fragment by attaching it to the sentence that comes after it or to the sentence that comes before it:
>
> After I stopped drinking coffee, I began sleeping better at night. (The fragment has been attached to the sentence that comes after it.)

---

*Some instructors refer to a dependent-word fragment as a *dependent clause*. A *clause* is simply a group of words having a subject and a verb. A clause may be *independent* (expressing a complete thought and able to stand alone) or *dependent* (not expressing a complete thought and not able to stand alone). A dependent clause by itself is a fragment. It can be corrected simply by adding an independent clause.

Brian sat nervously in the dental clinic while waiting to have his wisdom tooth pulled. (The fragment has been attached to the sentence that comes before it.)

Maria decided to throw away the boxes that had accumulated for years in the basement. (The fragment has been attached to the sentence that comes before it.)

Another way of correcting a dependent-word fragment is to eliminate the dependent word and make a new sentence:

I stopped drinking coffee.

He was waiting to have his wisdom tooth pulled.

They had accumulated for years in the basement.

Do not use this second method of correction too frequently, however, for it may cut down on interest and variety in your writing style.

TIPS

1. Use a comma if a dependent-word group comes at the *beginning* of a sentence (see also page 358):

    After I stopped drinking coffee, I began sleeping better at night.

    However, do not generally use a comma if the dependent-word group comes at the end of a sentence:

    Brian sat nervously in the dental clinic while waiting to have his wisdom tooth pulled.

    Maria decided to throw away the boxes that had accumulated for years in the basement.

2. Sometimes the dependent words *who, that, which,* or *where* appear not at the very start but *near* the start of a word group. A fragment often results.

    Today I visited Faye Cooper. A friend who is in the hospital.

    "A friend who is in the hospital" is not in itself a complete thought. We want to know in the same statement *who* the friend is. The fragment can be corrected by attaching it to the sentence that comes before it:

    Today I visited Faye Cooper, a friend who is in the hospital.

    (Here a comma is used to set off "a friend who is in the hospital," which is extra material placed at the end of the sentence.)

Practice	Turn each of the dependent-word groups into a sentence by adding a complete thought. Put a comma after the dependent-word group if a dependent word starts the sentence.
1	

EXAMPLES

Before I begin college

Before I begin college, I want to brush up on my math and English

skills.

The horoscope forecast that I read

The horoscope forecast that I read predicted new love, but I am happily

married.

1. Before I log off from the computer

   _____

   _____

2. Even though I cheated

   _____

   _____

3. Although my parents never went to college

   _____

   _____

4. The pills that the doctor prescribed

   _____

   _____

5. If I remember correctly

   _____

   _____

Underline the dependent-word fragment (or fragments) in each item. Then correct each fragment by attaching it to the sentence that comes before or the sentence that comes after—whichever sounds more natural. Put a comma after the dependent-word group if it starts the sentence.

Practice

2

1. Since she was afraid of muggers. Barbara carried a small can of pepper spray on her key ring. A hat pin was hidden under her coat lapel.

    _____

    _____

    _____

2. When I began watching the TV mystery movie. I remembered that I had seen it before. I already knew who had murdered the millionaire.

    _____

    _____

    _____

3. Tulips had only begun to bloom. When a freakish spring snowstorm blanketed the garden. The flowers perished in the unseasonable cold.

    _____

    _____

    _____

4. Whenever I'm in the basement and the phone rings. I don't run up to answer it. If the message is important. The person will call back.

    _____

    _____

    _____

5. Since she is a new student. Carla feels shy and insecure. She thinks she is the only person. Who doesn't know anyone else.

    _____

    _____

    _____

-ing and *to* Fragments

When a word ending in *-ing* or the word *to* appears at or near the start of a word group, a fragment may result. Such fragments often lack a subject and part of the verb.

Underline the word groups in the examples below that contain *-ing* words. Each is an *-ing* fragment.

EXAMPLE 1

I spent all day in the employment office. Trying to find a job that suited me. The prospects looked bleak.

EXAMPLE 2

Lola surprised Tony on the nature hike. Picking blobs of resin off pine trees. Then she chewed them like bubble gum.

EXAMPLE 3

Mel took an aisle seat on the bus. His reason being that he had more legroom.

People sometimes write *-ing* fragments because they think the subject in one sentence will work for the next word group as well. In the first example above, they might think the subject *I* in the opening sentence will also serve as the subject for "Trying to find a job that suited me." But the subject must actually be *in* the sentence.

How to Correct *-ing* Fragments

1. Attach the fragment to the sentence that comes before it or the sentence that comes after it, whichever makes sense. Example 1 above could read, "I spent all day in the employment office, trying to find a job that suited me." (Note that here a comma is used to set off "trying to find a job that suited me," which is extra material placed at the end of the sentence.)

2. Add a subject and change the *-ing* verb part to the correct form of the verb. Example 2 could read, "She picked blobs of resin off pine trees."

3. Change *being* to the correct form of the verb *be (am, are, is, was, were)*. Example 3 could read, "His reason was that he had more legroom."

How to Correct *to* Fragments

As noted earlier, when *to* appears at or near the start of a word group, a fragment sometimes results.

> To remind people of their selfishness. Otis leaves handwritten notes on cars that take up two parking spaces.

The first word group in the example above is a *to* fragment. It can be corrected by adding it to the sentence that comes after it.

> To remind people of their selfishness, Otis leaves handwritten notes on cars that take up two parking spaces.

(Note that here a comma is used to set off "To remind people of their selfishness," which is introductory material in the sentence.)

Underline the *-ing* fragment in each of the following selections. Then make the fragment a sentence by rewriting it, using the method described in parentheses.

Practice

3

EXAMPLE

The dog eyed me with suspicion. <u>Not knowing whether its master was at home.</u> I hesitated to open the gate.

(Add the fragment to the sentence that comes after it.)

Not knowing whether its master was at home, I hesitated to open

the gate.

1. Julie spent an hour at her desk. Staring at a blank piece of paper. She didn't know how to start her report.

   (Add the fragment to the preceding sentence.)

   _____

   _____

2. Rummaging around in the kitchen drawer. Tyrone found the key he had misplaced a year ago.

   (Add the fragment to the sentence that comes after it.)

   _____

   _____

3. I went back to get a carton of Tropicana. As a result, losing my place in the checkout line.

    (Add the subject *I* and change *losing* to the correct form of the verb, *lost.*)

    _____

    _____

Practice

4

Underline the *-ing* or *to* fragment in each item. Then rewrite the item correctly, using one of the methods of correction described on pages 88–89.

1. Last night, my bedroom was so hot I couldn't sleep. Tossing and turning for hours. I felt like a blanket being tumbled dry.

    _____

    _____

    _____

2. A sparrow landed on the icy windowsill. Fluffing its feathers to keep itself warm.

    _____

    _____

    _____

3. Alma left the party early. The reason being that she had to work the next day.

    _____

    _____

    _____

4. Grasping the balance beam with her powdered hands. The gymnast executed a handstand. Then she dismounted.

    _____

    _____

    _____

5. To cover his bald spot. Walt combed long strands of hair over the top of his head. Unfortunately, no one was fooled by this technique.

    _____

    _____

    _____

Added-Detail Fragments

Added-detail fragments lack a subject and a verb. They often begin with one of the following words or phrases.

also	**except**	**including**
especially	**for example**	**such as**

Underline the one added-detail fragment in each of these examples:

EXAMPLE 1

Tony has trouble accepting criticism. Except from Lola. She has a knack for tact.

EXAMPLE 2

My apartment has its drawbacks. For example, no hot water in the morning.

EXAMPLE 3

I had many jobs while in school. Among them, busboy, painter, and security guard.

People often write added-detail fragments for much the same reason they write *-ing* fragments. They think the subject and verb in one sentence will serve for the next word group as well. But the subject and verb must be in *each* word group.

How to Correct Added-Detail Fragments

1. Attach the fragment to the complete thought that precedes it. Example 1 could read, "Tony has trouble accepting criticism, except from Lola." (Note that here a comma is used to set off "except from Lola," which is extra material placed at the end of the sentence.)

2. Add a subject and a verb to the fragment to make it a complete sentence. Example 2 could read, "My apartment has its drawbacks. For example, there is no hot water in the morning."

3. Change words as necessary to make the fragment part of the preceding sentence. Example 3 could read, "Among the many jobs I had while in school were busboy, painter, and security guard."

Practice

5

Underline the fragment in each selection below. Then make it a sentence by rewriting it, using the method described in parentheses.

EXAMPLE

My husband and I share the household chores. <u>Including meals.</u> I do the cooking, and he does the eating.

(Add the fragment to the preceding sentence.)

My husband and I share the household chores, including meals.

1. My father has some nervous habits. For instance, folding a strip of paper into the shape of an accordion.

   (Correct the fragment by adding the subject *he* and changing *folding* to the proper form of the verb, *folds*.)

   _____

   _____

2. Marco stuffed the large green peppers. With hamburger meat, cooked rice, and chopped parsley. Next, using toothpicks, he reattached the stemmed pepper tops.

   (Add the fragment to the preceding sentence.)

   _____

   _____

3. My little brother is addicted to junk foods. For example, Bugles and Doritos. If something is good for him, he won't eat it.

   (Correct the fragment by adding the subject and verb *he craves*.)

   _____

   _____

Practice

6

Underline the added-detail fragment in each selection. Then rewrite that part of the selection needed to correct the fragment. Use one of the three methods of correction described on page 91.

1. My husband keeps all his old clothes. For instance, his faded sweatshirt from high school. He says it's the most comfortable thing he owns.

   _____

   _____

2. My sister has some very bad habits. For example, borrowing my sweaters. She also returns them without washing them.

    _____

    _____

3. To improve her singing, Amber practiced some odd exercises. Such as flapping her tongue and fluttering her lips.

    _____

    _____

4. When she spotted her ex-husband, Leona left the party. She did not want him to see how much she had changed. For example, put on forty pounds.

    _____

    _____

5. Stanley wanted a big birthday cake. With candles spelling out STAN. He wanted to see his name in lights.

    _____

    _____

Missing-Subject Fragments

In each example below, underline the word group in which the subject is missing.

EXAMPLE 1

One example of my father's generosity is that he visits sick friends in the hospital. And takes along get-well cards with a few dollars folded in them.

EXAMPLE 2

The weight lifter grunted as he heaved the barbell into the air. Then, with a loud groan, dropped it.

People write missing-subject fragments because they think the subject in one sentence will apply to the next word group as well. But the subject, as well as the verb, must be in *each* word group to make it a sentence.

> ## How to Correct Missing-Subject Fragments
>
> **1.** Attach the fragment to the preceding sentence. Example 1 could read, "One illustration of my father's generosity is that he visits sick friends in the hospital and takes along get-well cards with a few dollars folded in them."
>
> **2.** Add a subject (which can often be a pronoun standing for the subject in the preceding sentence). Example 2 could read, "Then, with a loud groan, he dropped it."

Practice

7

Underline the missing-subject fragment in each selection. Then rewrite that part of the selection to correct the fragment. Use one of the two methods of correction described above.

1. Embarrassed, Sandra looked around the laundromat. Then quickly folded her raggedy towels and faded sheets.

   _____

   _____

2. Wally took his wool sweaters out of storage. And found them full of moth holes.

   _____

   _____

3. My sister is taking a word-processing course. Also, is learning two computer languages. Machines don't frighten her.

   _____

   _____

4. When someone comes to the door, my dog races upstairs. Then hides under the bed. Strangers really terrify him.

   _____

   _____

5. A tiny bug crawled across my paper. And sat down in the middle of a sentence. There was suddenly one comma too many.

   _____

   _____

A REVIEW

How to Check for Fragments

1. Read your paper aloud from the *last* sentence to the *first*. You will be better able to see and hear whether each word group you read is a complete thought.

2. If you think any word group is a fragment, ask yourself, Does this contain a subject and a verb and express a complete thought?

3. More specifically, be on the lookout for the most common fragments.
   - Dependent-word fragments (starting with words like *after, because, since, when,* and *before*)
   - *-ing* and *to* fragments (*-ing* or *to* at or near the start of a word group)
   - Added-detail fragments (starting with words like *for example, such as, also,* and *especially*)
   - Missing-subject fragments (a verb is present but not the subject)

www.mhhe.com/langan

Collaborative Activity

Editing and Rewriting

Working with a partner, read the short paragraph below and underline the five fragments. Then correct the fragments. Feel free to discuss the rewrite quietly with your partner and refer back to the chapter when necessary.

¹Did you ever wonder how trainers get porpoises to do all those tricks, like leaping over a high bar or jumping through a hoop? ²Wild porpoises are first taught to eat fish from their trainer's hand. ³The trainer blows a whistle. ⁴When the animal accepts a fish. ⁵The porpoise associates the whistle with "correct" behavior. ⁶Once the porpoise touches a human hand to get a fish, it will touch other things. ⁷Like a red target ball. ⁸For example, the trainer will hold the ball high above the water while leaning over a kind of pulpit. ⁹Seeing the ball. ¹⁰The porpoise leaps out of the water. ¹¹Because it knows it will be rewarded with a fish.

continued

¹²A hoop can then be substituted for a ball, and the porpoise's behavior can be "shaped" so it will jump through the hoop. ¹³If the porpoise misses the hoop by jumping too low. ¹⁴The fish reward is withheld. ¹⁵The intelligent mammal will associate "no fish" with "wrong" behavior. ¹⁶Very quickly, the porpoise will be leaping gracefully through the center of the hoop.

Collaborative Activity

Creating Sentences

Working with a partner, make up your own short fragments test as directed. Write one or more of your sentences about the photo to the right.

1. Write a dependent-word fragment in the space below. Then correct the fragment by making it into a complete sentence. You may want to begin your fragment with the word *before, after, when, because*, or *if*.

   Fragment _____

   Sentence _____

2. Write an *-ing* fragment in the space below. Then correct the fragment by making it into a complete sentence. You may want to begin your fragment with the word *laughing, walking, shopping*, or *talking*.

   Fragment _____

   Sentence _____

3. Write an added-detail fragment in the space below. Then correct the fragment by making it into a complete sentence. You may want to begin your fragment with the word *also, especially, except*, or *including*.

   Fragment _____

   Sentence _____

Reflective Activity

1. Look at the paragraph about porpoises that you revised. How has removing fragments affected the reading of the paragraph? Explain.

2. Explain what it is about fragments that you find most difficult to remember and apply. Use an example to make your point clear. Feel free to refer to anything in this chapter.

Review Test   1

Turn each of the following word groups into a complete sentence. Use the space provided.

EXAMPLES

Feeling very confident

Feeling very confident, I began my speech.

Until the rain started

We played softball until the rain started.

1. Before you leave work today

2. When the game show came on

3. Since I have to gain some weight

4. While I was looking in the store window

5. Will be in town next week

6. Stanley, who has a terrible temper

7. Down in the basement

8. Flopping down on the couch

_____

9. Who fixed my car

_____

10. To wake up early

_____

Review Test 2

Underline the fragment in each selection. Then correct the fragment in the space provided.

EXAMPLE

Sam received all kinds of junk mail. Then complained to the post office. Eventually, some of the mail stopped coming.

Then he complained to the post office.

1. Since she was afraid of mussing her hair. Terry refused to go swimming.

_____

_____

2. The first time I took a college course, I was afraid to say anything in class. I didn't open my mouth. Not even to yawn.

_____

_____

3. Looking like a large dish of vanilla fudge ice cream. Our brown-and-white cat went to sleep on the table.

_____

_____

4. Fran read that a sure sign of age is forgetting things. She wanted to show the article to her doctor. But couldn't remember where it was.

_____

_____

5. Dave insisted on wearing a silly hat. That his girlfriend hated. It had two horns like a Viking helmet.

_____

_____

6. A box of frozen vegetables slipped out of Mark's grocery bag. And split open on the sidewalk. Little green peas rolled in every direction, while hard white onions bounced down the street.

_____

_____

7. Even though Laurie isn't disabled. She used to park in "handicapped only" parking spaces. After receiving several tickets, however, she gave up this selfish habit.

_____

_____

8. Thinking that the Halloween get-together was a costume party. Vince came dressed as a boxer. Unfortunately, the other guests were dressed normally.

_____

_____

9. My doctor is using disposable equipment. Such as paper examining gowns and plastic thermometers. He says these are more hygienic.

_____

_____

10. Stanley painted his house lemon-yellow. With orange shutters and a lime-green roof. People say his house looks like a fruit salad.

_____

_____

Review Test 3

In the space provided, write *C* in front of the five word groups that are complete sentences; write *frag* in front of the five fragments. The first two items are done for you.

_____*frag*_____   1. As I was driving my car to work last Monday morning.

_____*C*_____   2. I saw an animal die.

_____   3. It was a beautiful, breezy fall day.

_____   4. With colorful leaves swirling across the road.

_____   5. Suddenly, a squirrel darted out from the bushes.

_____   6. And began zigzagging in the path of approaching cars.

_____   7. Soundlessly, the car in front of me hit the animal.

_____   8. Sending its tiny gray-brown body flying off the road in a flurry of leaves.

_____   9. After the incident, I thought about how fragile life is.

_____   10. And how easily and quickly it can be taken away.

Now correct the fragments you have found. Attach each fragment to the sentence that comes before or after it, or make whatever other change is needed to turn the fragment into a sentence. Use the space provided. The first one is corrected for you.

1. _As I was driving my car to work last Monday morning, I saw an_
   animal die.

2. _____

   _____

3. _____

   _____

4. _____

   _____

5. _____

   _____

Review Test   4

Write quickly for five minutes about the high school you attended. Don't worry about spelling, punctuation, finding exact words, or organizing your thoughts. Just focus on writing as many words as you can without stopping.

After you have finished, go back and make whatever changes are needed to correct any fragments in your writing.

Fragments   MASTERY TEST 1

Each word group in the student paragraph below is numbered. In the space provided, write C if a word group is a complete sentence; write frag if it is a fragment. You will find ten fragments in the paragraph.

1. _____

2. _____

3. _____

4. _____

5. _____

6. _____

7. _____

8. _____

9. _____

10. _____

11. _____

12. _____

13. _____

14. _____

15. _____

16. _____

17. _____

18. _____

19. _____

20. _____

¹One of my favorite dishes to cook and eat is chili. ²The hotter the better. ³First, I chop onion, garlic, and sweet red and green peppers into small cubes. ⁴While I fry the vegetables in one pan. ⁵I brown some lean ground beef in another pan. ⁶Then combine the two mixtures. ⁷And add a can of shiny red kidney beans. ⁸Next, I decide what kind of seasonings to use. ⁹In addition to chili powder, hot pepper flakes, and Tabasco sauce. ¹⁰I sometimes add unusual ingredients. ¹¹Like molasses, cinnamon, chocolate, beer, red wine, or raisins. ¹²Stirring the bubbling pot and inhaling the spicy aromas. ¹³I occasionally taste the mixture to make sure it's good. ¹⁴ I cook the chili over a flame for as long as possible. ¹⁵To give the flavors time to mellow and blend together. ¹⁶Also, longer cooking time produces spicier chili. ¹⁷My chili has been known to burn people's tongues and cause beads of perspiration to form on their brows. ¹⁸And has made friends reach desperately for a glass of water. ¹⁹However, no one has ever complained. ²⁰Or forgotten to ask for a second helping.

NAME: _____

DATE: _____

MASTERY TEST 2 | # Fragments

Underline the fragment in each item. Then make whatever changes are needed to turn the fragment into a sentence.

EXAMPLE

In grade school, I didn't want to wear glasses. ^aAnd avoided having to get them by memorizing the Snellen eye chart.

1. Nita's sons kept opening and closing the refrigerator door. To see just when the little light inside went out.

2. Even though there are a million pigeons in the city. You never see a baby pigeon. It makes you wonder where they are hiding out.

3. Frank likes to get to work early. And spread papers all over his desk. Then he looks too busy to be given any more work.

4. Brenda's doctor warned her to cut out sweets. Especially ice cream and candy.

5. Dragging her feet in the paper slippers. The patient shuffled along the corridor. She hugged the wall closely as nurses and visitors bustled past her.

6. The children ignored the sign. That the lifeguard had posted. They raced around on the slick cement bordering the pool.

7. Pete flunked out of college. After only two semesters. The only thing he could pass was a football.

8. My neighbors' dog likes to borrow things. Today, I saw him trotting away from my back steps. Carrying one of my gardening shoes in his mouth.

9. Since cooking with a small toaster oven saves energy. I bought one to use for small meals and snacks.

10. My cousin sends me funny cards. Such as one with a picture of a lion hanging on to a parachute. It says, "Just thought I'd drop you a lion."

Fragments MASTERY TEST 3

Underline the fragment in each item. Then make whatever changes are needed to turn the fragment into a sentence.

1. As Robert twisted the front doorknob. It came off in his hand. He regretted the day he had bought the house as a "do-it-yourself special."

2. Large, spiky plants called *Spanish spears* bordered the path. The leaves brushed against my legs. And left little slash marks on my ankles.

3. Tim stockpiles canned and dried foods in his basement. In case of emergency. Some of his Campbell's soup is eight years old.

4. At the amusement park, we piled into a boat shaped like a hollowed-out log. Then, gripping the boat's sides and screaming in fear. We plunged through clouds of spray down a water-filled chute.

5. At the lumberyard, Clarence loaded his compact car. With ten-foot planks of raw pine. The car's open hatchback bounced and vibrated as he drove away.

6. Before the newly painted parking stripes had dried. Cars had begun driving over them. As a result, the lot was crisscrossed with pale white lines.

7. My father used to take me to ball games. He would always bring along a newspaper. To read between innings.

8. When Lucas goes on vacation, he fills the bathtub with an inch of water. Then puts his houseplants in the tub. This way, they don't die of thirst.

9. Terry carries her iPod everywhere she goes. For example, to the bookstore. She can't survive for ten minutes without her favorite songs.

10. The perfect shell glittered on the ocean bottom. The diver lifted it off the sand. And placed it in the bag hanging from his shoulder.

NAME: _____

DATE: _____

Fragments

Underline and then correct the five fragments in the following passage.

Did you know that one in every five children is overweight? If you think that these kids will simply outgrow their "baby fat." You're wrong. The number of overweight children in this country has doubled in the past twenty years. Creating a health epidemic. Too many children spend hours watching television. And playing video games when they should be outside playing. They consume sugary, high-calorie snacks. When they should be eating fresh fruits and low-fat yogurt. These children are at a higher risk for high cholesterol, high blood pressure, and type 2 diabetes. They are also more likely to miss school, endure teasing from their peers, and develop low self-esteem. These problems often follow them through adolescence and into adulthood. Sadly, overweight kids have a 70 percent greater chance of becoming overweight adults. Everyone, however, can make a difference. By being a positive role model. So live a healthy life. Turn off your television and take twenty-minute walk.

Fragments   MASTERY TEST 5

Underline and then correct the ten fragments in the following passage.

This summer, I discovered that nature offers some surprises to people. Who take the time to look and listen. After I began an exercise program of walking quickly a half hour a day. I soon slowed down because the world around me was so interesting. For one thing, becoming aware of the richness of the bird and animal life around me. I saw a robin with strands of newspaper in his mouth. And realized it was building a nest in a nearby tree. A family of quail exploded from hiding as I skirted a brushy field. I began to connect the birdsongs I heard with individual birds. For instance, I now know the lonely call of a mourning dove. And the happy buzz of a chickadee. After it rained. I discovered that creatures I have never seen before live in my neighborhood. In the mud beside my walking paths were various tracks. Among them, paws, hooves, and scaly feet. I also found that little dramas were taking place all the time. And that there are some grim moments in nature. I saw a swarm of maggots covering a dead mouse. I also came upon a fat snake spread across the path. I prodded it with a stick. To see if it would move. It shocked me by coughing up an entire frog. My walks have taught me there is a great deal to discover. When I open my eyes and ears.

Run-Ons

6

Introductory Activity

A run-on occurs when two sentences are run together with no adequate sign given to mark the break between them. Shown below are four run-on sentences and four correctly marked sentences. Complete the statement that explains how each run-on is corrected.

1. A man coughed in the movie theater the result was a chain reaction of copycat coughing. *Run-on*

   A man coughed in the movie theater. The result was a chain reaction of copycat coughing. *Correct*

The run-on has been corrected by using a _____ and a capital letter to separate the two complete thoughts.

2. I heard laughter inside the house, no one answered the bell. *Run-on*

   I heard laughter inside the house, but no one answered the bell. *Correct*

The run-on has been corrected by using a joining word, _____, to connect the two complete thoughts.

3. A car sped around the corner, it sprayed slush all over the pedestrians. *Run-on*

   A car sped around the corner; it sprayed slush all over the pedestrians. *Correct*

The run-on has been corrected by using a _____ to connect the two closely related thoughts.

4. I had a campus map, I still could not find my classroom building. *Run-on*

    Although I had a campus map, I still could not find my classroom building.   *Correct*

The run-on has been corrected by using the dependent word _____ to connect the two closely related thoughts.

Answers are on page 662.

What Are Run-Ons?

A *run-on* is two complete thoughts that are run together with no adequate sign given to mark the break between them. As a result of the run-on, the reader is confused, unsure of where one thought ends and the next one begins. Two types of run-ons are fused sentences and comma splices.

www.mhhe.com/langan

Some run-ons have no punctuation at all to mark the break between the thoughts. Such run-ons are known as *fused sentences:* they are fused or joined together as if they were only one thought.

Fused Sentence

Rosa decided to stop smoking she didn't want to die of lung cancer.

The exam was postponed the class was canceled as well.

In other run-ons, known as *comma splices*, a comma is used to connect or "splice" together the two complete thoughts.* However, a comma alone is not enough to connect two complete thoughts. Some connection stronger than a comma alone is needed.

Notes:
1. Some instructors feel that the term *run-ons* should be applied only to fused sentences, not to comma splices. Other instructors, and for our purposes in this book, the term *run-on* applies equally to fused sentences and comma splices. The bottom line is that you do not want either fused sentences or comma splices in your writing.
2. Some instructors refer to each complete thought in a run-on as an *independent clause*. A *clause* is simply a group of words having a subject and a verb. A clause may be *independent* (expressing a complete thought and able to stand alone) or *dependent* (not expressing a complete thought and not able to stand alone). A run-on is two independent clauses that are run together with no adequate sign given to mark the break between them.

Comma Splice

Rosa decided to stop smoking, she didn't want to die of lung cancer.

The exam was postponed, the class was canceled as well.

Comma splices are the most common kind of run-on. Students sense that some kind of connection is needed between thoughts, and so they put a comma at the dividing point. But the comma alone is not sufficient. A stronger, clearer mark is needed between the two thoughts.

A Warning: Words That Can Lead to Run-Ons

People often write run-ons when the second complete thought begins with one of the following words. Be on the alert for run-ons whenever you use them in your writing.

I	we	there	now
you	they	this	then
he, she, it		that	next

Correcting Run-Ons

Here are four common methods of correcting a run-on:

1. Use a period and a capital letter to separate the two complete thoughts. (In other words, make two separate sentences of the two complete thoughts.)

    Rosa decided to stop smoking. She didn't want to die of lung cancer.

    The exam was postponed. The class was canceled as well.

2. Use a comma plus a joining word (*and, but, for, or, nor, so, yet*) to connect the two complete thoughts.

    Rosa decided to stop smoking, for she didn't want to die of lung cancer.

    The exam was postponed, and the class was canceled as well.

3. Use a semicolon to connect the two complete thoughts.

Rosa decided to stop smoking; she didn't want to die of lung cancer.

The exam was postponed; the class was canceled as well.

4. Use subordination (put a dependent word at the beginning of one word group).

Because Rosa didn't want to die of lung cancer, she decided to stop smoking.

When the exam was postponed, the class was canceled as well.

The following pages will give you practice in all four methods of correcting run-ons. The use of subordination will be explained further on page 135, in a chapter that deals with sentence variety.

Method 1: Period and a Capital Letter

One way of correcting a run-on is to use a period and a capital letter at the break between the two complete thoughts. Use this method especially if the thoughts are not closely related or if another method would make the sentence too long.

Locate the split in each of the following run-ons. Each is a *fused sentence*—that is, each consists of two sentences fused or joined together with no punctuation at all between them. Reading each sentence aloud will help you "hear" where a major break or split in the thought occurs. At such a point, your voice will probably drop and pause.

Practice

1

Correct the run-on by putting a period at the end of the first thought and a capital letter at the start of the second thought.

EXAMPLE

Craig was not a success at his job. His mouth moved faster than his hands.

1. Michael gulped two cups of strong coffee his heart then started to flutter.

2. Elena defrosted the freezer in her usual impatient way she hacked at the thick ice with a screwdriver.

3. The engine was sputtering and coughing a strong smell of gas came from under the hood.

4. A bright yellow Volkswagen "bug" pulled up beside me it looked like a deviled egg on wheels.

5. The phone in the next apartment rings all the time the new tenants keep complaining about the sound.

6. Numbered Ping-Pong balls bounced in the machine we clutched our raffle tickets tightly.

7. The store clerk watched the girls closely they must have looked like shoplifters to her.

8. It's hard to discuss things with Lauren she interprets almost everything as criticism.

9. Kate's books look like accident victims they have cracked spines and torn covers.

10. I got to the sale too late the last ceiling fan had been sold just five minutes before.

Practice 2

Locate the split in each of the following run-ons. Some of the run-ons are fused sentences, and some of them are *comma splices*—run-ons spliced or joined together only with a comma. Correct each run-on by putting a period at the end of the first thought and a capital letter at the start of the next thought.

1. Human teenagers must be descended from cockroaches, both like to stay out late and eat junk food.

2. Only the female mosquito drinks blood the male lives on plant juices.

3. Sonja has the experience to be an excellent marriage counselor she's already been married four times.

4. My uncle's final words probably express everyone's feeling about death he said, "Wait a minute."

5. I remember every rainbow I've ever seen one actually circled the sun.

6. The beach was once beautiful now it is covered with soda cans, plastic six-pack rings, and cigarette butts.

7. In eighteenth-century Russia, smoking carried a death penalty the same is true of chain-smoking today.

8. The business school near our home just closed down it ran out of money.

9. The frankfurter or hot dog did not begin in Germany, in fact, it first appeared in China.

10. The man about to be shot by a firing squad had a last request he wanted to be given a bulletproof vest.

Write a second sentence to go with each sentence below. Start the second sentence with the word given in the margin.

EXAMPLE

It   My wireless all-in-one printer is so convenient. *It allows me to print, scan, copy, and fax documents.*

Then   1. The oysters were placed on the grill until their shells popped open.

_____

It   2. I need to update the anti-virus software on my computer. _____

_____

She   3. Ashlee sent me several urgent text messages last night. _____

_____

They 4. Students who take studio art classes spend hours on their projects.

_____

There 5. After the recent sewage spill, people were afraid to swim in the ocean. _____

Method 2: Comma and a Joining Word

Another way of correcting a run-on is to use a comma plus a joining word to connect the two complete thoughts. Joining words (also called *coordinating conjunctions*) include *and, but, for, or, nor, so,* and *yet.* The meaning of the four most common joining words is explained below.

and   in addition, along with

Lola was watching *Monday Night Football,* and she was doing her homework as well.

(*And* means *in addition:* Lola was watching *Monday Night Football;* in *addition,* she was doing her homework.)

but   however, except, on the other hand, just the opposite

I voted for the president two years ago, but I would not vote for him today.

(*But* means *however:* I voted for the president two years ago; *however,* I would not vote for him today.)

for   because, the reason why, the cause for something

Saturday is the worst day to shop, for people jam the stores.

(*For* means *because*: Saturday is the worst day to shop *because* people jam the stores.) If you are not comfortable using *for*, you may want to use *because* instead of *for* in the activities that follow. If you do use *because*, omit the comma before it.

so   as a result, therefore

Our son misbehaved again, so he was sent upstairs without dessert.

(*So* means *as a result*: Our son misbehaved again; *as a result*, he was sent upstairs without dessert.)

Practice **4**	Insert the comma and the joining word (*and, but, for, so*) that logically connects the two thoughts in each sentence.

EXAMPLE

      I hate to see animals in cages$\overset{so}{\wedge}$a trip to the zoo always depresses me.

1. We knew the old desk had a secret drawer no one could find it.

2. I had to retype my term paper my little boy had scrawled on it with a purple crayon.

3. Last year my nephew needed physical therapy the whole family pitched in to work with him.

4. My new car is a pleasure to drive it gets terrific mileage.

5. A cat food commercial came on Marie started to sing along with the jingle.

6. It rained a lot this summer we have not had to water our lawn.

7. I heard the grinding of the garbage truck I ran downstairs and grabbed the trash bags.

8. Ella wanted to take a break the boss wanted the inventory list right away.

9. The map was faded an ink stain had blotted out an entire country.

10. The two little boys had a giggling fit their father hustled them out of the church.

2. You should have looked at the label _____ you washed that wool sweater.

3. _____ the instructor announced that there were only ten minutes left in the test, students began writing even more quickly to finish their essay answers.

4. _____ you open the windows, the paint fumes will disappear more quickly.

5. The directions say to continue on the main highway _____ a large red barn and a small road appear on the right.

Rewrite the five sentences below so that one idea is subordinate to the other. In each case, use one of the dependent words from the box on the previous page.

Practice

10

> **HINT** As in the example, use a comma if a dependent statement starts a sentence.

EXAMPLE

I hate to see animals in cages; a trip to the zoo always depresses me.

Because I hate to see animals in cages, a trip to the zoo always

depresses me.

1. I had a campus map; I still could not find my classroom building.

_____

_____

2. A cat food commercial came on; Marie started to sing along with the jingle.

_____

_____

3. The phone in the next apartment rings constantly; I'm beginning to get used to the sound.

_____

_____

4. Michael gulped two cups of strong coffee; his heart began to flutter.

_____

_____

5. A car sped around the corner; it sprayed slush all over the pedestrians.

_____

_____

Collaborative Activity

Editing and Rewriting

Working with a partner, carefully read the short paragraph below and underline the five run-ons. Then correct them. Feel free to discuss the corrections quietly with your partner and refer back to the chapter when necessary.

[1]People do funny things when they get on an elevator. [2]They try to move into a corner or against a wall. [3]They all face forward their hands are kept in front or at their sides. [4]Most of all, they avoid eye contact with the other passengers, preferring to stare at the floor numbers. [5]Nobody teaches these people how to behave on an elevator however, everyone seems to obey the same rules. [6]Psychologists have a theory about elevator behavior that they feel explains these actions. [7]Elevators are small, enclosed spaces they force people into contact with one another. [8]The contact is a violation of a person's "personal space" this is the invisible shield we all carry with us. [9]We get nervous when a stranger stands too close to us we want to put that invisible shield back. [10]Therefore, an elevator isn't the place to try to get to know someone.

Collaborative Activity

Creating Sentences

Working with a partner, make up your own short run-ons test as directed.

1. Write a run-on sentence. Then rewrite it, using a period and capital letter to separate the thoughts into two sentences.

    Run-on _____

    _____

    Rewrite _____

    _____

2. Write a sentence that has two complete thoughts. Then rewrite it, using a comma and a joining word to correctly join the complete thoughts.

    Two complete thoughts _____

    _____

    Rewrite _____

    _____

3. Write a sentence that has two complete thoughts. Then rewrite it, using a semicolon to correctly join the complete thoughts.

    Two complete thoughts _____

    _____

    Rewrite _____

    _____

Reflective Activity

1. Look at the paragraph about elevators that you revised. Explain how run-ons interfered with your reading of the paragraph.

2. In your own written work, which type of run-on are you more likely to write: comma splices or fused sentences? Why?

3. Which method of correcting run-ons are you most likely to use in your own writing? Which are you least likely to use? Why?

Review Test 1

Some of the run-ons that follow are *fused sentences,* having no punctuation between the two complete thoughts; others are *comma splices,* having only a comma between the two complete thoughts.

Correct the run-ons by using one of the following three methods:

- Period and a capital letter
- Comma and a joining word (*and, but, for, so*)
- Semicolon

Use whichever method seems most appropriate in each case.

EXAMPLE

and
Fred pulled the cellophane off the cake⸝the icing came along with it.

1. The runner was called safe even he couldn't believe it.

2. I looked all over for my new shirt all I could find was the empty bag.

3. Lia tried to fold the road map neatly she gave up and stuffed it into the glove compartment.

4. First we can't wait to go on vacation, then we can't wait to come home again.

5. One step was sagging Martina hired a carpenter to fix the porch.

6. I ran toward the supermarket, the manager had just locked the doors.

7. Ted tried to assemble the barbecue, the instructions were impossible to understand.

8. I reached into the pretzel bag all that was left was salt.

9. Tina was starving she bought a limp sandwich from the vending machine.

10. Bev was bored she drew rocket ships in the margins of her notebook.

Review Test 2

Correct the run-on in each sentence by using subordination. Choose from among the following dependent words.

after	before	unless
although	even though	until
as	if	when
because	since	while

EXAMPLE

Tony hated going to a new barber, he was afraid of butchered hair.

Because Tony was afraid of butchered hair, he hated going to a new barber.

1. The fan started throwing beer cans onto the field security guards hustled him away.

2. I had three cups of coffee, my eyes looked like huge globes.

3. The boy didn't want to talk to his mother, he pretended to be asleep.

4. The check arrived in the mail we didn't really believe that we had won the contest.

5. We forgot to put film in the camera, the only pictures we have of our vacation are the ones in our memory.

6. I left school this afternoon hailstones as big as marbles were falling from the sky.

_____

_____

7. The plumber comes quickly our kitchen will look like a swamp.

_____

8. The man circled the crowded parking lot in their car, his wife ran into the store to return a sweater.

_____

_____

9. The boy was wearing headphones nearly everyone on the bus could hear the beat of the song on his iPod.

_____

_____

10. The computer went dead a message appeared on the screen saying, "System error."

_____

_____

Review Test 3

On separate paper, write six sentences, each of which has two complete thoughts. In two of the sentences, use a period and a capital letter between the thoughts. In another two sentences, use a comma and a joining word (*and, but, or, nor, for, so, yet*) to join the thoughts. In the final two sentences, use a semicolon to join the thoughts.

Review Test 4

Write quickly for five minutes about something that makes you angry. Don't worry about spelling, punctuation, finding exact words, or organizing your thoughts. Just focus on writing as many words as you can without stopping.

After you have finished, go back and make whatever changes are needed to correct any run-on sentences in your writing.

Run-Ons   MASTERY TEST 1

In the space provided, write R-O beside run-on sentences and C for sentences that are punctuated correctly. Some of the run-ons have no punctuation between the two complete thoughts; others have only a comma.

Correct each run-on by using (1) a period and a capital letter, (2) a comma and a joining word, or (3) a semicolon. Do not use the same method of correction in every sentence.

EXAMPLES

_____R-O_____ I applied for the job, *but* I never got called in for an interview.

_____R-O_____ Carla's toothache is getting worse; *s* she should go to a dentist soon.

_____ 1. This year's company picnic was not a success, it attracted more bears than people.

_____ 2. Chang is allergic to anything green, even houseplants make him sneeze.

_____ 3. I was falling asleep in a hurry, I couldn't keep my eyes open any longer.

_____ 4. Don't try to hand-feed the sharks you could end up feeding them more than your hand.

_____ 5. These days, getting married is a risky business, for over half of all marriages end in divorce.

_____ 6. We quickly switched from one news program to another each one had the same story.

_____ 7. An accident had happened on the bridge traffic was backed up in both directions.

_____ 8. On long car trips, my little brother drives me crazy he insists on reading all the road signs out loud.

_____ 9. Harold always finishes the ice cream then he puts the empty carton back in the freezer.

_____ 10. It was too hot indoors to read, so I took my book onto the front porch.

NAME: _____

DATE: _____

MASTERY TEST 2 | ## Run-Ons

In the space provided, write R-O beside run-on sentences. Write C beside the one sentence that is punctuated correctly. Some of the run-ons have no punctuation between the two complete thoughts; others have only a comma.

Correct each run-on by using (1) a period and capital letter, (2) a comma and joining word, or (3) a semicolon. Do not use the same method of correction for every sentence.

_____ 1. I work for about two hours on my homework I then spend about an hour watching television.

_____ 2. Sheets of heavy rain were pounding against my car windshield, I pulled over to the side of the road.

_____ 3. A bus pulled away slowly from the curb an elderly woman ran after it, waving her hand for it to stop.

_____ 4. Our apartment gets really cold at night the landlord refuses to turn up the heat.

_____ 5. The little boy was struggling with the top of the candy bag, it suddenly tore open and spilled Skittles all over the floor.

_____ 6. Dozens of restaurants open in the city every year, almost that many go out of business.

_____ 7. I got out of the shower to answer the telephone, but it stopped ringing as soon as I touched it.

_____ 8. The breakfast cereal is "new and improved" it doesn't taste any different to me.

_____ 9. The line at the cash register wasn't moving the cashier seemed to have gone home.

_____ 10. Several homeless men live under the bridge, their sleeping bags and shopping carts are always there.

Run-Ons   MASTERY TEST 3

In the space provided, write R-O *beside run-on sentences. Write* C *beside the one sentence that is punctuated correctly. Some of the run-ons have no punctuation between the two complete thoughts; others have only a comma.*

Correct each run-on by using (1) a period and a capital letter, (2) a comma and a joining word, or (3) a semicolon. Do not use the same method of correction for every sentence.

_____ 1. Americans spend millions of dollars each year on bottled water, critics argue that tap water is equally safe to drink.

_____ 2. Isaiah is confident that the trucking company will hire him he has a valid CDL license and a clean traffic abstract.

_____ 3. The mechanic said that many hybrid cars have transmission problems, I am glad that I purchased a gasoline-powered subcompact car, which is equally fuel efficient.

_____ 4. This summer brought record-breaking drought conditions, many farmers are being forced to plant fewer crops or irrigate their fields.

_____ 5. Sydney decided to use recycled plastic to build an outdoor deck, her children asked her to build a doghouse with the extra lumber.

_____ 6. Mark worried when the canned chili sauce he ate while on his camping trip was recalled for botulism, he did not experience any symptoms of food poisoning.

_____ 7. Parents who sign up their children for martial arts hope that the study will provide physical exercise, self-confidence, and personal discipline, their children, however, say that they are simply having fun.

_____ 8. The Ladies Professional Golf Association (LPGA) was founded in 1950, making it the oldest female professional sports organization in the United States.

_____ 9. Witnesses reported that the bank robber was a woman, security cameras revealed that the thief was a man carrying a handbag and wearing a wig and lipstick.

_____ 10. Today, the average American teenager works 16 hours per week parents and educators are concerned that these part-time jobs leave little time for homework or sleep.

NAME: _____

DATE: _____

MASTERY TEST 4 ## Run-Ons

In the space provided, write R-O *beside run-on sentences. Write* C *beside the one sentence that is punctuated correctly. Some of the run-ons have no punctuation between the two complete thoughts; others have only a comma.*

Correct each run-on by using (1) a period and capital letter, (2) a comma and joining word, or (3) a semicolon. Do not use the same method of correction for every sentence.

_____ 1. Flora carried heavy trays all day long her feet felt like hundred-pound lead weights.

_____ 2. The young woman paced anxiously while the laundry circled lazily in the dryer.

_____ 3. The musician strummed his most popular song the crowd waved cigarette lighters and chanted the words along with him.

_____ 4. That man has a million-dollar company he prefers to wear a stained T-shirt and torn jeans.

_____ 5. I finished writing the paper for my English class I started reading and taking notes on a chapter in my psychology text.

_____ 6. The detective burst into the crowded party he announced that he knew the murderer's identity.

_____ 7. Chicken and dumplings were cooking on the stove we set the table for dinner.

_____ 8. Sid is trying to smoke less, he cut all his cigarettes in half and can smoke only one of those an hour.

_____ 9. It was a beautiful springtime day full of sunshine and soft breezes the park was strangely empty.

_____ 10. Raoul sat on his sofa staring out at the cold gray snow he wondered what it would be like to live in Hawaii.

Sentence Variety I

This chapter will show you how to write effective and varied sentences. You'll learn more about two techniques—subordination and coordination—that you can use to expand simple sentences, making them more interesting and expressive. You'll also reinforce what you have learned in Chapters 5 and 6 about how subordination and coordination can help you correct fragments and run-ons in your writing.

Four Traditional Sentence Patterns

Sentences in English are traditionally described as *simple, compound, complex,* or *compound-complex.* Each is explained below.

The Simple Sentence

A simple sentence has a single subject-verb combination.

> Children play.

> The game ended early.

> My car stalled three times last week.

> The lake has been polluted by several neighboring streams.

A simple sentence may have more than one subject:

> Lola and Tony drove home.

> The wind and sun dried my hair.

or more than one verb:

The <u>children</u> <u>smiled</u> and <u>waved</u> at us.

The <u>lawn mower</u> <u>smoked</u> and <u>sputtered</u>.

or several subjects and verbs:

<u>Manny</u>, <u>Moe</u>, and <u>Jack</u> <u>lubricated</u> my car, <u>replaced</u> the oil filter, and <u>cleaned</u> the spark plugs.

Practice

1

On separate paper, write:

Three sentences, each with a single subject and verb

Three sentences, each with a single subject and a double verb

Three sentences, each with a double subject and a single verb

In each case, underline the subject once and the verb twice. (See pages 69–70 if necessary for more information on subjects and verbs.)

The Compound Sentence

A compound, or "double," sentence is made up of two (or more) simple sentences. The complete statements in a compound sentence are usually connected by a comma plus a joining word (*and, but, for, or, nor, so, yet*).

A compound sentence is used when you want to give equal weight to two closely related ideas. The technique of showing that ideas have equal importance is called *coordination.*

Following are some compound sentences. Each sentence contains two ideas that the writer considers equal in importance.

The rain increased, so the officials canceled the game.

Martha wanted to go shopping, but Fred refused to drive her.

Hollis was watching television in the family room, and April was upstairs on the phone.

I had to give up wood carving, for my arthritis had become very painful.

Combine the following pairs of simple sentences into compound sentences. Use a comma and a logical joining word (*and, but, for, so*) to connect each pair.

> HINT For a review of joining words, see pages 111–112.

EXAMPLE
- The children wanted to eat pizza.
- I picked up fried chicken on the way home.

The children wanted to eat pizza, but I picked up fried chicken on the way home.

1. • I am majoring in digital media arts.
   • I hope to find a job doing video-game animation.

   _____

   _____

2. • My children were spending too much time in front of the TV and computer.
   • I signed up my entire family for a one-year gym membership.

   _____

   _____

3. • Nicole's skin was blemished and sun damaged.
   • She consulted with a plastic surgeon about a chemical face peel.

   _____

   _____

4. • Riley insists on buying certified-organic fruits and vegetables.
   • I cannot distinguish organic from conventionally grown produce.

   _____

   _____

5. • I was recently promoted to shift manager at work.
   • I need to drop down to part-time status at school next semester.

   _____

   _____

On separate paper, write five compound sentences of your own about the photo below. Use a different joining word (*and, but, for, or, nor, so, yet*) to connect the two complete ideas in each sentence.

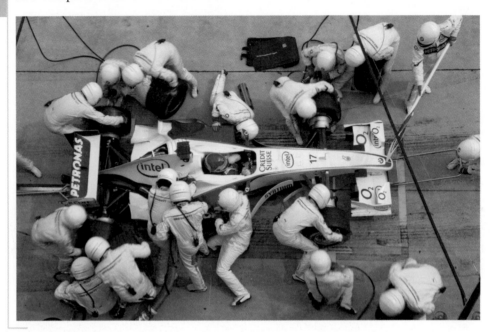

The Complex Sentence

A complex sentence is made up of a simple sentence (a complete statement) and a statement that begins with a dependent word.* Here is a list of common dependent words:

Dependent Words

after	if, even if	when, whenever
although, though	in order that	where, wherever
as	since	whether
because	that, so that	which, whichever
before	unless	while
even though	until	who
how	what, whatever	whose

---

*The two parts of a complex sentence are sometimes called an independent clause and a dependent clause. A *clause* is simply a word group that contains a subject and a verb. An *independent clause* expresses a complete thought and can stand alone. A *dependent clause* does not express a complete thought in itself and "depends on" the independent clause to complete its meaning. Dependent clauses always begin with a dependent or subordinating word.

A complex sentence is used when you want to emphasize one idea over another in a sentence. Look at the following complex sentence:

Because I forgot the time, I missed the final exam.

The idea that the writer wants to emphasize here—*I missed the final exam*—is expressed as a complete thought. The less important idea—*Because I forgot the time*—is subordinated to the complete thought. The technique of giving one idea less emphasis than another is called *subordination*.

Following are other examples of complex sentences. In each case, the part starting with the dependent word is the less emphasized part of the sentence.

While Aisha was eating breakfast, she began to feel sick.

I checked my money *before* I invited Pedro for lunch.

When Jerry lost his temper, he also lost his job.

Although I practiced for three months, I failed my driving test.

Use logical dependent words to combine the following pairs of simple sentences into complex sentences. Place a comma after a dependent statement when it starts the sentence.

Practice

4

EXAMPLES

- I obtained a credit card.
- I began spending money recklessly.
  When I obtained a credit card, I began spending money recklessly.

- Alan dressed the turkey.
- His brother greased the roasting pan.
  Alan dressed the turkey while his brother greased the roasting pan.

1. • The movie disgusted Dena.
   • She walked out after twenty minutes.

   _____

   _____

2. • The house had been burglarized.
   • Dave couldn't sleep soundly for several months.

   _____

   _____

3. • My vision begins to fade.
   • I know I'd better get some sleep.

   _____

   _____

4. • The family would need a place to sleep.
   • Fred told the movers to unload the mattresses first.

   _____

   _____

5. • The hurricane hit the coast.
   • We crisscrossed our windows with strong tape.

   _____

   _____

Practice 5

Rewrite the following sentences, using subordination rather than coordination. Include a comma when a dependent statement starts a sentence.

EXAMPLE

The hair dryer was not working right, so I returned it to the store.
Because the hair dryer was not working right, I returned it to the store.

1. The muffler shop advertised same-day service, but my car wasn't ready for three days.

   _____

   _____

2. The hypertension medication produced dangerous side effects, so the government banned it.

   _____

   _____

2. • Tess had worn glasses for fifteen years.
    • She decided to get contact lenses.
    • She would be able to see better.
    • She would look more glamorous.

    _____

    _____

    _____

    _____

3. • The children at the day care center took their naps.
    • They unrolled their sleeping mats.
    • They piled their shoes and sneakers in a corner.

    _____

    _____

    _____

4. • Jerry dialed the police emergency number.
    • He received a busy signal.
    • He dropped the phone and ran.
    • He didn't have time to call back.

    _____

    _____

    _____

5. • Louise disliked walking home from the bus stop.
    • The street had no overhead lights.
    • It was lined with abandoned buildings.

    _____

    _____

    _____

6. • The rain hit the hot pavement.
   • Plumes of steam rose from the blacktop.
   • Cars slowed to a crawl.
   • The fog obscured the drivers' vision.

   _____

   _____

   _____

   _____

7. • His car went through the automated car wash.
   • Harry watched from the sidelines.
   • Floppy brushes slapped the car's doors.
   • Sprays of water squirted onto the roof.

   _____

   _____

   _____

   _____

8. • The pipes had frozen.
   • The heat had gone off.
   • We phoned the plumber.
   • He couldn't come for two days.
   • He had been swamped with emergency calls.

   _____

   _____

   _____

   _____

9. • My car developed an annoying rattle.
   • I took it to the service station.
   • The mechanic looked under the hood.
   • He couldn't find what was wrong.

   _____

   _____

   _____

   _____

10. • The childproof cap on the aspirin bottle would not budge.
    • The arrows on the bottleneck and cap were lined up.
    • I pried the cap with my fingernails.
    • One nail snapped off.
    • The cap still adhered tightly to the bottle.

    _____

    _____

    _____

    _____

Review Test   1

Combine each group of short sentences into one sentence. Various combinations are possible. Choose the combination that reads most smoothly and clearly and that sounds most appropriate in the context of the surrounding sentences. Use separate paper.

Here is an example of a group of sentences and some possible combinations.

EXAMPLE

• Martha moved in the desk chair.
• Her moving was uneasy.
• The chair was hard.
• She worked at the assignment.
• The assignment was for her English class.

Martha moved uneasily in the hard desk chair, working at the assignment for her English class.

Moving uneasily in the hard desk chair, Martha worked at the assignment for her English class.

Martha moved uneasily in the hard desk chair as she worked at the assignment for her English class.

While she worked at the assignment for her English class, Martha moved uneasily in the hard desk chair.

> **HINT** In combining short sentences into one sentence, omit repeated words where necessary.

Our First Camping Trip

- My husband and I went camping for the first time.
- It was an experience.
- The experience is one we will never forget.

- We borrowed a tent.
- We borrowed a propane stove.
- We borrowed them from my brother-in-law.

- We arrived at the campground.
- We chose a spot.
- The spot was where we could pitch our tents.

- We had forgotten to bring the directions for setting up the tent.
- We had to put up the tent using a trial-and-error process.
- The process took us four hours.

- The tent suddenly collapsed.
- It was nearly dark.
- We had to put it up again.

- Later, we had difficulty making dinner.
- The stove at first refused to light.
- The food wouldn't cook.

- We finished cleaning up.
- We were exhausted.
- We crawled into our sleeping bags.

- A brief rain awoke us that night.
- We were so tired.
- We soon fell asleep again.

- Morning came.
- We were damp and miserable.

- We had learned the important lesson.
- It was that "roughing it" was too rough for us.

Review Test 2

Combine each group of short sentences into one sentence. Various combinations are possible. Choose the combination that reads most smoothly and clearly and that sounds most appropriate in the context of surrounding sentences. In combining short sentences into one sentence, omit repeated words where necessary. Use separate paper.

My Dishwashing Job

- I had one of the worst experiences of my life.
- This happened when I showed up for my first night of work.
- It was work as a restaurant dishwasher.

- I was to load the dirty dishes and silverware into the dishwashing machine.
- The dishes were cleaned and dried.

- Business at the restaurant started to pick up.
- This happened when dinnertime began.
- The dishes came in faster and faster.

- I tried to scrape and load the dishes as fast as I could.
- I couldn't keep up.

- The counter was piled high with dishes.
- The busboys began to stack pans of them on the floor.

- I was hot and sweaty.
- My arms were spotted with bits of food.
- My fingertips were burned from grabbing the clean dishes out of the machine.

- Then my boss burst through the double doors of the kitchen.
- He told me to hurry up.
- He told me the dining room was almost out of clean dishes.

- My back was aching.
- My head was splitting.
- I smelled like the garbage can next to me.
- This happened when the restaurant was ready to close.

- It took all my courage to return to this job the next night.
- I stuck it out.
- I needed the money.

- I hope never to have to be a dishwasher again.
- I did become an expert one.
- I did this after I had been on the job for a few days.

Sentence Variety I

Combine each group of short sentences into one sentence. Various combinations are possible. Choose the combination that reads most smoothly and clearly and that sounds most appropriate in the context of surrounding sentences. Use separate paper.

> HINT In combining short sentences into one sentence, omit repeated words where necessary.

Kids and Mud

- Two toddlers sit on the ground.
- They play in the wet and gooey mud.

- They keep busy for hours.
- They build all sorts of things.

- Kids can turn mud into cakes.
- They can turn twigs into candles.
- They do so when they are allowed to use their imagination.

- They don't need expensive toys.
- They don't even need a television set.

- What they need is some wet dirt.
- They also need patient parents.
- Patient parents won't yell about their muddy clothes.

NAME: _____

DATE: _____

MASTERY TEST 2 | # Sentence Variety I

Follow the instructions provided for Mastery Test 1.

> **HINT** In combining short sentences into one sentence, omit repeated words where necessary.

The Do-It-Yourself Special

- Kevin and Tyra decided to move out of their cramped apartment.
- They went to a real estate agent.
- The real estate agent was Kevin's high school friend.

- They looked at lots of houses.
- All the houses were too expensive.

- Finally, they found a house.
- They could afford the house.
- The house needed a lot of work.

- For example, the front steps had a railing.
- The railing was made of rusty pipes.
- The floors tilted a bit.
- The kitchen walls were covered in a crazy pattern of multicolored tiles.

- There was a great deal of work to be done.
- Kevin and Tyra bought the do-it-yourself special.
- They knew it was a place they could call home.

Standard English Verbs

Underline what you think is the correct form of the verb in each pair of sentences below.

That radio station once (play, played) top-forty hits.

It now (play, plays) classical music.

When Sherry was a little girl, she (hope, hoped) to become a movie star.

Now she (hope, hopes) to be accepted at law school.

At first, my father (juggle, juggled) with balls of yarn.

Now that he is an expert, he (juggle, juggles) raw eggs.

On the basis of the preceding examples, complete the following statements.

1. The first sentence in each pair refers to an action in (past time, the present time), and the regular verb has an _____ ending.

2. The second sentence in each pair refers to an action in (past time, the present time), and the regular verb has an _____ ending.

Answers are on page 664.

Many people have grown up in communities where nonstandard verb forms are used in everyday life. Such nonstandard forms include *they be, it done, we has, you was, she don't,* and *it ain't.* Community dialects have richness and power but are a drawback in college and the world at large, where standard English verb forms must be used. Standard English helps ensure clear communication among English-speaking people everywhere, and it is especially important in the world of work.

This chapter compares the community dialect and the standard English forms of a regular verb and three common irregular verbs.

Regular Verbs: Dialect and Standard Forms

The chart below compares community dialect (nonstandard) and standard English forms of the regular verb *talk.*

	Talk		
Community Dialect **(Do not use in your writing)**		*Standard English* **(Use for clear communication)**	
Present Tense			
I talks	we talks	I talk	we talk
you talks	you talks	you talk	you talk
he, she, it talk	they talks	he, she, it talks	they talk
Past Tense			
I talk	we talk	I talked	we talked
you talk	you talk	you talked	you talked
he, she, it talk	they talk	he, she, it talked	they talked

One of the most common nonstandard forms results from dropping the endings of regular verbs. For example, people might say "Rose work until ten o'clock tonight" instead of "Rose works until ten o'clock tonight." Or they'll say "I work overtime yesterday" instead of "I worked overtime yesterday." To avoid such nonstandard usage, memorize the forms shown above for the regular verb *talk.* Then do the activities that follow. These activities will help you make it a habit to include verb endings in your writing.

Present Tense Endings

The verb ending -s or -es is needed with a regular verb in the present tense when the subject is *he, she, it,* or any one person or thing.

He	He lifts weights.
She	She runs.
It	It amazes me.
One person	Their son Ted swims.
One person	Their daughter Terry dances.
One thing	Their house jumps at night with all the exercise.

All but one of the ten sentences that follow need -s or -es endings. Cross out the nonstandard verb forms and write the standard forms in the spaces provided. Mark the one sentence that needs no change with a *C.*

Practice

1

www.mhhe.com/langan

EXAMPLE

_____*ends*_____   The sale ~~end~~ tomorrow.

_____ 1. Lucille wear a wig to cover up her thinning gray hair.

_____ 2. My horoscope say that today is a good day for romance.

_____ 3. Huang subscribe to three newsmagazines to keep up with current events.

_____ 4. My mother believe in always trying her best.

_____ 5. A dog see only tones of gray, black, and white.

_____ 6. At Thanksgiving, our church distribute turkeys to the needy.

_____ 7. Andrea breaks her cigarettes in half before smoking them.

_____ 8. Chris feed chopped-up flies and mosquitoes to his tropical fish.

_____ 9. That diner overcook all its food.

_____ 10. He polish his shoes using a melted wax crayon and an old towel.

Practice

2

Rewrite the short selection below, adding present tense -*s* verb endings wherever needed.

> Lou work for a company that deliver singing telegrams. Sometimes he put on a sequined tuxedo or wear a Cupid costume. He compose his own songs for birthdays, anniversaries, bachelor parties, and other occasions. Then he show up at a certain place and surprise the victim. He sing a song that include personal details, which he get in advance, about the recipient of the telegram. Lou love the astonished looks on other people's faces; he also enjoy earning money by making people happy on special days.

_____

_____

_____

_____

_____

_____

_____

_____

Past Tense Endings

The verb ending -*d* or -*ed* is needed with a regular verb in the past tense.

Yesterday we finished painting the house.

I completed the paper an hour before class.

Fred's car stalled on his way to work this morning.

www.mhhe.com/langan

Practice

3

All but one of the ten sentences that follow need -*d* or -*ed* endings. Cross out the nonstandard verb forms and write the standard forms in the spaces provided. Mark the one sentence that needs no change with a *C*.

EXAMPLE

jumped   The cat ~~jump~~ on my lap when I sat down.

_____   1. The first time I baked a pound cake, it turn out to be a ton cake.

_____   2. The line drive slammed into the fence and bounce into the stands for a ground-rule double.

_____ 3. Ben page through the book, looking for the money he had hidden there.

_____ 4. Mario crush the sunglasses in his back pocket as he flopped on the sofa.

_____ 5. The sweating workers shoveled hot tar onto the road and then smoothed it out.

_____ 6. The surgeons wash their hands before they entered the operating room.

_____ 7. The detective crack the case after finding a key witness.

_____ 8. When she was a teenager, Rita collect pictures of her favorite rock stars.

_____ 9. As they struggled, the mugger pull the gold chain from Val's neck.

_____ 10. Ken knew he lack the ability to make the varsity team, but he tried out anyway.

Rewrite this selection below, adding past tense -d or -ed verb endings where needed.

Practice

4

Brad hate working long hours, but he need money to support his growing family and to pay for school. He start working at the auto body shop when he graduate from high school because he like cars, but the job bore him. He wish that he could spend more time at home with his wife and new baby girl. He also want to dedicate more time to his homework. Brad knew that he had made his own choices, so he decide to appreciate his job, his family, and his chance to move ahead in life.

_____

_____

_____

_____

_____

_____

_____

_____

_____

_____

_____

Three Common Irregular Verbs: Dialect and Standard Forms

The following charts compare the nonstandard and standard dialects of the common irregular verbs *be, have,* and *do.* (For more on irregular verbs, see the next chapter, beginning on page 159.)

Be

Community Dialect		Standard English	
(Do not use in your writing)		*(Use for clear communication)*	
Present Tense			
I be (*or* is)	we be	I am	we are
you be	you be	you are	you are
he, she, it be	they be	he, she, it is	they are
Past Tense			
I were	we was	I was	we were
you was	you was	you were	you were
he, she, it were	they was	he, she, it was	they were

Have

Community Dialect (Do not use in your writing)		Standard English (Use for clear communication)	

Present Tense

I ~~has~~	we ~~has~~	I have	we have
you has	you has	you have	you have
he, she, it have	they ~~has~~	he, she, it has	they have

Past Tense

I ~~has~~	we ~~has~~	I had	we had
you has	you has	you had	you had
he, she, it have	they ~~has~~	he, she, it had	they had

Do

Community Dialect (Do not use in your writing)		Standard English (Use for clear communication)	

Present Tense

I ~~does~~	we ~~does~~	I do	we do
you does	you does	you do	you do
he, she, it do	they ~~does~~	he, she, it does	they do

Past Tense

I ~~done~~	we ~~done~~	I did	we did
you done	you done	you did	you did
he, she, it done	they ~~done~~	he, she, it did	they did

TIP Many people have trouble with one negative form of *do*. They will say, for example, "She don't listen" instead of "She doesn't listen," or they will say "This pen don't work" instead of "This pen doesn't work." Be careful to avoid the common mistake of using *don't* instead of *doesn't*.

Practice

5

Underline the standard form of the irregular verb *be, have,* or *do.*

1. My brother Ronald (be, is) a normal, fun-loving person most of the time.

2. But he (have, has) a hobby that changes his personality.

3. He (be, is) an amateur actor with our community theater group.

4. When he (do, does) a part in a play, he turns into the character.

5. Once the company (done, did) a play about Sherlock Holmes, the detective.

6. In the show, Ronald (was, were) a frightened man stalked by a murderer.

7. The role (had, have) a strange effect on my brother.

8. At home, he (were, was) nervous and jittery.

9. I (done, did) my best to calm him.

10. However, he remained convinced that he (was, were) being followed.

Practice

6

www.mhhe.com/langan

Cross out the nonstandard verb form in each sentence. Then write the standard form of *be, have,* or *do* in the space provided.

_____ 1. That music store, Platters, be the largest in the area.

_____ 2. It have all the latest releases.

_____ 3. In addition, a special section have classic CDs at reasonable prices.

_____ 4. The salespeople is very knowledgeable about music.

_____ 5. They is willing to help a customer find any CD in the store.

_____ 6. They also does their best to order any CD available.

_____ 7. The owners of Platters does a good job promoting local recording artists, too.

_____ 8. The store have posters of local groups in the windows.

_____ 9. It do special promotions of their performances.

_____ 10. My friends and I be loyal and satisfied customers of Platters.

Fill in each blank with the standard form of *be, have,* or *do.*

My friend Tyrell _____ a real bargain hunter. If a store _____ a sale, he runs right over and buys two or three things, whether or not they _____ things he needs. Tyrell _____ his best, also, to get something for nothing. Last week, he _____ reading the paper and saw that the First National Bank's new downtown offices _____ offering gifts for new accounts. "Those freebies sure _____ look good," Tyrell said. So he went downtown, opened an account, and _____ the manager give him a Big Ben alarm clock. When he got back with the clock, he _____ smiling. "I _____ a very busy man," he told me, "and I really need the free time."

Review Test   1

Underline the standard verb form.

1. We (pay, pays) more for car insurance since the accident.
2. Two years ago, my brother and his wife (adopt, adopted) a special-needs child.
3. The baby (grasp, grasps) his mother's long hair in his tiny fist.
4. The original Frisbees (was, were) tin pie plates from a baking company.
5. Greta (don't, doesn't) approve of her brother's deer hunting.
6. My stepmother likes to work in the yard whenever the sun (be, is) shining.
7. Lorraine looks like a squirrel when she (chews, chew) a big wad of gum.
8. My little sister (has, have) an unusual ailment—an allergy to homework.
9. Louise (grease, greases) the casserole dish with melted chicken fat.
10. My brother (own, owns) a World War II flyer's leather jacket that belonged to our father.

Review Test   2

Cross out the nonstandard verb forms in the sentences that follow. Then write the standard English verb forms in the space above, as shown.

EXAMPLE

                                              played
    For most of yesterday morning, the children ~~play~~ quietly in the sandbox.

1. Usually Sandra dunk her chicken wings in sweet-and-sour sauce.

2. My parents locks themselves in the bathroom during arguments.

3. A suspicious-looking man ask if I wanted to buy a new microwave oven for fifty dollars.

4. My sister bite the erasers off her pencils.

5. Theo ride a bicycle to work in order to save money on gas.

6. The school don't allow anyone to use the darkroom without an appointment.

7. For the third time in the movie, a car bounce headlong down a cliff and burst into flames.

8. The mail carrier give us a pink slip when we have a package waiting at the post office.

9. The ceilings was ringed with water marks from the leaky roof.

10. Instead of a keyhole, each hotel room door have a slot for a magnetic card.

Standard English Verbs

Underline the correct words in the parentheses.

1. "Jim doesn't work," my father (claim, claims). "He just (push, pushes) pencils."

2. Because my engine (leak, leaks) oil, I (park, parks) my car in the street rather than in the driveway.

3. Perspiration (drip, dripped) off Tom's forehead as he (mix, mixed) sand into the new cement.

4. Every time our upstairs neighbor (do, does) his workout, we hear him grunt as he (lift, lifts) his barbell.

5. Lee (were, was) so famished that she (swallow, swallowed) the mouthful of hamburger without chewing it.

6. Uncle Arthur, who (is, be) as bald as a grapefruit, buys every new hair-growing tonic he (have, has) heard about on television.

7. You (frighten, frightened) me to death a minute ago when I (turn, turned) around and saw you standing in the doorway.

8. Before Sharon (take, takes) a bath, she (unplug, unplugs) the phone.

9. Why is it that whenever I (drop, drops) my toast, it (fall, falls) on the buttered side?

10. I just (finish, finished) reading a horror story about some creatures from outer space who (invade, invades) earth disguised as video games.

NAME: _____

DATE: _____

MASTERY TEST 2 | Standard English Verbs

Cross out the nonstandard verb form and write the correct form in the space provided.

EXAMPLE

___*seems*___ The job offer ~~seem~~ too good to be true.

_____ 1. Chung break into a rash when he eats strawberries.

_____ 2. It feel strange to get up before the sun rises.

_____ 3. Before he showed the movie, Carlos thread the film through the reels of the projector.

_____ 4. The driver of the huge moving van do a double take as a tiny VW passed him on the turnpike.

_____ 5. The bartender flattered my aunt when he ask her to prove she was of drinking age.

_____ 6. As Lonnie strolled casually into the singles bar, he unbutton the top three buttons of his sports shirt.

_____ 7. I intends to pay all my bills the minute I obtain some extra cash.

_____ 8. He's so lazy that if opportunity knock, he'd say no one was at home.

_____ 9. Whenever we see my sister and her family coming down the front walk, we pretends we aren't at home.

_____ 10. Kenny have an antique car that looks like an overturned bathtub.

Standard English Verbs   MASTERY TEST 3

PART 1

Fill in each blank with the appropriate standard verb form of be, have, *or* do *in the present or past tense.*

A small town in New England _____ the best kind of dogcatcher—the
            1
kind who _____ not want to hurt an animal. In this town, it _____
          2   3
the law to shoot on sight dogs that _____ running loose. It turned out that
                                        4
the local police _____ not want to enforce this law, so they asked the
                  5
dogcatcher. He answered, "I _____ never shot a dog in my life, and I
                             6
_____ not going to start shooting them now." Instead, he _____
  7   8
seen on several occasions picking up stray dogs and putting them in his car to
return them to their homes. He _____ often taken dogs to his own house
                                9
until he can find their owners. This man _____ certainly worthy of being
                                          10
called a dog's best friend.

PART 2

*Fill in each blank with the appropriate form of the regular verb shown in
parentheses. Use the present or past tense as needed.*

Ed's mother always (*clip*) _____ the cents-off coupons from the news-
                            11
paper and (*save*) _____ them for him. Every time he (*visit*) _____,
                   12   13
his mother (*refuse*) _____ to let him go without those little pieces of paper
                      14
that advertise "50¢ off on 3 cans" or "Save $1 on large economy size." Last week,
she even (*hand*) _____ him some coupons for dog food, although he has
                  15
never (*own*) _____ a dog in his life. Whenever he (*remember*) _____
              16   17
to take some of her coupons to the market, they have usually already (*expire*)
_____. But he never (*turn*) _____ them down, because he (*know*)
  18   19
_____ that his mother's coupons are her way of saying, "I love you."
  20

NAME: _____

DATE: _____

MASTERY TEST 4 Standard English Verbs

PART 1

Fill in each blank with the appropriate standard verb form of be, have, *or* do *in the present or past tense.*

My grandmother _____ an eccentric character. She _____ the
          1   2
idea that my name was Joe (which it _____ not), and she insisted on call-
                                    3
ing me that. She _____ also a miser; she _____ not hide money,
                    4   5
though—only candy. Under her bed _____ a suitcase full of spearmint
                                      6
leaves and licorice. Once, when she thought she _____ alone, I saw her
                                      7
count the candy pieces and then put them back. I'll never forget one thing she
_____. When I brought my girlfriend home for the first time, Grandma
        8
_____ sure we were married; she kept asking us if we _____ any
  9   10
children yet.

PART 2

Fill in each blank with the appropriate form of the regular verb shown in parentheses. Use the present or past tense as needed.

A funny thing (*happen*) _____ recently at the Port Authority Bus Ter-
                                 11
minal in New York City. This terminal (*serve*) _____ 168,000 riders every
                                          12
day, so commuters (*expect*) _____ all sorts of delays. In fact, someone
                              13
who (*ride*) _____ a bus can spend the first twenty minutes of the trip just
            14
waiting in line to buy a ticket. To reward these long-suffering commuters, the
Port Authority (*ask*) _____ a sculptor to create a statue in their honor.
                  15
When the statue (*arrive*) _____, it (*turn*) _____ out to be three cast
                     16   17
bronze commuters waiting in line. Then the statues were (*place*) _____
                                              18
in front of a gate, and a few commuters actually (*line*) _____ up behind
                                      19
the bronze figures. "The line (*seem*) _____ to be moving about as fast as
                                 20
usual," one commuter said.

Irregular Verbs

Introductory Activity

You may already have a sense of which common English verbs are regular and which are not. To test yourself, fill in the past tense and past participle of the verbs below. Five are regular verbs and so take *-d* or *-ed* in the past tense and past participle. For these verbs, write *R* under *Verb Type* and then write their past tense and past participle verb forms. Five are irregular verbs and will probably not sound right when you try to add *-d* or *-ed*. For these verbs, write *I* under *Verb Type*. Also, see if you can write in their irregular verb forms.

Present	Verb Type	Past	Past Participle
fall	*I*	*fell*	*fallen*
1. scream			
2. write			
3. steal			
4. ask			
5. kiss			
6. choose			
7. ride			
8. chew			
9. think			
10. dance			

Answers are on page 664.

A Brief Review of Regular Verbs

Every verb has four principal parts: present, past, past participle, and present participle. These parts can be used to build all the verb tenses (the times shown by a verb).

Most verbs in English are regular. The past and past participle of a regular verb are formed by adding *-d* or *-ed* to the present. The *past participle* is the form of the verb used with the helping verbs *have, has,* or *had* (or some form of *be* with passive verbs, which are explained on page 201). The *present participle* is formed by adding *-ing* to the present.

Here are the principal forms of some regular verbs:

Present	Past	Past Participle	Present Participle
laugh	laughed	laughed	laughing
ask	asked	asked	asking
touch	touched	touched	touching
decide	decided	decided	deciding
explode	exploded	exploded	exploding

List of Irregular Verbs

Irregular verbs have irregular forms in the past tense and past participle. For example, the past tense of the irregular verb *grow* is *grew*; the past participle is *grown*.

Almost everyone has some degree of trouble with irregular verbs. When you are unsure about the form of a verb, you can check the following list of irregular verbs. (The present participle is not shown on this list, because it is formed simply by adding *-ing* to the base form of the verb.) Or you can check a dictionary, which gives the principal parts of irregular verbs.

Present	Past	Past Participle
arise	arose	arisen
awake	awoke *or* awaked	awoke *or* awaked
be (am, are, is)	was (were)	been
become	became	become
begin	began	begun
bend	bent	bent
bite	bit	bitten
blow	blew	blown
break	broke	broken
bring	brought	brought

Present	Past	Past Participle
build	built	built
burst	burst	burst
buy	bought	bought
catch	caught	caught
choose	chose	chosen
come	came	come
cost	cost	cost
cut	cut	cut
do (does)	did	done
draw	drew	drawn
drink	drank	drunk
drive	drove	driven
eat	ate	eaten
fall	fell	fallen
feed	fed	fed
feel	felt	felt
fight	fought	fought
find	found	found
fly	flew	flown
freeze	froze	frozen
get	got	got *or* gotten
give	gave	given
go (goes)	went	gone
grow	grew	grown
have (has)	had	had
hear	heard	heard
hide	hid	hidden
hold	held	held
hurt	hurt	hurt
keep	kept	kept
know	knew	known
lay	laid	laid
lead	led	led
leave	left	left
lend	lent	lent
let	let	let
lie	lay	lain
light	lit	lit
lose	lost	lost
make	made	made
meet	met	met
pay	paid	paid

Present	Past	Past Participle
ride	rode	ridden
ring	rang	rung
rise	rose	risen
run	ran	run
say	said	said
see	saw	seen
sell	sold	sold
send	sent	sent
shake	shook	shaken
shrink	shrank *or* shrunk	shrunk *or* shrunken
shut	shut	shut
sing	sang	sung
sit	sat	sat
sleep	slept	slept
speak	spoke	spoken
spend	spent	spent
stand	stood	stood
steal	stole	stolen
stick	stuck	stuck
sting	stung	stung
swear	swore	sworn
swim	swam	swum
take	took	taken
teach	taught	taught
tear	tore	torn
tell	told	told
think	thought	thought
wake	woke *or* waked	woken *or* waked
wear	wore	worn
win	won	won
write	wrote	written

Practice

1

Cross out the incorrect verb form in each of the following sentences. Then write the correct form of the verb in the space provided.

EXAMPLE

began   When the mud slide started, the whole neighborhood ~~begun~~ going downhill.

_____   1. The boys taked cigarettes into the darkened theater.

_____   2. The fire department has finally chose two women for its training program.

_____   3. The daredevil catched a bullet in his teeth.

_____   4. Someone has stole the sound system from my car.

_____   5. After I seen my new haircut, I cried.

_____   6. I have went to the lost-and-found office several times, but my leather gloves haven't turned up yet.

_____   7. The stunt man has fell off hundreds of horses without injuring himself.

_____   8. Steve has swore to control his temper.

_____   9. The bacon strips in the pan had shrank into blackened stubs.

_____ 10. Why haven't you spoke up about your problems?

For each of the italicized verbs in the following sentences, fill in the three missing forms in the order shown in the box:

Practice

2

> a. Present tense, which takes an *-s* ending when the subject is *he, she, it,* or any *one person or thing* (see page 147)
>
> b. Past tense
>
> c. Past participle—the form that goes with the helping verb *have, has,* or *had*

EXAMPLE

My little nephew loves to *break* things. Every Christmas he (a) __*breaks*__ his new toys the minute they're unwrapped. Last year he (b) __*broke*__ five toys in seven minutes and then went on to smash his family's new china platter. His mother says he won't be happy until he has (c) __*broken*__ their hearts.

1. My husband always seems to *lose* things. He (a) _____ his eyeglasses about three times a day. Once he (b) _____ one of his running shoes while he was out jogging. He has (c) _____ so many car keys that we keep one taped inside the bumper of our car.

2. Jamie is often asked to *bring* her gorgeous sister to parties. Poor Jamie (a) _____ Vanessa and then fades into the wallpaper. Last week she (b) _____ Vanessa to a pool party. Jamie felt as if she had (c) _____ a human magnet instead of a sister, since all the guys clustered around Vanessa the entire night.

3. Small babies can be taught to *swim*. They don't (a) _____ like adults, but they do float and keep their heads above water. Babies are accustomed to a watery environment, since they (b) _____ inside their mothers' bodies in a bath of fluid. Babies who have (c) _____ in pools shortly after birth seem to become more confident swimmers as children.

4. My brother actually likes to *go* to the dentist. He (a) _____ at least every three months for a checkup. He (b) _____ last week just to have his teeth flossed. He has (c) _____ to his dentist so regularly that Dr. Ross has been able to afford a new sports car.

5. The vast crowd in the stadium waits for the rock concert to *begin*. The fans don't care if it (a) _____ late, since they are having a great time eating, drinking, and listening to iPods. In fact, if the concert (b) _____ on time, they would feel cheated. Once it has (c) _____, the stadium will vibrate from the screams of the fans and the roar of the music.

6. My little boy likes to *hide* from me. I usually find him, since he (a) _____ in obvious places, like under the bed or inside the closet. Once, however, he (b) _____ in an unusual place. I searched all over until I discovered that he had (c) _____ inside an empty garbage can.

7. I like to *choose* unusual items when I order from a restaurant menu. My friends always (a) _____ something safe and familiar, but I'm more adventurous. Once I (b) _____ stuffed calves' brains, which were delicious. I have (c) _____ items like squid, sea urchins, and pickled pigs' feet just to see how they would taste.

8. Last month I had to *speak* before the PTA members at my daughter's school. I can (a) _____ comfortably to small groups, but this was a meeting of hundreds of people in an auditorium. Before I gave my report, I (b) _____ to the principal and told him how nervous I was. He assured me that even though he had (c) _____ in public many times over the years, he still got butterflies in his stomach.

9. Sheila has to *take* her dog to the veterinarian. Whenever she (a) _____ him, though, he howls in the waiting room or lunges at the other pets. The last time Sheila (b) _____ Bruno, he had an accident on the linoleum floor. This time, however, Sheila has (c) _____ the precaution of keeping Bruno away from his water bowl for several hours.

10. Greg hates to *wake* up. When he does (a) _____ up, he is groggy and miserable. Once he (b) _____ up and yelled at his pet hamster for looking at him the wrong way. He has (c) _____ up this way so often that his family won't speak to him until noon.

Troublesome Irregular Verbs

Three common irregular verbs that often give people trouble are *be, have,* and *do.* See pages 150–151 for a discussion of these verbs. Three sets of other irregular verbs that can lead to difficulties are *lie-lay, sit-set,* and *rise-raise.*

Lie-Lay

The principal parts of *lie* and *lay* are as follows:

Present	Past	Past Participle
lie	lay	lain
lay	laid	laid

To lie means *to rest* or *recline. To lay* means *to put something down.*

To Lie	To Lay
Tony *lies* on the couch.	I *lay* the mail on the table.
This morning he *lay* in the tub.	Yesterday I *laid* the mail on the counter.
He has *lain* in bed all week with the flu.	I have *laid* the mail where everyone will see it.

Practice

3

Underline the correct verb.

> **HINT** Use a form of *lie* if you can substitute *recline*. Use a form of *lay* if you can substitute *place.*

1. Unknowingly, I had (lain, laid) my coat down on a freshly varnished table.
2. Like a mini solar collector, the cat (lay, laid) in the warm rays of the sun.
3. He was certain he had (lain, laid) the tiles in a straight line until he stepped back to look.
4. (Lying, Laying) too long in bed in the morning can give me a headache.
5. I (lay, laid) on the doctor's examining table, staring into the bright bars of fluorescent light on the ceiling.

Sit-Set

The principal parts of *sit* and *set* are as follows:

Present	Past	Past Participle
sit	sat	sat
set	set	set

To sit means *to take a seat* or *to rest. To set* means *to put* or *to place.*

To Sit	To Set
I *sit* down during work breaks.	Tony *sets* out the knives, forks, and spoons.
I *sat* in the doctor's office for three hours.	His sister already *set* out the dishes.
I have always *sat* in the last desk.	They have just *set* out the dinnerware.

Underline the correct form of the verb.

> **HINT** Use a form of *sit* if you can substitute *rest*. Use a form of *set* if you can substitute *place*.

1. Dillon had (sat, set) his iPod shuffle on the counter for only a few seconds before someone walked off with it.

2. Zena (sat, set) her heavy backpack down on the floor, and then she proceeded to take out her calculus textbook, graphing calculator, and class notes.

3. The cardiologist told me to (sit, set) down before she went over my X-ray results.

4. I (sat, set) a candle on the mantel in the living room to remember my younger sister, who died of leukemia last month.

5. Jackson was (sitting, setting) the hard drive down on the floor when he heard his spine crack.

Rise-Raise

The principal parts of *rise* and *raise* are as follows:

Present	Past	Past Participle
rise	rose	risen
raise	raised	raised

To rise means *to get up* or *to move up*. *To raise* (which is a regular verb with simple *-ed* endings) means *to lift up* or *to increase in amount*.

To Rise	**To Raise**
The soldiers *rise* at dawn.	I'm going to *raise* the stakes in the card game.
The crowd *rose* to applaud the batter.	I *raised* the shades to let in the sun.
Dracula has *risen* from the grave.	I would have quit if the company had not *raised* my salary.

Practice 5

Underline the correct verb.

> **HINT** Use a form of *rise* if you can substitute *get up* or *move up*. Use a form of *raise* if you can substitute *lift up* or *increase*.

1. When food prices (rise, raise), people living on Social Security suffer.

2. They have (risen, raised) their daughter to be a self-sufficient person.

3. As the crowd watched, the World War II veteran (rose, raised) the flag.

4. The reporters (rose, raised) as the president entered the room for the press conference.

5. The promising weather report (rose, raised) our hopes for an enjoyable camping trip.

Review Test 1

Cross out the incorrect verb form. Then write the correct form of the verb in the space provided.

_____ 1. The famous recording star first sung in his hometown church choir.

_____ 2. After Lola was bit by the parrot, her finger was sore for a week.

_____ 3. Last August, Carmen taked her family to Yellowstone National Park.

_____ 4. The plane would have ran off the runway if the pilot hadn't been so skillful.

_____ 5. He heard a frightening hissing sound before the pipes bursted.

_____ 6. I couldn't believe I got a B on the first paper I writed in college.

_____ 7. Stefano laid in a lounge chair, staring up at the moon through his new binoculars.

_____ 8. The class clown had went too far, and the students waited to see what the teacher would do.

_____ 9. The sun had already rose by the time I got home from the party.

_____ 10. As we approached the quiet pond, a beaver slid into the water and swum toward its underwater lodge.

Review Test 2

Write short sentences that use the form requested for the following irregular verbs.

EXAMPLE

Past of *ride:* _The Lone Ranger rode into the sunset._

1. Past of *drink* _____

2. Present of *bring* _____

3. Past participle of *grow* _____

4. Present of *swim* _____

5. Past participle of *write* _____

6. Past of *give* _____

7. Present of *do* _____

8. Past participle of *begin* _____

9. Past of *go* _____

10. Present of *know* _____

NAME: _____

DATE: _____

Irregular Verbs

Underline the correct word in the parentheses.

1. My girlfriend and I (saw, seen) a bad car accident yesterday.

2. Tina (weared, wore) her favorite jeans until the patches were paper-thin.

3. Fran (hurt, hurted) her hand when she tried to open the mayonnaise jar.

4. That new Cutlass (cost, costed) more than I was willing to pay.

5. We should have (took, taken) the dog to the vet sooner.

6. Ralph has (drawed, drawn) blueprints for the cabin he hopes to build.

7. Simone (sended, sent) Mike their divorce papers in the mail.

8. Ever since Nicole (became, become) a supervisor, she hasn't talked to us.

9. Art (catched, caught) pneumonia when he went camping in the mountains.

10. I (knew, knowed) the answer—I just couldn't think of it.

11. I must have (drove, driven) around the development for half an hour looking for my brother's new house.

12. Within a month, the baby had (grew, grown) two inches and gained three pounds.

13. Before my grandfather died, he (gave, given) me his gold pocket watch and Army medals.

14. That gray-haired lumberjack has (arose, arisen) every day at dawn for the past fifty years.

15. When I heard that my car still hadn't been repaired, I (lost, losted) my temper.

16. As soon as you have (ate, eaten) all your ice cream, you may have some spinach.

17. Sarita (choose, chose) soft pink shag carpeting for her bedroom.

18. After raking the leaves, Julio (lay, laid) down under a tree and fell sound asleep.

19. The dummy (sang, sung) in a clear voice, but the ventriloquist's lips never moved.

20. Valerie had (rode, ridden) the roller coaster five times before she started complaining that everything was going around in circles.

Irregular Verbs   MASTERY TEST 2

Cross out the incorrect verb form. Write the correct form in the space provided.

_____   1. Paul sweared loudly when the wasp stung him.

_____   2. I bited down hard on a caramel and lost a filling.

_____   3. As the car groaned and lurched from side to side, we realized that Lamont had never drove with a manual shift before.

_____   4. Because Fran had throwed away the receipt, she couldn't return the frying pan.

_____   5. Though the runner slided head first, he was still tagged out at home plate.

_____   6. Barry rung the bell for fifteen minutes and then decided that no one was home.

_____   7. After I ran three miles in ninety-degree heat, I drunk a whole quart of iced tea.

_____   8. Lenny hided his daughter's Christmas present so well that he couldn't find it.

_____   9. If I had knew better, I would never have left my car door unlocked.

_____   10. Maria broke her engagement but kept all the wedding presents.

_____   11. I stayed away from sick people and took extra vitamin C all winter, but I catched a cold anyway.

_____   12. On his first day of summer vacation, Danny sleeped until two in the afternoon.

_____   13. My new cotton sweater shrinked so much that it now fits my kid sister.

_____   14. Mac was instantly sorry he had writed such an angry e-mail, but there was no way to get it back.

_____   15. The hostess turned on soft music and lighted candles on the table before her guests arrived.

_____   16. I had runned out of cash before payday, so I had to ask my parents for a loan.

_____   17. Nobody believed the criminal's claim that Martians had maked him rob the bank.

_____   18. After the politician was invited to say a few words, he speaked for half an hour.

_____   19. Something private must be going on in the meeting, because a committee member just got up and shutted the door.

_____   20. The group of diners ordered the most expensive steaks, drank the best champagne, kept two waitresses busy all night, and then leaved only a two-dollar tip.

NAME: _____

DATE: _____

MASTERY TEST 3 | ## Irregular Verbs

Write in the space provided the correct form of the verb shown in the margin.

teach

1. When I was little, my parents _____ me how to find my way home if I got lost.

lend

2. My best friend _____ me ten dollars so I could buy Dad a birthday gift.

build

3. It took eight months before Andy's garage was finally _____.

wear

4. I used to fidget in class so much that I _____ a hole in my trousers.

write

5. Susie has read every romance novel Jennifer Crusie has _____.

fall

6. Frowning, the building inspector stood where the grocery store's sign had _____.

see

7. We _____ the other car coming, but we couldn't stop in time.

send

8. Rina and Marvin _____ telegrams to their families saying that they were eloping.

speak

9. I don't think he's heard a single word I have _____.

sleep

10. I must have _____ twelve hours before I finally work up.

Irregular Verbs   MASTERY TEST 4

Write in the space provided the correct form of the verb shown in the margin.

burst

1. As soon as little Davy stuck a pin in it, the balloon _____.

go

2. When the alarm rang, Fred shut it off and _____ back to sleep.

bring

3. Yesterday, my cousin _____ over his entire baseball card collection.

hurt

4. You really _____ my feelings when you told me you didn't like my new outfit.

keep

5. Whenever she rode in a car, my mother _____ reminding the driver when a turn was coming up or a light was changing.

shake

6. After the collision, we were badly _____ up, but we had no broken bones.

spend

7. Stanley _____ a fortune on fishing equipment, but all he ever caught was a cold.

shrink

8. When she saw the giant tomato reaching for her in her dream, Amy _____ back in horror.

buy

9. Because stick shifts made her nervous, Mei Lin _____ a car with an automatic transmission.

stick

10. Why have I _____ with this broken-down car for so long?

Subject-Verb Agreement

Introductory Activity

As you read each pair of sentences below, place a check mark beside the sentence that you think uses the underlined word correctly.

There <u>was</u> many applicants for the position. _____
There <u>were</u> many applicants for the position. _____

The pictures in that magazine <u>is</u> very controversial. _____
The pictures in that magazine <u>are</u> very controversial. _____

Everybody usually <u>watch</u> the lighted numbers in an elevator. _____
Everybody usually <u>watches</u> the lighted numbers in an elevator. _____

On the basis of the examples above, complete the following statements.

1. In the first two pairs of sentences, the subjects are _____

   and _____. Since both these subjects are plural, the verb

   must be plural.

2. In the last pair of sentences, the subject, *Everybody*, is a word that is

   always (singular, plural), and so that verb must be (singular, plural).

Answers are on page 665.

www.mhhe.com/langan

A verb must agree with its subject in number. A *singular subject* (one person or thing) takes a singular verb. A *plural subject* (more than one person or thing) takes a plural verb. Mistakes in subject-verb agreement are sometimes made in the following situations:

1. When words come between the subject and the verb
2. When a verb comes before the subject
3. With indefinite pronouns
4. With compound subjects
5. With *who, which,* and *that*

Each situation is explained on the following pages.

Words between the Subject and the Verb

Words that come between the subject and the verb do not change subject-verb agreement.

The breakfast cereals in the pantry are made mostly of sugar.

In the example above, the subject (*cereals*) is plural and so the verb (*are*) is plural. The words *in the pantry* that come between the subject and the verb do not affect subject-verb agreement. To help find the subject of certain sentences, you should cross out prepositional phrases (explained on pages 72–73):

One ~~of the crooked politicians~~ was jailed for a month.

The posters ~~on my little brother's wall~~ include hip-hop stars, athletes, and models in bathing suits.

Following is a list of common prepositions.

Common Prepositions

about	before	by	inside	over
above	behind	during	into	through
across	below	except	of	to
among	beneath	for	off	toward
around	beside	from	on	under
at	between	in	onto	with

Underline the subject. Then lightly cross out any words that come between the subject and the verb. Finally, double-underline the correct verb in parentheses.

EXAMPLE

The price ~~of the stereo speakers~~ (is, are) too high for my wallet.

1. The leaders of the union (has, have) called for a strike.

2. One of Omar's pencil sketches (hangs, hang) in the art classroom.

3. Three days of anxious waiting finally (ends, end) with a phone call.

4. The members of the car pool (chips, chip) in for the driving expenses.

5. The woman with the teased, sprayed hairdo (looks, look) as if she were wearing a plastic helmet.

6. The addition of heavy shades to my sunny windows (allows, allow) me to sleep during the day.

7. Several houses in the old whaling village (has, have) been designated as historical landmarks.

8. The stack of baseball cards in my little brother's bedroom (is, are) two feet high.

9. Gooey puddles of egg white (spreads, spread) over the stove as Mike cracks the shells against the frying pan.

10. The giant-size box of Raisinets (sells, sell) for four dollars at the theater's candy counter.

Verb before the Subject

A verb agrees with its subject even when the verb comes *before* the subject. Words that may precede the subject include *there, here,* and, in questions, *who, which, what,* and *where.*

Inside the storage shed are the garden tools.

At the street corner were two panhandlers.

There are times I'm ready to quit my job.

Where are the instructions for the DVD player?

> **TIP** If you are unsure about the subject, ask *who* or *what* of the verb. With the first sentence above, you might ask, "What are inside the storage shed?" The answer, garden *tools,* is the subject.

Underline the subject in each sentence. Then double-underline the correct verb in parentheses.

1. Lumbering along the road (was, were) six heavy trucks.

2. There (is, are) now wild coyotes wandering the streets of many California suburbs.

3. Lining the country lanes (is, are) rows of tall, thin poplar trees.

4. At the back of my closet (is, are) the high platform boots I bought ten years ago.

5. Helping to unload the heavy sofa from the delivery truck (was, were) a skinny young boy.

6. Nosing through the garbage bags (was, were) a furry animal with a hairless tail.

7. Here (is, are) the rug shampooer I borrowed last month.

8. Along the side of the highway (was, were) a sluggish little stream.

9. Where (is, are) the box of kitchen trash bags?

10. On the door of his bedroom (is, are) a sign reading, "Authorized personnel only."

Indefinite Pronouns

The following words, known as *indefinite pronouns,* always take singular verbs.

www.mhhe.com/langan

Indefinite Pronouns

(-one words)	*(-body words)*	*(-thing words)*	
one	nobody	nothing	each
anyone	anybody	anything	either
everyone	everybody	everything	neither
someone	somebody	something	

TIP *Both* always takes a plural verb.

Practice

3

Write the correct form of the verb in the space provided.

is, are
1. Neither of those last two books on the list _____ required for the course.

remembers, remember
2. Nobody _____ seeing a suspicious green car cruising the street.

fits, fit
3. Both of these belts _____ perfectly.

has, have
4. Somebody _____ been playing with my Xbox.

wanders, wander
5. Nobody _____ into those woods during hunting season without wearing bright-colored clothing.

needs, need
6. Each of those dogs _____ to be inoculated against rabies.

keeps, keep
7. One of my friends _____ a pet iguana in her dorm room.

sneaks, sneak
8. Everyone _____ stationery and pens out of our office.

is, are
9. Either of those motels _____ good enough for me.

eats, eat
10. One of my children _____ raw onions as if they were apples.

www.mhhe.com/langan

Compound Subjects

Subjects joined by *and* generally take a plural verb.

> <u>Yoga</u> and <u>biking</u> <u>are</u> Lola's ways of staying in shape.

> <u>Ambition</u> and <u>good luck</u> <u>are</u> the keys to his success.

When subjects are joined by *or, either . . . or, neither . . . nor, not only . . . but also,* the verb agrees with the subject closer to the verb.

> Either the restaurant <u>manager</u> or his <u>assistants</u> <u>deserve</u> to be fired for the spoiled meat used in the stew.

The nearer subject, *assistants,* is plural, and so the verb is plural.

Write the correct form of the verb in the space provided.

**seem,
seems**

1. The Pilates and spinning classes _____ to help me stay in shape, but the key to fitness is a sensible diet.

is, are

2. Either the tongue ring or the dragon tattoo _____ responsible for Zack's appeal.

is, are

3. A double shot of espresso and two pumps of hazelnut syrup _____ all I need to start my morning.

help, helps

4. The lecture podcasts and study guides _____ me prepare for exams.

**impress,
impresses**

5. Neither Mick Jagger nor my favorite rock band, the Rolling Stones, _____ my ten-year-old daughter, who prefers Disney's Hannah Montana.

Who, Which, and That

When *who, which,* and *that* are used as subjects, they take singular verbs if the word they stand for is singular and plural verbs if the word they stand for is plural. For example, in the sentence

Gary is one of those people <u>who</u> <u>are</u> very private.

the verb is plural because *who* stands for *people,* which is plural. On the other hand, in the sentence

Gary is a person <u>who</u> <u>is</u> very private.

the verb is singular because *who* stands for *person,* which is singular.

www.mhhe.com/langan

Write the correct form of the verb in the space provided.

**roams,
roam**

1. The dogs that _____ around this area are household pets abandoned by cruel owners.

**begins,
begin**

2. A sharp pain that _____ in the lower abdomen may signal appendicitis.

**thunders,
thunder**

3. The heavy trucks that _____ past my car make me feel as though I'm being blown off the road.

fears, fear   4. The canyon tour isn't for people who _____ heights.

tastes,   5. This drink, which _____ like pure sugar, is sup-
taste   posed to be 100 percent fruit juice.

Collaborative Activity

Editing and Rewriting

Working with a partner, read the short paragraph below and mark off the five mistakes in subject-verb agreement. Then use the space provided to correct the five agreement errors. Feel free to discuss the rewrite quietly with your partner and refer back to the chapter when necessary.

Sometimes I just don't understand people. For instance, my neighbors Adolfo and Janelle go to the gym almost every day. Adolfo rides an exercise bike, Janelle runs on the treadmill, and they both take aerobic classes. Neither of them like to pay for the gym membership. But, as Janelle says, "Fitness and good health is very important to us both." Now, I think it's great that anyone are trying to stay fit and healthy. But this is the part of their activities that don't make sense to me. In order to get to the gym, these fitness nuts drive half a mile. Then they come home and take the elevator three stories up to their apartment. Wouldn't plain old walking and climbing stairs burns calories as well as the exercise they do in an expensive gym?

_____   _____

_____   _____

_____

Collaborative Activity

Creating Sentences

Working with a partner, write sentences as directed. With each item, pay special attention to subject-verb agreement.

1. Write a sentence in which the words *in the cafeteria* or *on the table* come between the subject and verb. Underline the subject of your sentence and circle the verb.

2. Look at the photo in this box and write a sentence that begins with the words *there is* or *there are*. Underline the subject of your sentence and circle the verb.

3. Write a sentence in which the indefinite pronoun *nobody* or *anything* is the subject.

4. Write a sentence with the compound subjects *manager* and *employees*. Underline the subject of your sentence and circle the verb.

Reflective Activity

1. Look at the paragraph about Adolfo and Janelle that you revised. Which rule involving subject-verb agreement gave you the most trouble? How did you figure out the correct answer?

2. Explain which of the five subject-verb agreement situations discussed in this chapter is most likely to cause you problems.

Review Test 1

Complete each of the following sentences, using *is, are, was, were, have,* or *has.*
Underline the subject of each of these verbs.

EXAMPLE

The <u>hot dogs</u> in that luncheonette _____ *are hazardous to your health.* _____

1. Either of those small keys _____

_____

2. The practical joker in our office _____

_____

3. The rock star and his bodyguard _____

_____

4. He was the kind of customer who _____

_____

5. The memos posted on the office door _____

_____

6. There's always someone who _____

_____

7. The old boiler, along with the rusty water tanks, _____

_____

8. The air freshener hanging from her rearview mirror _____

_____

9. The first few times that I tried to roller-skate _____

_____

10. The spectators outside the courtroom _____

_____

Review Test 2

Underline the correct word in the parentheses.

1. The number of commercials between television shows (is, are) increasing.

2. Lani and Paco (works, work) overnight at the motel's registration desk.

3. A report on either book (counts, count) as extra credit.

4. Both the mattress and the box spring on this bed (is, are) filled with rusty, uncoiling springs.

5. Nobody in that class ever (argues, argue) with the professor.

6. Remembering everyone's birthday and organizing family reunions (is, are) my sister's main hobbies.

7. Lying like limp little dolls on the bed (was, were) the exhausted children.

8. The woman from the telephone company who (empties, empty) the pay phones wears a photo ID tag around her neck.

9. The illegal dogfights which (occurs, occur) regularly in our town are being investigated by the SPCA.

10. Sewn into the sweater's seam (was, were) an extra button and a small hank of matching yarn for repairs.

Review Test 3

There are eight mistakes in subject-verb agreement in the following passage. Cross out each incorrect verb and write the correct form above it. In addition, underline the subject of each of the verbs that must be changed.

What are the factors that makes a third-grade child aggressive and destructive? On the other hand, what experiences help a third-grader make friends easily and earn good grades in school? Years of research on a group of children from infancy through elementary school has provided an answer, or at least a new theory. A psychologist from one of our leading universities claim that success in the early grades are the direct result of a close relationship with the mother. Babies who have this relationship with a mother seems to gain the strength and self-esteem they need for future success in the classroom and in life. A strong, secure bond between a mother and child are formed when mothers respond quickly and consistently to their babies' needs. Both the speed and the attention is important in earning a baby's trust. The researcher points out that there are no evidence of a link between day care arrangements and weaker mother-baby attachments. It is the quality of the relationship, not the actual hours spent, that causes a child to feel secure.

Subject-Verb Agreement   MASTERY TEST 1

Underline the correct verb in the parentheses. Note that you will first have to determine the subject of each sentence. To help find subjects in certain sentences, you may find it helpful to cross out prepositional phrases.

1. Sadly, neither of the dogs rescued from the greyhound kennel (is, are) likely to be adopted.

2. One of my roommates in college (wants, want) to become a software engineer so that she can create cutting-edge video and computer games.

3. The cost of all my utilities, which include electricity, water, cable, and phone, (is, are) ridiculous.

4. High-speed chases and grisly car accidents (seems, seem) to be the focus on many reality television shows.

5. Not one of the red tag specials advertised in yesterday's newspaper (was, were) left on the shelf.

6. Once a year, Jackie and her girlfriends (takes, take) a weekend trip to Las Vegas for shopping, dining, and gambling.

7. The online articles that the librarian located for the student (was, were) originally published in print.

8. Squeaking from underneath the refrigerator (was, were) a tiny mouse caught in a forgotten, rusty, spring-based trap.

9. Neither Dad nor my brother Miguel (wants, want) to talk about his experiences as a combat soldier in the Iraq War.

10. There (was, were) a laptop computer left in one of the carrels at the library.

11. A kleptomaniac will steal anything that (is, are) not nailed down.

12. A few girls at my daughter's high school (plans, plan) to try out for the football team.

13. Not only the air ducts but also the plumbing in the abandoned building (is, are) infested with rats.

14. Everyone in my history class (believes, believe) that the professor grades unfairly, but nobody is willing to approach her.

NAME: _____

DATE: _____

MASTERY TEST 2 | Subject-Verb Agreement

In the space provided, write the correct form of the verb shown in the margin.

comes, come   1. All the wrinkles in a drip-dry shirt _____ out with a cool iron.

Is, Are   2. _____ all the bracelets Toshiko wears made of real gold?

does, do   3. Alcoholic beverages and allergy pills _____ not make a good combination.

was, were   4. No one _____ willing to take the blame for the spilled paint.

is, are   5. Under the sofa _____ a year's supply of dust.

was, were   6. Neither of the jackets I was looking for _____ in the closet.

sees, see   7. Krista and Eve _____ better with contact lenses than they saw with glasses.

is, are   8. Three of the books Sandy borrowed from the library _____ overdue.

was, were   9. A complete list of complaints and demands _____ read at the beginning of the tenants' meeting.

is, are   10. At the intersection of Pleasant Grove Lane and Valley View Road _____ the future location of the new shopping mall.

Subjects-Verb Agreement **MASTERY TEST 3**

Cross out the incorrect form of the verb. In addition, underline the subject that goes with the verb. Then write the correct form of the verb in the space provided. Mark the one sentence that is correct with a C.

_____ 1. There is some unpleasant surprises among this month's bills.

_____ 2. Those piles of dirty laundry does not belong to me.

_____ 3. The lilies that we planted last year has grown to over six feet tall.

_____ 4. My counselor and my English instructor has agreed to write job recommendations for me.

_____ 5. Everyone in my neighborhood under the age of ten believe in Santa Claus.

_____ 6. Neither Gale nor Jerry plans to look for a job this summer.

_____ 7. Many gas stations on that highway stays open all night.

_____ 8. The mayor, along with the council members, are helping carry sandbags for flood control.

_____ 9. Lying across all the lanes of the highway were a jackknifed tractor-trailer.

_____ 10. Emil's parents, who have been seeing a marriage counselor, has decided to get a divorce.

NAME: _____

DATE: _____

MASTERY TEST 4 | Subject-Verb Agreement

Cross out the incorrect form of the verb. In addition, underline the subject that goes with the verb. Then write the correct form of the verb in the space provided. Mark the one sentence that is correct with a **C.**

_____ 1. At the back of my mother's closet hang an old-fashioned muskrat fur coat with padded shoulders.

_____ 2. Anyone who punches in late more than once get an official warning from the personnel department.

_____ 3. Many pages of Naomi's diary contains R-rated material.

_____ 4. His toy soldiers and stamp collection is the only things that mean anything to him.

_____ 5. Leaning against the lamppost with his hands in his pockets were a dangerous-looking character.

_____ 6. When I was seven, being alone in the house and hearing the walls creak in the wind were the scariest things in my life.

_____ 7. Something seem odd about Uncle Rico this evening; he's remembering everything people are saying.

_____ 8. The plastic trash bags that never bursts on TV always break in my kitchen.

_____ 9. Thick white fur and black skin acts like a greenhouse, trapping heat and keeping a polar bear warm in the coldest weather.

_____ 10. When is Lew and Marian going to return the camping equipment they borrowed from us?

Consistent Verb Tense

Introductory Activity

Underline the two mistakes in verb tense in the following selection.

When Computer Warehouse had a sale, Alex decided to buy a new laptop. He planned to set up a home office and hoped to connect to the Internet right away. When he arrived home, however, Alex discovers that setting up his wireless connection was complicated and confusing. The directions sounded as if they had been written for electrical engineers. After two hours of frustration, Alex gave up and calls a technician for help.

Now complete the following statement:

Verb tenses should be consistent. In the selection above, two verbs have to be changed because they are mistakenly in the (*present, past*) _____ tense while all the other verbs in the selection are in the (*present, past*) _____ tense.

Answers are on page 666.

Keeping Tenses Consistent

Do not shift tenses unnecessarily. If you begin writing a paper in the present tense, don't shift suddenly to the past. If you begin in the past, don't shift without reason to the present. Notice the inconsistent verb tenses in the following example:

> Smoke spilled from the front of the overheated car. The driver opens up the hood, then jumped back as steam billows out.

The verbs must be consistently in the present tense:

> Smoke spills from the front of the overheated car. The driver opens up the hood, then jumps back as steam billows out.

Or the verbs must be consistently in the past tense:

> Smoke spilled from the front of the overheated car. The driver opened up the hood, then jumped back as steam billowed out.

Practice 1

In each item, one verb must be changed so that it agrees in tense with the other verbs. Cross out the incorrect verb and write the correct form in the space at the left.

EXAMPLE

learned   I donated blood at the American Red Cross after I ~~learn~~ that someone in the U.S. will need blood every two or three seconds.

_____ 1. Dirk, a devoted single father, cooks his children breakfast, drives them to school, takes them to soccer practice, prepared dinner at night, and helps them with their homework.

_____ 2. Before meeting friends, Jordan stopped at the ATM to withdraw fifty dollars and fills his car up with gas.

_____ 3. Worried that I would be late for class, I parked in a stall reserved for faculty. When I returned to my car a few hours later, I find that the security guard had given me a citation.

_____ 4. After the labor union voted to enforce mandatory drug testing, my co-workers begin to talk about ways to cheat on the test, such as eating poppy seeds and drinking detox teas.

_____ 5. Some people argue that Americans are too materialistic. After all, there were more shopping malls than high schools in this country.

_____ 6. Donald and I divorced five years ago. He remarried the following year but separate from that wife a year later.

_____ 7. In the workplace, employees are discouraged from making personal phone calls. Many of them, however, sent personal e-mail messages while at work.

_____ 8. Madeline spends her weekends going to garage sales, auctions, and thrift stores. She collects military antiques, which she sold for a profit online.

_____ 9. Last month, Tommy wanted to sign up for a satellite TV service, but the property manager at his condominium says that he would be violating his lease agreement.

_____ 10. When my dog is left home alone, he liked to pull dirty laundry from the hamper and rummage through the wastebaskets.

Review Test 1

Change the verbs where needed in the following selection so that they are consistently in the past tense. Cross out each incorrect verb and write the correct form above it, as shown in the example. You will need to make ten corrections.

Making a foul shot that won a basketball game was a special moment for me. For most of the year, I sat on the bench. The coach put me on the team after the tryouts and then ~~forgets~~ _forgot_ about me. Then my chance appears near the end of the Rosemont High School game. The score was tied 65 to 65. Because of injuries and foul-outs, most of the substitutes, except me, were in the game. Then our last first-stringer, Larry Toner, got an elbow in the eye and leaves the game. The coach looked at me and said, "Get in there, Watson." The clock showed ten seconds to go. Rosemont had the ball when, suddenly, one of their players misses a pass. People scramble for the ball; then our center, Kevin, grabbed it and starts down the court. He looked around and saw me about twenty feet from the basket. I caught his pass, and before I could decide whether to shoot or pass, a Rosemont player fouls me. The referee's whistle blew, and I had two free throws with two seconds left in the game. My stomach churns as I stepped to the foul line. I almost couldn't hold the ball because my hands were so damp with sweat. I shot and missed, and the Rosemont crowd sighs with relief. My next shot would mean a win for us or overtime. I looked at the hoop, shot, and waited for what seemed like forever. The ball circles the rim and dropped in, and then the buzzer sounded. Everyone on the team slapped me on the back and the coach smacks my rear end, saying, "All right, Watson!" I'll always remember that moment.

Review Test   2

Change verbs as necessary in the following selection so that they are consistently in the past tense. Cross out each incorrect verb and write the correct form above it. You will need to make ten corrections in all.

According to an old Greek myth, the goddess of the harvest had one child, a beautiful daughter. One day, as the daughter was gathering flowers, the god of the underworld drove by in his chariot. He sees her and fell madly in love with her. He reaches out, grabbed the frightened girl, and pulled her into the chariot beside him. The daughter's screams were useless as the two drove below the surface of the earth. Soon they reached the land of the dead, where he forces her to become his wife. Not long afterward, the goddess realizes her daughter was missing. She searched for her all over the world. When she could not find the girl, she became so grief-stricken that she neglects her duties, and all over the earth, the crops weakened and died. Finally she threatened that nothing would grow until her daughter was returned to her. Zeus, king of the gods, then commanded that the daughter has to be released—but only if she had not eaten anything. The god of the underworld agreed to let her go, but he tricks her into eating six pomegranate seeds before she leaves. Because the girl had eaten the food of Death, she had to live

_____ 8. I forced myself to read the *boring* textbook, but I remembered very little of what I had read.

_____ 9. *Copying* my classmate's notes is a poor substitute for attending class on my own.

_____ 10. *To quit* smoking, Blaise stopped going to places where he would usually smoke, such as nightclubs and bars.

Active and Passive Verbs

When the subject of a sentence performs the action of a verb, the verb is in the *active voice.* When the subject of a sentence receives the action of a verb, the verb is in the *passive voice.*

www.mhhe.com/langan

The passive form of a verb consists of a form of the verb *be* plus the past participle of the main verb. Look at the active and passive forms of the verbs below.

Active	Passive
Lola *ate* the vanilla pudding. (The subject, *Lola,* is the doer of the action.)	The vanilla pudding *was eaten by* Lola. (The subject, *pudding,* does not act. Instead, something happens to it.)
The plumber *replaced* the water heater. (The subject, *plumber,* is the doer of the action.)	The water heater *was replaced by* the plumber. (The subject, *heater,* does not act. Instead, something happens to it.)

In general, active verbs are more effective than passive ones. Active verbs give your writing a simpler and more vigorous style. The passive form of verbs is appropriate, however, when the performer of the action is unknown or is less important than the receiver of the action. For example,

My house was vandalized last night.
(The performer of the action is unknown.)

Troy was seriously injured as a result of your negligence.
(The receiver of the action, *Troy,* is being emphasized.)

Practice 3

Change the following sentences from the passive to the active voice. Note that you may have to add a subject in some cases.

EXAMPLES

The moped was ridden by Tony.
Tony rode the moped.

The basketball team was given a standing ovation.
The crowd gave the basketball team a standing ovation.

(Here a subject had to be added.)

1. Carla's long hair was snipped off by the beautician.

   _____

2. The teachers' strike was protested by the parents.

   _____

3. The silent alarm was tripped by the alert bank teller.

   _____

4. The escaped convicts were tracked by relentless bloodhounds.

   _____

5. The new PET scanner was donated to the hospital.

   _____

6. A gallon glass jar of pickles was dropped in the supermarket aisle by a stock clerk.

   _____

7. The deer was struck as it crossed the highway.

   _____

8. I was referred by my doctor to a specialist in hearing problems.

   _____

9. One wall of my living room is covered by family photographs.

   _____

10. The town was gripped by fear during the accident at the nuclear power plant.

    _____

Review Test 1

On separate paper, write three sentences apiece that use:

1. Present perfect tense

2. Past perfect tense

3. Present progressive tense

4. Past progressive tense

5. Infinitive

6. Participle

7. Gerund

8. Passive voice (when the subject is unknown or is less important than the receiver of an action—see page 201)

NAME: _____

DATE: _____

| MASTERY TEST 1 | Additional Information about Verbs |

PART A

*In each space, write the **present perfect tense** form of the verb shown.*

occur

1. In the past few years, several shark attacks _____ off the shores of Maui.

grow up

2. Millions of children _____ reading *Harry Potter* books.

testify

3. Thousands of people _____ in support of children's health care legislation.

PART B

*In each space, write the **past perfect tense** form of the verb shown.*

finish

4. Miho _____ taking her English and math placement tests before she received a call from the hospital about her father.

write

5. After two months, I _____ only three pages of my term paper.

PART C

*In each space, write the **present progressive tense** form of the verb shown.*

take

6. I _____ insulin to control my diabetes, but my endocrinologist says that I can control the disease through exercise and diet.

organize

7. Gayle _____ several Take Back the Night events at the Women's Center in March.

PART D

*In each space, write the **past progressive tense** form of the verb shown.*

raise

8. The students in Mr. Pascual's sixth-grade class _____ money for their trip to Washington, D.C. by recycling aluminum cans and glass bottles.

play

9. Until last year, my daughter _____ with Bratz dolls, but now all she wants to do is play computer and video games.

present

10. The mayor _____ a speech at the neighborhood board meeting when the civil defense siren sounded.

Additional Information about Verbs   MASTERY TEST 2

PART 1

In the space provided, identify the italicized word as a participle (P), *an infinitive* (I), *or a gerund* (G).

_____ 1. Karen worries that her toddler will swallow *chipped* paint, which might contain lead.

_____ 2. Mark, who works twice as hard as his teammates, joined the collegiate *wrestling* team as a walk-on.

_____ 3. My seventeen-year-old son wants *to buy* a car, but he expects his parents to pay for the insurance and gasoline.

_____ 4. Over fifty college students have died of alcohol *poisoning* since 2000.

_____ 5. The Tex-Mex restaurant in town is known for its *sizzling* fajita steaks.

PART 2

Change the following sentences from the passive to the active voice. Note that you may have to add a subject in some cases.

1. The celebrities on the red carpet were photographed by the clamoring paparazzi.

   _____

2. A five-day extension on the research project was given to students by the professor.

   _____

3. Blood was drawn by a phlebotomist to randomly test employees for illegal drug use.

   _____

4. Thousands of dollars have been gambled away by Keith playing online video poker.

   _____

5. "Gently used" prom and bridal dresses were donated by women of all ages to high school girls in need of gowns.

   _____

   _____

Pronoun Reference, Agreement, and Point of View

13

Introductory Activity

Read each pair of sentences below, noting the underlined pronouns. Then circle the correct letter in each of the statements that follow.

1. a. Neither of the finalists in the talent competition showed their anxiety as the envelope was being opened.
   b. Neither of the finalists in the talent competition showed her anxiety as the envelope was being opened.

2. a. At the mall, they are already putting up Christmas decorations.
   b. At the mall, shop owners are already putting up Christmas decorations.

3. a. I go to the steak house often because you can get inexpensive meals there.
   b. I go to the steak house often because I can get inexpensive meals there.

In the first pair, (a, b) uses the underlined pronoun correctly because the pronoun refers to *Neither,* which is a singular word.

In the second pair, (a, b) is correct because otherwise the pronoun reference would be unclear.

In the third pair, (a, b) is correct because the pronoun point of view should not be shifted unnecessarily.

Answers are on page 666.

Pronouns are words that take the place of nouns (words for persons, places, or things). In fact, the word *pronoun* means *for a noun.* Pronouns are shortcuts that keep you from unnecessarily repeating words in writing. Here are some examples of pronouns:

Meena shampooed *her* dog. (*Her* is a pronoun that takes the place of *Meena's.*)

As the door swung open, *it* creaked. (*It* replaces *door.*)

When the motorcyclists arrived at McDonald's, *they* removed *their* helmets. (*They* replaces *motorcyclists; their* replaces *motorcyclists'.*)

This chapter presents rules that will help you avoid three common mistakes people make with pronouns. The rules are as follows:

1. A pronoun must refer clearly to the word it replaces.
2. A pronoun must agree in number with the word or words it replaces.
3. Pronouns should not shift unnecessarily in point of view.

Pronoun Reference

A sentence may be confusing and unclear if a pronoun appears to refer to more than one word, as in this sentence:

I locked my suitcase in my car, and then it was stolen.

What was stolen? It is unclear whether the suitcase or the car was stolen.

I locked my suitcase in my car, and then my car was stolen.

A sentence may also be confusing if the pronoun does not refer to any specific word. Look at this sentence:

We never buy fresh vegetables at that store because they charge too much.

Who charges too much? There is no specific word that *they* refers to. Be clear.

We never buy fresh vegetables at that store because the owners charge too much.

Here are additional sentences with unclear pronoun reference. Read the explanations of why they are unclear and look carefully at the ways they are corrected.

Unclear	Clear
Lola told Gina that she had gained weight.	Lola told Gina, "You've gained weight."
(*Who* had gained weight: Lola or Gina? Be clear.)	(Quotation marks, which can sometimes be used to correct an unclear reference, are explained in Chapter 25.)
My older brother is an electrician, but I'm not interested in it.	My older brother is an electrician, but I'm not interested in becoming one.
(There is no specific word that *it* refers to. It would not make sense to say, "I'm not interested in electrician.")
Our instructor did not explain the assignment, which made me angry.	I was angry that our instructor did not explain the assignment.
(Does *which* mean that the instructor's failure to explain the assignment made you angry, or that the assignment itself made you angry. Be clear.)

Practice 1

Rewrite each of the following sentences to make clear the vague pronoun reference. Add, change, or omit words as necessary.

EXAMPLE

Lana thanked Denise for the gift, which was very thoughtful of her.
Lana thanked Denise for the thoughtful gift.

1. At the gas station, they told us one of our tires looked soft.

_____

_____

2. Nora dropped the heavy ashtray on her foot and broke it.

_____

_____

3. Vicki asked for a grade transcript at the registrar's office, and they told her it would cost three dollars.

_____

_____

4. Don't touch the freshly painted walls with your hands unless they're dry.

_____

_____

5. Maurice stays up half the night watching *Chiller Theater,* which really annoys his wife.

_____

_____

6. Robin went to the store's personnel office, where they are interviewing for sales positions.

_____

_____

7. Leon told his brother that he needed to lose some weight.

_____

_____

8. I wrote to the insurance company, but they haven't answered my letters.

_____

_____

9. Because my eyes were itchy and bloodshot, I went to the doctor to see what he could do about it.

_____

_____

10. I took the loose pillows off the chairs and sat on them.

_____

_____

Pronoun Agreement

A pronoun must agree in number with the word or words it replaces. If the word a pronoun refers to is singular, the pronoun must be singular; if the word is plural, the pronoun must be plural. (Note that the word a pronoun refers to is known as the *antecedent.*)

www.mhhe.com/langan

Lola agreed to lend me her Billie Holiday albums.

The gravediggers sipped coffee during their break.

In the first example, the pronoun *her* refers to the singular word *Lola;* in the second example, the pronoun *their* refers to the plural word *gravediggers.*

| Practice | Write the appropriate pronoun (*they, their, them, it*) in the blank space in each of the following sentences. |

2   **EXAMPLE**

My credit cards got me into debt, so I shredded ____*them*____.

1. Even though I should replace my disposable contact lenses every week, I often forget to change _____ out.

2. Several legislators proposed a bill to establish a registry of convicted murderers, but these lawmakers still need to determine the cost of _____ proposal.

3. Many educators have had to change the way that _____ teach in order to comply with the No Child Left Behind Act of 2001.

4. After I promised my children that I would take them to the movies on Friday, I had to tell _____ that the hospital needed me to work an additional shift.

5. Less than a week after I placed a backorder for my textbook, the bookstore called to say that _____ had arrived.

Indefinite Pronouns

The following words, known as *indefinite pronouns,* are always singular.

Indefinite Pronouns

(-one words)	(-body words)	
one	nobody	each
anyone	anybody	either
everyone	everybody	neither
someone	somebody	

Either of the apartments has its drawbacks.

One of the girls lost her skateboard.

Everyone in the class must hand in his paper tomorrow.

In each example, the pronoun is singular because it refers to one of the indefinite pronouns. There are two important points to remember about indefinite pronouns.

Point 1

The last example above suggests that everyone in the class is male. If the students were all female, the pronoun would be *her*. If the students were a mixed group of males and females, the pronoun form would be *his or her*.

Everyone in the class must hand in *his or her* paper tomorrow.

Some writers still follow the traditional practice of using *his* to refer to both men and women. Many now use *his or her* to avoid an implied sexual bias. Perhaps the best practice, though, is to avoid using either *his* or the somewhat awkward *his or her*. This can often be done by rewriting a sentence in the plural:

All students in the class must hand in *their* papers tomorrow.

Here are some examples of sentences that can be rewritten in the plural.

A young child is seldom willing to share her toys with others.
Young children are seldom willing to share their toys with others.

Anyone who does not wear his seat belt will be fined.
People who do not wear their seat belts will be fined.

A newly elected politician should not forget his or her campaign promises.
Newly elected politicians should not forget their campaign promises.

Point 2

In informal spoken English, *plural* pronouns are often used with indefinite pronouns. Instead of saying

Everybody has *his or her* own idea of an ideal vacation.

we are likely to say

Everybody has *their* own idea of an ideal vacation.

Here are other examples:

> Everyone in the class must pass in *their* papers.
>
> Everybody in our club has *their* own idea about how to raise money.
>
> No one in our family skips *their* chores.

In such cases, the indefinite pronouns are clearly plural in meaning. Also, the use of such plurals helps people avoid the awkward *his or her*. In time, the plural pronoun may be accepted in formal speech or writing. Until that happens, however, you should use the grammatically correct singular form in your writing.

Practice

3

Underline the correct pronoun.

EXAMPLE

Neither of those houses has (<u>its</u>, their) own garage.

1. Girls! Did everyone remember to bring (her, their) insect repellent?
2. Anyone can pass our men's physical education course if (he, they) will laugh at all the instructor's jokes.
3. Each of the lead actresses had (her, their) own dressing room.
4. Neither of the Mets' relief pitchers was able to get (his, their) curve ball across.
5. If any student wants to apply for the scholarship offered by the women's college, (she, they) will need two recommendations.
6. Either type of video recording system has (its, their) drawbacks.
7. Each ballerina stretched for an hour to prepare for (her, their) audition.
8. Three boys were suspected, but nobody would confess to leaving (his, their) fingerprints all over the window.
9. All women leaving the room should pick up (her, their) lab reports.
10. During the fire, any one of those men could have lost (his, their) balance on that narrow ledge.

Pronoun Point of View

Pronouns should not shift their point of view unnecessarily. When writing a paper, be consistent in your use of first-, second-, or third-person pronouns.

Type of Pronoun	Singular	Plural
First-person pronouns	**I (my, mine, me)**	**we (our, us)**
Second-person pronouns	**you (your)**	**you (your)**
Third-person pronouns	**he (his, him)** **she (her)** **it (its)**	**they (their, them)**

> **TIP** Any person, place, or thing, as well as any indefinite pronoun like *one, anyone, someone,* and so on (page 210), is a third-person word.

For instance, if you start writing in the first-person *I*, don't jump suddenly to the second-person *you*. Or if you are writing in the third-person *they*, don't shift unexpectedly to *you*. Look at the examples.

Inconsistent

One reason that *I* like living in the city is that *you* always have a wide choice of sports events to attend.

(The most common mistake people make is to let a *you* slip into their writing after they start with another pronoun.)

Someone who is dieting should have the help of friends; *you* should also have plenty of willpower.

Students who work while *they* are going to school face special problems. For one thing, *you* seldom have enough study time.

Consistent

One reason that *I* like living in the city is that *I* always have a wide choice of sports events to attend.

Someone who is dieting should have the help of friends; *he* or *she* should also have plenty of willpower.

Students who work while *they* are going to school face special problems. For one thing, *they* seldom have enough study time.

Practice

4

Cross out inconsistent pronouns in the following sentences and write the correction above the error.

EXAMPLE

me

I work better when the boss doesn't hover over ~~you~~ with instructions.

1. When we drive through the Pennsylvania countryside, you see some of the horse-drawn buggies used by the Amish people.

2. One of the things I like about the corner store is that you can buy homemade sausage there.

3. In our family, we had to learn to keep our bedrooms neat before you were given an allowance.

4. No matter how hard we may be working, the minute you relax, the supervisor will be watching.

5. People shouldn't discuss cases outside of court if you serve on a jury.

6. As I read the daily papers, you get depressed by all the violent crime occurring in this country.

7. I never eat both halves of a hamburger bun, because you save calories that way.

8. If someone started a bakery or donut shop in this town, you could make a lot of money.

9. Fran likes to shop at the factory outlet because you can buy discount clothing there.

10. I can't wait for summer, when you can stop wearing heavy coats and itchy sweaters.

Review Test   1

Underline the correct word in the parentheses.

1. John spent all morning bird-watching and didn't see a single (one, bird).

2. Of the six men on the committee, no one was prepared to give (his, their) report, so the deadline was extended.

3. If a student in that women's college wants to get a good schedule, (she, you) must enroll as soon as possible.

4. Neither of the luncheonettes near our office has a very wide choice of sandwiches on (its, their) menu.

5. My father has cut down on salt because it can give (you, him) high blood pressure.

6. Well, gentlemen, if anyone objects to the plan, (he, they) should speak up now.

7. I put my wet umbrella on the porch until (it, the umbrella) was dry.

8. I don't like that fast-food restaurant, because (they, the employees) are inefficient.

9. Doctors make large salaries, but (you, they) often face the pressure of dealing with life and death.

10. After eight hours in the cramped, stuffy car, I was glad (it, the trip) was over.

Review Test 2

Cross out the pronoun error in each sentence and write the correction in the space provided at the left. Then circle the letter that correctly describes the type of error that was made.

EXAMPLES

_____People_____ ~~Anyone~~ turning in their papers late will be penalized.

Mistake in: a. pronoun reference   (b.) pronoun agreement

_____Paul_____ When Clyde takes his son Paul to the park, ~~he~~ enjoys himself.

Mistake in: (a.) pronoun reference   b. pronoun point of view

_____we_____ From where we stood, ~~you~~ could see three states.

Mistake in: a. pronoun agreement   (b.) pronoun point of view

_____ 1. In our company, you have to work for one year before getting vacation time.

   Mistake in: a. pronoun agreement   b. pronoun point of view

_____ 2. Amy signed up for a word-processing course because she heard that they are in demand.

   Mistake in: a. pronoun reference   b. pronoun agreement

_____ 3. We did not eat much of the fruit; you could tell that it was not fresh.

   Mistake in: a. pronoun agreement   b. pronoun point of view

_____ 4. Eric visited the counseling center because they can help him straighten out his schedule.

   Mistake in: a. pronoun reference   b. pronoun agreement

_____   5. Every student who was in the chemistry lab has their own memories of the fire.

Mistake in: a. pronoun reference   b. pronoun agreement

HINT You may want to rewrite item 5 in the plural, using the lines below.

_____

_____

_____   6. After LaTanya put cheese slices on the hamburgers, the dog ate them.

Mistake in: a. pronoun reference   b. pronoun point of view

_____   7. If people feel that they are being discriminated against in jobs or housing, you should contact the appropriate federal agency.

Mistake in: a. pronoun agreement   b. pronoun point of view

_____   8. Norma told her neighbor that her house needed a new coat of paint.

Mistake in: a. pronoun reference   b. pronoun agreement

_____   9. One of the actors forgot their lines and tried to ad-lib.

Mistake in: a. pronoun agreement   b. pronoun point of view

_____   10. If anyone wants a tryout, they should be at the gym at four o'clock.

Mistake in: a. pronoun reference   b. pronoun agreement

HINT You may want to rewrite item 10 in the plural, using the lines below.

_____

_____

Pronoun Reference, Agreement, and Point of View | MASTERY TEST 1

Underline the correct word in the parentheses.

1. Each of my daughters had to get (her, their) own lunch before leaving for school.

2. Lonnell needed his writing folder from the file cabinet, but he couldn't find (it, the folder).

3. In our office we have to work for six months before (we, you) get a raise.

4. Shoppers seem to like the new store because (you, they) rarely have to wait in line.

5. Although I liked my math teacher, I never really understood (it, math).

6. The bellhop discovered that someone had left (his, their) expensive suit in one of the hotel closets.

7. If you want to lose weight by exercising, (one, you) should begin with a sensible program of light workouts.

8. Every player on the Rangers' bench pulled on (his, their) helmet and jumped onto the ice as soon as the fight broke out.

9. John's neighbor called to tell him that someone had parked in (his, John's) spot.

10. Whenever I go to that post office, (they, the clerks) act as if I'm troubling them when I ask for stamps.

11. On the first day of school, students spend most of the time getting (your, their) schedule in order and finding classrooms.

12. The cat sat staring at the bird in the cage, and (the bird, it) was very upset.

13. Elise treated Ariana to lunch at the restaurant that (she, Elise) likes best.

14. As we walked toward the accident site, (they, police officers) told us to stay out of the way.

15. Steve watches movies of all kinds, because he's interested in (it, making movies) as a possible career.

16. A person has to be self-confident to go to a party where (you, he or she) doesn't know anyone.

17. Felice stopped at the bakery to pick up the cake she'd ordered, but (he, the baker) was not finished decorating it.

18. I don't know anybody who has (their, his or her) report finished yet.

19. When I got my bike out of the garage, I noticed that (it, the garage) really needed cleaning.

20. There was a pretty bow on my present, but I threw (it, the bow) into the trash.

NAME: _____

DATE: _____

MASTERY TEST 2 | Pronoun Reference, Agreement, and Point of View

In the space provided, write PE *for sentences that contain pronoun errors.*
Write C *for the three sentences that use pronouns correctly. Then cross out*
each pronoun error and write a correction above it.

EXAMPLE

_____PE_____

                                      his

    Each of the boys explained ~~their~~ project.

_____ 1. Drew told his boss that he needed more time to finish the report.

_____ 2. Each musician carried his or her own instrument onto the bus.

_____ 3. In this course, people can sit in class for weeks before the instructor calls
on them.

_____ 4. Harold refuses to take his children to amusement parks because he doesn't
like them.

_____ 5. Everyone who parks on that street has had their car windows smashed.

_____ 6. Carl says he has problems taking lecture notes because they all talk too fast.

_____ 7. I hate standing in bakery lines where you have to take a number.

_____ 8. "Anyone even suspected of cheating," warned the instructor at the boys'
school, "forfeits his chance of passing this test."

_____ 9. The ace pilots flew in formation over the crowded stadium, which was
breathtaking.

_____ 10. He avoids foods that might give you heartburn.

Pronoun Reference, Agreement, and Point of View   MASTERY TEST 3

In the space provided, write PE *for sentences that contain pronoun errors.*
Write C *for the two sentences that use pronouns correctly. Then cross out each*
pronoun error and write a correction above it.

_____   1. Pam called Ellen to tell her that the instructor had read her paper to the class.

_____   2. Danny's favorite Christmas toy is the robot you must wind up.

_____   3. Neither contestant answered her bonus question about the Civil War battles

correctly.

_____   4. Jesse won't go for the job interview because he says they hire only college

graduates.

_____   5. If you send in your ticket order in advance, one can be sure of getting

good seats.

_____   6. With rain in the forecast, just about everybody in the stadium had an

umbrella by their side.

_____   7. The old man asked me to move my suitcase off the bench so he could sit on it.

_____   8. Hana is really a generous person, but she keeps it hidden.

_____   9. Whenever we take our children on a trip, we have to remember to bring

snacks and toys to keep them occupied.

_____   10. One of the men in our cab company just got their license revoked.

NAME: _____

DATE: _____

MASTERY TEST 4 Pronoun Reference, Agreement, and Point of View

In the space provided, write PE *for sentences that contain pronoun errors. Write* C *for the sentence that uses pronouns correctly. Then cross out each pronoun error and write a correction above it.*

_____ 1. After Erica put the candles on her twin sons' birthday cakes, the dog ate them.

_____ 2. None of the women in the class was eager to have their presentation put on video.

_____ 3. The cheeseburgers we were served were so thick that you could hardly bite into them.

_____ 4. The citizens protested at City Hall because they had raised taxes for the second year in a row.

_____ 5. Tina knew Ed was still angry, but he wouldn't talk about it.

_____ 6. Devon asked Spencer to try out his new motorbike.

_____ 7. Carol was told to sign on the dotted line with her ballpoint pen, but she couldn't find it.

_____ 8. Either the dog or the cat had spilled water from its dish all over the kitchen floor.

_____ 9. Davy complained to his brother that he always got asked to walk the puppy.

_____ 10. The grounder took a bad hop and bounced over the shortstop's head; this resulted in two runs scoring.

Pronoun Types

Introductory Activity

In each pair, write a check beside the sentence that you think uses pronouns correctly.

_____ Ali and *I* enrolled in a computer course.

_____ Ali and *me* enrolled in a computer course.

_____ The police officer pointed to my sister and *me*.

_____ The police officer pointed to my sister and *I*.

_____ Lola prefers men *whom* take pride in their bodies.

_____ Lola prefers men *who* take pride in their bodies.

_____ The players are confident that the league championship is *theirs'*.

_____ The players are confident that the league championship is *theirs*.

_____ *Them* concert tickets are too expensive.

_____ *Those* concert tickets are too expensive.

_____ Our parents should spend some money on *themself* for a change.

_____ Our parents should spend some money on *themselves* for a change.

Answers are on page 667.

This chapter describes some common types of pronouns: subject and object pronouns, relative pronouns, possessive pronouns, demonstrative pronouns, and reflexive pronouns.

Subject and Object Pronouns

Pronouns change their form depending on the place they occupy in a sentence. Here is a list of subject and object pronouns:

Subject Pronouns	Object Pronouns
I	me
you	you (no change)
he	him
she	her
it	it (no change)
we	us
they	them

Subject Pronouns

www.mhhe.com/langan

Subject pronouns are subjects of verbs.

They are getting tired. (*They* is the subject of the verb *are getting*.)

She will decide tomorrow. (*She* is the subject of the verb *will decide*.)

We women organized the game. (*We* is the subject of the verb *organized*.)

Several rules for using subject pronouns, and mistakes people sometimes make, are explained starting below.

Rule 1

Use a subject pronoun in a sentence with a compound (more than one) subject.

Incorrect	Correct
Dwayne and *me* went shopping yesterday.	Dwayne and *I* went shopping yesterday.
Him and *me* spent lots of money.	*He* and *I* spent lots of money.

If you are not sure which pronoun to use, try each pronoun by itself in the sentence. The correct pronoun will be the one that sounds right. For example, "*Me* went shopping yesterday" does not sound right; "*I* went shopping yesterday" does.

Rule 2

Use a subject pronoun after forms of the verb *be*. Forms of *be* include *am, are, is, was, were, has been, have been,* and others.

It was *I* who telephoned.

It may be *they* at the door.

It is *she.*

The sentences above may sound strange and stilted to you, since this rule is seldom actually followed in conversation. When we speak with one another, forms such as "It was me," "It may be them," and "It is her" are widely accepted. In formal writing, however, the grammatically correct forms are still preferred. You can avoid having to use a subject pronoun after *be* simply by rewording a sentence. Here is how the preceding examples could be reworded:

I was the one who telephoned.

They may be at the door.

She is here.

Rule 3

Use subject pronouns after *than* or *as* when a verb is understood after the pronoun.

You read faster than I (read). (The verb *read* is understood after *I.*)

Tom is as stubborn as I (am). (The verb *am* is understood after *I.*)

We don't go out as much as they (do). (The verb *do* is understood after *they.*)

TIPS

1. Avoid mistakes by mentally adding the "missing" verb at the end of the sentence.

2. Use object pronouns after *as* or *than* when a verb is not understood after the pronoun.

   The law applies to you as well as me.

   Our boss paid Monica more than me.

Object Pronouns

Object pronouns (*me, him, her, us, them*) are the objects of verbs or prepositions. (Prepositions are connecting words like *for, at, about, to, before, by, with,* and *of.* See also page 72.)

> Nika chose *him.* (*Him* is the object of the verb *chose.*)
>
> We met *them* at the ball park. (*Them* is the object of the verb *met.*)
>
> Don't mention UFOs to *us.* (*Us* is the object of the preposition *to.*)
>
> Between you and *me,* I don't trust that woman. (*Me* is the object of the preposition *between.*)

People are sometimes uncertain about what pronoun to use when two objects follow the verb.

Incorrect	Correct
I spoke to George and *he.*	I spoke to George and *him.*
She pointed at Hana and *I.*	She pointed at Hana and *me.*

> **TIP** If you are not sure what pronoun to use, try each pronoun by itself in the sentence. The correct pronoun will be the one that sounds right. For example, "I spoke to he" doesn't sound right; "I spoke to him" does.

Practice 1

Underline the correct subject or object pronoun in each of the following sentences. Then show whether your answer is a subject or an object pronoun by circling the *S* or *O* in the margin. The first one is done for you as an example.

S Ⓞ   1. I left the decision to (her, she).

S O   2. At a sale, my mother and (I, me) get bargain-hunting fever.

S O   3. As he gazed at (she, her) and the children, he knew he was happy.

S O   4. The panhandler asked my brother and (I, me) for some change.

S O   5. Without (she, her) and (he, him), this club would be a disaster.

S O   6. Suki can change a tire faster than (I, me).

S O   7. (We, Us) athletes always have to stay in shape.

S O   8. It was (she, her) who noticed that the phone was off the hook.

S O   9. The bad feelings between you and (I, me) have lasted too long.

S O   10. Before the wedding, Romeo and (he, him) tried, without much luck, to put on the cummerbunds that came with the tuxedos.

For each sentence, in the space provided, write an appropriate subject or object pronoun. Try to use as many different pronouns as possible. The first one is done for you as an example.

1. Dina ran after Kris and _____*me*_____ to return the keys she had borrowed.

2. That video equipment belongs to Barry and _____.

3. Sally and _____ decided to open a bookstore together.

4. Herb has worked at the welding shop longer than _____.

5. Take that box of candy from the shelf and give it to _____.

6. Why do you and _____ always get stuck with the cleaning up?

7. I really envy _____ for their ability to get along with people.

8. The police caught Val and _____ as they were trying to break into the boarded-up store.

9. My neighbor and _____ are soap-opera addicts.

10. Neither Ron nor _____ is afraid of walking through the cemetery at night.

Relative Pronouns

Relative pronouns do two things at once. First, they refer to someone or something already mentioned in the sentence. Second, they start a short word group that gives additional information about this someone or something. Here is a list of relative pronouns, followed by some example sentences:

Relative Pronouns	
who	which
whose	that
whom	

The only friend *who* really understands me is moving away.
The child *whom* Ben and Arlene adopted is from Korea.
Chocolate, *which* is my favorite food, upsets my stomach.
I guessed at half the questions *that* were on the test.

In the example sentences, *who* refers to *friend,* *whom* refers to *child,* *which* refers to *chocolate,* and *that* refers to *questions.* In addition, each of these relative pronouns begins a group of words that describes the person or thing being referred to. For example, the words *whom Ben and Arlene adopted* tell which child the sentence is about, and the words *which is my favorite food* give added information about chocolate.

Points to Remember about Relative Pronouns

Point 1

Whose means *belonging to whom.* Be careful not to confuse *whose* with *who's,* which means *who is.*

Point 2

Who, whose, and *whom* all refer to people. *Which* refers to things. *That* can refer to either people or things.

> I don't know *whose* book this is.
>
> He mistakenly sat on the blue chair, *which* is broken.
>
> Let's build a house *that* is energy-efficient.

Point 3

Who, whose, whom, and *which* can also be used to ask questions. When they are used in this way, they are called *interrogative* pronouns:

> *Who* murdered the secret agent?
>
> *Whose* fingerprints were on the bloodstained knife?
>
> To *whom* have the detectives been talking?
>
> *Which* suspect is going to confess?

> **TIP** In informal usage, *who* is generally used instead of *whom* as an interrogative pronoun. Informally, we can say or write, "*Who* are you rooting for in the game?" or "*Who* did the instructor fail?" More formal usage would use *whom:* "*Whom* are you rooting for in the game?" and "*Whom* did the instructor fail?"

Point 4

Who and *whom* are used differently. *Who* is a subject pronoun. Use *who* as the subject of a verb:

> Let's see *who* will be teaching the course.

Whom is an object pronoun. Use *whom* as the object of a verb or a preposition:

> Dr. Martinez is the instructor *whom* I like best.

> I haven't decided for *whom* I will vote.

You may want to review the material on subject and object pronouns found on pages 222–224.

Here is an easy way to decide whether to use *who* or *whom*. Find the first verb after the place where the *who* or *whom* will go. See if it already has a subject. If it does have a subject, use the object pronoun *whom*. If there is no subject, give it one by using the subject pronoun *who*. Notice how *who* and *whom* are used in the sentences that follow:

> I don't know *who* sideswiped my car.

> The suspect *whom* the police arrested finally confessed.

In the first sentence, *who* is used to give the verb *sideswiped* a subject. In the second sentence, the verb *arrested* already has a subject, *police*. Therefore, *whom* is the correct pronoun.

Underline the correct pronoun in each of the following sentences.

1. Alexandre Dumas, (who, which) wrote *The Three Musketeers,* once fought a duel in which his pants fell down.

2. The power failure, (who, which) caused the stage to go black, happened during the singer's performance of "You Light Up My Life."

3. The football coach wasn't very encouraging toward Mark, (who, whom) he advised to get extra health insurance.

4. A national animal-protection society honored a high school student (who, whom) refused to dissect a frog in her biology class.

5. Several of the students (who, which) were taking College Survival Skills dropped out before the end of the semester.

Practice

3

On separate paper, write five sentences using *who, whose, whom, which,* and *that.*

Practice

4

Possessive Pronouns

Possessive pronouns show ownership or possession.

> Clyde shut off the engine of *his* motorcycle.
>
> The keys are *mine*.

Here is a list of possessive pronouns:

www.mhhe.com/langan

Possessive Pronouns	
my, mine	our, ours
your, yours	your, yours
his	their, theirs
her, hers	
its	

Points to Remember about Possessive Pronouns

Point 1

A possessive pronoun *never* uses an apostrophe. (See also page 329.)

Incorrect	Correct
That coat is *hers'*.	That coat is *hers*.
The card table is *theirs'*.	The card table is *theirs*.

Point 2

Do not use any of the following nonstandard forms to show possession.

Incorrect	Correct
I met a friend of *him*.	I met a friend of *his*.
Can I use *you* car?	Can I use *your* car?
Me sister is in the hospital.	*My* sister is in the hospital.
That magazine is *mines*.	That magazine is *mine*.

Practice

5

Cross out the incorrect pronoun form in each of the sentences that follow. Write the correct form in the space at the left.

EXAMPLE

___My___   ~~Me~~ stomach is growling, so I will have a light snack before dinner.

_____ 1. Is this BlackBerry hers'?

_____ 2. The sushi without horseradish is mines.

_____ 3. My husband came home and told me that the new Chevrolet Suburban SUV in the driveway is ours'.

_____ 4. The wireless router has a dozen cables running from it's parts.

_____ 5. Marisa and Jo often remind they children that they need to budget their money if they want to go to Disney World next summer.

Demonstrative Pronouns

Demonstrative pronouns point to or single out a person or thing. There are four demonstrative pronouns:

Demonstrative Pronouns	
this	these
that	those

Generally speaking, *this* and *these* refer to things close at hand; *that* and *those* refer to things farther away.

Is anyone using *this* spoon?

I am going to throw away *these* magazines.

I just bought *that* silver Prius at the curb.

Pick up *those* toys in the corner.

> **TIP** Do not use *them, this here, that there, these here,* or *those there* to point out. Use only *this, that, these,* or *those.*

Incorrect	Correct
Them tires are badly worn.	*Those* tires are badly worn.
This here book looks hard to read.	*This* book looks hard to read.
That there candy is delicious.	*That* candy is delicious.
Those there squirrels are pests.	*Those* squirrels are pests.

Practice

6

Cross out the incorrect form of the demonstrative pronoun and write the correct form in the space provided.

EXAMPLE

Those   ~~Them~~ clothes need washing.

_____ 1. This here waitress will take your order.

_____ 2. Them sunglasses make you look really sharp.

_____ 3. These here phones are out of order.

_____ 4. Them batteries won't fit my camera.

_____ 5. I didn't know that there gun was loaded.

Practice

7

Look at the photo above and write four sentences about it using *this, that, these,* and *those.*

_____

_____

_____

_____

Reflexive Pronouns

Reflexive pronouns are pronouns that refer to the subject of a sentence. Here is a list of reflexive pronouns:

Reflexive Pronouns		
myself	herself	ourselves
yourself	itself	yourselves
himself		themselves

Sometimes the reflexive pronoun is used for emphasis:

You will have to wash the dishes *yourself.*

We *ourselves* are willing to forget the matter.

The president *himself* turns down his living room thermostat.

Points to Remember about Reflexive Pronouns

Point 1

In the plural *-self* becomes *-selves.*

Lola soaks *herself* in lavender bath oil.

They treated *themselves* to a vacation in Bermuda.

Point 2

Be careful that you do not use any of the following incorrect forms as reflexive pronouns.

Incorrect	Correct
He believes in *hisself.*	He believes in *himself.*
We drove the children *ourself.*	We drove the children *ourselves.*
They saw *themself* in the fun house mirror.	They saw *themselves* in the fun house mirror.
I'll do it *meself.*	I'll do it *myself.*

Practice 8

Cross out the incorrect form of the reflexive pronoun and write the correct form in the space at the left.

EXAMPLE

themselves   She believes that God helps those who help ~~themself~~.

_____ 1. We painted the kitchen ourself.

_____ 2. The mayor hisself spoke to the striking bus drivers.

_____ 3. Marian's sons don't like being left by theirselves in the house.

_____ 4. You must get the tickets yourselfs.

_____ 5. Bill and I cooked the dinner ourself.

Review Test 1

Underline the correct word in the parentheses.

EXAMPLE

Tomas and (I, me) have already seen the movie.

1. It looks as if (this, this here) DVD player is out of order.

2. I exercise twice as much as (she, her), and I'm in worse shape.

3. The only thing for Jack and (I, me) to eat was cold rice.

4. That folding umbrella you just picked up is (our's, ours).

5. Since Paula and (he, him) are engaged, we should give them a party.

6. Why do our parents always embarrass (we, us) kids by showing those old home movies?

7. The manager (hisself, himself) plans to take a cut in salary.

8. They knew the stolen clock radios were (theirs, their's), but they couldn't prove it.

9. If you put (them, those) vegetables in the microwave, they'll defrost in a few minutes.

10. My nephews couldn't stop giggling after they saw (theirselves, themselves) in their Halloween costumes.

Review Test 2

Cross out the pronoun error in each sentence and write the correct form above it.

EXAMPLE

You and ~~me~~ *I* have to stick together.

1. I asked the dentist's receptionist for appointments for my sister and I.

2. I can't tell if them potatoes are cooked all the way through or not.

3. Since the fault is your's, you owe me the cost of the repairs.

4. When the will was read, my cousin and me had inherited a thousand dollars each.

5. After we got our income tax refund, we rewarded ourself and the kids with a vacation.

6. Demetri's car had it's antenna broken off while it was parked outside the mall.

7. Nothing is more bothersome to he than having to fix things around the house.

8. This here town needs a tough sheriff.

9. Since I take better notes than him, we studied from mine for the exam.

10. In small claims court, the judges themself decide the cases and award damages.

Review Test 3

On separate paper, write sentences that correctly use each of the following words or word groups.

EXAMPLE

Peter and him   *The coach suspended Peter and him.*

1. you and I   6. taller than I

2. yours   7. yourselves

3. Kathy and me   8. with Roberto and him

4. Leon and he   9. those

5. the neighbors and us   10. Lisa and them

NAME: _____

DATE: _____

Pronoun Types

Underline the correct word in parentheses.

1. (Them, Those) doves nest in our cedar tree every year.

2. I suspect that those dirty dishes are (yours, your's).

3. Horror movies don't scare my friends and (I, me) one bit.

4. The four boys finally had the house all to (themself, themselves).

5. Laura and (I, me) have been engaged for over three years.

6. (That, That there) woman is a helicopter pilot.

7. Without asking for permission, (he, him) and Nelson began cutting up the cake.

8. My new Buick got (its, it's) first scratch when I parked too close to a fence.

9. Bernie decided to buy (hisself, himself) a reward for sticking to his diet for one solid month.

10. The plumber showed Elaine and (I, me) the corroded lead pipes under the sink.

11. Terry's foul-shooting percentage isn't as good as (mine, mines).

12. Lonnie needs some sleep right now more than he needs (we, us).

13. Marla is taking more courses this semester than (I, me).

14. I don't understand how (this, this here) formula is used.

15. Does anyone know how (those, them) screens got torn?

16. Any friend of the Newtons is a friend of (our's, ours).

17. The team members (theirselves, themselves) are selling candy door to door.

18. I wish (those, those there) babies would stop crying.

19. When you're finished with the radio, return it to either Roberta or (I, me).

20. Those power tools are (hers, hers').

Pronoun Types MASTERY TEST 2

Cross out the incorrect pronoun in each sentence and write the correct form in the space provided at the left.

_____ 1. If we offered Michael and she some money, would they accept it?

_____ 2. Every one of those there courses is filled.

_____ 3. We caught a lot more fish than them.

_____ 4. Them mountains in the distance are the Catskills.

_____ 5. Lenny hisself decided to confess to the robbery.

_____ 6. My dog and me usually eat our meals at the same time.

_____ 7. Our station wagon can hold more people than their's.

_____ 8. These here boots will hurt you until they're fully broken in.

_____ 9. This will be the first time in weeks we've had dinner by ourself.

_____ 10. Those garden tools of your's are getting rusty.

_____ 11. The sweaters Gloria knitted for Ron and I came out two sizes too small.

_____ 12. Every girl at the party wore jeans except Michelle and I.

_____ 13. The chief showed we rookie firefighters what to do when an alarm sounded.

_____ 14. You can't park here, because this here space is reserved for the supervisor.

_____ 15. Are these binoculars her's?

_____ 16. Matina and him have nothing to discuss.

_____ 17. Of all my grandchildren, Chris and him wear me out the fastest.

_____ 18. Check the pockets of that there bathrobe for your glasses.

_____ 19. His bicycle had its' tires slashed overnight.

_____ 20. They've decided to repair the engine by themselfs.

Adjectives and Adverbs

15

Introductory Activity

Write in an appropriate word or words to complete each of the sentences below.

1. The teenage years were a _____ time for me.

2. The mechanic listened _____ while I described my car problem.

3. Basketball is a _____ game than football.

4. My brother is the _____ person in our family.

Now complete the following sentences.

The word inserted in the first sentence is an (adjective, adverb); it describes the word *time*.

The word inserted in the second sentence is an (adjective, adverb); it probably ends in the two letters _____ and describes the word *listened*.

The word inserted in the third sentence is a comparative adjective; it may be preceded by *more* or end in the two letters _____.

The word inserted in the fourth sentence is a superlative adjective; it may be preceded by *most* or end in the three letters _____.

Answers are on page 667.

Adjectives and adverbs are descriptive words. Their purpose is to make the meaning of the words they describe more specific.

Adjectives

What Are Adjectives?

Adjectives describe nouns (names of persons, places, or things) or pronouns.

www.mhhe.com/langan

> Charlotte is a *kind* woman. (The adjective *kind* describes the noun *woman*.)
>
> He is *tired*. (The adjective *tired* describes the pronoun *he*.)

An adjective usually comes before the word it describes (as in *kind woman*). But it can also come after forms of the verb *be (is, are, was, were*, and so on). Less often, an adjective follows verbs such as *feel, look, smell, sound, taste, appear, become*, and *seem*.

> The bureau is *heavy*. (The adjective *heavy* describes the bureau.)
>
> These pants are *itchy*. (The adjective *itchy* describes the pants.)
>
> The children seem *restless*. (The adjective *restless* describes the children.)

Describe this painting, using as many specific details as possible. How many adjectives did you use? Circle them.

www.mhhe.com/langan

Using Adjectives to Compare

For most short adjectives, add *-er* when comparing two things and *-est* when comparing three or more things.

> I am *taller* than my brother, but my father is the *tallest* person in the house.

> The farm market sells *fresher* vegetables than the corner store, but the *freshest* vegetables are the ones grown in my own garden.

For most *longer* adjectives (two or more syllables), add *more* when comparing two things and *most* when comparing three or more things.

> Backgammon is *more enjoyable* to me than checkers, but chess is the *most enjoyable* game of all.

> My mother is *more talkative* than my father, but my grandfather is the *most talkative* person in the house.

Points to Remember about Adjectives

Point 1

Be careful not to use both an *-er* ending and *more,* or both an *-est* ending and *most.*

Incorrect	Correct
Football is a *more livelier* game than baseball.	Football is a *livelier* game than baseball.
Tod Traynor was voted the *most likeliest* to succeed in our high school class.	Tod Traynor was voted the *most likely* to succeed in our high school class.

Point 2

Pay special attention to the following words; each has irregular forms.

	Comparative (Two)	Superlative (Three or More)
bad	worse	worst
good, well	better	best
little	less	least
much, many	more	most

Fill in the comparative or superlative forms for the following adjectives. The first two are done for you as examples.

	Comparative (Two)	Superlative (Three or More)
fast	*faster*	*fastest*
timid	*more timid*	*most timid*
kind	_____	_____
ambitious	_____	_____
generous	_____	_____
fine	_____	_____
likable	_____	_____

Add to each sentence the correct form of the word in the margin.

EXAMPLE

bad   The _____*worst*_____ day of my life was the one when my house caught fire.

thick   1. I attempted to bite into the _____ sandwich I had ever seen.

lazy   2. Each perfect summer day was _____ than the last.

harsh   3. The judge pronounced the _____ sentence possible on the convicted robber.

flexible 4. My new hairbrush is _____ than my old one and doesn't pull out as many hairs.

bad   5. I felt even _____ after I had taken the anti-motion-sickness pills.

good   6. The _____ seats in the stadium are completely sold out.

little   7. I'm looking for a cereal with _____ sugar than "Candy Flakes."

vulnerable   8. The body's central trunk is _____ to frostbite than the hands and feet.

wasteful   9. Many people throughout the world feel that Americans are the _____ people on earth.

shiny   10. My hair looked _____ than usual after I began taking vitamins.

Adverbs

What Are Adverbs?

Adverbs describe verbs, adjectives, or other adverbs. An adverb usually ends in *-ly.*

Charlotte spoke *kindly* to the confused man. (The adverb *kindly* describes the verb *spok*e.)

The man said he was *completely* alone in the world. (The adverb *completely* describes the adjective *alone*.)

Charlotte listened *very* sympathetically to his story. (The adverb *very* describes the adverb *sympathetically.)*

A Common Mistake with Adjectives and Adverbs

Perhaps the most common mistake that people make with adjectives and adverbs is to use an adjective instead of an adverb after a verb.

Incorrect	Correct
Tony breathed *heavy.*	Tony breathed *heavily.*
I rest *comfortable* in that chair.	I rest *comfortably* in that chair.
She learned *quick.*	She learned *quickly.*

Practice 3

Underline the adjective or adverb needed.

1. She walked (hesitant, hesitantly) into the room.

2. I could have won the match (easy, easily) if I had concentrated more.

3. After turning the motorcycle (sharp, sharply), Marilyn tried to regain her balance.

4. The bus stopped (abrupt, abruptly), and the passengers were thrown forward.

5. The candidate waged an (aggressive, aggressively) campaign, and the voters turned against him.

6. The man talked (regretful, regretfully) about the chances he had missed.

7. The instructor spoke so (quick, quickly) that we gave up taking notes.

8. The students eat so (messy, messily) that the cafeteria must be cleaned twice a day.

9. The boy was (envious, enviously) of his brother's new cowboy boots.

10. Maureen worked (terrible, terribly) hard at her job, yet she managed to find time for her children.

Well and Good

Two words often confused are *well* and *good*. *Good* is an adjective; it describes nouns. *Well* is usually an adverb; it describes verbs. *Well* (rather than *good*) is also used as an adjective when referring to a person's health. Here are some examples:

I became a *good* swimmer. (*Good* is an adjective describing the noun *swimmer*.)

For a change, two-year-old Rodney was *good* during the church service. (*Good* is an adjective describing Rodney and comes after *was*, a form of the verb *be*.)

Maryann did *well* on that exam. (*Well* is an adverb describing the verb *did*.)

I explained that I wasn't feeling *well*. (*Well* is used in reference to health.)

Write *well* or *good* in the sentences that follow.

1. As a manager, I am always looking for _____ employees—people who are reliable, work hard, and get along with others.

2. My friends assure me George, my blind date this Saturday night, is a _____ man.

3. The Army buddy who gave my uncle's eulogy knew him _____.

4. Horacio told the therapist that he was feeling _____, but he was still having nightmares and anxiety attacks.

5. I suspected that I was doing _____ in my world civilization class, but I never thought that I would score a 98 percent on the final exam.

Practice

4

Review Test   1

Cross out the adjective or adverb error in each sentence and write the correction in the space at the left.

EXAMPLES

frequently   My boss ~~frequent~~ tells me to slow down.

harder   For me, the country is a ~~more harder~~ place to live than the city.

_____ 1. I knew she wasn't feeling good when I saw her put her head in her hands.

_____ 2. It is best for me now to be in school than to have a full-time job.

_____ 3. The mother pressed the baby against her shoulder and sang soft in his ear.

_____ 4. After the two-week camping trip, Donna gazed grateful at her warm bathroom and clean towels.

_____ 5. That show is the most dullest one on television.

_____ 6. Squirming restless in the seat next to her date, Carol felt uneasy during the violent movie scene.

_____ 7. My sister Ella is the kinder of the four children in our family.

_____ 8. Clutching a box of chocolate-flavored cereal, the boy stood in the supermarket aisle and looked imploring at his mother.

_____ 9. He had done good on the first test, so he decided not to study for the next one.

_____ 10. Peering suspicious at the can of corn, the woman peeled back the new price label that had been stuck over the old one.

Review Test 2

Write a sentence that uses each of the following adjectives and adverbs correctly.

1. nervous _____

2. nervously _____

3. good _____

4. well _____

5. carefully _____

6. most honest _____

7. easier _____

8. best _____

9. more useful _____

10. loudest _____

NAME: _____

DATE: _____

MASTERY TEST 1 | Adjectives and Adverbs

PART **1**

Cross out the incorrect adjectival or adverbial form in each sentence. Then write the correct form in the space provided.

_____ 1. Clark runs good for a person who's thirty pounds overweight.

_____ 2. The car's brakes were acting strange, so the mechanic checked the fluid.

_____ 3. The girls sang beautiful, but the faulty microphones spoiled the show.

_____ 4. That actor's inexperience is real obvious.

_____ 5. Janelle tiptoed careful past the guest room, not wanting to wake the sleeping children.

PART **2**

Cross out the error in comparison in each sentence. Then write the correct form in the space provided.

_____ 6. The ad tried to prove which model's hair was the most glossiest by using a light meter.

_____ 7. My sister does more well on standardized tests than I do.

_____ 8. The longer Luis waited in line at the bank, the impatienter he got.

_____ 9. My awkwardest moment came when I tried to introduce my wife to my boss and forgot both their names.

_____ 10. This has been the most productivest session we've had yet.

Adjectives and Adverbs   MASTERY TEST 2

PART 1

Cross out the incorrect adjectival and adverbial form in each sentence. Then write the correct form in the space provided.

_____ 1. Sherry ate quick so she wouldn't miss the beginning of the early show.

_____ 2. Xavier decided he wasn't feeling good enough to bowl for the team.

_____ 3. I had a terrible high fever and a deep cough.

_____ 4. Hakim makes friends easy because he is so sure of himself.

_____ 5. Paul gripped the handle tight and told the barman to let the mechanical bull loose.

PART 2

Add to each sentence the correct form of the word in the margin.

loud   6. During the spring thunderstorm, each booming clap of thunder was

_____ than the preceding one.

tried   7. After doing fifty push-ups, I was _____ than I had been in years.

cheap   8. You'll need binoculars if you sit in the _____ seats in the stadium.

bad   9. The _____ clashes of the war occurred in the hot jungles of some small South Pacific islands.

little   10. This semester, I'm making _____ money at my after-school job, but I have more free time.

Misplaced Modifiers

16

Introductory Activity

Because of misplaced words, each of the sentences below has more than one possible meaning. In each case, see if you can explain both the intended meaning and the unintended meaning.

1. The farmers sprayed the apple trees wearing masks.

   Intended meaning: _____

   Unintended meaning: _____

2. The woman reached out for the faith healer who had a terminal disease.

   Intended meaning: _____

   Unintended meaning: _____

Answers are on page 668.

What Misplaced Modifiers Are and How to Correct Them

www.mhhe.com/langan

Misplaced modifiers are words that, because of awkward placement, do not describe the words the writer intended them to describe. Misplaced modifiers often confuse the meaning of a sentence. To avoid them, place words as close as possible to what they describe.

Misplaced Words	Correctly Placed Words
They could see the Goodyear blimp *sitting on the front lawn.*	Sitting on the front lawn, they could see the Goodyear blimp.
(The *Goodyear blimp* was sitting on the front lawn?)	(The intended meaning—that the Goodyear blimp was visible from the front lawn—is now clear.)
We had a hamburger after the movie, *which was too greasy for my taste.*	After the movie, we had a hamburger, which was too greasy for my taste.
(The *movie* was too greasy for your taste?)	(The intended meaning—that the hamburger was greasy—is now clear.)
Our phone *almost rang* fifteen times last night.	Our phone rang almost fifteen times last night.
(The phone *almost rang* fifteen times, but in fact did not ring at all?)	(The intended meaning—that the phone rang a little under fifteen times—is now clear.)

Other single-word modifiers to watch out for include *only, even, hardly, nearly,* and *often.* Such words should be placed immediately before the word they modify.

Underline the misplaced word or words in each sentence. Then rewrite the sentence, placing related words together to make the meaning clear.

EXAMPLE

Anita returned the hamburger to the supermarket <u>that was spoiled.</u>

Anita returned the hamburger that was spoiled to

the supermarket.

1. We noticed several dead animals driving along the wooded road.

_____

_____

2. Maya envisioned the flowers that would bloom in her mind.

_____

_____

3. I watched my closest friends being married in my tuxedo.

_____

_____

Practice

1

4. Zoe carried her new coat on her arm, which was trimmed with fur.

_____

_____

5. We just heard that all major highways were flooded on the radio.

_____

_____

6. Fresh-picked blueberries almost covered the entire kitchen counter.

_____

_____

7. Betty licked the homemade peach ice cream making sounds of contentment.

_____

_____

8. The salesman confidently demonstrated the vacuum cleaner with a grin.

_____

_____

9. Natasha is delivering singing telegrams dressed in a top hat and tails.

_____

_____

10. The local drama group needs people to build scenery badly.

_____

_____

Practice 2

Rewrite each sentence, adding the _italicized_ words. Make sure that the intended meaning is clear and that two different interpretations are not possible.

EXAMPLE

I use a flash drive to store my computer files. (Insert _that I keep on my key chain._)

I use a flash drive that I keep on my key chain to store my computer files.

1. I rolled down my car window only a few inches for the police officer. (Insert *using caution*.)

   _____

   _____

2. Tabloids publish unflattering photos of celebrities who are arrested for drunk driving or for possession of illicit drugs. (Insert *all over the world*.)

   _____

   _____

3. The mongoose was brought to Hawaii to kill rats but has since destroyed much of the native plant life. (Insert *which resembles the ferret*.)

   _____

   _____

4. Led Zeppelin's fourth album has sold 22 million copies. (Insert *almost*.)

   _____

   _____

5. Elisa decided to undergo laser eye surgery to correct her astigmatism. (Insert *at the university medical center*.)

   _____

   _____

Review Test 1

Write *M* for *misplaced* or *C* for *correct* in the space to the left of each sentence.

_____ 1. Books don't sell well in the bookstores with hard covers.

_____ 2. Books with hard covers don't sell well in the bookstores.

_____ 3. Marilyn went to the door to let in the plumber wearing her nightgown.

_____ 4. Wearing her nightgown, Marilyn went to the door to let in the plumber.

_____ 5. Franco spent nearly three hours in the doctor's office.

_____ 6. Franco nearly spent three hours in the doctor's office.

_____ 7. I spent three days in a hospital watching TV reruns recovering from surgery.

_____ 8. Recovering from surgery, I spent three days in a hospital watching TV reruns.

_____ 9. Paula searched through the closet for something to wear on her date.

_____ 10. Paula searched for something to wear on her date through the closet.

_____ 11. Nick and Fran found six boxes of pictures of their vacation in the attic.

_____ 12. Nick and Fran found six boxes of pictures in the attic of their vacation.

_____ 13. In the attic, Nick and Fran found six boxes of pictures of their vacation.

_____ 14. Mrs. Liu mistakenly put the milk container which was leaking in the refrigerator.

_____ 15. Mrs. Liu mistakenly put the milk container in the refrigerator which was leaking.

_____ 16. Susie whispered a silent prayer before the exam began under her breath.

_____ 17. Susie whispered a silent prayer under her breath before the exam began.

_____ 18. Under her breath, Susie whispered a silent prayer before the exam began.

_____ 19. On the patio, we ate roast beef sandwiches dripping with gravy.

_____ 20. We ate roast beef sandwiches on the patio dripping with gravy.

Review Test 2

Underline the five misplaced modifiers in the passage below. Then, in the spaces that follow, show how you would correct them.

¹The tired hikers almost slept for ten hours in the trail shelter. ²Then Rick awakened and hurried out of his cot when he saw a black spider looking out of the corner of his eye. ³At this point, his brother Hal woke up with a start and sneezed several times. ⁴Because Hal was coming down with a cold, Rick agreed to prepare the breakfast. ⁵He first fetched a canteen of orange juice from a nearby stream which had cooled overnight. ⁶Next, he started a fire and set about boiling water for coffee and frying up some bacon and eggs. ⁷Meanwhile, Hal sniffled, sipped some orange juice, and waited by the fire for a cup of coffee wearing a heavy sweatshirt and gloves. ⁸After both had eaten, Rick was ready to plan another day's hiking. ⁹But Hal was interested only in hiking to the bus on the nearby highway that could drop him a block from his house.

1. _____

_____

_____

2. _____

_____

_____

3. _____

_____

_____

4. _____

_____

_____

5. _____

_____

_____

NAME: _____

DATE: _____

MASTERY TEST 1 | Misplaced Modifiers

Underline the misplaced word or words in each sentence. Then rewrite the sentence, placing related words together and making the meaning clear.

1. Leroy stepped on the worm without shoes on.

   _____

2. Scott purchased an expensive ticket from a scalper that turned out to be a fake.

   _____

   _____

3. I watched a woman board a bus wearing a dress that was several sizes too small.

   _____

   _____

4. A tray of donuts had been placed on the counter which smelled delicious.

   _____

   _____

5. The student tried to study in the noisy library with great concentration.

   _____

   _____

6. Craig was spotted by a teacher cheating on an examination.

   _____

   _____

7. I stayed at the cabin window watching the bear in my pajamas.

   _____

   _____

8. Tri Lee almost read the whole psychology assignment in two hours.

   _____

   _____

NAME: _____

DATE: _____

Misplaced Modifiers

Underline the misplaced word or words in each sentence. Then rewrite the sentence, placing related words together and making the meaning clear.

1. I bought the used car from a friend with a bad exhaust system.

    _____

2. The news featured a man who played basketball in a wheelchair with no legs.

    _____

    _____

3. Our neighbor received a reward for returning the puppy to its family that had been missing for a week.

    _____

    _____

4. We saw a commercial for a company that promises to remodel any bathroom on television.

    _____

    _____

5. The hungry lions crept up behind the big game hunter who had fallen asleep without making a sound.

    _____

    _____

6. Larissa watched her sons toss a baseball back and forth through her living room picture window.

    _____

    _____

7. We were notified that we had won a trip to Disney World by telegram.

    _____

    _____

8. I woke up this morning thinking I had a paper due in a cold sweat.

    _____

Dangling Modifiers

17

Introductory Activity

Because of dangling words, each of the sentences below has more than one possible meaning. In each case, explain both the intended meaning and the unintended meaning.

1. Munching leaves from a tall tree, the children were fascinated by the eighteen-foot-tall giraffe.

   Intended meaning: _____

   _____

   Unintended meaning: _____

   _____

2. Arriving home after ten months in the army, Michael's neighbors threw a block party for him.

   Intended meaning: _____

   _____

   Unintended meaning: _____

   _____

Answers are on page 668.

Note

Some instructors might consider the first example a misplaced modifier, since the subject of the phrase *munching leaves from a tall tree*—the giraffe—does appear later in the sentence. However, correcting the error would involve changing words. Therefore, this type of error is classified as a dangling modifier in *Sentence Skills*.

www.mhhe.com/langan

What Dangling Modifiers Are and How to Correct Them

A modifier that opens a sentence must be followed immediately by the word it is meant to describe. Otherwise, the modifier is said to be *dangling,* and the sentence takes on an unintended meaning. For example, look at this sentence:

> While sleeping in his backyard, a Frisbee hit Bill on the head.

The unintended meaning is that the *Frisbee* was sleeping in his backyard. What the writer meant, of course, was that *Bill* was sleeping in his backyard. The writer should have placed *Bill* right after the modifier, revising the rest of the sentence as necessary:

> While sleeping in his backyard, *Bill* was hit on the head by a Frisbee.

The sentence could also be corrected by adding the missing subject and verb to the opening word group:

> While *Bill* was sleeping in his backyard, a Frisbee hit him on the head.

Other sentences with dangling modifiers follow. Read the explanations of why they are dangling, and look carefully at how they are corrected.

Dangling	Correct
Having almost no money, my survival depended on my parents.	Having almost no money, *I* depended on my parents for survival.
(*Who* has almost no money? The answer is not *survival* but *I.* The subject *I* must be added.)	*Or:* Since *I* had almost no money, I depended on my parents for survival.
Riding his bike, a German shepherd bit Tony on the ankle.	Riding his bike, *Tony* was bitten on the ankle by a German shepherd.
(*Who* is riding the bike? The answer is not *German shepherd,* as it unintentionally seems to be, but *Tony.* The subject *Tony* must be added.)	*Or:* While *Tony* was riding his bike, a German shepherd bit him on the ankle.
When trying to lose weight, all snacks are best avoided.	When trying to lose weight, *you* should avoid all snacks.
(*Who* is trying to lose weight? The answer is not *snacks* but *you.* The subject *you* must be added.)	*Or:* When *you* are trying to lose weight, avoid all snacks.

These examples make clear two ways of correcting a dangling modifier. Decide on a logical subject and do one of the following:

1. Place the subject *within* the opening word group:

Since *I* had almost no money, I depended on my parents for survival.

In some cases an appropriate subordinating word such as *since* must be added, and the verb may have to be changed slightly as well.

2. Place the subject right *after* the opening word group:

Having almost no money, *I* depended on my parents for survival.

Sometimes even more rewriting is necessary to correct a dangling modifier. What is important to remember is that a modifier must be placed as close as possible to the word that it modifies.

Practice

1

Rewrite each sentence to correct the dangling modifier. Mark the one sentence that is correct with a *C.*

1. Foaming at the mouth, the dog warden had the stray put to sleep.

   _____

   _____

2. Kicked carelessly under the bed, Marian finally found her slippers.

   _____

   _____

3. Rusty with disuse, I tried out the old swing set.

   _____

   _____

4. Having given up four straight hits, the manager decided to replace his starting pitcher.

   _____

   _____

5. Having frozen on the vines, the farmers lost their entire tomato crop.

   _____

   _____

6. While I was pouring out the cereal, a coupon fell into my bowl of milk.

_____

_____

7. Dancing on their hind legs, the audience cheered wildly as the elephants paraded by.

_____

_____

8. Burned beyond all recognition, Marta took the overdone meat loaf from the oven.

_____

_____

9. Tattered, faded, and hanging in shreds, we decided to replace the dining room wallpaper.

_____

_____

10. When sealed in plastic, a person can keep membership cards clean.

_____

_____

Complete the following sentences. In each case, a logical subject should follow the opening words.

Practice

2

EXAMPLE

Checking my monthly credit card statement, _I discovered that the_ _restaurant had charged me twice for my meal._

1. Since starting college, _____.

2. After finishing the first semester, _____.

3. While listening to music downloads, _____.

4. Before starting a family, _____.

5. At the age of sixteen, _____.

Review Test   1

Write *D* for *dangling* or *C* for *correct* in front of each sentence. Remember that the opening words are a dangling modifier if they are not followed immediately by a logical subject.

_____   1. Yellowed with age, the young journalist could hardly read the old newspaper clipping.

_____   2. The young journalist could hardly read the old newspaper clipping, which was yellowed with age.

_____   3. Tired and exasperated, the fight we had was inevitable.

_____   4. Since we were tired and exasperated, the fight we had was inevitable.

_____   5. After signing the repair contract, I had second thoughts.

_____   6. After signing the repair contract, second thoughts made me uneasy.

_____   7. At the age of twelve, several colleges had already accepted the boy genius.

_____   8. At the age of twelve, the boy genius had already been accepted by several colleges.

_____   9. While setting up the board, several game pieces were missing.

_____   10. While setting up the board, we noticed that several game pieces were missing.

_____   11. Walking to class, a gorgeous white Corvette sped by me at sixty miles an hour.

_____   12. As I was walking to class, a gorgeous white Corvette sped by me at sixty miles an hour.

_____   13. While waiting for the dentist to see her, Vicky became more nervous.

_____   14. While waiting for the dentist to see her, Vicky's nervousness increased.

_____   15. While she was waiting for the dentist to see her, Vicky became more nervous.

_____   16. Protected with slipcovers, my mother lets us put our feet on the living room furniture.

_____   17. My mother lets us put our feet on the living room furniture, since it is protected with slipcovers.

_____   18. Packed tightly in a tiny can, Fran had difficulty removing the anchovies.

_____   19. Since they were packed tightly in a tiny can, Fran had difficulty removing the anchovies.

_____   20. Packed tightly in a tiny can, the anchovies were difficult for Fran to remove.

Review Test   2

Underline the five dangling modifiers in this passage. Then correct them in the spaces provided.

[1]For years, students have been using the same methods of cheating on exams. One tried-and-true technique is the casual glance. [2]Pretending to stare thoughtfully out the window, peripheral vision will be used to look at another student's paper. [3]Another all-time favorite method, the pencil or pen drop, requires a helper. [4]Dropping a pen and then diving for it, "Number seventeen" (or the number of some other question) is whispered. [5]Then, making a similar pen drop, the answer is whispered by the helper. [6]The most elaborate system, though, is writing up cheat sheets. [7]Tucked up a shirtsleeve, pages of textbook material are condensed into tiny scraps of paper. [8]No matter how smooth a cheater's style is, however, the time-tested methods are often ineffective. [9]Having been a student at one time, the same ones are probably familiar to the instructor.

1. _____

_____

_____

2. _____

_____

_____

3. _____

_____

_____

4. _____

_____

_____

5. _____

_____

_____

NAME: _____

DATE: _____

MASTERY TEST 1 Dangling Modifiers

Underline the dangling modifier in each sentence. Then rewrite the sentence, correcting the dangling modifier.

1. Being made of clear glass, the children kept bumping into the sliding door.

2. Still green, Helen put the tomato in sunlight to ripen.

3. Though somewhat warped, my grandfather still enjoys playing his record collection from the forties.

4. Having turned crispy and golden, I removed the chicken from the pan.

5. Bigger than ever, Aunt Clara predicted that this year's watermelon entry would win first prize at the county fair.

6. After changing the bait, the fish started to bite.

7. Coming home without a job, the comedies on television only made Helen feel depressed.

8. Having rehearsed his speech several times, Amal's presentation to the staff went smoothly.

Dangling Modifiers   MASTERY TEST 2

Underline the dangling modifier in each sentence. Then rewrite the sentence, correcting the dangling modifier.

1. Being too heavy to lift, Jo asked Bob to help her move the sofa.

2. Parched and dry, the ice-cold Coke soothed my throat.

3. Clutching a handful of silver and a portable TV set, our neighbor's watchdog surprised a burglar.

4. Living in a tent for two weeks, the camping trip made us appreciate hot showers and dry towels.

5. Thrown on the floor in a heap, we could not tell if the clothes were clean or dirty.

6. Afraid to look his father in the eye, Danny's head remained bowed.

7. Straining at the leash, I could see my neighbor's Great Dane getting ready for his walk.

8. While lying in bed with a cold, my cat jumped on me and curled up on my stomach.

Faulty Parallelism

18

Introductory Activity

Read aloud each pair of sentences below. Place a check mark beside the sentence that reads more smoothly and clearly and sounds more natural.

Pair 1

_____ I use my computer to write papers, to search the Internet, and for playing video games.

_____ I use my computer to write papers, to search the Internet, and to play video games.

Pair 2

_____ One option the employees had was to take a cut in pay; the other was longer hours of work.

_____ One option the employees had was to take a cut in pay; the other was to work longer hours.

Pair 3

_____ Dad's favorite chair has a torn cushion, the armrest is stained, and a musty odor.

_____ Dad's favorite chair has a torn cushion, a stained armrest, and a musty odor.

Answers are on page 669.

Parallelism Explained

Words in a pair or a series should have parallel structure. By balancing the items in a pair or a series so that they have the same kind of structure, you will make the sentence clearer and easier to read. Notice how the parallel sentences that follow read more smoothly than the nonparallel ones.

Nonparallel (Not Balanced)	Parallel (Balanced)
Fran spends her free time reading, listening to music, and she works in the garden.	Fran spends her free time reading, listening to music, and working in the garden.
	(A balanced series of *-ing* words: *reading, listening, working.*)
After the camping trip I was exhausted, irritable, and wanted to eat.	After the camping trip I was exhausted, irritable, and hungry.
	(A balanced series of descriptive words: *exhausted, irritable, hungry.*)
My hope for retirement is to be healthy, to live in a comfortable house, and having plenty of money.	My hope for retirement is to be healthy, to live in a comfortable house, and to have plenty of money. (A balanced series of *to* verbs: *to be, to live, to have.*)
Nightly, Alexei puts out the trash, checks the locks on the doors, and the burglar alarm is turned on.	Nightly, Alexei puts out the trash, checks the locks on the doors, and turns on the burglar alarm.
	(Balanced verbs and word order: *puts out the trash, checks the locks, turns on the burglar alarm.*)

Balanced sentences are not a skill you need to worry about when you are writing first drafts. But when you rewrite, you should try to put matching words and ideas into matching structures. Such parallelism will improve your writing style.

Practice

1

The unbalanced part of each sentence is italicized. Rewrite this part so that it matches the rest of the sentence.

EXAMPLE

In the afternoon, I changed two diapers, ironed several shirts, and *was watching* soap operas. _watched_____

1. As the home team scored the winning touchdown, the excited fans screamed, cheered, and *pennants were waved.*

   _____

2. Would you prefer to go for a walk outside or *staying indoors?*

   _____

3. Before Pete could assemble the casserole, he had to brown the meat, dice the vegetables, and *a cream sauce had to be made.*

   _____

4. Please feed the dog, *the heat must be turned down,* and lock the doors.

   _____

5. That restaurant specializes in *hamburgers that are overdone,* wilted salads, and stale pastries.

   _____

6. The old Ford sputtered, *was coughing,* and finally stopped altogether.

   _____

7. The hospital patients can sometimes be cranky, *make a lot of demands,* and ungrateful.

   _____

8. After eating a whole pizza, *two milk shakes,* and sampling a bag of chips, Ernest was still hungry.

   _____

9. As soon as she gets up, she starts the coffee machine, turns on the radio, and *a frozen waffle is put into the toaster.*

   _____

10. The boss told Vern that he had only two options: to work harder or *leaving the company.*

    _____

Complete the following statements. The first two parts of each statement are parallel in form; the part that you add should be parallel in form as well.

EXAMPLE

Three things I could not live without are my cell phone, my laptop, and *my morning coffee.*

1. The new reality TV show is disappointing: the premise is absurd, the cast members are uninteresting, and _____.

2. As a parent, I promise to love my child unconditionally, to provide for my child's needs, and _____.

3. As the students waited for the professor to arrive for class, they rummaged through their backpacks, silenced their phones, and _____.

4. During my first year in my own apartment, I learned how to fix leaky toilets and torn screens, how to survive on instant ramen and frozen pizzas, and

_____.

5. Online dating is popular, unpredictable, and _____.

Collaborative Activity

Editing and Rewriting

Working with a partner, carefully read the short paragraph below and mark the five instances of faulty parallelism. Then correct the instances of faulty parallelism. Feel free to discuss the rewrite quietly with your partner and refer back to the chapter when necessary.

[1]For the 10 percent of the American population that is left-handed, life is not easy. [2]Using a pair of scissors or to write in a spiral notebook can be very difficult. [3]The scissors and the notebook are two items designed for right-handers. [4]Also, have you ever seen a "southpaw" take notes or writing an exam at one of those right-handed half-desks? [5]The poor "lefty" has to twist like a yoga devotee or in the style of a circus acrobat in order to reach the paper. [6]But a recent study proves that

continued

being left-handed can be psychologically damaging as well as tax a person physically. [7]A survey of 2,300 people showed that 20 percent more left-handers than right-handers smoked. [8]Perhaps left-handed people smoke to relieve the tension or they are forgetting the problems of living in a right-handed world.

Collaborative Activity

Creating Sentences

Working with a partner, make up your own short test on faulty parallelism, as directed.

1. Write a sentence that includes three things you want to do tomorrow. One of those things should not be in parallel form. Then correct the faulty parallelism.

   Nonparallel _____

   _____

   Parallel _____

   _____

2. Write a sentence that names three positive or three negative qualities of a person you know.

   Nonparallel _____

   _____

   Parallel _____

   _____

3. Write a sentence that includes three everyday things that annoy you.

   Nonparallel _____

   _____

   Parallel _____

   _____

Reflective Activity

1. Look at the paragraph about being left-handed that you revised on page 265. How does parallel form improve the paragraph?

2. How would you evaluate your use of parallel form in your writing? Do you use it almost never, at times, or often? How would you benefit from using it more?

Review Test 1

Cross out the unbalanced part of each sentence. Then rewrite the unbalanced part so that it matches the other item or items in the sentence.

EXAMPLE

I enjoy watering the grass and to work in the garden.

working

1. The traffic cop blew his whistle, was waving his hands, and nodded to the driver to start moving.

2. Mike's letter of application was smudged, improperly spaced, and it had wrinkles.

3. Kendra spoke vividly and with force at the student government meeting.

4. I like Mariah Carey; Beyoncé is preferred by my sister.

5. Darkening skies, branches that were waving, and scurrying animals signaled the approaching storm.

6. The pitcher wiped his brow, straightened his cap, and he was tugging at his sleeve.

7. The driving instructor told me to keep my hands on the wheel, to drive defensively, and the use of caution at all times.

_____

8. The customer made choking noises, turned red, and was pointing to his throat.

_____

9. My sister eats spaghetti without sauce, cereal without milk, and doesn't put mustard on hot dogs.

_____

10. The scratches on my car's hood were caused by rocks hitting it, people who sat on it, and cats jumping on it.

_____

Review Test 2

On separate paper, write five sentences of your own that use parallel structure. Each sentence should contain three items in a series.

Review Test 3

There are six nonparallel parts in the following passage. The first is corrected for you as an example. Underline the other five and write corrections in the space provided.

¹Consumers have several sources of information they can use in the never-ending war against poor services and merchandise that is shoddy. ²For one thing, consumers can take advantage of the Better Business Bureau. ³If you plan to contract the Fly-By-Night Company to paint your house or the replacement of siding, you should first phone your local Better Business Bureau to learn about any complaints against that company. ⁴Second, consumers can refer to helpful information available from the U.S. Government Printing Office. ⁵You can learn, for instance, how to buy a house, shopping for health insurance, or protect yourself

from auto repair rip-offs. [6]Finally, careful buyers can turn to *Consumer Reports,* an independent magazine and one which is nonprofit that tests and rates a wide range of consumer products. [7]For example, if you are thinking about buying a certain car, *Consumer Reports* will give you information on its comfort level, safety features, fuel economy, and record for repair. [8]If consumers remember to look before they leap and are taking advantage of the above sources of information, they are more likely to get a fair return on their hard-earned dollars.

1. *shoddy merchandise* _____
2. _____
3. _____
4. _____
5. _____
6. _____

NAME: _____

DATE: _____

MASTERY TEST 1 | Faulty Parallelism

The unbalanced part of each sentence is italicized. Rewrite this part so that it matches the rest of the sentence.

1. The bus squealed, grunted, and then *there was a hiss* as it shifted gears.

   _____

2. *With grace* and skillfully, Charles took aim and tossed a quarter into the basket at the toll booth.

   _____

3. Sue beats the blues by taking a hot bubble bath, cuddling up in a cozy quilt, and *eats her favorite snack.*

   _____

4. They didn't want a black-and-white set, but *a color set couldn't be afforded.*

   _____

5. We stayed at a country inn and dined on tender steak, baked Idaho potatoes, and *vegetables that were homegrown.*

   _____

6. When she learned she had won the gymnastic contest, Nikki gasped, screamed, and *all teammates were kissed by her.*

   _____

7. I avoid camping because I don't like to eat half-cooked food, sleep on rocks and twigs, or *the biting of insects.*

   _____

8. Make sure you have proofread your paper, stapled it, and *there are numbers on the pages* before you turn it in.

   _____

9. Unless you are either very noisy or *persist,* you won't wake me up.

   _____

10. Kerry uses his roller skates to get to school, to go to the store, and *for going to football practice.*

    _____

Faulty Parallelism   **MASTERY TEST 2**

Draw a line under the unbalanced part of each sentence. Then rewrite the unbalanced part so that it matches the other items in the sentence.

1. Stan was so hungry he could have eaten a horse—roasted, broiled, or in a stew.

   _____

2. In the last game, Julio had one single, a two-base hit, and one triple.

   _____

3. Bill told us to help ourselves at the buffet and that we could fix our own drinks in the kitchen.

   _____

4. My grandfather must have foods that are easy to cook and digestible.

   _____

5. The awards show was filled with splashy dance numbers, film clips that were boring, and long-winded speeches.

   _____

6. My driving instructor told me to keep both hands on the wheel, to use caution at all times, and don't take my eyes off the road.

   _____

7. Jackie sucked in her stomach, stopped breathing, and was trying to pull the zipper up again.

   _____

8. Phil was so sick that all he was good for was lying in bed and to look up at the ceiling.

   _____

9. When she gets very angry, Gale works off her anger by cleaning out her desk drawers, windows getting washed, or scrubbing the bathtub.

   _____

10. The movie about the "mad slasher" was violent, it caused shock, and demeaning to women.

   _____

Sentence Variety II

Like Chapter 7, this chapter will show you several ways to write effective and varied sentences. You will increase your sense of the many ways available to you for expressing your ideas. The practices here will also reinforce much of what you have learned in this section about modifiers and the use of parallelism.

-ing Word Groups

Use an -ing word group at some point in a sentence. Here are examples:

> The doctor, *hoping* for the best, examined the X-rays.

> *Jogging* every day, I soon raised my energy level.

More information about -ing words, also known as *present participles,* appears on page 200.

Practice

1

Combine each pair of sentences below into one sentence by using an -ing word and omitting repeated words. Use a comma or commas to set off the -ing word group from the rest of the sentence.

EXAMPLE

- The diesel truck chugged up the hill.
- It spewed out smoke.

  Spewing out smoke, the diesel truck chugged up the hill.

  or *The diesel truck, spewing out smoke, chugged up the hill.*

1. • The sparrow tried to keep warm.
    • It fluffed out its feathers.

    _____

    _____

2. • I managed to get enough toothpaste on my brush.
    • I squeezed the tube as hard as I could.

    _____

    _____

3. • The janitor started up the enormous boiler.
    • He checked the glass-faced gauges.

    _____

    _____

4. • The runner set his feet into the starting blocks.
    • He stared straight ahead.

    _____

    _____

5. • The produce clerk cheerfully weighed bags of fruit and vegetables.
    • He chatted with each customer.

    _____

    _____

On separate paper, write five sentences of your own that contain *-ing* word groups.

Practice

2

-ed Word Groups

Use an *-ed* word group at some point in a sentence. Here are examples:

> *Tired* of studying, I took a short break.
>
> Mary, *amused* by the joke, told it to a friend.
>
> I opened my eyes wide, *shocked* by the red "F" on my paper.

More information about *-ed* words, also known as *past participles,* appears on page 200.

Practice

3

Combine each of the following pairs of sentences into one sentence by using an *-ed* word and omitting repeated words. Use a comma or commas to set off the *-ed* word group from the rest of the sentence.

EXAMPLE

- Tim woke up with a start.
- He was troubled by a dream.
  Troubled by a dream, Tim woke up with a start.

or *Tim, troubled by a dream, woke up with a start.*

1. • I dozed off.
   • I was bored with the talk show.

   _____

   _____

2. • The old dollar bill felt like tissue paper.
   • It was crinkled with age.

   _____

   _____

3. • The students acted nervous and edgy.
   • They were crowded into a tiny, windowless room.

   _____

   _____

4. • I waited for someone to open the door.
   • I was loaded down with heavy bags of groceries.

   _____

   _____

5. • Ron bought a green-striped suit.
   • He was tired of his conservative wardrobe.

   _____

   _____

Practice

4

On separate paper, write five sentences of your own that contain *-ed* word groups.

-*ly* Openers

Use an -*ly* word to open a sentence. Here are examples:

Gently, he mixed the chemicals together.

Anxiously, the contestant looked at the game clock.

Skillfully, the quarterback rifled a pass to his receiver.

More information about -*ly* words, which are also known as *adverbs,* appears on page 240.

Combine each of the following pairs of sentences into one sentence by starting with an -*ly* word and omitting repeated words. Place a comma after the opening -*ly* word.

Practice

5

EXAMPLE

- • I gave several yanks to the starting cord of the lawn mower.
- • I was angry.

  Angrily, I gave several yanks to the starting cord of the lawn mower.

1. • Clarissa hung up on the telemarketer.
   • She was abrupt.

   _____

   _____

2. • The thief slipped one of the watches into her coat sleeve.
   • She was casual.

   _____

   _____

3. • I tugged on my shoes and pants as the doorbell rang.
   • I was swift.

   _____

   _____

4. • The defense lawyer cross-examined the witnesses.
   • He was gruff.

   _____

   _____

5. • Estelle poked the corner of a handkerchief into her eye.
   • She was careful.

   _____

   _____

On separate paper, write five sentences of your own that begin with *-ly* words.

To Openers

Use a *to* word group to open a sentence. Here are examples.

To succeed in that course, you must attend every class.

To help me sleep better, I learned to quiet my mind through meditation.

To get good seats, we went to the game early.

The *to* in such a group is also known as an *infinitive*, as explained on page 200.

Combine each of the following pairs of sentences into one sentence by starting with a *to* word group and omitting repeated words. Use a comma after the opening *to* word group.

EXAMPLE

- I fertilize the grass every spring.
- I want to make it greener.
  To make the grass greener, I fertilize it every spring.

1. • We set bricks on the ends of the picnic table.
   • We did this to anchor the flapping tablecloth.

   _____

   _____

2. • Darryl scraped the windshield with a credit card.
   • He did this to break up the coating of ice.

   _____

   _____

3. • We gave our opponents a ten-point advantage.
   • We wanted to make the basketball game more even.

   _____

   _____

4. • I offered to drive the next five hundred miles.
   • I wanted to give my wife a rest.

   _____

   _____

5. • Fran added Hamburger Helper to the ground beef.
   • She did this to feed the unexpected guests.

   _____

   _____

On separate paper, write five sentences of your own that begin with *to* word groups.

Prepositional Phrase Openers

Use prepositional phrase openers. Here are examples:

> *From* the beginning, I disliked my boss.
>
> *In spite* of her work, she failed the course.
>
> *After* the game, we went to a movie.

TIP Prepositional phrases include words like *in, from, of, at, by,* and *with.*
A full list is on page 72.

Practice

9

Combine each of the following groups of sentences into one sentence by omitting repeated words. Start each sentence with a suitable prepositional phrase and put the other prepositional phrases in places that sound right. Generally, you should use a comma after the opening prepositional phrase.

EXAMPLE

- A fire started.
- It did this at 5 A.M.
- It did this inside the garage.
  At 5 A.M., a fire started inside the garage.

1. • The old man wrote down my address.
   • He did this on the bus.
   • He did this with a stubby pencil.

   _____

   _____

2. • Special bulletins interrupted regular programs.
   • They did this during the day.
   • The bulletins were about the election returns.

   _____

   _____

3. • My clock radio turned itself on.
   • It did this at 6:00 A.M.
   • It did this with a loud blast.
   • The loud blast was of rock music.

   _____

   _____

4. • The security guard looked.
   • He did this at the concert.
   • He did this in Sue's pocketbook.
   • He did this for concealed bottles.

   _____

   _____

5. • A plodding turtle crawled.
   • It did this on the highway.
   • It did this toward the grassy shoulder of the road.

   _____

   _____

On separate paper, write five sentences of your own, each beginning with a prepositional phrase and containing at least one other prepositional phrase.

Practice

10

Series of Items

Use a series of items. Following are two of the many items that can be used in a series: adjectives and verbs. The section on parallelism (page 263) gives you practice in some of the other kinds of items that can be used in a series.

Adjectives in Series

Adjectives are descriptive words. Here are examples:

The *husky young* man sanded the *chipped, weather-worn* paint off the fence.

Husky and *young* are adjectives that describe *man; chipped* and *weather-worn* are adjectives that describe *paint*. More information about adjectives appears on page 237.

Practice

11

Combine each of the following groups of sentences into one sentence by using adjectives in a series and omitting repeated words. Use a comma between adjectives only when *and* inserted between them sounds natural.

EXAMPLE

- I sewed a set of buttons onto my coat.
- The buttons were shiny.
- The buttons were black.
- The coat was old.
- The coat was green.

I sewed a set of shiny black buttons onto my old green coat.

1. • The child gazed at the gift box.
   • The child was impatient.
   • The child was excited.
   • The gift box was large.
   • The gift box was mysterious.

   _____

   _____

2. • Juice spurted out of the caterpillar.
   • The juice was sticky.
   • The caterpillar was fuzzy.
   • The caterpillar was crushed.

   _____

   _____

3. • The car dangled from the crane.
   • The car was battered.
   • The crane was gigantic.
   • The crane was yellow.

   _____

   _____

4. • Patty squeezed her feet into the shoes.
   • Patty's feet were swollen.
   • Patty's feet were tender.
   • Patty's feet were sunburned.
   • The shoes were tight.

   _____

   _____

5. • The cook flipped the hamburgers on the grill.
   • The cook was tall.
   • The cook was white-aproned.
   • The hamburgers were thick.
   • The hamburgers were juicy.
   • The grill was grooved.
   • The grill was metal.

   _____

   _____

On separate paper, write five sentences of your own that contain a series of adjectives.

Practice

12

Verbs in Series

Verbs are words that express action. Here are examples:

In my job as a cook's helper, I *prepared* salads, *sliced* meat and cheese, and *made* all kinds of sandwiches.

Basic information about verbs appears on pages 70–75.

Combine each group of sentences below into one sentence by using verbs in a series and omitting repeated words. Use a comma between verbs in a series.

Practice

13

EXAMPLES

- At the gym, Dirk asked his friend to spot him on the free weights.
- He did several lateral pull-downs.
- He jumped on the elliptical machine for twenty minutes.

At the gym, Dirk asked his friend to spot him on the bench press,

did several lateral pull-downs, and jumped on the elliptical machine

for twenty minutes.

1. • In the sports bar, Tanner placed a bet on his favorite basketball team.
   • He took a swig from his bottle of Budweiser.
   • He sat back to watch the NBA playoff semifinals.

   _____

   _____

   _____

2. • The robber scanned the liquor store for a surveillance camera.
   • He fidgeted with his dark sunglasses and baseball cap.
   • He signaled to the clerk behind the counter that he had a handgun.

   _____

   _____

   _____

3. • The phlebotomist pressed down on Logan's forearm.
   • She slid the needle into his arm.
   • She let out a heavy sigh as the needle missed his vein.

   _____

   _____

4. • The comedy hypnotist invited a volunteer to the stage.
   • He quickly brought her into a trance.
   • He offered her a clove of garlic, which she thought was a cashew nut.

   _____

   _____

   _____

5. • The paparazzo stalked the Hollywood actor on vacation.
    • He adjusted his telephoto lens.
    • He snapped hundreds of candid photos.

    _____

    _____

On separate paper, write five sentences of your own that use verbs in a series.

Practice

14

Review Test   1

On separate paper, combine each group of sentences into one sentence. Various combinations are possible. Choose the combination that reads most smoothly and clearly and that sounds most appropriate in the context of surrounding sentences.

> HINT In combining short sentences into one sentence, omit repeated words where necessary.

English Class
  • The teacher said, "Name three famous poets."
  • She was looking at John.
  • The teacher repeated the question when John didn't answer.
  • She did this in an encouraging voice.
  • John sat up straight.
  • He did this quickly.
  • John named Shakespeare and Frost.
  • He couldn't name a third poet.
  • The teacher was feeling sorry for John.
  • The teacher decided to give him a hint.
  • She was smiling warmly.
  • She asked, "What's taking you so long, fellow?"

- Many long seconds passed, and then John blurted, "Longfellow."
- John was happy.
- John heard the other students laughing.
- The students were behind him.
- The laughing was loud.
- One student called out, "What took you so long, fellow?"
- The student did so in a teasing tone.
- John realized why everyone was laughing.
- He was embarrassed.
- But John joined in the laughter.
- He had a good sense of humor.

Review Test 2

On separate paper, combine each group of sentences into one sentence. Various combinations are possible. Choose the combination that reads most smoothly and clearly and that sounds most appropriate in the context of surrounding sentences.

> HINT In combining short sentences into one sentence, omit repeated words where necessary.

Practical Joker
- My brother Mark was handing me what looked like a kaleidoscope.
- Mark is my older brother.
- He said to me, "Twist this tube and watch the patterns of glass."
- I twisted the tube.
- I said that I couldn't see anything.

- Mark said, "You must be blind."
- As he said this, he was laughing loudly.

- I knew that Mark was a practical joker.
- I looked in a mirror.
- I saw a black ring around my right eye.

- However, Mark outsmarted himself.
- He did this one Sunday evening.
- It was an evening when I took a shower to be ready for school the next day.

- Mark had unscrewed the showerhead.
- He had poured in a packet of dye.
- He replaced the showerhead.
- He waited for his victim to take a shower.

- While Mark was in the kitchen, my father headed for the bathroom.
- This was unfortunate.
- My father was wearing his robe.
- His robe was red-and-white striped.

- Soon, a shout pierced the bathroom walls.
- The shout was deafening.
- The shout was angry.

- My father burst through the door.
- He was splattered in navy blue.

- Mark did the sensible thing.
- Mark took off through the back door.
- He ran till he was out of sight.
- He didn't return until my father cooled off.

NAME: _____

DATE: _____

MASTERY TEST 1 | # Sentence Variety II

Combine each group of short sentences into one sentence. A variety of combinations is possible. Choose the combination that reads most smoothly and clearly and that sounds most appropriate in the context of surrounding sentences. Use separate paper. The story continues in the next mastery test.

> **HINT** In combining short sentences into one sentence, omit repeated words where necessary.

Bargain Flight

- Ramon missed his grandparents.
- He decided to visit them.
- His grandparents are in Florida.
- He decided to do this during the semester break.

- Ramon needed to save money and time.
- He looked for a flight to Miami.
- He looked for a cheap flight.
- He looked for a direct flight.

- Florida Express Airline offered a fare.
- It was a no-frills fare.
- It was a nonstop fare.
- It was a hundred-dollar fare.

- Ramon was excited about the good deal.
- He bought a ticket.
- He packed his bags.

- However, Ramon began to have doubts about his bargain flight.
- He did this as he entered the terminal.
- The terminal was dingy.
- The terminal was little-used.

Sentence Variety II   MASTERY TEST 2

Follow the directions given for Mastery Test 1.

Bargain Flight (Continued)

- An airline clerk charged Ramon ten dollars to check in his suitcase.
- The clerk was rude.
- This happened at the counter.

- Ramon and the other passengers had to sprint onto the runway.
- They did this to board the plane.
- They did this when the boarding announcement was yelled out.

- Ramon was sweaty and annoyed.
- He wedged himself into a narrow seat.
- The seat was worn.
- He did this after pushing his way down the crowded aisle.

- The flight attendant sold Ramon a snack and a soda.
- This happened once the plane took off.
- The snack was five dollars.
- The snack was stale.

- Ramon calculated that he hadn't saved any money on the flight.
- He swore he'd never take a bargain flight again.
- This happened by the time the plane landed.

Paper Format

Introductory Activity

This chapter will discuss the guidelines for preparing a paper. Which of the paper openings below seems clearer and easier to read?

A

	Finding Faces
	It takes just a little imagination to find faces in the
	objects around you. For instance, clouds are sometimes
	shaped like faces. If you lie on the ground on a partly

B

	"finding faces"
	It takes just a little imagination to find faces in the objects
	around you. For instance, clouds are sometimes shaped like
	faces. If you lie on the ground on a partly cloudy day, chan-
	ces are you will be able to spot many well-known faces

What are three reasons for your choice?

_____

_____

_____

_____

Answers are on page 670.

Guidelines for Preparing a Paper

Here are guidelines to follow in preparing a paper for an instructor.

1. Use full-size theme or printer paper, 8½ by 11 inches.

2. Leave wide margins (1 to 1½ inches) all around the paper. In particular, do not crowd the right-hand or bottom margin. This white space makes your paper more readable; also, it gives the instructor room for comments.

3. If you write by hand,

   - Use a pen with blue or black ink (*not* a pencil).

   - Be careful not to overlap letters and not to make decorative loops on letters.

   - On narrow-ruled paper, write on every other line.

   - Make all your letters distinct. Pay special attention to *a, e, i, o,* and *u*—five letters that people sometimes write illegibly.

4. Center the title of your paper on the first line of the first page. Do not put quotation marks around the title. Do not underline the title. Capitalize all the major words in a title, including the first word. Short connecting words within a title, such as *of, for, the, in,* and *to,* are not capitalized.

5. Skip a line between the title and the first line of your text. Indent the first line of each paragraph about five spaces (half an inch) from the left-hand margin.

6. Make commas, periods, and other punctuation marks firm and clear. Leave a slight space after each period.

7. If you break a word at the end of a line, break only between syllables (see page 384). Do not break words of one syllable.

8. Put your name, date, and course number where your instructor asks for them.

Remember these points about the title and the first sentence of your paper.

9. The title should be several words that tell what the paper is about. It should usually *not* be a complete sentence. For example, if you are writing a paper about your jealous sister, the title could simply be "My Jealous Sister."

10. Do not rely on the title to help explain the first sentence of your paper. The first sentence must be independent of the title. For instance, if the title of your paper is "My Jealous Sister," the first sentence should *not* be "She has been this way as long as I can remember." Rather, the first sentence might be "My sister has always been a jealous person."

Practice 1

Identify the mistakes in format in the following lines from a student theme. Explain the mistakes in the spaces provided. One mistake is described for you as an example.

	"Too small to fight back"
	Until I was ten years old, I was at the mercy of my
	parents. Because they were bigger than I was, they
	could decide when we were going out, where we were going,
	and how long it would take to get there. I especially hated
	the long weekend trips that we would take even during

1. *Do not use quotation marks around the title.*

2. _____

3. _____

4. _____

5. _____

Practice 2

As already stated, a title should tell in several words what a paper is about. Often a title can be based on the sentence that expresses the main idea of a paper.

Following are five main-idea sentences from student papers. Write a suitable and specific title for each paper, basing the title on the main idea.

EXAMPLE

Title: *Aging Americans as Outcasts*

Our society treats aging Americans as outcasts in many ways.

1. Title: _____
   I will never forget my first-grade teacher.

2. Title: _____
   The first year of college was the hardest year of my life.

3. Title: _____
   My father has a wonderful sense of humor.

4. Title: _____
   There are several ways that Americans could conserve energy.

5. Title: _____
   In the past few years I have become concerned about the amount of violence in movies.

In four of the five sentences that follow, the writer has mistakenly used the title to help explain the first sentence. But as has already been stated, you must *not* rely on the title to help explain your first sentence.

Rewrite the sentences so that they stand independent of the title. Then write *Correct* under the one sentence that is independent of the title.

EXAMPLE

Title: Finishing a Marathon

First sentence: I managed to do this because I followed a strict training
    schedule.

Rewritten: *I managed to finish a marathon because I followed a strict*

training schedule.

1. Title: Effective Communication

   First sentence: This is often the key to a healthy relationship.

   Rewritten: _____

   _____

2. Title: Reality TV Shows

   First sentence: They are popular for several reasons.

   Rewritten: _____

   _____

3. Title: My First Day of College

   First sentence: My first day of college was the most nervous day of my
       adult life.

   Rewritten: _____

   _____

4. Title: The Best Vacation I Ever Had

   First sentence: It began when my friends from high school booked a one-
       week trip to Cancun, Mexico.

   Rewritten: _____

   _____

5. Title: Professional Athletes on Steroids
    First sentence: Most of them say that they don't use it to enhance athletic
        performance.

    Rewritten: _____

    _____

Review Test

Use the space provided below to rewrite the following sentences from a student
paper, correcting the mistakes in format.

	"my first Blind Date"
	It is an occasion I will not easily forget. I was only thirt-
	een and had not gone out very much at all, but since I was
	so young, it hardly mattered. Then, one day, my mother
	came back from her appointment at the hairdresser's, smiling
	from ear to ear. She informed me that I was going out on

Paper Format MASTERY TEST 1

Identify the five mistakes in paper format in the student paper that follows. From the box below, choose the letter that describes the five mistakes and write those letters in the spaces provided in the order in which they appear in the paper.

a.	The title should not be underlined.
b.	The title should not be set off in quotation marks.
c.	There should not be a period at the end of the title.
d.	All the major words in a title should be capitalized.
e.	The title should just be several words and not a complete sentence.
f.	The first sentence of a paper should stand independent of the title.
g.	A line should be skipped between the title and the first line of the paper.
h.	The first line of a paper should be indented.
i.	The right-hand margin should not be crowded.
j.	Hyphenation should occur only between syllables.

	"Kicking the habit"
	After twenty years, I finally quit smoking. I started smoking in
	high school as a way to fit in with my friends and look "cool."
	Back then, I could buy a pack of cigarettes for about a dollar
	from vending machines throughout the city. After I graduated
	and starting selling cars, I found myself smoking a pack a day,
	sometimes two packs. There were no anti-smoking laws back then,
	so I could smoke at work. Sometimes I smoked out of boredom,
	but other times I smoked to relieve stress. Although my wife
	begged me to stop, I kept on smoking. Last year, my dad died of
	lung cancer. He was a smoker for over sixty years. When I saw
	what smoking had done to him, I quit by going "cold turkey."

1. _____   2. _____   3. _____   4. _____   5. _____

NAME: _____

DATE: _____

Paper Format

Identify the five mistakes in paper format in the student paper that follows. From the box below, choose the letter that describes the five mistakes and write those letters in the spaces provided in the order in which they appear in the paper.

---

a. The title should not be underlined.

b. The title should not be set off in quotation marks.

c. There should not be a period at the end of the title.

d. All the major words in a title should be capitalized.

e. The title should just be several words and not a complete sentence.

f. The first sentence of a paper should stand independent of the title.

g. A line should be skipped between the title and the first line of the paper.

h. The first line of a paper should be indented.

i. The right-hand margin should not be crowded.

j. Hyphenation should occur only between syllables.

	<u>cheating</u>
	Teachers warn students about dangers of it, but they shou-
	ld encourage their students to cheat at least once. When I was
	a senior in high school, I cheated on a take-home history test.
	Although I studied, I was not able to answer all the questions,
	so I looked online and copied down information from a few web
	sites. I was so worried that I would be caught that I could not
	look directly at my teacher when I turned in my test. All week,
	I thought that he would confront me about my cheating. Inst-
	ead, my teacher gave me an "A" on the test. I felt so guilty that
	I vowed never to cheat again, and I have never cheated since.

1. _____   2. _____   3. _____   4. _____   5. _____

Capital Letters

21

Introductory Activity

You probably already know a good deal about the uses of capital letters. Answering the questions below will help you check your knowledge before you begin the chapter.

1. Write the full name of a good friend: _____

2. In what city and state were you born? _____

3. What is your present street address? _____

4. Name a country where you would like to travel: _____

5. Name a school that you attended: _____

6. Give the name of a store where you buy food: _____

7. Name a company where you or anyone you know works:

   _____

8. Which day of the week gives you the best chance to relax? _____

9. What holiday is your favorite? _____

10. Which brand of toothpaste do you use? _____

11. Give the brand name of candy or chewing gum you like: _____

12. Name a song or a television show you enjoy: _____

13. Write the title of a magazine or newspaper you read:

    _____

Three capital letters are needed in the example below. Underline the words you think should be capitalized. Then write them, capitalized, in the spaces provided.

[14]on Super Bowl Sunday, my roommate said, [15]"let's buy some snacks and invite a few friends over to watch the game." [16]i knew my plans to write a term paper would have to be changed.

14. _____   15. _____   16. _____

Answers are on page 671.

Main Uses of Capital Letters

www.mhhe.com/langan

Capital letters are used with

1. First word in a sentence or direct quotation
2. Names of persons and the word *I*
3. Names of particular places
4. Names of days of the week, months, and holidays
5. Names of commercial products
6. Titles of books, magazines, articles, films, television shows, songs, poems, stories, papers that you write, and the like
7. Names of companies, associations, unions, clubs, religious and political groups, and other organizations

Each use is illustrated on the pages that follow.

First Word in a Sentence or Direct Quotation

Our company has begun laying people off.

The doctor said, "This may hurt a bit."

"My husband," said Sheryl, "is a light eater. When it's light, he starts to eat."

In the third example above, *My* and *When* are capitalized because they start new sentences. But *is* is not capitalized, because it is part of the first sentence.

Names of Persons and the Word *I*

At the picnic, I met Tony Curry and Lola Morrison.

Names of Particular Places

After graduating from Gibbs High School in Houston, I worked for a summer at a nearby Holiday Inn on Clairmont Boulevard.

But Use small letters if the specific name of a place is not given.

After graduating from high school in my hometown, I worked for a summer at a nearby hotel on one of the main shopping streets.

Names of Days of the Week, Months, and Holidays

Memorial Day falls on the last Monday in May.

But Use small letters for the seasons—summer, fall, winter, spring.

In the early summer and fall, my hay fever bothers me.

Names of Commercial Products

The consumer magazine gave high ratings to Cheerios breakfast cereal, Breyer's ice cream, and Progresso chicken noodle soup.

But Use small letters for the *type* of product (breakfast cereal, ice cream, chicken noodle soup, and the like).

Titles of Books, Magazines, Articles, Films, Television Shows, Songs, Poems, Stories, Papers That You Write, and the Like

My oral report was on *The Diary of a Young Girl,* by Anne Frank.

While watching *The Young and the Restless* on television, I thumbed through *Cosmopolitan* magazine and *The New York Times.*

Names of Companies, Associations, Unions, Clubs, Religious and Political Groups, and Other Organizations

A new bill before Congress is opposed by the National Rifle Association.

My wife is Jewish; I am Roman Catholic. We are both members of the Democratic Party.

My parents have life insurance with Prudential, auto insurance with Allstate, and medical insurance with Blue Cross and Blue Shield.

Write a paragraph describing the advertisement shown here so that a person who has never seen it will be able to visualize it and fully understand it. Once you have written your paragraph, check to make sure you have used capital letters properly throughout.

Practice

1

In the sentences that follow, cross out the words that need capitals. Then write the capitalized forms of the words in the space provided. The number of spaces tells you how many corrections to make in each case.

EXAMPLE

Rhonda said, "~~Why~~ should I bother to *eat* this ~~hershey~~ bar? I should just apply it directly to my hips." _____Why_____ _____Hershey_____

1. My sister, a greeting card addict, sends cards on the fourth of july and veterans' day.

   _____ _____ _____ _____

2. My lazy brother George said, "when I get the urge to exercise, i lie down until it goes away."

   _____ _____

3. When Len's toyota ran out of gas on the long island expressway, he hitched a ride to the nearest filling station.

   _____ _____ _____ _____

4. According to the latest issue of *entertainment weekly,* sixty minutes is still the most popular show in its time slot.

   _____ _____ _____ _____

5. Alberta opened an account at the First national bank in order to get the free samsung clock radio offered to new depositors.

   _____ _____ _____

6. Teresa works part time at the melrose diner and takes courses at the Taylor business institute.

   _____ _____ _____ _____

7. In a story by Ray Bradbury called "a sound of thunder," tourists of the future can travel back in time to observe living dinosaurs.

   _____ _____ _____

8. Stacy, whose ambition is to be a hairdresser, studies at the pacific school of cosmetology.

   _____ _____ _____

9. Last night there was a fire at the sears store on ninth street.

   _____ _____ _____

10. For breakfast, I mixed a slim–fast shake and fried some boca sausage.

    _____ _____

Other Uses of Capital Letters

Capital letters are also used with

1. Names that show family relationships
2. Titles of persons when used with their names
3. Specific school courses
4. Languages
5. Geographic locations
6. Historical periods and events
7. Races, nations, and nationalities
8. Opening and closing of a letter

Each use is illustrated on the pages that follow.

Names That Show Family Relationships

Aunt Fern and Uncle Jack are selling their house.

I asked Grandfather to start the fire.

Is Mom feeling better?

But Do not capitalize words like *mother, father, grandmother, grandfather, uncle, aunt,* and so on when they are preceded by *my* or another possessive word.

My aunt and uncle are selling their house.

I asked my grandfather to start the fire.

Is my mom feeling better?

Titles of Persons When Used with Their Names

I wrote an angry letter to Senator Blutt.

Can you drive to Dr. Stein's office?

We asked Professor Bushkin about his attendance policy.

But Use small letters when titles appear by themselves, without specific names.

I wrote an angry letter to my senator.

Can you drive to the doctor's office?

We asked our professor about his attendance policy.

Specific School Courses

My courses this semester include Accounting I, Introduction to Web Design, Business Law, General Psychology, and Basic Math.

But Use small letters for general subject areas.

This semester I'm taking mostly business courses, but I have a psychology course and a math course as well.

Languages

Yasmin speaks English and Spanish equally well.

Geographic Locations

I lived in the South for many years and then moved to the West Coast.

But Use small letters in giving directions.

Go south for about five miles and then bear west.

Historical Periods and Events

One essay question dealt with the Battle of the Bulge in World War II.

Races, Nations, Nationalities

The census form asked whether I was Caucasian, African American, Native American, Latino, or Asian.

Last summer I hitchhiked through Italy, France, and Germany.

The city is a melting pot for Koreans, Vietnamese, and Mexican Americans.

But Use small letters when referring to *whites* or *blacks.*

Both whites and blacks supported our mayor in the election.

Opening and Closing of a Letter

Dear Sir:	Sincerely yours,
Dear Madam:	Truly yours,

TIP Capitalize only the first word in a closing.

Cross out the words that need capitals in the following sentences. Then write the capitalized forms of the words in the spaces provided. The number of spaces tells you how many corrections to make in each case.

1. My uncle david, who has cirrhosis of the liver, added his name to the national waiting list for organ transplants.

    _____   _____

2. My daughter asked me to buy her a magenta pink motorola razr phone and bluetooth headset for her sixteenth birthday.

    _____   _____   _____

3. Former united states president jimmy carter received the nobel peace prize in 2002.

    _____   _____   _____   _____

    _____   _____   _____   _____

4. Terisa spoke to the class about her experience as a pacific islander from samoa who is now living on the east coast.

    _____   _____   _____   _____

    _____

5. Next semester, I want to register for principles of marketing and two other business courses.

    _____   _____

Unnecessary Use of Capitals

Many errors in capitalization are caused by adding capitals where they are not needed. Cross out the incorrectly capitalized letters in the following sentences and write the correct forms in the spaces provided. The number of spaces tells you how many corrections to make in each sentence.

1. In our High School, the vice-Principal was in charge of Discipline.

    _____   _____   _____

2. My Father settled in to watch his favorite *Twilight Zone* rerun, the one in which a man sitting in a plane sees a weird Creature out on the Wing.

    _____   _____   _____

3. A group called Project Bigfoot offers a thousand-dollar reward to anyone finding the Skull, Hair, or Bones of the legendary Bigfoot.

   _____   _____   _____

4. In Salt Lake City, Utah, there is a Monument to the sea gulls that saved the first Settlers' crops by eating a Plague of Locusts.

   _____   _____   _____   _____

5. "My brand-new Motorcycle was crushed by a Tractor-Trailer in the Motel parking lot," moaned Gene.

   _____   _____   _____   _____

Collaborative Activity

Editing and Rewriting

Working with a partner, read the short paragraph that follows and mark off the ten spots with missing capital letters. Then rewrite the passage, adding the necessary capital letters. Feel free to discuss the rewrite quietly with your partner and refer back to the chapter when necessary.

[1]Some seventh-graders in a pittsburgh school have gone into the candy-making business. [2]It all started one january when a parent showed the children how to make chocolates. [3]the first week, the children made 775 chocolate-covered pretzels and sold the entire batch. [4]Then the frick foundation, a charitable organization, donated $2,100. [5]With this money, the students bought candy molds and began taking orders for $800 worth of easter candy. [6]They also produced red heart lollipops for Valentine's day. [7]The children have even gotten good at packaging their products. [8]They proudly tell their parents, "we are learning how to keep our own financial records!" [9]They are now planning a line of candies for Christmas, to be delivered by their own Santa claus. [10]It is good to hear that one school in america has experienced the sweet smell of success.

Collaborative Activity

Creating Sentences

Working with a partner, write a sentence (or two) as directed. Pay special attention to capital letters.

1. Write about a place you like (or want) to visit. Be sure to include the name of the place, including the city, state, or country where it is located.

2. Write a sentence (or two) in which you state the name of your elementary school, your favorite teacher or subject, and your least favorite teacher or subject.

3. Write a sentence (or two) that mentions three brand-name products you often use. You may begin the sentence with the words, "Three brand-name products I use every day are . . ."

4. Think of the name of your favorite musical artist or performer. Then write a sentence in which you include the musician's name and the title of one of his or her songs.

5. Write a sentence in which you describe something you plan to do two days from now. Be sure to include the date and day of the week in your sentence.

Reflective Activity

1. What would writing be like without capital letters? Use an example or two to help show how capital letters are important to writing.

2. What three uses of capital letters are most difficult for you to remember? Explain, giving examples.

Review Test   1

Cross out the words that need capitals in the following sentences. Then write the capitalized forms of the words in the spaces provided. The number of spaces tells you how many corrections to make in each sentence.

EXAMPLE

During halftime of the ~~Saturday~~ afternoon football game, my sister said, "~~Let's~~ get some hamburgers from ~~Wendy's~~ or put a pizza in the oven."

_____Saturday_____   _____Let's_____   _____Wendy's_____

1. Mom put on a johnny mathis CD, and the outside world faded away.

   _____   _____

2. After uncle Bruce returned from his trip to florida, he showed us endless slides of the everglades and the miami Zoo.

   _____   _____   _____   _____

3. As grandma turned on *wheel of fortune,* we slipped out of the living room and began a serious game of monopoly in the den.

   _____   _____   _____   _____

4. This saint patrick's day, the local school band is going to march down fifth avenue.

   _____   _____   _____   _____

   _____

5. Jackie yelled, "you kids have seen that episode of *star trek* at least fifteen times!"

   _____   _____   _____

6. Last spring, in my introduction to anthropology course, we had to start fires without using matches or flints.

   _____   _____

7. After he watched the miss america contest on television, Norman dreamed that miss texas wanted to make him king for a day.

   _____   _____   _____   _____

8. In namibia, a country in africa, a small herd of elephants survives in an area where it hasn't rained for five years.

   _____   _____

9. During our visit to the west coast, we ate dinner on the *queen Mary,* the old british luxury liner docked in Long Beach.

   _____ _____ _____ _____

10. "Since last september," said Dmitri, "i've been repossessing cars for a collection agency. I've had to collect everything from a small toyota to a rolls-royce."

    _____ _____ _____ _____

    _____

Review Test 2

On separate paper, write:

- Seven sentences demonstrating the seven main uses of capital letters.
- Eight sentences demonstrating the eight other uses of capital letters.

Capital Letters MASTERY TEST 1

Cross out the two capitalization errors in each of the following sentences.
Then write the corrections in the spaces provided.

_____ 1. My Sister Tanya is studying french this semester.
_____

_____ 2. Bill Cosby's comedy routine focused on his childhood in philadelphia and
_____   his exploits at Temple university.

_____ 3. I ordered a Big Mac, and the cashier said, "you're at Burger king, you
_____   know."

_____ 4. Alice found two milky way wrappers and a peach pit in the shag rug.
_____

_____ 5. The Frank Sinatra version of "my way" was blasting from the diner's
_____   jukebox.

_____ 6. I traded in my kodak for an olympus camera with a telephoto lens.
_____

_____ 7. As soon as mrs. Werner pulled into the gas station, the children headed
_____   for the pepsi machine.

_____ 8. Rita always breaks her New year's resolutions long before Valentine's day.
_____

_____ 9. Terry said, "did you read the *National Enquirer* story about the woman
_____   who was locked in an Attic for forty-seven years?"

_____ 10. My little brother really annoyed dr. Thompson by asking, "Is your
_____   Malpractice insurance paid up?"

NAME: _____

DATE: _____

MASTERY TEST 2 Capital Letters

Cross out the two capitalization errors in each of the following sentences. Then write the corrections in the spaces provided.

_____ 1. I fed my plants with miracle-gro so often that they died from overeating.

_____

_____ 2. It would take eighteen hours to drive to chicago, so Brad suggested that we stay one night in a Holiday inn.

_____

_____ 3. Every fourth of july, my dog howls when he hears the fireworks.

_____

_____ 4. "it's so dull in this town," said Joe, "that sometimes we go down to the shoprite store just to watch them restock the toothpaste."

_____

_____ 5. The tigers played well in Florida but started losing when they got back to detroit.

_____

_____ 6. To curb her impulse buying, Toni cut up her visa and J. C. penney charge cards.

_____

_____ 7. During the argument, my brother accused me of needing scope mouthwash and I told him to buy some right Guard deodorant.

_____

_____ 8. On his way to california, the hitchhiker rode in a moving van, a 1972 ford, and a 1993 Cadillac.

_____

_____ 9. Because I hadn't gotten the new *TV guide,* I didn't know whether there was anything on monday night I wanted to watch.

_____

_____ 10. The red Cross poster urged, "have a heart and give blood."

Capital Letters　MASTERY TEST 3

Cross out the two capitalization errors in each of the following sentences.
Then write the corrections in the spaces provided.

_____　1. "with friends like you, George," said Pat, "a person doesn't need Enemies."

_____

_____　2. Every payday, we treat ourselves to dinner at a Steak house on baltimore
_____　　　Pike.

_____　3. Bill bought three Lottery tickets and a pack of gum at marv's News.

_____

_____　4. When my Aunt was pregnant, she craved raw green Peppers sprinkled
_____　　　with salt.

_____　5. Next to my neighbor's german shepherd, my toy poodle looks like a
_____　　　Mosquito.

_____　6. Every time I buy a box of wheat thins, the price goes up three cents.

_____

_____　7. Kelly almost fell over backward trying to see the top of the empire state
_____　　　Building.

_____　8. When my issue of *time* arrives, i turn to the "Entertainment" section first.

_____

_____　9. An infielder for the terrible New York mets team of 1962 once hit a Triple
_____　　　and was called out because he forgot to touch first base.

_____　10. The prentices, who live in the next Apartment, have a new baby that cries
_____　　　all the time.

NAME: _____

DATE: _____

| MASTERY TEST 4 | Capital Letters

Cross out the two capitalization errors in each of the following sentences. Then write the corrections in the spaces provided.

_____ 1. Maxine begins classes at the university of miami this fall.

_____ 2. My Grandmother starts buying Christmas presents in august.

_____ 3. The press conference was carried live on all three Networks the evening before thanksgiving.

_____ 4. The disk jockey promised to play a track from the Beatles' album *abbey road* after the commercial.

_____ 5. The history professor announced that there would be a quiz on Friday about the revolutionary war.

_____ 6. "I've just gotten a request," said the disk jockey, "to play some elton john for the night crew at McNeil Industries."

_____ 7. I suddenly realized that my lunch consisted of an english muffin, swiss cheese, and German potato salad.

_____ 8. Last Summer, we drove to San Francisco in our chevy van.

_____ 9. A tractor-trailer loaded with Chemicals had flipped over at the intersection of Oakdale and Cherry streets.

_____ 10. I ordered two corned beef sandwiches and a pound of Cole slaw from the dee-lish Delicatessen.

Numbers and Abbreviations

22

Introductory Activity

This chapter will introduce you to the specific rules for using numbers and abbreviations in your writing. Write a check mark beside the item in each pair that you think uses numbers correctly.

_____ I finished the exam by 8:55, but my grade was only 65 percent.

_____ I finished the exam by eight-fifty-five, but my grade was only sixty-five percent.

_____ 9 people are in my biology lab, but there are 45 in my lecture group.

_____ Nine people are in my biology lab, but there are forty-five in my lecture group.

Write a check mark beside the item in each pair that you think uses abbreviations correctly.

_____ Both of my bros. were treated by Dr. Lewis after the mt. climbing accident.

_____ Both of my brothers were treated by Dr. Lewis after the mountain climbing accident.

_____ I spent two hrs. finishing my Eng. paper and handed it to my teacher, Ms. Peters, right at the deadline.

_____ I spent two hours finishing my English paper and handed it to my teacher, Ms. Peters, right at the deadline.

Answers are on page 671.

Numbers

Rule 1

Spell out numbers that take no more than two words. Otherwise, use numerals—the numbers themselves.

> Last year Tina bought nine new CDs.
>
> Ray struck out fifteen batters in Sunday's softball game.

But

> Tina now has 114 CDs in her collection.
>
> Already this season Ray has recorded 168 strikeouts.

You should also spell out a number that begins a sentence:

> One hundred fifty first-graders throughout the city showed flu symptoms today.

Rule 2

Be consistent when you use a series of numbers. If some numbers in a sentence or paragraph require more than two words, then use numerals throughout the selection.

> This past spring, we planted 5 rhodos, 15 azaleas, 50 summersweet, and 120 myrtle around our house.

Rule 3

Use numbers to show dates, times, addresses, percentages, exact sums of money, and parts of a book.

> John Kennedy was killed on November 22, 1963.
>
> My job interview was set for 10:15. (*But:* Spell out numbers before *o'clock.* For example: The time was then changed to eleven o'clock.)
>
> Lee's new address is 118 North 35th Street.
>
> Almost 40 percent of my meals are eaten at fast-food restaurants.
>
> The cashier rang up a total of $18.35. (*But:* Round amounts may be expressed as words. For example: The movie has a five-dollar admission charge.)
>
> Read Chapter 6 in your math textbook and answer questions 1 to 5 on page 250.

Use the three rules to make the corrections needed in these sentences.

1. This semester, Mohammed is taking 5 classes and two labs.

2. My dog Missy, an adorable Maltese, is 11 years old—that's 77 in people years.

3. Every day Mike gets up at 5 o'clock to run 4 miles.

4. During the summer, I like to stay up until two-thirty A.M. playing video games and chatting online with my gamer friends.

5. Americans waste over fifteen percent of the food that they purchase from supermarkets and restaurants.

6. An adult human body has two hundred and six bones.

7. Dr. Martin Luther King, Jr., was born on January fifteenth.

8. Someone ate over 200 pickled jalapeno peppers at the State Fair of Texas.

9. My cousin went to Las Vegas to get married on July seventh, two-thousand-and-seven, supposedly the luckiest day of the year.

10. Akira Kurosawa's film *The 7 Samurai* was nominated for an Academy Award in 1954.

Abbreviations

While abbreviations are a helpful time-saver in note taking, you should avoid most abbreviations in formal writing. Listed below are some of the few abbreviations that can acceptably be used in compositions. Note that a period is used after most abbreviations.

www.mhhe.com/langan

1. **Mr., Mrs., Ms., Jr., Sr., and Dr. when used with proper names:**

   Mr. Rollin   Ms. Peters   Dr. Coleman

2. **Time references:**

   A.M., or A.M., or a.m.   P.M., or P.M., or p.m.   B.C., or B.C.; A.D. or A.D.

3. **First or middle initial in a signature:**

   T. Alan Parker   Linda M. Evans

4. **Organizations, technical words, and trade names known primarily by their initials:**

   ABC   CIA   UNESCO   GM   AIDS   DNA

Practice

2

Cross out the words that should not be abbreviated and correct them in the spaces provided.

1. My mother can't go into a dept. store without making an impulse purch.

   _____   _____

2. Driving along Rt. 90 in Fla., we saw armadillos along the roadside.

   _____   _____

3. The heaviest man who ever lived in Amer. weighed over nine hundred lbs. and was buried in a piano crate.

   _____   _____

4. This Swiss army knife has everything from a pr. of scissors to a six-in. ruler.

   _____   _____

5. The first appt. my eye dr., Dr. C. I. Glass, could give me was for early next mo.

   _____   _____   _____

6. After I study in the lib. for fifteen min., I get bored and open a mag.

   _____   _____   _____

7. Only a tsp. of watery Fr. dressing was sprinkled over the limp lettuce salad.

   _____   _____

8. Mandy lost her lic. when she was arrested for driv. on the wrong side of the rd.

   _____   _____   _____

9. How can I be expected to fin. my assign. by 9 P.M. if there isn't one ball-pt. pen in the house?

   _____   _____   _____

10. The *CBS Evening News* suggested that if we don't approve of the new speed lim., we should let our state sen. or rep. know.

   _____   _____   _____

Review Test

Cross out the mistake or mistakes in numbers and abbreviations and correct them in the spaces provided.

1. The Liberty Bell cracked several yrs. after the Amer. Revolution.

   _____ _____

2. The power failure happened at exactly five-twenty A.M. and lasted for almost 2 hours.

   _____ _____

3. I mailed my letter at the p.o. on Grant and Carter Sts.

   _____ _____

4. Juan's insect collection includes seventeen grasshoppers, eight moths, and 148 fireflies.

   _____ _____

5. I didn't have time to study for my chem. test because I had to study for my Span. final.

   _____ _____

6. I arrive at the Hartford Ins. Build. at 8 o'clock every morning.

   _____ _____ _____

7. How can I write a 3-page paper on a poem that's only 14 lines along?

   _____ _____

8. Every Mon. morning I wake up wishing it were Fri.

   _____ _____

9. Tom found a great bargain today—a wool jacket and 2 pairs of pants for ninety dollars and ninety-nine cents.

   _____ _____

10. This is the 3rd time since New Year's that I've tried to lose 10 lbs.

    _____ _____ _____

NAME: _____

DATE: _____

MASTERY TEST 1 | Numbers and Abbreviations

Cross out the mistake in numbers or abbreviations in each sentence and correct it in the space provided.

_____ 1. *Consumer Reports* rated 2 of twelve brands of bacon it tested as "unacceptable."

_____ 2. When the air cond. broke down, the supermarket employees packed shaved ice around the dairy products.

_____ 3. After her husband died in eighteen sixty one, Queen Victoria went into mourning for twenty-five years.

_____ 4. One pg. of the science textbook showed the stone tools of prehistoric people.

_____ 5. I managed to fit the entire contents of my apt. into the back of my brother's station wagon.

_____ 6. The team of six bank robbers got away with less than 1,000 dollars.

_____ 7. The telephone book lists one hundred and nine Richard Browns and 41 Dick Browns.

_____ 8. The six of us left Cleveland in a camper and headed for Daytona Beach, Fla.

_____ 9. One page 122 of the tax guide is a sample form showing a typical joint return filed by a couple with 4 dependents.

_____ 10. By 9:30, every student in my ten o'clock psychology class was already in the examination rm.

NAME: _____

DATE: _____

Numbers and Abbreviations MASTERY TEST 2

Cross out the mistake in numbers or abbreviations in each sentence and correct it in the space provided. Mark the one sentence that is correct with a C.

_____ 1. As soon as Karina finished 6 months of work, she will get one week's paid vacation.

_____ 2. Tonight, I have to read two chaps. in my English textbook.

_____ 3. The new puppy chewed the wooden legs on our dining rm. chairs.

_____ 4. Sherry answered 16 of the twenty test questions correctly.

_____ 5. There's a smudge on page seventy three that looks like chocolate syrup and one on page 90 that looks like coffee.

_____ 6. The pres. waved to the crowd as he left on the flight to California.

_____ 7. When the astronauts landed on the moon in nineteen sixty nine, they had traveled over 244,000 miles.

_____ 8. If I go without a cigarette for several hrs., I begin to feel nervous.

_____ 9. Half of all the people in the United States live in just eight of the fifty states.

_____ 10. The flight from San Juan, Puerto Rico, to N. Y. was delayed for more than three hours.

End Marks

23

Introductory Activity

A sentence always ends with a period, a question mark, or an exclamation point. Each of these will be discussed in turn on the following pages. First, see if you can add the end mark needed in each of the following sentences.

1. All week I have been feeling depressed
2. What is the deadline for handing in the paper
3. The man at the door wants to know whose car is double-parked
4. That truck ahead of us is out of control

Answers are on page 671.

Period (.)

www.mhhe.com/langan

Use a period after a sentence that makes a statement.

> More single parents are adopting children.
> It has rained for most of the week.

Use a period after most abbreviations.

Mr. Sanchez	B.A.	Dr. Patel
Ms. Peters	A.M.	Tom Ricci, Jr.

Question Mark (?)

Use a question mark after a *direct* question.

> When is your paper due?
>
> How is your cold?
>
> Tom asked, "When are you leaving?"
>
> "Why doesn't everyone take a break?"
> Marisol suggested.

Do not use a question mark after an *indirect* question (a question not in the speaker's exact words).

> She asked when the paper was due.
>
> He asked how my cold was.
>
> Tom asked when I was leaving.
>
> Marisol suggested that everyone take a break.

www.mhhe.com/langan

FREE BONUS ITEMS!

WITH PURCHASE

Is the exclamation point used correctly in this sign? If not, what should be done to fix the sign?

Exclamation Point (!)

Use an exclamation point after a word or sentence that expresses strong feeling.

> Come here!
>
> Ouch! This pizza is hot!
>
> That truck just missed us!

www.mhhe.com/langan

> **TIP** Be careful not to overuse exclamation points.

Add a period, a question mark, or an exclamation point, as needed, to each of the following sentences.

Practice 1

1. Why can't I find my car keys when I'm rushing out the door

2. My husband asked me if I wanted a back rub or a foot massage

3. The pedestrian yelled to the speeding motorist, "Watch out, jerk "

4. When Chandra told me that she had been raped, I was shocked

5. Dr. Klein is not a medical doctor; he earned his doctorate in psychology

6. Fred, who loved practical jokes and silly pranks, would often say, "Gotcha "

7. Famous actors, musicians, and athletes have posed with milk mustaches in popular "Got milk?" ads

8. Ratsami asked me if I knew of anyone who could repair the roof that had been damaged in the storm

9. Jordan answered my question by asking me, "What do *you* think "

10. Ms. Caraway will replace Mr. Lee as the chief financial officer

Review Test

Add a period, question mark, or exclamation point as needed to each of the following sentences.

1. Why do these mashed potatoes look green

2. The group that donates the most blood wins free T-shirts

3. Watch out so you don't step in that broken glass

4. The artist throws buckets of paint at a huge canvas on the wall

5. Did you know that Trina has a twin brother

6. There's the man who stole my wallet

7. The dinosaurs in that movie looked like overgrown lizards

8. Have you read the new book by Stephen King

9. All that remained after the car accident was a bloodstain

10. Be careful not to run over that turtle on the highway

NAME: _____

DATE: _____

End Marks   MASTERY TEST 1

Add a period, question mark, or exclamation point, as needed, to each of the following sentences.

> **HINT** End marks always go *inside* the quotation marks that appear in sentences in this test.

1. Andy wondered whether he would look better if he shaved off his beard

2. "My hand's as swollen as a baseball glove," moaned Flora

3. Suddenly, someone yelled, "Get off that wet cement "

4. During the electrical storm, the nervous mother asked all her children to put on their rubber sneakers

5. When Rob woke up, his tongue felt as though it were wearing a woolly sock

6. "How many people here believe in ESP?" the speaker asked

7. If I pay for the gas, will you do all the driving

8. Hurry, grab the fire extinguisher

9. Darlene slammed the phone down and yelled, "Don't call me again "

10. Audrey asked, "Is the dinosaur the biggest animal that ever lived "

11. Sylvia wondered if she would ever see Sam again

12. On a bet, Pasquale drank a glassful of horseradish

13. I yelled as my spoon touched something squishy in the coffee cup

14. The TV evangelist exclaimed to his audience, "If you've been born again, raise your hand "

15. Why does the same pair of jeans cost more in the women's department than in the men's

16. Does a snake really shed its skin all in one piece

17. Would someone give me a hand with this window

18. Three people have asked me for a match already

19. Will you please save my seat for me

20. In the movies, it seems that only two minutes after a woman goes into labor, someone shouts, "It's a boy "

NAME: _____

DATE: _____

End Marks

Add a period, question mark, or exclamation point, as needed, to each of the following sentences.

> HINT End marks always go *inside* the quotation marks that appear in sentences in this test.

1. The coach screamed, "That runner was safe "

2. "For someone so wrapped up in himself," Dora snapped, "Steve makes a pretty small package "

3. The stereo ad asked, "Are you ready for wall-to-wall sound "

4. When she goes out, Edith worries about what her children are watching on TV

5. The teenagers in the back row threw Milk Duds at the people in front

6. The headline in the yellowing old newspaper read, "Horsecar Strikes Pedestrian "

7. "I can't believe you gave my favorite jacket to the Salvation Army " Nick yelled

8. When did our instructor say the paper would be due

9. Please fill up the tank and check the oil

10. It's strange that no one has ever told Vince that he needs to use mouthwash

11. Ken put the money in a safe place and then couldn't find it

12. Debbie asked her mother, "If I don't keep my dentist appointment, will my teeth fall out "

13. I was told I could pick up this suit on Wednesday afternoon

14. Can we stop for lunch soon

15. The zookeeper yelled, "Close the cage "

16. He wondered whether the mail had arrived yet

17. I wish my boss would stop looking over my shoulder and asking when the project will be done

18. Emmet remarked, "Can this be the same hotel we stayed at five years ago "

19. Jan, expecting the glass door to open automatically, got a painful surprise

20. He is afraid of only two things: snakes and the IRS

Apostrophe

24

Introductory Activity

Carefully look over the three items below. Then see if you can answer the questions that follow each item.

1. She is my best friend.   =   She's my best friend.

   I am afraid of snakes.   =   I'm afraid of snakes.

   Do not watch too much TV.   =   Don't watch too much TV.

   They are a perfect match.   =   They're a perfect match.

   It is a terrible movie.   =   It's a terrible movie.

What is the purpose of the apostrophe in the examples above?

_____

_____

2. the desk of the editor   =   the editor's desk

   the car of Giovanni   =   Giovanni's car

   the teeth of my cat   =   my cat's teeth

   the smile of the child   =   the child's smile

   the briefcase of my mother   =   my mother's briefcase

What is the purpose of the apostrophe in the examples above?

_____

_____

continued

3. Several families were affected by the flood. One family's car floated away and was found in a field more than a mile away.

Why does the apostrophe belong in the second sentence but not the first?

_____

_____

Answers are on page 671.

The two main uses of the apostrophe are

1. To show the omission of one or more letters in a contraction.
2. To show ownership or possession.

Each use is explained on the pages that follow.

Apostrophe in Contractions

www.mhhe.com/langan

A contraction is formed when two words are combined to make one word. An apostrophe is used to show where letters are omitted in forming the contraction. Here are two contractions:

have + not = haven't (the *o* in *not* has been omitted)
  I + will = I'll (the *wi* in *will* has been omitted)

The following are some other common contractions:

I	+ am	= I'm	it	+ is	= it's
I	+ have	= I've	it	+ has	= it's
I	+ had	= I'd	is	+ not	= isn't
who	+ is	= who's	could	+ not	= couldn't
do	+ not	= don't	I	+ would	= I'd
did	+ not	= didn't	they	+ are	= they're
let	+ us	= let's	there	+ is	= there's

> **TIP** The combination *will* + *not* has an unusual contraction: *won't.*

Combine the following words into contractions. One is done for you.

Practice

1

they + will = _they'll_   they + are = _____

should + not = _____   can + not = _____

does + not = _____   who + is   = _____

is + not = _____   would + not = _____

will + not = _____   are + not = _____

Write the contraction for the words in parentheses.

Practice

2

EXAMPLE

He (could not) _couldn't_ come.

1. When you hear the whistle blow, (you will) _____ know (it is) _____ quitting time.

2. Because he (had not) _____ studied the owner's manual, he (could not) _____ figure out how to start the power mower.

3. There (is not) _____ a rug in this house that (does not) _____ have stains on it.

4. (I am) _____ fine in the morning if (I am) _____ left alone.

5. (Where is) _____ the idiot (who is) _____ responsible for leaving the front door wide open?

> **TIP** Even though contractions are common in everyday speech and in written dialogue, usually it is best to avoid them in formal writing.

Write five sentences using the apostrophe in different contractions.

Practice

3

1. _____

2. _____

3. _____

4. _____

5. _____

Four Contractions to Note Carefully

Four contractions that deserve special attention are *they're, it's, you're,* and *who's.* Sometimes these contractions are confused with the possessive words *their, its, your,* and *whose.* The following chart shows the difference in meaning between the contractions and the possessive words.

Contractions	Possessive Words
they're (means *they are*)	their (means *belonging to them*)
it's (means *it is* or *it has*)	its (means *belonging to it*)
you're (means *you are*)	your (means *belonging to you*)
who's (means *who is*)	whose (means *belonging to whom*)

Possessive words are explained further on page 329.

Practice 4

Underline the correct form (the contraction or the possessive word) in each of the following sentences. Use the contraction whenever the two words of the contraction (*they are, it is, you are, who is*) would also fit.

1. (It's, Its) the rare guest who knows when (it's, its) time to go home.
2. If (they're, their) going to bring (they're, their) vacation pictures, I'm leaving.
3. (You're, Your) a difficult kind of person because you always want (you're, your) own way.
4. I don't know (who's, whose) fault it was that the window got broken, but I know (who's, whose) going to pay for it.
5. Unless (it's, its) too much trouble, could you make it (you're, your) business to find out (who's, whose) been throwing garbage into my yard?

Apostrophe to Show Ownership or Possession

To show ownership or possession, we can use such words as *belongs to, owned by,* or (most commonly) *of.*

the knapsack *that belongs to* Lola

the grades *possessed by* Travis

the house *owned by* my mother

the sore arm *of* the pitcher

But the apostrophe plus *s* is often the quickest and easiest way to show possession. Thus we can say:

Lola's knapsack
Travis's grades
my mother's house
the pitcher's sore arm

Points to Remember

1. The *'s* goes with the owner or possessor (in the examples given, *Lola, Travis, mother,* and *pitcher*). What follows is the person or thing possessed (in the examples given, *knapsack, grades, house,* and *sore arm*). An easy way to determine the owner or possessor is to ask the question "Who owns it?" In the first example, the answer to the question "Who owns the knapsack?" is *Lola.* Therefore, the *'s* goes with *Lola.*

2. In handwriting, there should always be a break between the word and the *'s.*

Lola's   not   Lola's
Yes   No

3. A singular word ending in *-s* (such as *Travis*) also shows possession by adding an apostrophe plus *s* (Travis's).

Rewrite the italicized part of each of the sentences below, using the *'s* to show possession. Remember that the *'s* goes with the owner or possessor.

Practice

5

EXAMPLES

The motorcycle owned by Clyde is a frightening machine.
Clyde's motorcycle

The roommate of my brother is a sweet and friendly person.
My brother's roommate

1. The *rifle of the assassin* failed to fire.

2. The playboy spent *the inheritance of his mother* within six months.

3. *The throat of Ali* tightened when the doorbell rang.

_____

4. The new salesman took *the parking space of Sam.*

_____

5. *The hat of the chef* fell into the pea soup.

_____

6. A big man wearing sunglasses stayed near *the wife of the president.*

_____

7. *The hand of the mugger* closed over the victim's mouth.

_____

8. The *briefcase of Harry* was still there, but the documents were gone.

_____

9. *The shoulder bag of Sandy* had vanished from her locker.

_____

10. *The leash of the dog* was tangled around a fire hydrant.

_____

Practice 6

Underline the word in each sentence that needs an 's. Then write the word correctly in the space at the left. One is done for you as an example.

ex-husband's 1. Julie is always upset after one of her ex-husband visits.

_____ 2. My instructor worst habit is leaving her sentences unfinished.

_____ 3. The astrologer predictions were all wrong.

_____ 4. Ellen jeans were so tight that she had to lie flat in order to zip them.

_____ 5. The lemonade bitter flavor assaulted my taste buds.

_____ 6. My sister life is like a soap opera.

_____ 7. Brian gold wedding band slid into the garbage disposal.

_____ 8. Nita ten-year-old Volvo is still dependable.

_____ 9. We didn't believe any of Uncle Ted stories.

_____ 10. The hypnotist piercing eyes frightened Kelly.

Add an *'s* to each of the following words to make it the possessor or owner of something. Then write sentences using the words. Your sentences can be serious or playful. One is done for you as an example.

1. Aaron ___Aaron's___

    Aaron's girlfriend sends him more than forty text messages a day.

2. bus _____

    _____

3. computer _____

    _____

4. Ross _____

    _____

5. pizza _____

    _____

Apostrophe versus Possessive Pronouns

Do not use an apostrophe with possessive pronouns. They already show ownership. Possessive pronouns include *his, hers, its, yours, ours,* and *theirs.*

Incorrect	Correct
The bookstore lost its' lease.	The bookstore lost its lease.
The racing bikes were theirs'.	The racing bikes were theirs.
The change is yours'.	The change is yours.
His' problems are ours', too.	His problems are ours, too.
His' skin is more tanned than hers'.	His skin is more tanned than hers.

Apostrophe versus Simple Plurals

When you want to make a word plural, just add an *s* at the end of the word. Do *not* add an apostrophe. For example, the plural of the word *movie* is *movies,* not *movie's* or *movies'.* Look at this sentence:

When Korie's cat began catching birds, the neighbors called the police.

The words *birds* and *neighbors* are simple plurals, meaning more than one bird, more than one neighbor. The plural is shown by adding *-s* only. (More information about plurals starts on page 397.) On the other hand, the *'s* after *Korie* shows possession—that Korie owns the cat.

Are the apostrophes used correctly in this sign? If not, what should be done to fix the sign?

Practice	In the spaces provided under each sentence, add the one apostrophe needed and explain why the other words ending in *s* are simple plurals.
8	**EXAMPLE**

Originally, the cuffs of mens pants were meant for cigar ashes.

cuffs: *simple plural meaning more than one cuff*

mens: *men's, meaning "belonging to men"*

ashes: *simple plural meaning more than one ash*

1. Phil thinks that the restaurants hamburgers taste better than sirloin steaks.

   restaurants: _____

   hamburgers: _____

   steaks: _____

2. San Franciscos cable cars can go up hills at a sixty-degree angle.

   San Franciscos: _____

   cars: _____

   hills: _____

3. My twelve-year-old brothers collection of baseball cards is in six shoe boxes.

   brothers: _____

   cards: _____

   boxes: _____

4. Only women shaped like toothpicks look decent in this years fashions.

   toothpicks: _____

   years: _____

   fashions: _____

5. Pedros blood pressure rose when he drove around the mall for twenty minutes and saw that there were no parking spaces.

   Pedros: _____

   minutes: _____

   spaces: _____

6. The write-ups of Rubys promotion made her co-workers jealous.

   write-ups: _____

   Rubys: _____

   coworkers: _____

7. My sons backyard fort is made from pieces of scrap lumber, old nails, and spare roof shingles.

   sons: _____

   pieces: _____

   nails: _____

   shingles: _____

8. The mayors double-talk had reporters scratching their heads and scribbling in their notebooks.

   mayors: _____

   reporters: _____

   heads: _____

   notebooks: _____

9. Two cuts over the boxers left eye prompted the referee to stop the fight after six rounds.

cuts: _____

boxers: _____

rounds: _____

10. As rock music blared over the cafeterias loudspeakers, Theresa tried to study for her exams.

cafeterias: _____

loudspeakers: _____

exams: _____

Apostrophe with Plural Words Ending in -s

Plurals that end in -s show possession simply by adding the apostrophe, rather than an apostrophe plus s.

Both of my *neighbors'* homes have been burglarized recently.

The many *workers'* complaints were ignored by the company.

All the *campers'* tents were damaged by the hailstorm.

www.mhhe.com/langan

Practice

9

In each sentence, cross out the one plural word that needs an apostrophe. Then write the word correctly, with the apostrophe, in the space provided.

EXAMPLE

_____*bosses'*_____ My two ~~bosses~~ tempers are much the same: explosive.

_____ 1. Bobby wanted to look in all the mall stores windows.

_____ 2. Why are all my friends problems easier to solve than my own?

_____ 3. Dad hopes that the Dallas Cowboys new quarterback will get them into the Super Bowl.

_____ 4. The students insect collections were displayed in a glass case.

_____ 5. The poll showed that the voters wish was to replace all the politicians in office.

Collaborative Activity

Editing and Rewriting

Working with a partner, read the short paragraph below. Then rewrite the paragraph, adding ten apostrophes where needed to indicate contractions and possessives. Feel free to discuss the rewrite quietly with your partner and refer back to the chapter when necessary.

¹If youre going to visit someone in the hospital, dont be gloomy.

²Other peoples problems wont help someone whos sick to feel better.

³But you dont have to limit yourself to "safe" topics like todays weather.

⁴You can even discuss the patients condition, as long as neither of you

gets upset. ⁵Also, dont stay too long. ⁶Patients are usually weak and

cant talk for long periods. ⁷Leave before the patient gets tired.

Collaborative Activity

Creating Sentences

Working with a partner, write sentences that use apostrophes as directed.

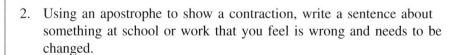

1. Write a sentence describing something a friend owns. For instance, you might mention a pet or a material possession.

   _____

2. Using an apostrophe to show a contraction, write a sentence about something at school or work that you feel is wrong and needs to be changed.

   _____

3. Write a sentence that correctly uses the word *teachers*. Then write a second sentence that correctly uses the word *teacher's*.

   _____

   _____

Reflective Activity

1. Look at the paragraph about the hospital visit that you revised. How has adding apostrophes affected the reading of the paragraph?

2. Explain what it is about apostrophes that you find most difficult to remember and apply. Use an example to make your point clear.

Review Test 1

In each sentence cross out the two words that need apostrophes. Then write the words correctly in the spaces provided.

1. That restaurants menu hasnt changed its selections since ten years ago.

   _____   _____

2. Steve doesnt begin writing his papers until the day before theyre due.

   _____   _____

3. My fathers habit is never to root for a team until he thinks its going to lose.

   _____   _____

4. The toddler knocked his mothers sewing box onto the floor; then, he dropped her calculator into the dogs water bowl.

   _____   _____

5. Part of Colins nursing training consists of a stint in the local hospitals trauma center.

   _____   _____

6. "Youre daring someone to steal that camera if you carry it to the rock concert," warned Tinas dad.

   _____   _____

7. Ever since my sister passed her drivers test, she keeps asking for the keys to our parents car.

   _____   _____

8. The department store wouldnt exchange Carols birthday gift, since earrings cannot be returned.

   _____   _____

9. I use Sids dry-cleaning service because he will clean anyones American flag free.

   _____   _____

10. When Dannys cut was being stitched up, he asked the doctor why he didnt use a sewing machine.

    _____   _____

Review Test 2

Rewrite the following sentences, changing the underlined words into either a contraction or a possessive.

1. I wanted to buy the house of my uncle but could not get a mortgage.

   _____

   _____

2. The issue of this week of *Newsweek* features a report on the campaign of the president to raise educational standards.

   _____

   _____

3. The programs of next week always look better than what is on now.

   _____

   _____

4. The tires of the car are as smooth as the eggs of a hen.

   _____

   _____

5. The voice of the instructor boomed in the ears of Marie as she sat in the front row.

   _____

   _____

NAME: _____

DATE: _____

MASTERY TEST 1 | # Apostrophe

In each sentence, cross out the word that needs an apostrophe. Then write the word correctly in the space provided.

_____ 1. She is nobodys fool when money is involved.

_____ 2. The ducks beak had been taped shut.

_____ 3. That was Ronnies third car accident this year.

_____ 4. A hawks wings beat faster when it is about to dive at its prey.

_____ 5. The safecrackers eyes gleamed as the lock clicked open.

_____ 6. My dentists worst habit is asking me questions when my mouth is stuffed with cotton.

_____ 7. Its been estimated that the typical American consumes one hundred pounds of white sugar a year.

_____ 8. When the insurance companys check arrived, I ran to the bank.

_____ 9. The doctors waiting room was stuffy and crowded.

_____ 10. The resorts policy is to give a partial refund if the weather is poor.

Apostrophe | MASTERY TEST 2

In the space provided under each sentence, add the one apostrophe needed and explain why the other word ending in s *is a simple plural.*

EXAMPLE

Joans hair began to fall out two days after she dyed it.

Joans: *Joan's, meaning "the hair belonging to Joan"*

Days: *simple plural meaning more than one day*

1. The elderly womans long, knotty fingers show a lifetime of wear.

    womans: _____

    fingers: _____

2. Studies show that a rooms color can affect our moods.

    rooms: _____

    moods: _____

3. Kens homework is not yet done because of the two football games on TV today.

    Kens: _____

    games: _____

4. The raccoons tracks led from a hole in the backyard fence to our garbage can.

    raccoons: _____

    tracks: _____

5. In my mothers picture collection, my grandparents posed against a backdrop of painted scenery.

    mothers: _____

    grandparents: _____

MASTERY TEST 3 | Apostrophe

In each sentence two apostrophes are missing or are used incorrectly. Cross out the two errors and write the corrections in the spaces provided.

_____ 1. I cant understand why our neighbors disturb the evenings quiet with their electronic bug zapper.

_____

_____ 2. My sisters habit of tying up the phone for hours' drives my parents crazy.

_____

_____ 3. I wonder whos responsible for making childrens clothes so expensive.

_____

_____ 4. The gunslinger barged through the saloons swinging door's.

_____

_____ 5. Qualifying for the Olympic's is an amateur athletes crowning achievement.

_____

_____ 6. The stores photographer used a variety of anties' to get the children to smile.

_____

_____ 7. While her mother paid the clerk, Michelle wandered over to the supermarkets gum-ball machine's.

_____

_____ 8. The suspect couldn't have committed the crime, for his shoe size did not match the burglars footprints.

_____

_____ 9. At twelve oclock, the factorys whistle blows, and the shift changes.

_____

_____ 10. Dewdrops' glistened on the bicycles vinyl seat.

_____

NAME: _____

DATE: _____

Apostrophe **MASTERY TEST 4**

In each sentence two apostrophes are missing or are used incorrectly. Cross out the two errors and write the corrections in the spaces provided.

_____ 1. Sandys brown eyes filled with tears as she listened to Jims explanation.

_____

_____ 2. My sons toys were strewn all over the Greenfields driveway.

_____

_____ 3. Mikes Saint Bernard has a custom-built shelter as big as a childs playhouse.

_____

_____ 4. Monday mornings *Press* omitted several popular comic strip's.

_____

_____ 5. Stans behavior at the Bradleys party surprised everyone.

_____

_____ 6. When the jurys verdict was announced, both defendants' looked stunned.

_____

_____ 7. When Franks phone bill comes in, hes likely to rip it into little pieces.

_____

_____ 8. Helens mistake was to trust the strength of the fraying hammock in her fathers yard.

_____

_____ 9. Two firefighter's rushed into the burning building to rescue the familys pet dog.

_____

_____ 10. When she cant handle her two toddlers, Madge takes them to her mothers house.

_____

Quotation Marks

25

Introductory Activity

Read the following scene and underline all the words enclosed within quotation marks. Your instructor may also have you dramatize the scene, with one person reading the narration and three others acting the speaking parts—Len, Tina, and Mario. The speakers should imagine the scene as part of a stage play and try to make their words seem as real and true-to-life as possible.

At a party that Len and his wife Tina hosted recently, Len got angry at a guy named Mario who kept bothering Tina. "Listen, man," Len said, "what's this thing you have for my wife? There are lots of other women at this party."

"Relax," Mario replied. "Tina is very attractive, and I like talking with her."

"Listen, Mario," Tina said. "I've already told you three times that I don't want to talk to you anymore. Please leave me alone."

"Look, there's no law that says I can't talk to you if I want to," Mario challenged.

"Mario, I'm only going to say this once," Len warned. "Lay off my wife, or leave this party *now*."

Mario grinned at Len smugly. "You've got good liquor here. Why should I leave? Besides, I'm not done talking with Tina."

Len went to his basement and was back a minute later holding a two-by-four. "I'm giving you a choice," Len said. "Leave by the door or I'll slam you out the window."

Mario left by the door.

1. On the basis of this selection, what is the purpose of quotation marks?

   _____

2. Do commas and periods that come after a quotation go inside or outside the quotation marks?

   _____

Answers are on page 672.

The two main uses of quotation marks are

1. To set off the exact words of a speaker or writer
2. To set off the titles of short works

Each use is explained on the pages that follow.

Quotation Marks to Set Off the Words of a Speaker or Writer

Use quotation marks when you want to show the exact words of a speaker or writer:

www.mhhe.com/langan

"Who left the cap off the toothpaste?" Lola demanded. (Quotation marks set off the exact words that Lola spoke.)

Ben Franklin wrote, "Keep your eyes wide open before marriage, half shut afterward." (Quotation marks set off the exact words that Ben Franklin wrote.)

"You're never too young," my Aunt Fern often tells me, "to have a heart attack." (Two pairs of quotation marks are used to enclose the aunt's exact words.)

Maria complained, "I look so old some days. Even makeup doesn't help. I feel as though I'm painting a corpse!" (Note that the end quotes do not come until the end of Maria's speech. Place quotation marks before the first quoted word of a speech and after the last quoted word. As long as no interruption occurs in the speech, do not use quotation marks for each new sentence.)

Complete the following statements that explain how capital letters, commas, and periods are used in quotations. Refer to the four examples as guides.

> **HINT** In the four preceding examples, notice that a comma sets off the quoted part from the rest of the sentence. Also observe that commas and periods at the end of a quotation always go *inside* quotation marks.

- Every quotation begins with a _____ letter.
- When a quotation is split (as in the sentence about Aunt Fern), the second part does not begin with a capital letter unless it is a _____ sentence.
- _____ are used to separate the quoted part of a sentence from the rest of the sentence.
- Commas and periods that come at the end of a quotation go _____ quotation marks.

The answers are *capital, new, Commas,* and *inside.*

Practice 1

Insert quotation marks where needed in the sentences that follow.

1. This is the tenth commercial in a row, complained Niko.
2. The police officer said sleepily, I could really use a cup of coffee.
3. My boss asked me to step into his office and said, Joanne, how would you like a raise?
4. I'm out of work again, Miriam sighed.
5. I didn't know this movie was R-rated! Lorraine gasped.
6. Why does my dog always wait until it rains before he wants to go out? Donovon asked.
7. A sign over the box office read, Please form a single line and be patient.
8. Unless I run three miles a day, Marty said, my legs feel like lumpy oatmeal.
9. I had an uncle who knew when he was going to die, claimed Dan. He saw the date in a dream.
10. The unusual notice in the newspaper read, Young farmer would be pleased to hear from young lady with tractor. Send photograph of tractor.

Rewrite the following sentences, adding quotation marks where needed. Use a capital letter to begin a quotation, and use a comma to set off a quoted part from the rest of the sentence.

EXAMPLE

I can't eat another bite Jeremy told his grandmother.

"I can't eat another bite," Jeremy told his grandmother.

1. The firefighter asked the neighbors, Is there anyone else still in the building?

    _____

    _____

2. You'll have to remove your sunglasses, the security guard reminded the customers at the bank.

    _____

    _____

3. Upon eating a few drops of Horacio's homemade habanero sauce, Trudy yelped, That's hot!

    _____

    _____

4. Good things come to those who wait, Zhao told himself as he waited in line for hours to buy an iPhone.

    _____

    _____

5. If at first you don't succeed, my wife joked, you should read the directions.

    _____

    _____

1. Write three quotations that appear in the first part of a sentence.

EXAMPLE

"Let's go shopping," I suggested.

a. _____

b. _____

c. _____

2. Write three quotations that appear at the end of a sentence.

EXAMPLE

Bob asked, "Have you had lunch yet?"

a. _____

b. _____

c. _____

3. Write three quotations that appear at the beginning and end of a sentence.

EXAMPLE

"If the bus doesn't come soon," Mary said, "we'll freeze."

a. _____

b. _____

c. _____

Indirect Quotations

An indirect quotation is a rewording of someone else's comments rather than a word-for-word direct quotation. The word *that* often signals an indirect quotation.

Direct Quotation

George said, "My son is a dare-devil."

(George's exact spoken words are given, so quotation marks are used.)

Carol's note to Arnie read, "I'm at the neighbors' house. Give me a call."

(The exact words that Carol wrote in the note are given, so quotation marks are used.)

Indirect Quotation

George said that his son is a dare-devil.

(We learn George's words *indi-rectly*, so no quotation marks are used.)

Carol left a note for Arnie that said she would be at the neighbors' house and he should give her a call.

(We learn Carol's words *indirectly*, so no quotation marks are used.)

Rewrite the following sentences, changing words as necessary to convert the sentences into direct quotations. The first one is done for you as an example.

1. Luis asked Marian if she had had a bad day at work.
   Luis asked Marian, "Did you have a bad day at work?"

2. Marian said that it was the worst day of her life.

   _____

3. Luis said to tell him all about it.

   _____

4. Marian insisted that he wouldn't understand her job problems.

   _____

5. Luis said he would certainly try.

   _____

Rewrite the following sentences, converting each direct quotation into an indirect statement. In each case you will have to add the word *that* or *if* and change other words as well.

EXAMPLE

The barber asked Reggie, "Have you noticed how your hair is thinning?"
The barber asked Reggie if he had noticed how his hair was thinning.

1. He said, "I need a vacation."

   _____

2. Gretchen said, "Purple is my favorite color."

   _____

3. She asked the handsome stranger, "Could I buy you a drink?"

   _____

4. My brother asked, "Has anyone seen my frog?"

   _____

5. Françoise complained, "I married a man who falls asleep during horror movies."

   _____

   _____

Quotation Marks to Set Off the Titles of Short Works

Titles of short works are usually set off by quotation marks, while titles of long works are underlined or italicized. Use quotation marks to set off the titles of short works such as articles in books, newspapers, or magazines; chapters in a book; short stories; poems; and songs. On the other hand, you should underline or italicize the titles of books, newspapers, magazines, plays, movies, CDs, and television shows. See the following examples.

Quotation Marks	Underlines
the article "The Toxic Tragedy"	in the book Who's Poisoning America
the article "New Cures for Headaches"	in the newspaper the New York Times
the article "When the Patient Plays Doctor"	in the magazine Family Health
the chapter "Connecting with Kids"	in the book Straight Talk
the story "The Dead"	in the book Dubliners
the poem "Birches"	in the book The Complete Poems of Robert Frost
the song "House of Cards"	in the album In Rainbows
the episode "One of Us"	in the television show Lost
	the movie Rear Window

> **TIP** In published work, the titles of long works are set off by italics. In handwritten papers, these titles should be underlined.

Practice 6

Use quotation marks or underlines as needed.

1. My recently divorced sister refused to be in the talent show when she was told she'd have to sing Love Is a Many-Splendored Thing.

2. Disgusted by the constant dripping noise, Brian opened his copy of Handy Home Repairs to the chapter titled Everything about the Kitchen Sink.

3. My little brother has seen Star Wars at least eight times.

4. Before they bought new car tires, Nick and Fran studied the article Testing Tires in the February, 2007, issue of Consumer Reports.

5. Many people mistakenly think that Huckleberry Finn and The Adventures of Tom Sawyer are children's books only.

6. I just found out that the musical My Fair Lady is based on a play by George Bernard Shaw called Pygmalion.

7. The ending of Shirley Jackson's story The Lottery really surprised me.

8. I sang the song Mack the Knife in our high school production of The Threepenny Opera.

9. Unless he's studied the TV Guide listings thoroughly, my father won't turn on his television.

10. Stanley dreamed that both Time and Newsweek had decided to use him in their feature article Person of the Year.

Other Uses of Quotation Marks

1. **To set off special words or phrases from the rest of a sentence (italics are also used for this purpose):**

   Many people spell the words "all right" as one word, "alright," instead of correctly spelling them as two words.

   I have trouble telling the difference between "principal" and "principle."

2. **To mark off a quote within a quote. For this purpose, single quotes (') are used:**

   Ben Franklin said, "The noblest question in the world is, 'What good may I do in it?'"

   "If you want to have a scary experience," Eric told Lynn, "read Stephen King's story 'The Mangler' in his book *Night Shift*."

Collaborative Activity

Editing and Rewriting

Working with a partner, read the short passage below and circle the ten sets of quotation mark mistakes. Then, on separate paper, rewrite the passage, adding the ten sets of quotation marks. Feel free to discuss the rewrite quietly with your partner and refer back to the chapter when necessary.

¹Fran put aside her books to answer the phone. ² Hello, she said.

³ Hey, Fran, take a break, said Nick. ⁴ There's a great party going on here. ⁵Why don't you come over?

⁶Fran hesitated. ⁷She was tired and bored; the party was tempting. ⁸She felt like a cartoon character with a devil perched on one shoulder and an angel on the other.

⁹ Go to the party, the devil said. ¹⁰ Forget this studying.

¹¹ Stay home," the angel whispered, or you'll regret it tomorrow.

¹²Interrupting Fran's thoughts, Nick urged, Oh, come on, you can cram when you get home.

¹³Fran felt an imaginary stab from the devil's pitchfork. ¹⁴ I want to, Nick, she said.

¹⁵Then she gave in to the imaginary angel. ¹⁶ But I can't. ¹⁷I really have to pass this test.

Collaborative Activity

Creating Sentences

Working with a partner, write sentences that use quotation marks as directed.

1. Write a sentence in which you quote a favorite expression of someone you know. Identify the person's relationship to you.

EXAMPLE

My brother Sam often says after a meal, "That wasn't bad at all."

2. Write a quotation that contains the words *Tony asked Lola*. Write a second quotation that includes the words *Lola replied*.

3. Write a sentence that interests or amuses you from a book, magazine, or newspaper. Identify the title and author of the book, magazine, or newspaper article.

EXAMPLE

In her book At Wit's End, Erma Bombeck advises, "Never go to a doctor whose office plants have died."

Reflective Activity

1. Look at the paragraph about Fran and Nick that you revised on page 348. How has adding quotation marks affected the reading of the paragraph?

2. What would writing be like without quotation marks? Using an example, explain how quotation marks are important to understanding writing.

3. Explain what it is about quotation marks that is most difficult for you to remember and apply. Use an example to make your point clear. Feel free to refer back to anything in this chapter.

Review Test   1

Place quotation marks around the exact words of a speaker or writer in the sentences that follow.

1. Look at the dent in my car! André cried.

2. My mother always says to me, When in doubt, don't.

3. Franklin Roosevelt said, The only thing we have to fear is fear itself.

4. It's much too quiet in here, whispered Vince as he entered the library.

5. The sign on the manager's desk reads: I'd like to help you out. Which way did you come in?

6. Clutching his partner's hands in midair, the trapeze artist murmured, We've got to stop meeting like this.

7. I've got two tickets on the fifty-yard line! the scalper shouted as the fans filed into the stadium.

8. Looking at the football fan who had removed his shirt in subzero weather, Lonnie said, There's a guy whose elevator doesn't go to the top.

9. I can't believe it, he muttered. I put the hammer right there a minute ago, and now it's gone.

10. Why doesn't anyone ever get hungry at the beach? Dad asked. When we didn't answer, he explained, Because of all the sand which is there.

Review Test   2

Go through the comics section of a newspaper to find a comic strip that amuses you. Be sure to choose a strip in which two or more characters are speaking to each other. Write a full description that will enable people who have not read the comic strip to visualize it clearly and appreciate its humor. Describe the setting and action in each panel and enclose the words of the speakers in quotation marks.

Quotation Marks   MASTERY TEST 1

Place quotation marks or underlines where needed.

1. The lifeguard shouted, No ball playing in the water!

2. Kathy insisted in a loud voice, I'm not really overweight. I'm just six inches too short.

3. If today were a blackboard, Terrence said, I'd erase it and start over.

4. In her diet book, Miss Piggy advises, Never eat anything at one sitting that you can't lift.

5. Something is wrong with my radio, Fred said to the mechanic. It won't work unless the windshield wipers are turned on.

6. You creep! Zella yelled to the tailgater behind her. I've got small children in this car!

7. The first chapter in the book How to Train Your Dog is titled Training the Master.

8. Why do I skydive? the elderly man repeated to the news reporter. Well, I guess because I'm terrible at checkers.

9. I'll only warn you this time, said the officer. But next time you'd better drive more slowly or be prepared to open your wallet.

10. When I was a child, said Cindy, I thought that if you swallowed a watermelon seed, a watermelon would grow in your stomach.

MASTERY TEST 2 | Quotation Marks

Place quotation marks or underlines where needed.

1. Darla said, To err is human. That's why I do it so much.

2. At breakfast, Terry said, I'll trade the sports section and a piece of bacon for the comics.

3. Danny's second-grade teacher asked, How many months have twenty-eight days?

4. All twelve of them, Danny answered.

5. And the winner, announced the host, is Miss Mexico!

6. I'm not hungry, said Bertha. I'm starved.

7. The bumper sticker on the car ahead of us read, If you get any closer, introduce yourself.

8. Where are you going? asked Carrie sarcastically. A Halloween party?

9. If you guys don't start hustling, warned the coach, you're going to see football scholarships start vanishing into thin air.

10. The episode titled Finding a Voice on the television series Nova describes how some people with cerebral palsy are now speaking through the use of computers that have artificial voices.

NAME: _____

DATE: _____

Quotation Marks   MASTERY TEST 3

Place quotation marks or underlines where needed.

1. Minds are like parachutes, the teacher said. They work only when they're open.

2. If you refrigerate candles before using them, said the household hints book, they'll last longer and won't drip.

3. In Psychology Today magazine, the author of the article called The Techniques of the Artful Salesman suggests that successful salespeople almost hypnotize their customers.

4. When I wake up in the morning, said Fran, I sometimes have dream hangovers. For several hours, I can't shake the emotions I felt in my dream.

5. My insomnia is terrible these days, said Stan. I can't even sleep on the job.

6. I turned the radio up when Carl Perkins's classic song Blue Suede Shoes came on.

7. I read a horror story titled Children of the Kingdom, in which giant slugs that eat people live in the sewers of New York City.

8. As the miser was taking a walk, a robber pressed a gun into his ribs and demanded, Your money or your life!

9. Take my life, said the miser. I'm saving my money for my old age.

10. The sign on Toshio's desk reads, In the rat race, only the rats win.

NAME: _____

DATE: _____

MASTERY TEST 4 Quotation Marks

Place quotation marks or underlines where needed.

1. When I saw Raiders of the Lost Ark, my grandfather said, it reminded me of the old adventure serials we watched in the thirties and forties.

2. Before she asked her boss for a raise, Nadine said timidly, Are you in a good mood, Mr. Huff?

3. The newspaper headline read, Good Humor Man Slays Ten.

4. The driver leaned out and handed two dollars to the toll collector, saying, I'm paying for the car behind me, too.

5. Did you know, he said to the expectant mother, that it now costs $125,000 to raise a child to the age of eighteen?

6. The TV announcer warned, The latest figures indicate there will be a billion cars on the road by the year 2010. So if you want to cross the street, you'd better do it now.

7. My six-year-old nephew stared at me and asked, How did you break your kneecap with that big, heavy cast on your leg?

8. I never go back on my word, he promised. I might just go around it a little, though.

9. After Kay read a book called Chocolate: The Consuming Passion, she ran out and bought six Hershey bars.

10. Reassuring me that my diseased elm would recover, the tree surgeon said, Don't worry. Its bark it worse than its blight.

Comma

26

Introductory Activity

Commas often (though not always) signal a minor break or pause in a sentence. Each of the six pairs of sentences below illustrates one of six main uses of the comma. Read each pair of sentences and choose the rule that applies from the box on the next page. Each of these rules will be discussed in detail in the pages that follow.

_____ 1. Joel watched the eleven o'clock news, a movie, a *Honeymooners* rerun, and an hour-long infomercial.

Please endorse your check, write your account number on the back, and fill out a deposit slip.

_____ 2. Even though I was safe indoors, I shivered at the thought of the bitter cold outside.

To start the car, press the accelerator and then turn the ignition key.

_____ 3. The opossum, like the kangaroo, carries its young in a pouch.

George Derek, who was arrested, was a classmate of mine.

_____ 4. I enrolled in the course, but my name was not on the class list.

A police cruiser blocked the busy intersection, and an ambulance pulled up on the sidewalk near the motionless victims.

_____ 5. Emily said, "Why is it so hard to remember your dreams the next day?"

"After I left the interview," said David, "I couldn't remember a word I had said."

continued

_____ 6. Mike has driven over 1,500,000 accident-free miles in his job as a long-distance trucker.

The Gates Trucking Company of 1800 Industrial Highway, Jersey City, New Jersey, gave Mike an award on January 26, 2007, for his superior safety record.

> a. separate items in a series (list)
> b. separate introductory material from the sentence
> c. separate words that interrupt the sentence
> d. separate complete thoughts in a sentence
> e. separate direct quotations from the rest of the sentence
> f. separate numbers, addresses, and dates in everyday writing

Answers are on page 674.

Six Main Uses of the Comma

Commas are used mainly as follows:

1. To separate items in a series
2. To set off introductory material
3. On both sides of words that interrupt the flow of thought in a sentence
4. Between two complete thoughts connected by *and, but, for, or, nor, so, yet*
5. To set off a direct quotation from the rest of a sentence
6. For certain everyday material

You may find it helpful to remember that the comma often marks a slight pause, or break, in a sentence. These pauses or breaks occur at the points where the six main comma rules apply. Read aloud the sentence examples given on the following pages for each of the comma rules and listen for the minor pauses or breaks that are signaled by commas.

At the same time, you should keep in mind that commas are far more often overused than underused. As a general rule, you should *not* use a comma unless a given comma rule applies or unless a comma is otherwise needed to help a sentence read clearly. A good rule of thumb is that "when in doubt" about whether to use a comma, it is often best to "leave it out."

After reviewing each of the comma rules that follow, you will practice adding commas that are needed and omitting commas that are not needed.

Comma between Items in a Series

Use a comma to separate items in a series.

Magazines, paperback novels, and textbooks crowded the shelves.

Hard-luck Harold needs a loan, a good-paying job, and a close friend.

Pat sat in the doctor's office, checked her watch, and chewed gum nervously.

Lola bit into the ripe, juicy apple.

More and more people entered the crowded, noisy stadium.

A comma is used between two descriptive words in a series only if *and* inserted between the words sounds natural. You could say:

Lola bit into the ripe *and* juicy apple.

More and more people entered the crowded *and* noisy stadium.

But notice in the following sentences that the descriptive words do not sound natural when *and* is inserted between them. In such cases, no comma is used.

The model wore a light sleeveless blouse. ("A light *and* sleeveless blouse" doesn't sound right, so no comma is used.)

Dr. Van Helsing noticed two tiny puncture marks on his patient's neck. ("Two *and* tiny puncture marks" doesn't sound right, so no comma is used.)

Practice 1

Place commas between items in a series.

1. Mae-Lin tossed her sunglasses a bottle of water and a recent issue of *Every Day with Rachael Ray* into her tote bag.

2. Stephen uses the computer to check e-mail play games surf the Internet download music and send instant messages.

3. In the neighbors' backyard are an igloo-shaped doghouse several plastic toys trampled flowers and a cracked ceramic gnome.

Practice 2

For each item, cross out the one comma that is not needed. Add the one comma that is needed between items in a series.

1. A metal tape measure, a pencil a ruler, and a hammer dangled, from the carpenter's pockets.

2. The fortune-teller uncovered the crystal ball peered into it, and began, to predict my future.

3. That hairdresser is well known, for her frizzy perms butchered haircuts, and brassy hair colorings.

Comma after Introductory Material

Use a comma to set off introductory material.

Fearlessly, Lola picked up the slimy slug.

Just to annoy Tony, she let it crawl along her arm.

Although I have a black belt in karate, I decided to go easy on the demented bully who had kicked sand in my face.

Mumbling under her breath, the woman picked over the tomatoes.

TIPS

a. If the introductory material is brief, the comma is sometimes omitted. In the activities here, however, you should include the comma.

b. A comma is also used to set off extra material placed at the end of a sentence. Here are two sentences in which this comma rule applies:

I spent all day at the employment office, trying to find a job that suited me.

Tony has trouble accepting criticism, except from Lola.

Practice

3

Place commas after introductory material.

1. With shaking hands the frightened baby-sitter dialed 911.

2. During the storm snow drifted through cracks in the roof of the cabin.

3. Ashamed to ask for help Betty glanced around nervously at the other students to see how they were filling out the computer questionnaire.

Practice

4

For each item, cross out the one comma that is not needed. Add the one comma that is needed after introductory material.

1. In order to work at that fast-food restaurant you have to wear a cowboy hat and six-shooters. In addition, you have to shout "Yippee!" every time, someone orders the special Western-style double burger.

2. Barely awake, the woman slowly rocked, her crying infant. While the baby softly cooed the woman fell asleep.

3. When I painted the kitchen, I remembered to cover the floor with newspapers. Therefore I was able to save the floor from looking, as if someone had thrown confetti on it.

Comma around Words
Interrupting the Flow of Thought

Use a comma before and after words that interrupt the flow of thought in a sentence.

The car, cleaned and repaired, is ready to be sold.

Joanne, our new neighbor, used to work as a bouncer at Rexy's Tavern.

Taking long walks, especially after dark, helps me sort out my thoughts.

Usually you can "hear" words that interrupt the flow of thought in a sentence. However, when you are not sure if certain words are interrupters, remove them from the sentence. If it still makes sense without the words, you know the words are interrupters and that the information they give is nonessential. Such nonessential information is set off with commas. In the following sentence,

Susie Hall, who is my best friend, won a new car in the *Reader's Digest* sweepstakes.

the words *who is my best friend* are extra information, not needed to identify the subject of the sentence, *Susie Hall.* Put commas around such nonessential information. On the other hand, in the sentence

The woman who is my best friend won a new car in the *Reader's Digest* sweepstakes.

the words *who is my best friend* supply essential information needed for us to identify the woman. If the words were removed from the sentence, we would no longer know which woman won the sweepstakes. Commas are not used around such essential information.

Here is another example:

The Shining, a novel by Stephen King, is the scariest book I've ever read.

Here the words *a novel by Stephen King* are extra information, not needed to identify the subject of the sentence, *The Shining.* Commas go around such nonessential information. On the other hand, in the sentence

Stephen King's novel *The Shining* is the scariest book I've ever read.

the words *The Shining* are needed to identify the novel. Commas are not used around such essential information.

Most of the time you will be able to "hear" words that interrupt the flow of thoughts in a sentence and will not have to think about whether the words are essential or nonessential.*

---

*Some instructors refer to nonessential or extra information that is set off by commas as a *nonrestrictive* clause. Essential information that interrupts the flow of thought is called a *restrictive* clause. No commas are used to set off a restrictive clause.

Practice

5

Add commas to set off interrupting words.

1. This all-purpose kitchen gadget ladies and gentlemen sells for only $19.98!

2. Tigers because they eat people do not make good house pets.

3. A practical joker had laid a dummy its straw-filled "hands" tied with rope across the railroad tracks.

Practice

6

For each item, cross out the one comma that is not needed. Add the comma that is needed to completely set off interrupting words.

1. My brother, who likes only natural foods would rather eat a soybean patty, than a cheeseburger.

2. That room with its filthy rug, and broken dishwasher, is the nicest one in the building.

3. My aunt who claims she is an artist, painted her living room ceiling, to look like the sky at midnight.

Comma between Complete Thoughts Connected by a Joining Word

Use a comma between two complete thoughts connected by *and, but, for, or, nor, so, yet.*

My parents threatened to throw me out of the house, so I had to stop playing the drums.

The polyester bedsheets had a gorgeous design on them, but they didn't feel as comfortable as plain cotton sheets.

The teenage girls walked the hot summer streets, and the teenage boys drove by in their shined-up cars.

The comma is optional when the complete thoughts are short:

Calvin relaxed but Robert kept working.

The soda was flat so I poured it away.

Be careful not to use a comma in sentences having *one* subject and a *double* verb. The comma is used only in sentences made up of two complete thoughts (two subjects and two verbs). In the sentence

Dawn lay awake that stormy night and listened to the thunder crashing.

there is only one subject (*Dawn*) and a double verb (*lay* and *listened*). No comma is needed. Likewise, the sentence

The quarterback kept the ball and plunged across the goal line for a touchdown.

has only one subject (*quarterback*) and a double verb (*kept* and *plunged*); therefore, no comma is needed.

Place a comma before a joining word that connects two complete thoughts (two subjects and two verbs). The three sentences that have only one subject and a double verb do not need commas; mark these *C* as "correct."

1. Vince has to make sixty sandwiches an hour or he'll lose his job at Burgerland.
2. The doctor assured me that my back was fine but it still felt as rigid as an iron rod.
3. That new video store gets all the latest releases and it provides free popcorn for customers who rent two or more movies.
4. My new toaster is more hi-tech than my old one but it burns toast just as often.
5. Carol and Barbara pulled the volleyball net as tight as they could and then lashed it to a convenient pair of trees.
6. Ralph refuses to pay rent to his parents and will not do any chores at home.
7. Frieda wore a pair of wooden clogs while housecleaning and the people in the apartment next door could hear her clomping up and down the stairs.
8. William kept the cookie in his mouth until its chocolate coating melted and then he crunched the naked wafer into bits.
9. My little sister loves to call strangers on the telephone but she hangs up as soon as anyone answers.
10. Ronnie plans to make a million dollars by the time he's twenty-five and then write a book about his experiences.

Comma with Direct Quotations

Use a comma to set off a direct quotation from the rest of a sentence.

"Please take a number," said the deli clerk.

Fred told Martha, "I've just signed up for a knitting class."

"Those who sling mud," a famous politician once said, "usually lose ground."

"Reading this book," complained Stan, "is about as interesting as watching paint dry."

> **TIP** A comma or a period at the end of a quotation goes inside quotation marks. See also page 342.

Practice

8

In each sentence, add the one or more commas needed to set off the quoted material.

1. Frowning, the clerk asked "Do you have a driver's license and two major credit cards for identification?"

2. In my high school yearbook, my best friend wrote "2 Good 2 B 4 Gotten."

3. "The only thing that man couldn't talk his way out of" said Richie "is a coffin."

Practice

9

In each sentence, cross out the one comma that is not needed. Add the comma that is needed to set off a quotation from the rest of the sentence.

1. "Could you spare a quarter," the boy asked passersby, in the mall "for a video game?"

2. "Man does not live by words alone" wrote Adlai Stevenson, "despite the fact, that sometimes he has to eat them."

3. "That actress," said Velma "has promoted everything, from denture cleaner to shoelaces."

www.mhhe.com/langan

Comma with Everyday Material

Use a comma with certain everyday material as shown in the following sections.

Persons Spoken To

Sally, I think that you should go to bed.

Please turn down the stereo, Jo.

Please, sir, can you spare a dollar?

Dates

My best friend got married on April 29, 2005, and he became a parent on January 7, 2007.

Addresses

Lola's sister lives at Greenway Village, 342 Red Oak Drive, Los Angeles, California 90057.

> **TIP** No comma is used before the zip code.

Openings and Closings of Letters

Dear Vanessa,	Sincerely,
Dear John,	Truly yours,

> **TIP** In formal letters, a colon is used after the opening:
>
> Dear Sir:
>
> Dear Madam:

Numbers

Government officials estimate that Americans spend about 785,000,000 hours a year filling out federal forms.

Place commas where needed.

Practice

10

1. I am sorry sir but you cannot sit at this table.
2. On May 6 1954 Roger Bannister became the first person to run a mile in under four minutes.
3. Redeeming the savings certificate before June 30 2010 will result in a substantial penalty.
4. A cash refund of one dollar can be obtained by sending proof of purchase to Seven Seas P.O. Box 760 El Paso TX 79972.
5. Leo turn off that TV set this minute!

Unnecessary Use of Commas

Remember that if no clear rule applies for using a comma, it is usually better not to use a comma. As stated earlier, "When in doubt, leave it out." Following are some typical examples of unnecessary commas.

Incorrect

Sharon told me, that my socks were different colors. (A comma is not used before *that* unless the flow of thought is interrupted.)

The union negotiations, dragged on for three days. (Do not use a comma between a simple subject and verb.)

I waxed all the furniture, and cleaned the windows. (Use a comma before *and* only with more than two items in a series or when *and* joins two complete thoughts.)

Sharon carried, the baby into the house. (Do not use a comma between a verb and its object.)

I had a clear view, of the entire robbery. (Do not use a comma before a prepositional phrase.)

Practice

11

Cross out the one comma that does not belong in each sentence. Do not add any commas.

1. A new bulletproof material has been developed, that is very lightweight.

2. The vet's bill included charges, for a distemper shot.

3. Since the firehouse, is directly behind Ken's home, the sound of its siren pierces his walls.

4. Hard sausages, and net-covered hams hung above the delicatessen counter.

5. The students in the dance class, were dressed in a variety of bright tights, baggy sweatshirts, and woolly leg warmers.

6. A woman in the ladies' room asked me, if she could borrow a safety pin.

7. Telephone books, broken pencils, and scraps of paper, littered the reporter's desk.

8. The frenzied crowd at the game cheered, and whistled.

9. Splitting along the seams, the old mattress spilled its stuffing, on the ground.

10. To satisfy his hunger, Enrique chewed on a piece of dry, rye bread.

Collaborative Activity

Editing and Rewriting

Working with a partner, carefully read the short paragraph below and mark the ten places where commas are missing. Then, in the space between the lines, insert the ten additional commas needed. Feel free to discuss the rewrite quietly with your partner and refer back to the chapter when necessary.

¹You may have heard of Robinson Crusoe but there is an even stranger story of shipwreck and survival. ²In 1757 a Scottish whaling ship sank in the icy polar seas of the Arctic. ³Only one man Bruce Gordon survived. ⁴Without food or shelter Gordon spent his lonely first night huddled on the ice. ⁵The next day the whaling ship—upside-down—rose to the surface of the sea and lodged tightly in the ice floes. ⁶Gordon using some of the shipwreck debris managed to break into a cabin window. ⁷He survived for a year in the freezing world of the upside-down ship by using some stored coal to build a fire. ⁸Eventually Bruce Gordon was rescued by a band of Inuit hunters. ⁹After living for more than five years in the native village the shipwrecked sailor finally made it back to Scotland.

Collaborative Activity

Creating Sentences

Working with a partner, write sentences that use commas as directed.

1. Write a sentence mentioning three items that can be found in this photo.

   _____

   _____

2. Write two sentences describing how you relax after getting home from school or work. Start the first sentence with *After* or *When*. Start the second sentence with *Next*.

   _____

   _____

3. Write a sentence that tells something about your favorite movie, book, television show, or song. Use the words *which is my favorite movie* (or *book, television show,* or *song*) after the name of the movie, book, television show, or song.

   _____

   _____

4. Write a sentence containing two complete thoughts about a person you know. The first thought should mention something that you like about the person. The second thought should mention something you don't like. Join the two thoughts with *but*.

   _____

   _____

5. Invent a line that Lola might say to Tony. Use the words *Lola said* in the sentence. Then include Tony's reply, using the words *Tony responded*.

   _____

   _____

6. Write a sentence about an important event in your life. Include in your sentence the day, month, and year of the event.

_____

_____

Reflective Activity

1. Look at the paragraph about Bruce Gordon that you revised. Explain how adding commas has affected the reading of the paragraph.

2. What would writing be like without the comma? How do commas help writing?

3. What comma rule is the most difficult for you to remember and apply? Explain, giving an example.

Review Test   1

Insert commas where needed. In the space provided under each sentence, summarize briefly the rule that explains the use of the comma or commas.

1. During the sudden downpour people covered their heads with folded newspapers.

_____

2. Helen's sister always stopped her from buying expensive items by saying "You have champagne taste and a beer budget."

_____

3. The damp musty shadowy cellar was our favorite playground.

_____

4. My favorite pillow a sad specimen leaking chunks of foam is over ten years old.

_____

5. Mary Ann started work as a file clerk on June 21 2007 and quit on June 22.

_____

6. Phan agreed to sit in the window seat but he kept his eyes tightly shut during the takeoff and landing.

   _____

7. The massive fullback his uniform torn and bloodied hobbled back to the huddle.

   _____

8. Martin Luther King wrote "A man can't ride on your back unless it's bent."

   _____

9. If you want to avoid that run-down feeling you should look both ways before crossing the street.

   _____

10. My brother who is a practical joker once put a plastic shark in our bathtub.

    _____

Review Test 2

Insert commas where needed. One sentence does not need commas; mark this sentence *C* for "correct."

1. Thelma and Louise a corn snake who lived at the San Diego Zoo was popular with visitors.

2. She wasn't popular because corn snakes which are harmless are at all rare.

3. In fact corn snakes are among the most common North American snakes.

4. Thelma and Louise was a perfectly ordinary snake except for one little thing.

5. She had believe it or not two heads.

6. Scientists say that two-headed snakes are born fairly often but they usually don't survive long.

7. Because their two heads often want to go in different directions such snakes are slow and clumsy.

8. The two-headed babies are quickly caught and eaten by hawks raccoons skunks and other animals.

9. But in the safety of the zoo Thelma and Louise lived a long life.

10. She even gave birth to fifteen normal babies.

Review Test 3

On separate paper, write six sentences, each demonstrating one of the six main comma rules.

NAME: _____

DATE: _____

MASTERY TEST 1 Comma

Add commas where needed. Then refer to the box below and write, in the space provided, the letter of the comma rule that applies in each sentence.

a. Between items in a series	d. Between complete thoughts
b. After introductory material	e. With direct quotations
c. Around interrupters	f. With everyday material

_____ 1. Tasha makes her studying more bearable by having plenty of Triscuits pretzels and Skittles close by.

_____ 2. Because Jim is the company's top salesperson he receives special attention from the boss.

_____ 3. "You look different" said Lily. "Have you lost weight?"

_____ 4. My Uncle Al who is hard of hearing always asks me to repeat what I just said.

_____ 5. "I really appreciate the ride" the hitchhiker said. "A hundred cars must have passed me."

_____ 6. My little sister loves to ride on the back of my motorcycle but my parents worry about her falling off.

_____ 7. I have to pay $8,250 by June 30 2010 before I officially own my car.

_____ 8. Will emptied his piggy bank and sorted the nickels dimes and quarters into three shiny piles.

_____ 9. Huddled under a large piece of plastic we waited out the rain delay in the ball game.

_____ 10. The vacationing boys slept in the car that night for they'd spent too much on meals and souvenirs.

Comma   MASTERY TEST 2

*Cross out the one comma in each sentence that is not needed. Then add the
one comma that is needed and in the space provided write the letter of the
rule that applies for each comma you added.*

a. Between items in a series	d. Between complete thoughts
b. After introductory material	e. With direct quotations
c. Around interrupters	

_____ 1. *Harry Potter and the Deathly Hallows,* the seventh and final book in the *Harry Potter* series sold over eight million copies, on the first day of its release.

_____ 2. Pretending to be a babysitter the shoplifter slipped several DVDs, into her baby stroller.

_____ 3. Emmett, who recently adopted a baby girl, rushed to the supermarket, to buy infant formula, baby wipes and disposable diapers.

_____ 4. "Before I leave on my business trip" Emily told her two children, "I want both of you to promise me, that you will *not* torment the dog or Dad."

_____ 5. Brandie, a breast cancer survivor religiously wears her pink, "awareness bracelet" to remember her victory over the disease.

_____ 6. Recognizing the deadly effects of cigarette smoking the Walt Disney Company has banned depictions of smoking, in its films.

_____ 7. Kurt rehearsed the exact moment for months but he still stumbled over his own words, when he asked Keisha to marry him.

_____ 8. Everyone at the barbecue party enjoyed the mustard-coated oil-drizzled Alaskan, Copper River sockeye salmon fillets roasted on cedar planks.

_____ 9. Mahatma Gandhi, was wise when he said "We must be the change we wish to see."

_____ 10. The substitute teacher tried to enforce the class rules yet students misbehaved by sending text messages, and playing games on their cell phones.

NAME: _____

DATE: _____

MASTERY TEST 3 Comma

Add commas where needed. Then refer to the box below and write, in the space provided, the letter of the comma rule that applies in each sentence.

a. Between items in a series	d. Between complete thoughts
b. After introductory material	e. With direct quotations
c. Around interrupters	f. With everyday material

_____ 1. My friend Tina lives at 333 Virginia Avenue Atlantic City.

_____ 2. I went to her house one night recently and the two of us watched television for several hours.

_____ 3. Tina who is always hungry suggested we go to Tony's Grill for a pizza.

_____ 4. Along with about a dozen other drivers I parked in a tiny lot with a "No Parking" sign.

_____ 5. I believed foolishly enough that my car would be safe there.

_____ 6. We had our pizza left the restaurant and returned to the lot.

_____ 7. A 1975 Chevy and a tow truck were parked in the lot but my Honda and all the other cars had vanished.

_____ 8. After walking twenty blocks back to Tina's house I called the towing company.

_____ 9. A recorded voice said "Come to 26 Texas Avenue tomorrow morning with seventy-five dollars in cash."

_____ 10. Whenever Tina craves pizza I now buy a frozen pie at the local convenience store.

Comma   MASTERY TEST 4

Add commas where needed. Then refer to the box below and write, in the space provided, the letter of the comma rule that applies in each sentence.

> a. Between items in a series
> b. After introductory material
> c. Around interrupters
> d. Between complete thoughts
> e. With direct quotations

_____   1. Matt's first car a 1960 Chevy Impala had enormous tail fins.

_____   2. Kia called from upstairs "Could you turn the TV down?"

_____   3. The broken-down farm housed a swaybacked horse a blind cow and two lame chickens.

_____   4. In Phil's job as toll collector he takes quarters from over 5,500 drivers every day.

_____   5. In the middle of the love scene two little boys in the audience began to giggle.

_____   6. The combination of milk stains peanut butter splotches and jelly smears made the toddler's face look like a finger painting.

_____   7. Though public transportation saves her money Dotty prefers driving to work.

_____   8. "Better to keep your mouth shut and be thought a fool" my father always says "than to open it and remove all doubt."

_____   9. The fried eggs as they sizzled in the rusty iron skillet began to turn red.

_____   10. The road map must have been out of date for the highway it showed no longer existed.

Other Punctuation Marks

Introductory Activity

The main purpose of this chapter is to explain and illustrate five other punctuation marks not previously discussed. They are the colon (:), semi-colon (;), dash (—), hyphen (-), and parentheses ( ). Each sentence below needs one of these punctuation marks. See if you can insert the correct mark in each case.

1. The following items were on Ted's grocery list soda, potato chips, chocolate chip cookies, ice cream, and carrots.

2. A life size statue of her cat adorns the living room of Diana's penthouse.

3. Sigmund Freud 1856–1939, the pioneer of psychoanalysis, was a habitual cocaine user.

4. As children, we would put pennies on the railroad track we wanted to see what they would look like after being run over by a train.

5. The stuntwoman was battered, broken, and barely breathing but alive.

Answers are on page 675.

Colon (:)

The colon is a mark of introduction. Use the colon at the end of a complete statement to do the following:

www.mhhe.com/langan

1. **Introduce a list.**

   My little brother has three hobbies: playing video games, racing his Hot Wheels cars all over the floor, and driving me crazy.

2. **Introduce a long quotation.**

   Janet's paper was based on a passage from George Eliot's novel *Middlemarch:* "If we had a keen vision and feeling of all ordinary human life, it would be like hearing the grass grow and the squirrel's heart beat, and we should die of that roar which lies on the other side of silence. As it is, the quickest of us walk about well wadded with stupidity."

3. **Introduce an explanation.**

   There are two ways to do this job: the easy way and the right way.

Two minor uses of the colon are after the opening in a formal letter (*Dear Sir or Madam:*) and between the hour and the minute when writing the time (*The bus will leave for the game at 11:45*).

Place colons where needed.

1. A comedian once defined mummies as follows Egyptians who are pressed for time.

2. The manager boasted that his restaurant was full of good things good food, good selections, and good prices.

3. In her book *The Plug-In Drug,* Marie Winn describes the effect of television on family life "By its domination of the time families spend together, it destroys the special quality that distinguishes one family from another, a quality that depends to a great extent on what a family *does,* what special rituals, games, recurrent jokes, familiar songs, and shared activities it accumulates."

Practice

1

Semicolon (;)

The semicolon signals more of a pause than the comma alone but not quite the full pause of a period. Use a semicolon to do the following:

www.mhhe.com/langan

1. **Join two complete thoughts that are not already connected by a joining word such as *and, but, for,* or *so.***

   The chemistry lab blew up; Professor Thomas was fired.

   I once stabbed myself with a pencil; a black mark has been under my skin ever since.

2. **Join two complete thoughts that include a transitional word such as *however, otherwise, moreover, furthermore, therefore,* or *consequently.***

I cut and raked the grass; moreover, I weeded the lawn.

Sally finished typing the paper; however, she forgot to bring it to class.

> **TIP** The first two uses of the semicolon listed here are treated in more detail on pages 113–116.

3. **Mark off items in a series when the items themselves contain commas.**

This fall I won't have to work on Labor Day, September 7; Veterans Day, November 11; or Thanksgiving Day, November 26.

At the final Weight Watchers' meeting, prizes were awarded to Sally Johnson, for losing 20 pounds; Irving Ross, for losing 26 pounds; and Betty Mills, the champion loser, who lost 102 pounds.

Practice 2

Place semicolons where needed.

1. Be sure to plug up all unused electrical outlets otherwise, your toddler might get a severe shock.

2. In the old horror movie, the incredible shrinking man battled a black widow spider he finally speared it with a straight pin.

3. Having nothing better to do, Laurie watched the *Today* show from 7:00 to 9:00 A.M. a rerun of *Good Morning, Miami,* from 9:00 to 10:00 and soap operas from 12:30 to 4:00 P.M.

www.mhhe.com/langan

Dash (—)

A dash signals a degree of pause longer than a comma but not as complete as a period. Use the dash to set off words for dramatic effect.

I suggest—no, I insist—that you stay for dinner.

The prisoner walked toward the electric chair—grinning.

A meaningful job, a loving wife, and a car that wouldn't break down all the time—these are the things he wanted in life.

Place dashes where needed.

1. Our dishwasher doesn't dry very well the glasses look as if they're crying.

2. After I saw two museums, three monuments, and the governor's mansion, there was only one other place I wanted to see my hotel room.

3. I hoped no, I prayed that the operation would be successful.

Hyphen (-)

Use a hyphen in the following ways:

www.mhhe.com/langan

1. With two or more words that act as a single unit describing a noun.

The society ladies nibbled at the deep-fried grasshoppers.

A white-gloved waiter then put some snails on their table.

TIP Your dictionary will often help when you are unsure about whether to use a hyphen between words.

---

2. To divide a word at the end of a line of writing or typing.

Although it had begun to drizzle, the teams decided to play the championship game that day.

TIPS

1. Divide a word between syllables. Use your dictionary (see page 384) to be sure of correct syllable divisions.

2. Do not divide words of one syllable.

3. Do not divide a word if you can avoid dividing it.

Place hyphens where needed.

1. Sideway Inn, a hole in the wall diner located in the newly gentrified part of town, serves both comfort food and upscale, hoity toity dishes.

2. Grandpa needs to throw out his console TV and rabbit ear antenna and buy a new high definition TV.

3. The people in my hometown are honest, hard working folks, but they aren't very friendly to out of towners.

Parentheses ( )

www.mhhe.com/langan

Use parentheses to do the following:

1. **Set off extra or incidental information from the rest of a sentence.**

    The chapter on drugs in our textbook (pages 142–178) contains some frightening statistics.

    The normal body temperature of a cat (101 to 102°) is 3° higher than the temperature of its owner.

2. **Enclose letters or numbers that signal items in a series.**

    Three steps to follow in previewing a textbook are to (1) study the title, (2) read the first and last paragraphs, and (3) study the headings and subheadings.

> **TIP** Do not use parentheses too often in your writing.

Add parentheses where needed.

1. The high ticket prices fifty to ninety dollars made Rodney think twice about going to the concert.

2. In the last election the April primary, only 20 percent of eligible voters showed up at the polls.

3. When you come to take the placement test, please bring with you 1 two sharpened pencils and 2 an eraser.

Review Test 1

At the appropriate spot or spots, place the punctuation mark shown in the margin.

EXAMPLE

;   The singles dance was a success; I met several people I wanted to see again.

:   1. Fascinated, Corey read two unusual recipes in *The Joy of Cooking* roasted saddle of moose and woodchuck smothered with onions.

—   2. Sam's Pizza Heaven is advertising a Friday-night special on lasagna all you can eat for $2.99.

-     3. Very few older cars have front wheel drive.

( )   4. The sign on my instructor's office door read, "Available only during office hours 2 to 4 P.M."

:   5. In *Walden,* Thoreau wrote "I went to the woods because I wished to live deliberately, to front only the essential facts of life, and see if I could not learn what it had to teach, and not, when I came to die, discover that I had not lived."

;   6. Mosquitoes prefer to bite children rather than adults they are also more attracted to blonds than to brunettes.

—   7. Please go to the White Hen it's that convenience store in the middle of the next block and get a carton of milk.

-     8. We can't afford to see first run movies anymore.

( )   9. Four hints for success in taking exams are 1 review your notes the night before, 2 be on time for the exam, 3 sit in a quiet place, and 4 read all directions carefully before you begin to write.

;   10. My neighbor's boxer, Dempsey, is a great watchdog in fact, he can sit on my porch and watch me for hours.

Review Test 2

On separate paper, write two sentences for each of the following punctuation marks: colon, semicolon, dash, hyphen, parentheses.

NAME: _____

DATE: _____

MASTERY TEST 1 | # Other Punctuation Marks

At the appropriate spot (or spots), place the punctuation mark shown in the margin.

;

1. There are several ways to save money on your grocery bills for example, never go shopping on an empty stomach.

:

2. There are only two ways to get there hike or hitch a ride.

—

3. "The cooking at this restaurant," said the dissatisfied customer, "lacks just one thing good taste."

-

4. Pete's over the shoulder catch brought the crowd to its feet.

( )

5. Call your local office of the IRS Internal Revenue Service if you think you're entitled to a refund.

—

6. Annabelle gave Harold back his engagement ring without the diamond.

:

7. That new ice cream place has great flavors blueberry cheesecake, pineapple, bubble gum, and Oreo cookie.

—

8. Some teenage boys there they go around the corner just stole that man's wallet.

-

9. I'm waiting for the day when someone invents low calorie junk food.

;

10. In a study, people were asked who in their family got the most smiles and touches 44 percent said the family pet.

Other Punctuation Marks   MASTERY TEST 2

Add colons, semicolons, dashes, hyphens, or parentheses as needed. Each sentence requires only one of the five kinds of punctuation marks.

1. It's impossible for two blue eyed parents to have a brown-eyed child.

2. People watch more television than most of us realize the average set is on for more than six hours a day.

3. My aunt loves giving blow by blow accounts of all her operations.

4. Electrical storms, inflation, and my little brother's jokes these are the things that bother me the most.

5. My car was losing power I asked a gas station attendant to check the battery.

6. To cure hiccups, try one of the following methods put a paper bag over your head, hold your breath, or eat a teaspoonful of sugar.

7. A portion of the sociology text pages 150–158 deals with the changing roles of women.

8. My mother likes to listen to talk shows she feels less lonely if there's a conversation going on.

9. Our math instructor said "Standard units of measurement used to be set by parts of the body; for example, King Henry I of England defined a yard as the distance from his nose to his outstretched thumb."

10. From my second row seat at the movies, I could count the leading lady's eyelashes.

Dictionary Use

28

Introductory Activity

The dictionary is an indispensable tool, as will be apparent if you try to answer the following questions *without* using the dictionary.

1. Which one of the following words is spelled incorrectly?

   fortutious   macrobiotics   stratagem

2. If you wanted to hyphenate the following word correctly, at which points would you place the syllable divisions?

   h i e r o g l y p h i c s

3. What common word has the sound of the first *e* in the word *chameleon*?

   _____

4. Where is the primary accent in the following word?

   o c / t o / g e / n a r / i / a n

5. What are the two separate meanings of the word *earmark*?

   _____

   _____

Your dictionary is a quick and sure authority on all these matters: spelling, syllabication, pronunciation, and word meanings. And as this chapter will show, it is also a source for many other kinds of information.

Answers are on page 675.

But Dr Johnson ov wat yuse wil this dicshunary of yors be?

The dictionary is a valuable tool. To take advantage of it, you need to understand the main kinds of information that a dictionary gives about a word. Look at the information provided for the word *dictate* in the following entry from the *American Heritage Dictionary,* fourth paperback edition.*

Spelling and syllabication   **Pronunciation**   **Part of speech**

dic•tate (dĭk′tāt′, dĭk-tāt′) *v.* **-tat•ed, -tat•ing.**
1. To say or read aloud for transcription.
2. To prescribe or command with authority.
—*n.* (dĭk′tāt′). **1.** A directive; command.
2. A guiding principle: *the dictates of conscience.* [< Lat. *dictāre.* < *dīcere, say*]
—**dic•ta′tion** *n.*

Meanings

Example

Etymology

Other form of the word

Spelling

The first bit of information, in the boldface (heavy type) entry itself, is the spelling of *dictate*. You probably already know the spelling of *dictate*, but if you didn't, you could find it by pronouncing the syllables in the word carefully and then looking it up in the dictionary.

Use your dictionary to correct the spelling of the following words:

responsable _____	delite _____
thorogh _____	duble _____
akselerate _____	carefull _____
finaly _____	luckyer _____
refiree _____	dangrous _____
shizophrenic _____	accomodate _____
prescripshun _____	envalope _____
hankercheif _____	prenatel _____
marryed _____	progres _____
alright _____	jeneric _____
fotographer _____	excelent _____
krucial _____	persue _____

Syllabication

The second bit of information that the dictionary gives, also within the boldface entry, is the syllabication of *dic•tate*. Note that a dot separates each syllable (or part) of the word. Use your dictionary to mark the syllable divisions in the following words. Also indicate how many syllables are in each word.

c o n t a c t	(_____ syllables)
m a g n e t i c	(_____ syllables)
d e h u m a n i z e	(_____ syllables)
s e n t i m e n t a l i z e	(_____ syllables)

Noting syllable divisions will enable you to *hyphenate* a word: divide it at the end of one line of writing and complete it at the beginning of the next line. You can correctly hyphenate a word only at a syllable division, and you may have to check your dictionary to make sure of the syllable divisions for a particular word.

Pronunciation

The third bit of information in the dictionary entry is the pronunciation of *dictate:* (dĭk′tāt′) or (dĭk-tāt′). You already know how to pronounce *dictate*, but if you did not, the information within the parentheses would serve as your guide. Use your dictionary to complete the pronunciation exercises on the next page.

Vowel Sounds

You will probably use the pronunciation key in your dictionary mainly as a guide to pronouncing different vowel sounds (*vowels* are the letters *a, e, i, o,* and *u*). Here is the pronunciation key that appears in the front of the paperback *American Heritage Dictionary:*

ă pat ā pay â care ä father ĕ pet ē be ĭ pit ī tie î pier ŏ pot ō toe
ô paw, for oi noise ŏŏ took $\overline{oo}$ boot ou out th thin *th* this ŭ cut
û urge y$\overline{oo}$ abuse zh vision ə about, item, edible, gallop, circus

This key tells you, for example, that the short *a* is pronounced like the *a* in *pat*, the long *a* is like the *a* in *pay*, and the short *i* is like the *i* in *pit*.

Now look at the pronunciation key in your own dictionary. The key is probably located in the front of the dictionary or at the bottom of every page. What common word in the key tells you how to pronounce each of the following sounds?

ĕ _____   ō _____

ī _____   ŭ _____

ŏ _____ $\overline{oo}$ _____

> **TIP** Note that a long vowel always has the sound of its own name.

The Schwa (ə)

The symbol ə looks like an upside-down *e*. It is called a *schwa*, and it stands for the unaccented sound in such words as *about, item, edible, gallop,* and *circus*. More approximately, it stands for the sound *uh*—like the *uh* that speakers sometimes make when they hesitate. Perhaps it would help to remember that *uh*, as well as ə, could be used to represent the schwa sound.

Here are three of the many words in which the schwa sound appears: *socialize* (sō′shə līz or sō′shuh līz); *legitimate* (lə jĭt′ə mĭt or luh jĭt′ uh mĭt); *oblivious* (ə blĭv′ē əs or uh blĭv′ē uhs). Open your dictionary to any page, and you will almost surely be able to find three words that make use of the schwa in the pronunciation in parentheses after the main entry. Write three such words and their pronunciations in the following spaces:

1. _____

2. _____

3. _____

Accent Marks

Some words contain both a primary accent, shown by a heavy stroke ($'$), and a secondary accent, shown by a lighter stroke ($'$). For example, in the word *vicissitude* (vĭ sĭs′ĭ tōōd′), the stress, or accent, goes chiefly on the second syllable (sĭs′) and, to a lesser extent, on the last syllable (tōōd′).

Use your dictionary to add stress marks to the following words:

soliloquy (sə lĭl ə kwē)

diatribe (dī ə trīb)

rheumatism (rōō mə tīz əm)

representation (rĕp rĭ zĕn tā shən)

Full Pronunciation

Use your dictionary to write out the full pronunciation (the information given in parentheses) for each of the following words:

1. germane _____
2. jettison _____
3. juxtapose _____
4. catastrophic _____
5. alacrity _____
6. exacerbate _____
7. sporadic _____
8. cacophony _____
9. intrepid _____
10. oligarchy _____
11. raucous _____
12. temerity _____
13. forensic _____
14. megalomania _____
15. perpetuity _____

Now practice pronouncing each word. Use the pronunciation key in your dictionary as an aid to sounding out each syllable. Do *not* try to pronounce a word all at once; instead, work on mastering *one syllable at a time.* When you can pronounce each of the syllables in a word successfully, then say them in sequence, add the accent, and pronounce the entire word.

> **TIP** Online dictionaries offer spoken pronunciations of words. For example, if you go to www.merriam-webster.com, you will see a speaker icon next to each word entry. If you click on this icon, the word will be pronounced for you.

Other Information about Words

Parts of Speech

The dictionary entry for *dictate* includes the abbreviation *v.* This means that the meanings of *dictate* as a verb will follow. The abbreviation *n.* is then followed by the meanings of *dictate* as a noun.

At the front of your dictionary, you will probably find a key that will explain the meanings of abbreviations used in the dictionary. Use the key to fill in the meanings of the following abbreviations:

pl. = _____   adj. = _____

sing. = _____   adv. = _____

Principal Parts of Irregular Verbs

Dictate is a regular verb and forms its principal parts by adding *-d, -d,* and *-ing* to the stem of the verb. When a verb is irregular, the dictionary lists its principal parts. For example, with *begin* the present tense comes first (the entry itself, *begin*). Next comes the past tense (*began*), and then the past participle (*begun*)—the form of the verb used with such helping words as *have, had,* and *was.* Then comes the present participle (*beginning*)—the *-ing* form of the word.

Look up the principal parts of the following irregular verbs and write them in the spaces provided. The first one has been done for you.

Present	Past	Past Participle	Present Participle
see	*saw*	*seen*	*seeing*
go	_____	_____	_____
ride	_____	_____	_____
speak	_____	_____	_____

Plural Forms of Irregular Nouns

The dictionary supplies the plural forms of all irregular nouns (regular nouns form the plural by adding *-s* or *-es*). Give the plurals of the following nouns:

country   _____

volcano   _____

curriculum   _____

woman   _____

See page 397 for more information about plurals.

Meanings

When a word has more than one meaning, the meanings are numbered in the dictionary, as with the verb *dictate*. In many dictionaries, the most common meanings are presented first. The introductory pages of your dictionary will explain the order in which meanings are presented.

Use the sentence context to try to explain the meaning of the underlined word in each of the following sentences. Write your definition in the space provided. Then look up and record the dictionary meaning of the word. Be sure you pick out the meaning that fits the word as it is used in the sentence.

1. The insurance company <u>compensated</u> Jean for the two weeks she missed work.

   Your definition: _____

   Dictionary definition: _____

2. Howard is in excellent <u>condition</u> from running two miles a day.

   Your definition: _____

   Dictionary definition: _____

3. The underworld chief attained power by <u>liquidating</u> his competitors.

   Your definition: _____

   Dictionary definition: _____

Etymology

Etymology refers to the history of a word. Many words have origins in foreign languages, such as Greek (abbreviated Gk in the dictionary) or Latin (L). Such information is usually enclosed in brackets and is more likely to be present in a hardbound desk dictionary than in a paperback one. A good desk dictionary will tell you, for example, that the word *cannibal* derives from the name of the man-eating tribe, the Caribs, that Christopher Columbus discovered on Cuba and Haiti.

The following are good desk dictionaries:

The American Heritage Dictionary

Random House College Dictionary

Merriam–Webster's Collegiate Dictionary

Webster's New World Dictionary

See if your dictionary says anything about the origins of the following words.

derrick _____

_____

berserk _____

_____

boycott _____

_____

chauvinism _____

_____

Usage Labels

As a general rule, use only standard English words in your writing. If a word is not standard English, your dictionary will probably give it a usage label such as *informal, nonstandard, slang, vulgar, obsolete, archaic,* or *rare.*

Look up the following words and record how your dictionary labels them. Remember that a recent hardbound desk dictionary will always be the best source of information about usage.

messed up _____

peppy _____

techie _____

ain't _____

gross out (meaning *to fill with disgust*) _____

Synonyms

A *synonym* is a word that is close in meaning to another word. Using synonyms helps you avoid unnecessary repetition of the same word in a paper. A paperback dictionary is not likely to give you synonyms for words, but a good desk dictionary will. (You might also want to own a *thesaurus,* a book that lists synonyms and antonyms. An *antonym* is a word approximately opposite in meaning to another word.)

Consult a desk dictionary that gives synonyms for the following words, and write some of the synonyms in the spaces provided.

frighten _____

giant _____

insane _____

Review Test

Use your dictionary to answer the following questions.

1. How many syllables are in the word *magnanimous?* _____

2. Where is the primary accent in the word *detrimental?* _____

3. In the word *tractable,* the second *a* is pronounced like
   a. short *a.*
   b. long *a.*
   c. short *i.*
   d. schwa.

4. In the word *officiate,* the second *i* is pronounced like
   a. short *i.*
   b. long *i.*
   c. long *e.*
   d. schwa.

5. In the word *sedentary,* the first *e* is pronounced like
   a. short *e.*
   b. long *e.*
   c. short *i.*
   d. schwa.

There are five misspelled words in the following sentence. Cross out each misspelled word and write the correct spelling in the spaces provided.

Our physicle education instructer, Mrs. Stevens, constently tells us that people who exersize every day have a more positive atitude toward life than people who never work out.

6. _____

7. _____

8. _____

9. _____

10. _____

NAME: _____

DATE: _____

MASTERY TEST 1 | Dictionary Use

ITEMS **1–5**

Use your dictionary to answer the following questions.

1. How many syllables are in the word *incongruous?* _____

2. Where is the primary accent in the word *culmination?* _____

3. In the word *periphery,* the *i* is pronounced like
   a. long *i.*
   b. short *i.*
   c. long *e.*
   d. short *e.*

4. In the word *acquiesce,* the *i* is pronounced like
   a. long *i.*
   b. short *i.*
   c. long *e.*
   d. short *e.*

5. In the word *apostasy,* the first *a* is pronounced like
   a. long *a.*
   b. short *a.*
   c. short *o.*
   d. schwa.

ITEMS **6–10**

There are five misspelled words in the following sentence. Cross out each misspelled word and write in the correct spelling in the spaces provided.

Altho there were legal suits filed against him, the mayer decided to run for reelection, but the citazens of our town were not anxous to give him a second oportunity at public office.

6. _____   8. _____   10. _____

7. _____   9. _____

Dictionary Use　MASTERY TEST 2

ITEMS 1–5

Use your dictionary to answer the following questions.

1. How many syllables are in the word *pandemonium?* _____

2. Where is the primary accent in the word *unremitting?* _____

3. In the word *expatriate,* the *i* is pronounced like a
   a. long *i.*
   b. short *i.*
   c. long *e.*
   d. short *e.*

4. In the word *recapitulate,* the *i* is pronounced like a
   a. long *i.*
   b. short *i.*
   c. long *e.*
   d. short *e.*

5. In the word *frivolous,* the first *o* is pronounced like a
   a. long *o.*
   b. short *o.*
   c. short *u.*
   d. schwa.

ITEMS 6–10

There are five misspelled words in the following sentence. Cross out each misspelled word and write in the correct spelling in the spaces provided.

We regreted that we could not attend your anniversery celabration. Our station wagon broke down on the freeway, leaveing us with no means of transpertation.

6. _____　　8. _____　　10. _____

7. _____　　9. _____

Spelling Improvement

Introductory Activity

See if you can circle the word that is misspelled in each of the following pairs:

akward	*or*	awkward
exercise	*or*	exercize
business	*or*	buisness
worried	*or*	worryed
shamful	*or*	shameful
begining	*or*	beginning
partys	*or*	parties
sandwichs	*or*	sandwiches
heroes	*or*	heros

Answers are on page 675.

Poor spelling often results from bad habits developed in the early school years. With work, such habits can be corrected. If you can write your name without misspelling it, there is no reason why you can't do the same with almost any word in the English language. Following are seven steps you can take to improve your spelling.

Step 1: Using the Dictionary

Get into the habit of using the dictionary. When you write a paper, allow yourself time to look up the spelling of all the words you are unsure about. Do not underestimate the value of this step just because it is such a simple one. By using the dictionary, you can probably make yourself a 95 percent better speller.

Step 2: Keeping a Personal Spelling List

Keep a list of words you misspell, and study those words regularly. Use the chart on the inside front cover of this book as a starter. When you accumulate additional words, you may want to use a back page of your English notebook.

> **TIP** When you have trouble spelling long words, try to break each word into syllables and see whether you can spell the syllables. For example, *misdemeanor* can be spelled easily if you can hear and spell in turn its four syllables: *mis-de-mean-or.* The word *formidable* can be spelled easily if you hear and spell in turn its four syllables: *for-mi-da-ble.* Remember, then: try to see, hear, and spell long words in terms of their syllables.

Step 3: Mastering Commonly Confused Words

Master the meanings and spellings of the commonly confused words on pages 413–432. Your instructor may assign twenty words for you to study at a time and give you a series of quizzes until you have mastered all the words.

Step 4: Using a Computer's Spell-Checker

Most word-processing programs feature a *spell-checker* that will identify incorrect words and suggest correct spellings. If you are unsure how to use yours, consult the program's "help" function. Spell-checkers are not fool-proof; they will fail to catch misused homonyms like the words *your* and *you're*.

Step 5: Understanding Basic Spelling Rules

Explained briefly here are three rules that may improve your spelling. While exceptions sometimes occur, these rules hold true most of the time.

1. **Changing y to i.**

   When a word ends in a consonant plus *y,* change *y* to *i* when you add an ending.

try + ed = tried	marry + es = marries
worry + es = worries	lazy + ness = laziness
lucky + ly = luckily	silly + est = silliest

2. **Final silent e.**

   Drop a final *e* before an ending that starts with a vowel (the vowels are *a, e, i, o,* and *u*).

hope + ing = hoping	sense + ible = sensible
fine + est = finest	hide + ing = hiding

   Keep the final *e* before an ending that starts with a consonant.

use + ful = useful	care + less = careless
life + like = lifelike	settle + ment = settlement

3. **Doubling a final consonant.**

   Double the final consonant of a word when all the following are true:

   a. The word is one syllable or is accented on the last syllable.

   b. The word ends in a single consonant preceded by a single vowel.

   c. The ending you are adding starts with a vowel.

sob + ing = sobbing	big + est = biggest
drop + ed = dropped	omit + ed = omitted
admit + ing = admitting	begin + ing = beginning

Combine the following words and endings by applying the three rules above.

1. carry   + ed   = _____   6. permit + ed   = _____

2. revise + ing = _____   7. glide   + ing = _____

3. study   + es   = _____   8. angry + ly   = _____

4. wrap   + ing = _____   9. rebel   + ing = _____

5. horrify + ed   = _____   10. grudge + es   = _____

Step 6: Understanding Plurals

Most words form their plurals by adding *-s* to the singular.

Singular	Plural
blanket	blankets
pencil	pencils
street	streets

Some words, however, form their plurals in special ways, as shown in the rules that follow.

1. **Words ending in *-s, -ss, -z, -x, -sh,* or *-ch* usually form the plural by adding *-es*.**

    kiss   kisses   inch   inches

    box   boxes   dish   dishes

2. **Words ending in a consonant plus *y* form the plural by changing *y* to *i* and adding *-es*.**

    party   parties   county   counties

    baby   babies   city   cities

3. **Some words ending in *f* change the *f* to *v* and add *-es* in the plural.**

    leaf   leaves   life   lives

    wife   wives   yourself   yourselves

4. **Some words ending in *o* form their plurals by adding *-es*.**

    potato   potatoes   mosquito   mosquitoes

    hero   heroes   tomato   tomatoes

5. Some words of foreign origin have irregular plurals. When in doubt, check your dictionary.

antenna	antennae	crisis	crises
criterion	criteria	medium	media

6. Some words form their plurals by changing letters within the word.

man	men	foot	feet
tooth	teeth	goose	geese

7. Combined words (words made up of two or more words) form their plurals by adding -*s* to the main word.

brother-in-law	brothers-in-law
passerby	passersby

Practice 2

Complete these sentences by filling in the plural of the word at the left.

bus   1. Nathan told his boss that the metro _____ were running late this morning.

patch   2. Jorge collects military insignia _____ from World War II.

therapy   3. The endocrinologist told Elisa about several new _____ for people with diabetes.

batch   4. I baked three _____ of chocolate chip cookies for my son's sixth-grade graduation ceremony.

reef   5. The scuba divers explored the coral _____ on the island.

avocado   6. Tyler mashed three ripe _____ for the guacamole.

fifty   7. Jarik stopped at the ATM to withdraw two _____ but later wondered if he should have taken out an additional twenty.

knife   8. The security guard uses a hand-held metal detector to find concealed _____ and other weapons.

daughter-in-law   9. Lynette wishes that at least one of her _____ will get pregnant so that she can become a grandmother.

thesis   10. I wrote several tentative _____ for my argument essay.

Step 7: Mastering a Basic Word List

Make sure you can spell all the words in the following list. They are some of the words used most often in English. Your instructor may assign twenty words for you to study at a time and give you a series of quizzes until you have mastered the words.

www.mhhe.com/langan

ability	balance	condition
absent	bargain	conversation 60
accident	beautiful	daily
across	because	danger
address	become	daughter
advertise	before	death
advice	begin	decide
after	being	deposit
again	believe	describe
against	between	different
all right	bottom 40	direction
almost	breathe	distance
a lot	building	doubt
although	business	dozen
always	careful	during
among	careless	each
angry	cereal	early
animal	certain	earth
another	change	education
answer 20	cheap	either
anxious	chief	English
apply	children	enough 80
approve	church	entrance
argue	cigarette	everything
around	clothing	examine
attempt	collect	exercise
attention	color	expect
awful	comfortable	family
awkward	company	flower

foreign		money		ready	
friend		month		really	
garden		morning		reason	
general		mountain		receive	
grocery		much		recognize	
guess		needle		remember	
happy		neglect		repeat	**180**
heard		newspaper		restaurant	
heavy		noise		ridiculous	
height		none	**140**	said	
himself		nothing		same	
holiday		number		sandwich	
house	**100**	ocean		send	
however		offer		sentence	
hundred		often		several	
hungry		omit		shoes	
important		only		should	
instead		operate		since	
intelligence		opportunity		sleep	
interest		original		smoke	
interfere		ought		something	
kitchen		pain		soul	
knowledge		paper		started	
labor		pencil		state	
language		people		straight	
laugh		perfect		street	
leave		period		strong	**200**
length		personal		student	
lesson		picture		studying	
letter		place	**160**	success	
listen		pocket		suffer	
loneliness		possible		surprise	
making	**120**	potato		teach	
marry		president		telephone	
match		pretty		theory	
matter		problem		thought	
measure		promise		thousand	
medicine		property		through	
middle		psychology		ticket	
might		public		tired	
million		question		today	
minute		quick		together	
mistake		raise		tomorrow	

tongue	upon	watch
tonight	usual	welcome
touch	value	window
travel **220**	vegetable	would
truly	view	writing
understand	visitor	written
unity	voice	year
until	warning	yesterday **240**

Can you find the spelling mistake in the sign pictured here?

Review Test

Use the three spelling rules to spell the following words.

1. date   + ing = _____
2. hurry + ed   = _____
3. drive + able = _____
4. try   + es   = _____
5. swim + ing = _____
6. guide + ed   = _____
7. happy + est = _____
8. bare + ly   = _____

Circle the correctly spelled plural in each pair.

9. gooses   geese
10. richs   riches
11. heros   heroes
12. wolfs   wolves
13. pantries   pantrys
14. lifes   lives

Circle the correctly spelled word (from the basic word list) in each pair.

15. dout   doubt
16. written   writen
17. a lot   alot
18. exercize   exercise
19. origenal   original
20. anser   answer

Spelling Improvement

Use the three spelling rules to spell the following words.

1. palate + able = _____

2. silly + est = _____

3. fate + ful = _____

4. drag + ing = _____

5. plan + er = _____

6. healthy + ly = _____

7. cause + ing = _____

8. prefer + ed = _____

Circle the correctly spelled plural in each pair.

9. chiefs   chievs   12. candys   candies

10. sandwichs   sandwiches   13. vetoes   vetos

11. yourselfs   yourselves   14. supplys   supplies

Circle the correctly spelled word (from the basic word list) in each pair.

15. compeny   company   18. opportunity   oppertunity

16. hieght   height   19. restaurant   restarant

17. loneliness   lonliness   20. importent   important

NAME: _____

DATE: _____

Spelling Improvement

Use the three spelling rules to spell the following words.

1. drip   + ed   = _____

2. merry + ment = _____

3. escape + ing   = _____

4. expel   + ed   = _____

5. finance + ing = _____

6. accuse + er   = _____

7. happy + ness = _____

8. spite   + ful = _____

Circle the correctly spelled plural in each pair.

9. indexs	indexes	12. babies	babys
10. echos	echoes	13. lifes	lives
11. gifts	giftes	14. scratchs	scratches

Circle the correctly spelled word (from the basic word list) in each pair.

15. temorrow	tomorrow	18. straght	straight
16. truely	truly	19. ready	readdy
17. vegetable	vegtable	20. condition	condishun

Omitted Words and Letters

30

Introductory Activity

See if you can find the six places in the passage below where letters or words have been dropped. Supply whatever is missing.

Two glass bottle of apple juice lie broken the supermarket aisle. Suddenly, a toddler who has gotten away from his parents appears at the head of the aisle. He spots the broken bottles and begins to run toward them. His chubby body lurches along like windup toy, and his arm move excitedly up and down. Luckily, alert shopper quickly reacts to the impending disaster and blocks the toddler's path. Then the shopper waits with crying, frustrated little boy until his parents show up.

Answers are on page 675.

Some people drop small connecting words such as *a, an, in, of,* or *the* when they write. They may also drop the *-s* endings of plural nouns. Be careful not to leave out words or letters when you write, as this may confuse and irritate your readers. They may not want to read what they regard as careless work.

Finding Omitted Words and Letters

Finding omitted words and letters, like finding many other sentence-skills mistakes, is a matter of careful proofreading. You must develop your ability to look carefully at a page to find places where mistakes may exist.

The exercises here will give you practice in finding omitted words and omitted -s endings on nouns. Another section of this book (pages 146–149) gives you practice in finding omitted -s endings on verbs.

Practice

1

Add the missing word (*a, an, the, of,* or *to*) as needed.

EXAMPLE

Some people regard television as tranquilizer that provides temporary relief from pain and anxiety modern life.

1. In the rest room, Jeff impatiently rubbed his hands under mechanical dryer, which blew out feeble puffs cool air.

2. On February 10, 1935, the *New York Times* reported that eight-foot alligator had been dragged out of city sewer by three teenage boys.

3. Dave dressed up as stuffed olive for Halloween by wearing green plastic garbage bag and a red knitted cap.

4. Mrs. Chan nearly fainted when she opened health insurance bill and saw enormous rate increase.

5. At 4 A.M., all-night supermarket where I work hosts assortment of strange shoppers.

6. With loud hiss, inflated beach ball suddenly shrank to size of orange.

7. The boiling milk bubbled over the sides the pot, leaving a gluey white film on stove top.

8. Susan turned the answer page of the crossword book, pretended herself that she hadn't, and turned back to her puzzle.

9. In order avoid stepping on the hot blacktop of parking lot, the barefoot boy tiptoed along the cooler white lines.

10. The messy roommates used hubcaps for ashtrays scribbled graffiti on their own bathroom walls.

The Omitted -s Ending

The plural form of regular nouns usually ends in *-s*. One common mistake that some people make with plurals is to omit this *-s* ending. People who drop the ending from plurals when speaking also tend to do it when writing. This tendency is especially noticeable when the meaning of the sentence shows that a word is plural.

> Ed and Mary pay eight hundred dollar a month for an apartment that has only two room.

The *-s* ending has been omitted from *dollars* and *rooms*.

The activities that follow will help you correct the habit of omitting the *-s* endings from plurals.

Add *-s* endings where needed.

Practice 2

EXAMPLE

Kyle beat me at several game$_\wedge^s$ of darts.

1. Can you really get fifteen shave from one of those razor blade?

2. With perfect timing, the runner's powerful leg glided smoothly over a dozen hurdle.

3. One of the strangest fad of the 1950s was the promotion of chocolate-covered ant by candy manufacturers.

4. Because pet owner abandoned them, small bands of monkey are now living in southern Florida.

5. The photographer locked themselves in steel cages in order to film great white shark in their underwater environment.

6. The breeze blew dandelion spore and dry brown leave through the air.

7. Jim made twelve circular cage from chicken wire and set them around his growing tomato plant.

8. The special this week is three pound of grape for eighty-nine cent.

9. The rope sole on my summer shoe have begun to disintegrate.

10. The skinny man ordered two double cheeseburger and three vanilla shake.

Practice

3

Write sentences that use plural forms of the following pairs of words.

EXAMPLE

file, folder *I save my computer files in folders on the desktop.*

1. gambler, casino _____

   _____

2. recycling bin, bottle _____

   _____

3. diver, shark _____

   _____

4. sports fan, game _____

   _____

5. cherry, grape _____

   _____

TIP People who drop the *-s* ending on nouns also tend to omit endings on verbs. Pages 146–149 will help you correct the habit of dropping endings on verbs.

Review Test   1

In each of the following sentences, two small connecting words are needed. Write them in the spaces provided, and write a caret (ʌ) at each place in the sentence where a connecting word should appear.

_____   1. Suffering from horrible head cold, Susan felt as though she
_____   were trying breathe under water.

_____   2. Because he forgot the key his padlock, Al asked gym attendant
_____   to saw the lock off his locker.

_____   3. The store made mistake when it sent me a letter saying that I
_____   hadn't paid any my bills for six months.

_____ 4. The children laughed with delight when small dog jumped on
_____   circus clown's back.

_____ 5. Dr. Marini recommends that my grandfather drink one glass wine
_____   every day to stimulate appetite and improve his circulation.

Review Test 2

Correctly write the two words missing -s endings for each sentence.

_____ 1. The whites of Sam's eyes were red from broken blood vessel,
_____   and his forehead was a mass of purple bruise.

_____ 2. Ray has held five different job in four different cities in the
_____   past two year.

_____ 3. I've been to several specialist, but I still don't know what's
_____   causing these terrible headache.

_____ 4. Lian watched with dread as a bulldozer began knocking down
_____   tree and shrub in the patch of woods next door.

_____ 5. Vance was driving eighty mile an hour when two police car
_____   stopped him.

NAME: _____

DATE: _____

MASTERY TEST 1 Omitted Words and Letters

PART 1

In the spaces provided, write in the two short connecting words needed in each sentence. Use carets (∧) within the sentences to show where these words belong.

_____ 1. Returning her car, Sarah found she'd left the keys the ignition.

_____

_____ 2. Tony has superstitious habit of dribbling the ball exactly six times before

_____   he shoots free throw.

_____ 3. Carefully, Joanne pasted small strips correction tape over each typing

_____   mistake on page.

_____ 4. I know easy way to get an A in that course—just agree with everything

_____   instructor says.

_____ 5. Andy dreaded tests he would have to undergo even more than operation

_____   itself.

PART 2

Correctly write the two words missing -s endings for each sentence.

_____ 6. Marcy ate an entire jar of olive and left a pile of pit on the coffee table.

_____

_____ 7. Shards of green glass glittered on the pavement where those teenager had

_____   smashed a whole six-pack of empty beer bottle.

_____ 8. Our supermarket's deli section sells tray of party cold cut.

_____

_____ 9. Hector's tight-fitting new shoes have worn hole in all his sock.

_____

_____ 10. Those heavy rainstorm have flattened all my tomato plant.

_____

Omitted Words and Letters   MASTERY TEST 2

PART 1

In the spaces provided, write in the two short connecting words needed in each sentence. Use carets (∧) within the sentences to show where these words belong.

_____

_____   1. This weekend, we're going replace all the shingles that have fallen off roof.

_____

_____   2. My favorite snacks this restaurant are the crispy baked-potato skins the

marinated mushrooms.

_____   3. The eyes of woman on billboard seemed to follow me as I drove by.

_____

_____   4. When I sat down, three quarters fell out of pants pocket and rolled

under sofa.

_____   5. My pet turtles live in large, galvanized tin tub in garage.

_____

PART 2

Correctly write the two words missing -s endings for each sentence.

_____   6. After I had read several horror book, I began listening for weird sound.

_____

_____   7. I love to eat exotic dessert, but my husband likes only vanilla ice cream

_____   cone.

_____   8. All the neighbor comment on my mother's garden of roses and daffodil.

_____

_____   9. I slowed the car when I noticed a pair of kitchen chair that had been set

_____   out along with three garbage can.

_____   10. The old man sold me two bag of cookie from a homemade stand in front

of his house.

Commonly Confused Words

31

Introductory Activity

This chapter will introduce you to words that people often confuse in their writing. Circle the five words that are misspelled in the following passage. Then write their correct spellings in the spaces provided.

If your a resident of a temperate climate, you may suffer from feelings of depression in the winter and early spring. Scientists are now studying people who's moods seem to worsen in winter, and there findings show that the amount of daylight a person receives is an important factor in "seasonal depression." When a person gets to little sunlight, his or her mood darkens. Its fairly easy to treat severe cases of seasonal depression; the cure involves spending a few hours a day in front of full-spectrum fluorescent lights that contain all the components of natural light.

1. _____
2. _____
3. _____
4. _____
5. _____

Answers are on page 676.

Homonyms

The commonly confused words shown below are known as *homonyms;* they have the same sounds but different meanings and spellings. Complete the activities for each set of words, and check off and study the words that give you trouble.

Common Homonyms

all ready	knew	principal	to
already	new	principle	too
brake	know	right	two
break	no	write	wear
coarse	pair	than	where
course	pear	then	weather
hear	passed	their	whether
here	past	there	whose
hole	peace	they're	who's
whole	piece	threw	your
its	plain	through	you're
it's	plane		

all ready	completely prepared
already	previously, before

We were *all ready* to go, for we had eaten and packed *already* that morning.

Fill in the blanks: Eliza has _____ phoned them twice to ask if they'll be _____ to go by nine o'clock.

Write sentences using *all ready* and *already.*

_____

_____

brake	stop
break	come apart; an interruption

Dot slams the *brake* pedal so hard that I'm afraid I'll *break* my neck in her car.

Fill in the blanks: I hit the _____ pedal so hard that my car spun around on the slick highway; luckily, there was a _____ in the traffic at that point.

Write sentences using *brake* and *break*.

_____

_____

coarse	rough
course	part of a meal; a school subject; direction; certainly (with *of*)

During the *course* of my career as a waitress, I've dealt with some very *coarse* customers.

Fill in the blanks: As her final project in the weaving _____, Maria made a tablecloth out of _____ fibers in shades of blue.

Write sentences using *coarse* and *course*.

_____

_____

hear	perceive with the ear
here	in this place

If I *hear* another insulting ethnic joke *here,* I'll leave.

Fill in the blanks: Do you want to _____ about what happened to the last visitors who stayed _____ at the count's castle?

Write sentences using *hear* and *here.*

_____

_____

hole	an empty spot
whole	entire

If there is a *hole* in the tailpipe, I'm afraid we will have to replace the *whole* exhaust assembly.

Fill in the blanks: He walked the _____ way, despite the _____ in the sole of his right shoe.

Write sentences using *hole* and *whole.*

_____

_____

its	belonging to it
it's	shortened form for *it is* or *it has*

The kitchen floor has lost *its* shine because *it's* been used as a roller skating rink by the children.

Fill in the blanks: _____ foolish to wear your flimsy jacket with _____ thin hood in this downpour.

Write sentences using *its* and *it's*.

_____

_____

knew	past tense of *know*
new	not old

We *knew* that the *new* television comedy would be canceled quickly.

Fill in the blanks: Georgia _____ that a _____ plasma flat screen would tempt the children to spend more hours parked in front of the TV.

Write sentences using *knew* and *new*.

_____

_____

know	to understand
no	a negative

I never *know* who might drop in even though *no* one is expected.

Fill in the blanks: Now that we _____ how the movie ends—thanks to you—there will be _____ pleasure in watching it.

Write sentences using *know* and *no*.

_____

_____

pair	**a set of two**
pear	**a fruit**

The dessert consisted of a *pair* of thin biscuits topped with vanilla ice cream and poached *pear* halves.

Fill in the blanks: The _____ of infant overalls has a _____ embroidered on the bib.

Write sentences using *pair* and *pear.*

_____

_____

passed	**went by; succeeded in; handed to**
past	**a time before the present;**
	by, as in "I drove past the house"

After Emma *passed* the driver's test, she drove *past* all her friends' houses and honked the horn.

Fill in the blanks: As his mother _____ around her traditional Christmas cookies, Terry remembered all the times in the _____ when he had left some of those very cookies on a plate for Santa Claus.

Write sentences using *passed* and *past.*

_____

_____

peace	calm
piece	**a part**

The *peace* of the little town was shattered when a *piece* of a human body was found in the town dump.

Fill in the blanks: I won't give you any _____ unless you share that _____ of coconut cake with me.

Write sentences using *peace* and *piece.*

_____

_____

plain	**simple**
plane	**aircraft**

The *plain* box contained a very expensive model *plane* kit.

Fill in the blanks: The black-and-silver _____ on the runway looked exotic next to the _____ ones surrounding it.

Write sentences using *plain* and *plane.*

_____

_____

| principal | main; a person in charge of a school; amount of money borrowed |
| principle | a law or standard |

My *principal* goal in child rearing is to give my daughter strong *principles* to live by.

Fill in the blanks: The _____ sport at our high school, basketball, was coached by a man whose guiding _____ was team play.

Write sentences using *principal* and *principle.*

_____

_____

> **TIP** It might help to remember that the *le* in *principle* is also in *rule*—the meaning of *principle.*

| right | correct; opposite of *left;* privilege |
| write | what you do in English |

It is my *right* to refuse to *write* my name on your petition.

Fill in the blanks: As I rested my fractured _____ arm on his desk, I asked the doctor to _____ out a prescription for a painkiller.

Write sentences using *right* and *write.*

_____

_____

than	used in comparisons
then	at that time

I glared angrily at my boss, and *then* I told him our problems were more serious *than* he suspected.

Fill in the blanks: Frankenstein's monster played peacefully with the little girl;

_____ he was chased by the villagers, who were more hysterical

_____ stampeding turkeys.

Write sentences using *than* and *then*.

_____

_____

TIP It might help to remember that *then* is a time signal.

---

their	belonging to them
there	at that place; a neutral word used with verbs like *is, are, was, were, have,* and *had*
they're	shortened form of *they are*

The tenants *there* are complaining because *they're* being cheated by *their* landlords.

Fill in the blanks: _____ has been an increase in burglaries in

_____ neighborhood, so _____ planning to install

an alarm.

Write sentences using *their, there,* and *they're.*

_____

_____

_____

| threw | past tense of *throw* |
| through | from one side to the other; finished |

When a character in a movie *threw* a cat *through* the window, I had to close my eyes.

Fill in the blanks: As Darryl picked _____ the clothes in the dryer,

he _____ the still-damp towels aside.

Write sentences using *threw* and *through*.

_____

_____

to	a verb part, as in *to smile;* toward, as in "I'm going to heaven."
too	overly, as in "The pizza was too hot"; also, as in "The coffee was hot, too."
two	the number 2

Lola drove *to* the store *to* get some ginger ale. (The first *to* means *toward;* the second *to* is a verb part that goes with *get.*)

The jacket is *too* tight; the pants are tight, *too.* (The first *too* means *overly;* the second *too* means *also.*)

The *two* basketball players leaped for the jump ball. (2)

Fill in the blanks: I don't know how _____ such different people

were attracted _____ each other and made a happy marriage,

_____.

Write sentences using *to, too,* and *two.*

_____

_____

_____

| wear | to have on |
| where | in what place |

I work at a nuclear reactor, *where* one must *wear* a radiation-detection badge at all times.

Fill in the blanks: At the restaurant _____ I work, the waiters _____ cowboy hats and Western snap-front shirts.

Write sentences using *wear* and *where*.

_____

_____

| weather | atmospheric conditions |
| whether | if it happens that; in case; if |

Because of the threatening *weather,* it's not certain *whether* the game will be played.

Fill in the blanks: The _____ vane was once a valuable agricultural tool, indicating _____ the wind was coming from the north, south, east, or west.

Write sentences using *weather* and *whether.*

_____

_____

whose	belonging to whom
who's	shortened form for *who is* and *who has*

The man *who's* the author of the latest diet book is a man *whose* ability to cash in on the latest craze is well known.

Fill in the blanks: The substitute teacher, _____ lack of experience was obvious, asked, "_____ the person who threw that spitball?"

Write sentences using *whose* and *who's*.

_____

_____

your	belonging to you
you're	shortened form of *you are*

Since *your* family has a history of heart disease, *you're* the kind of person who should take extra health precautions.

Fill in the blanks: I may not like _____ opinion, but _____ certainly entitled to express it in this class.

Write sentences using *your* and *you're*.

_____

_____

Other Words Frequently Confused

Following is a list of other words that people frequently confuse. Complete the activities for each set of words, and check off and study the ones that give you trouble.

Commonly Confused Words

a	among	desert	learn
an	between	dessert	teach
accept	beside	does	loose
except	besides	dose	lose
advice	can	fewer	quiet
advise	may	less	quite
affect	clothes	former	though
effect	cloths	latter	thought

> **a**   Both *a* and *an* are used before other words to mean,
> **an**   approximately, *one.*

Generally you should use *an* before words starting with a vowel (*a, e, i, o, u*):

an absence   an exhibit   an idol   an offer   an upgrade

Generally you should use *a* before words starting with a consonant (all other letters):

a pen   a ride   a digital clock   a movie   a neighbor

Fill in the blanks: In _____ instant, he realized that _____ diamond-patterned snake was slithering over his shoe.

Write sentences using *a* and *an.*

_____

_____

accept	receive; agree to
except	exclude; but

If I *accept* your advice, I'll lose all my friends *except* you.

Fill in the blanks: The crowd couldn't _____ the judges' decision; _____ for some minor mistakes, Jones had clearly won the fight.

Write sentences using *accept* and *except.*

_____

_____

advice	noun meaning *an opinion*
advise	verb meaning *to counsel, to give advice*

Jake never listened to his parents' *advice,* and he ended up listening to a cop *advise* him of his rights.

Fill in the blanks: I asked a plumber to _____ me, since the _____ in the do-it-yourself book had been disastrous.

Write sentences using *advice* and *advise.*

_____

_____

> affect   verb meaning *to influence*
> effect   verb meaning *to bring about something;*
> noun meaning *result*

My sister Nicole cries for *effect,* but my parents caught on and her act no longer *affects* them.

Fill in the blanks: A dangerous flooding _____ is created when the full moon _____ s the tides in the spring.

Write sentences using *affect* and *effect.*

_____

_____

> among   implies three or more
> between   implies only two

We selfishly divided the box of candy *between* the two of us rather than *among* all the members of the family.

Fill in the blanks: _____ the heads of lettuce in the bin was one with a large insect nestled _____ the wrapper and the outer leaf.

Write sentences using *among* and *between.*

_____

_____

| beside | along the side of |
| besides | in addition to |

Fred sat *beside* Teresa. *Besides* them, there were ten other people at the Tupperware party.

Fill in the blanks: _____ the broken leg, he suffered a deep cut _____ his mouth.

Write sentences using *beside* and *besides*.

_____

_____

| can | refers to the ability to do something |
| may | refers to permission or possibility |

If you *can* work overtime on Saturday, you *may* take Monday off.

Fill in the blanks: Although that mole _____ be removed, it _____ be better to leave it alone.

Write sentences using *can* and *may*.

_____

_____

clothes	articles of dress
cloths	pieces of fabric

I tore up some old *clothes* to use as polishing *cloths*.

Fill in the blanks: Maxine used inexpensive dust _____ to make

_____ for her daughter's doll.

Write sentences using *clothes* and *cloths*.

_____

_____

desert	noun meaning *a stretch of dry land;* verb meaning *to abandon one's post or duty*
dessert	noun meaning *last part of a meal*

Don't *desert* us now; order a sinful *dessert* along with us.

Fill in the blanks: Guests began to _____ the banquet room after

the strawberry shortcake _____ had been cleared away.

Write sentences using *desert* and *dessert*.

_____

_____

does	form of the verb *do*
dose	an amount of medicine

Elena *does* not realize that a *dose* of brandy is not the best medicine for the flu.

Fill in the blanks: If this _____ of cough syrup _____ its work, I'll be able to give my speech.

Write sentences using *does* and *dose*.

_____

_____

fewer	used with things that can be counted
less	refers to amount, value, or degree

I missed *fewer* classes than Rafael, but I wrote *less* effectively than he did.

Fill in the blanks: Larry took _____ chances after the accident; he was _____ sure of his driving ability.

Write sentences using *fewer* and *less.*

_____

_____

> | former | refers to the first of two items named |
> |--------|--|
> | latter | refers to the second of two items named |

I turned down both the service station job and the shipping clerk job; the *former* involved irregular hours and the *latter* offered very low pay.

Fill in the blanks: She eats lots of raisins and strawberries; the _____ contain iron and the _____ are rich in vitamin C.

Write sentences using *former* and *latter.*

_____

_____

> **TIP** Be sure to distinguish *latter* from *later* (meaning *after some time*).

> | learn | to gain knowledge |
> |-------|-------------------|
> | teach | to give knowledge |

After Keisha *learns* the new dance, she is going to *teach* it to me.

Fill in the blanks: If Beth can _____ sign language, we can _____ her parents how to communicate with her.

Write sentences using *learn* and *teach.*

_____

_____

| loose | not fastened; not tight-fitting |
| lose | misplace; fail to win |

I am afraid I'll *lose* my ring: it's too *loose* on my finger.

Fill in the blanks: When he discovered that his pet turtles had gotten _____ he worried that he might _____ some of them.

Write sentences using *loose* and *lose.*

_____

_____

| quiet | peaceful |
| quite | entirely; really; rather |

After a busy day, the children were still not *quiet,* and their parents were *quite* tired.

Fill in the blanks: Chuck couldn't keep _____ about the scholarship his daughter had won; it was really _____ an honor.

Write sentences using *quiet* and *quite.*

_____

_____

| though | despite the fact that |
| thought | past tense of *think* |

Though I enjoyed the dance, I *thought* the cover charge of $10 was too high.

Fill in the blanks: _____ everyone claimed the silvery object was

an airplane, I _____ it was a UFO.

Write sentences using *though* and *thought*.

_____

_____

Incorrect Word Forms

Following is a list of incorrect word forms that people sometimes use in their writing. Complete the activities for each word, and check off and study the words that give you trouble.

Incorrect Word Forms

being that	could of	would of
can't hardly	must of	irregardless
couldn't hardly	should of	

| being that | Incorrect! Use *because* or *since*. |

I'm going to bed now ~~being that~~ *because* I must get up early tomorrow.

Correct the following sentences.

1. Being that the boss heard my remark, I doubt if I'll get the promotion.

2. I'll have more cake, being that my diet is officially over.

3. Peter knows a lot about cars, being that his dad is a mechanic.

| can't hardly | **Incorrect! Use *can hardly* or *could hardly*.** |
| couldn't hardly | |

Small store owners ~~can't~~ ^can^ hardly afford to offer large discounts.

Correct the following sentences.

1. I couldn't hardly enjoy myself at the theater because my brother gave me a play-by-play account of the entire movie, which he had seen three times.

2. I can't hardly believe that I spent over fifty dollars on gasoline to fill up my SUV.

3. By one o'clock in the afternoon, everyone can't hardly keep from falling asleep in class.

could of	
must of	**Incorrect! Use *could have, must have,***
should of	***should have, would have.***
would of	

I should ~~of~~ ^have^ applied for a loan when my credit was good.

Correct the following sentences.

1. Thelma must of painted the walls by herself.

2. You should of left the tip on the table.

3. I would of been glad to help if you had asked politely.

4. No one could of predicted that accident.

> irregardless   **Incorrect! Use *regardless*.**

Regardless
~~Irregardless~~ of what anyone says, he will not change his mind.

Correct the following sentences.

1. Irregardless of what anybody else does, I'm wearing jeans to the meeting.

2. Irregardless of the weather, the parade will go on as scheduled.

3. Irregardless of what my parents say, I will continue to see Elena.

Review Test   1

These sentences check your understanding of *its, it's; there, their, they're; to, too, two;* and *your, you're.* Underline the correct word in the parentheses. Rather than guess, look back at the explanations of the words when necessary.

1. As I walked (to, too, two) the car, I stepped in the freshly laid cement that (to, too, two) workers had just smoothed over.

2. (Its, It's) safe (to, too, two) park (your, you're) car over (there, their, they're).

3. "(Your, You're) wearing (your, you're) shoes on the wrong feet," Carla whispered to her little sister.

4. (There, Their, They're) are more secrets about (there, their, they're) past than (there, their, they're) willing to share.

5. The (to, too, two) of us plan to go to (your, you're) party, (to, too, two).

6. (Its, It's) been a long time since (your, you're) car has had (its, it's) transmission checked.

7. (To, Too, Two) get into the dance, (your, you're) friend will have to pay (to, too, two).

8. (Its, It's) a shame that (your, you're) being laid off from your job (there, their, they're).

9. (Its, It's) rumored that the team has lost (its, it's) best pitcher for the rest of the season.

10. (There, Their, They're) is a mistake on (there, their, they're) check, so they are speaking (to, too, two) the manager.

Review Test 2

The sentences that follow check your understanding of a variety of commonly confused words. Underline the correct word in the parentheses. Rather than guess, look back at the explanations of the words when necessary.

1. My sister is better at math (than, then) I am, but I (right, write) more easily.

2. I was (all ready, already) (to, too, two) sign up for (your, you're) (coarse, course) when I discovered it had (all ready, already) closed.

3. He is the kind of person who (accepts, excepts) any (advice, advise) he is given, even if (its, it's) bad.

4. I (know, no) you want to (hear, here) the (hole, whole) story.

5. (There, Their, They're) is no (plain, plane) paper in the house, only a (pair, pear) of lined pads.

6. Our team got a real (brake, break) when Pete's pop fly fell (among, between) (to, too, two) infielders for a base hit.

7. I (can't hardly, can hardly) (hear, here) the instructor in that (coarse, course) without making (a, an) effort.

8. If (your, you're) going to have (desert, dessert), pick something with (fewer, less) calories than chocolate cheesecake.

9. Looking (threw, through) his front window, Felipe could see a (pair, pear) of squirrels getting (there, their, they're) food ready for the cold (weather, whether) to come.

10. When I (learn, teach) you to drive a stick-shift, we'll go (to, too, two) a (quiet, quite) country road where (there, their, they're) won't be much traffic.

Review Test 3

On separate paper, write short sentences using the ten words shown below.

there	then	you're	affect	who's
past	advise	too (meaning *also*)	its	break

NAME: _____

DATE: _____

MASTERY TEST 1   Commonly Confused Words

For each sentence, choose the correct words and write them in the spaces provided.

_____
_____

1. When (you're, your) looking for the (right, write) career, it's helpful to talk to other people about their jobs.

_____
_____

2. Carol keeps a special (pair, pear) of (lose, loose) trousers with tough patches on the knees to wear while gardening.

_____
_____

3. (There, Their, They're) the (right, write) size, but these screws still don't fit.

_____
_____

4. "It's a matter of (principal, principle)," the editor said. "I won't print anything unless it's the (hole, whole) truth."

_____
_____

5. By twenty (passed, past) eight o'clock, I was (all ready, already) for my ten o'clock interview.

_____
_____

6. We went (through, threw) the entrance to the amusement park's haunted house and were met by (to, too, two) scary-looking creatures.

_____
_____

7. We all (past, passed) the midterm exam, (accept, except) for the student who had shown up for only three classes.

_____
_____

8. I (can hardly, can't hardly) see (through, threw) my windshield, since it's covered with squashed bugs and grit.

_____
_____

9. (Weather, Whether) or not Duane (loses, looses) his license depends on the outcome of the court hearing.

_____
_____

10. The tragic (affect, effect) of one car's faulty (brakes, breaks) was a six-car pileup.

Commonly Confused Words

For each sentence, choose the correct words and write them in the spaces provided.

_____   1. We were expected to (know, no) the (principals, principles) of
_____   photosynthesis for the biology test.

_____   2. (You're, Your) the first professor to ask me to (right, write) a sixty-page
_____   term paper.

_____   3. I took a (coarse, course) in speed-reading and can now read (to, too, two)
_____   books in the time it once took to read one.

_____   4. "It's (all ready, already) eight o'clock, and nobody's (hear, here) yet," Fran
_____   complained.

_____   5. I ate so much that I was (quiet, quite) full before (desert, dessert)
_____   arrived.

_____   6. (Among, Between) the three of us, we (though, thought) we could scrape up
_____   enough money for a large pizza.

_____   7. You (should of, should have) saved the last (peace, piece) of chicken
_____   for me.

_____   8. At the back of my (cloths, clothes) closet, I discovered a (pair, pear) of old,
_____   mildewed sneakers.

_____   9. (Whose, Who's) willing to sit (beside, besides) me in the back seat?

_____   10. The (plain, plane) truth is that (fewer, less) Americans feel financially
_____   secure these days.

NAME: _____

DATE: _____

MASTERY TEST 3 | Commonly Confused Words

Cross out the two mistakes in usage in each sentence. Then write the correct words in the spaces provided.

_____   1. Dose anyone know who's glasses these are?

_____

_____   2. Your a lot taller then I was when I was your age.

_____

_____   3. Monica went too the mall for one item but came home with a armful of packages.

_____

_____   4. I told my brother that he should except my advise on all matters.

_____

_____   5. With his fingers, Gene attempted to brake off a piece of the crusty, course bread.

_____

_____   6. In August 1945, a lone plain passed over the city of Hiroshima. Than a living hell began for the city's inhabitants.

_____

_____   7. Marilyn, a housewife whose returning to college, has been excepted in the medical technicians' program.

_____

_____   8. We divided the huge hero sandwich, with it's layers of salami and cheese, between the three of us.

_____

_____   9. Irregardless of the rumors, nobody could of guessed that the business would close.

_____

_____   10. Their go the obnoxious fans who through bottles onto the field.

_____

Commonly Confused Words MASTERY TEST 4

Cross out the two mistakes in usage in each sentence. Then write the correct words in the spaces provided.

_____   1. As soon as my jeans get to tight, I know its time to cut out junk food.

_____

_____   2. I must of read the assignment five times, but I couldn't hardly make any sense out of it.

_____

_____   3. After we drove passed the same diner for the third time, we new we were lost.

_____

_____   4. I put my paycheck under my pillow, being that I was afraid I was going to loose it.

_____

_____   5. As the wind blew threw the rafters, we wondered weather or not the old boathouse would survive the storm.

_____

_____   6. I couldn't decide on which of the too costumes to where to the party.

_____

_____   7. Knew desserts are being created all over the world by the careless destruction of trees.

_____

_____   8. The plane brown pears in the fruit bowl are sweeter then they look.

_____

_____   9. Although I could here it's pitiful cries, I couldn't reach the animal caught under the caved-in shed.

_____

_____   10. Before I took this writing coarse, I would brake into a cold sweat every time I picked up a pen.

_____

Effective Word Choice

32

Introductory Activity

Place a check mark beside the sentence in each pair that makes more effective and appropriate use of words.

1. _____ After a bummer of a movie, we pigged out on a pizza.

   _____ After a disappointing movie, we devoured a pizza.

2. _____ Feeling blue about the death of his best buddy, Tennyson wrote the tearjerker "In Memoriam."

   _____ Mourning the death of his best friend, Tennyson wrote the moving poem "In Memoriam."

3. _____ The personality adjustment inventories will be administered on Wednesday in the Student Center.

   _____ Psychological tests will be given on Wednesday in the Student Center.

4. _____ The referee in the game, in my personal opinion, made the right decision in the situation.

   _____ I think the referee made the right decision.

Now see if you can circle the correct number in each case:

Pair (1, 2, 3, 4) contains a sentence with slang; pair (1, 2, 3, 4) contains a sentence with a cliché; pair (1, 2, 3, 4) contains a sentence with pretentious words; and pair (1, 2, 3, 4) contains a wordy sentence.

Answers are on page 677.

Choose your words carefully when you write. Always take the time to think about your word choices, rather than simply using the first word that comes to mind. You want to develop the habit of selecting words that are appropriate and exact for your purposes. One way you can show sensitivity to language is by avoiding slang, clichés, pretentious words, and wordiness.

Slang

We often use slang expressions when we talk because they are so vivid and colorful. However, slang is usually out of place in formal writing. Here are some examples of slang expressions:

www.mhhe.com/langan

> Last night's party was a *real train wreck.*
>
> I don't want to *lay a guilt trip* on you.
>
> My boss *dissed* me last night; he said I was a bad employee.
>
> Dad *flipped out* when he learned that Jan had *totaled* the car.
>
> Someone *ripped off* Jay's new running shoes from his locker.
>
> After the game, we *stuffed our faces* at the diner.
>
> I finally told my parents to *get off my case.*
>
> The movie really *grossed me out.*

Slang expressions have a number of drawbacks. They go out of date quickly, they become tiresome if used excessively in writing, and they may communicate clearly to some readers but not to others. Also, the use of slang can be an evasion of the specific details that are often needed to make one's meaning clear in writing. For example, in "Last night's party was a real train wreck," the writer has not provided the specific details about the party necessary for us to understand the statement clearly. Was it the setting, the food and drink (or lack of them), the guests, the music, or the hosts that made the party such a dreadful experience? In general, you should avoid slang in your writing. If you are in doubt about whether an expression is slang, it may help to check a recently published hardbound dictionary.

Rewrite the following sentences, replacing the italicized slang words with more formal ones.

1

EXAMPLE

I was *so bummed* when my teacher *got on my case.*
I was discouraged when my teacher scolded me.

1. When I confronted my ex-boyfriend about *two-timing* me, he simply shrugged and said, "*My bad.*"

_____

_____

2. My friend thinks that Chantel is *phat,* but I think she's too *emo.*

_____

_____

3. Rayna is on her cell phone *24-7,* but *it's all good.*

_____

_____

4. Joe wanted to *blow* the family dinner so that he could *hook up* with his friends.

_____

_____

5. They were *psyched* about the party, but they knew they'd have to *bail* early.

_____

_____

Clichés

Clichés are expressions that have been worn out through constant use. Some typical clichés are listed on the following page.

Common Clichés

all work and no play	sad but true
at a loss for words	saw the light
better late than never	short and sweet
drop in the bucket	sigh of relief
easier said than done	singing the blues
had a hard time of it	taking a big chance
in the nick of time	time and time again
in this day and age	too close for comfort
it dawned on me	too little, too late
it goes without saying	took a turn for the worse
last but not least	under the weather
make ends meet	where he (*or* she) is coming from
needless to say	word to the wise
on top of the world	work like a dog

Clichés are common in speech but make your writing seem tired and stale. Also, they are often an evasion of the specific details that you must work to provide in your writing. You should, then, avoid clichés and try to express your meaning in fresh, original ways.

Underline the cliché in each of the following sentences. Then substitute specific, fresh words for the trite expression.

Practice

2

EXAMPLE

My parents supported me through some <u>trying times</u>.

rough years
_____

1. Salespeople who are rude make my blood boil.

_____

2. Doug has been down in the dumps ever since his girlfriend broke up with him.

_____

3. That new secretary is one in a million.

_____

4. We decided to hire a hall and roll out the red carpet in honor of our parents' silver wedding anniversary.

    _____

5. The minute classes let out for the summer, I feel free as a bird.

    _____

Practice

3

Write a short paragraph describing the kind of day you had. Try to put as many clichés as possible into your writing. For example, "I had a long hard day. I had a lot to get done, and I kept my nose to the grindstone." By making yourself aware of clichés in this way, you should lessen the chance that they will appear in your writing.

Pretentious Words

Some people feel they can improve their writing by using fancy, elevated words rather than more simple, natural words. They use artificial and stilted language that more often obscures their meaning than communicates it clearly. Here are some unnatural-sounding sentences:

The football combatants left the gridiron.

His instructional technique is a very positive one.

At the counter, we inquired about the arrival time of the aircraft.

I observed the perpetrator of the robbery depart from the retail establishment.

The same thoughts can be expressed more clearly and effectively by using plain, natural language, as below:

The football players left the field.

He is a good instructor.

At the counter, we asked when the plane would arrive.

I saw the robber leave the store.

Following is a list of some other inflated words and the simple words that could replace them.

Inflated Words	Simpler Words
component	part
delineate	describe
facilitate	help
finalize	finish
initiate	begin
manifested	shown
subsequent to	after
to endeavor	to try
transmit	send

Cross out the two pretentious words in each sentence. Then substitute clear, simple language for the pretentious words.

Practice

4

EXAMPLE

Sally was ~~terminated~~ from her ~~employment~~.

Sally was fired from her job.

1. I do not comprehend that individual's behavior.

   _____

2. He eradicated all the imperfections in his notes.

   _____

3. She contemplated his utterance.

   _____

4. The police officer halted the vehicle.

   _____

5. Inez told the counselor about her vocational aspirations.

   _____

Wordiness

Wordiness—using more words than necessary to express a meaning—is often a sign of lazy or careless writing. Your readers may resent the extra time and energy they must spend when you have not done the work needed to make your writing direct and concise.

Here is a list of some wordy expressions that could be reduced to single words.

Wordy Form	Short Form
a large number of	many
a period of a week	a week
arrive at an agreement	agree
at an earlier point in time	before
at the present time	now
big in size	big
due to the fact that	because
during the time that	while
five in number	five
for the reason that	because
good benefit	benefit
in every instance	always
in my opinion	I think
in the event that	if
in the near future	soon
in this day and age	today
is able to	can
large in size	large
plan ahead for the future	plan
postponed until later	postponed
red in color	red
return back	return

Here are examples of wordy sentences:

At this point in time in our country, the amount of violence seems to be increasing every day.

I called to the children repeatedly to get their attention, but my shouts did not get any response from them.

Omitting needless words improves these sentences:

Violence is increasing in our country.

I called to the children repeatedly, but they didn't respond.

Rewrite the following sentences, omitting needless words.

EXAMPLE

Starting as of the month of June, I will be working at the store on a full-time basis.

As of June, I will be working at the store full-time.

1. In light of the fact that I am a vegetarian, I don't eat meat.

   _____

2. On Tuesday of last week, I started going to college classes on a full-time basis.

   _____

3. On account of the fact that all my money is gone and I am broke, I can't go to the movies.

   _____

4. I repeated over and over again that I refused to go under any circumstances, no matter what.

   _____

5. Regardless of what I say, regardless of what I do, my father is annoyed by my words and behavior.

   _____

Review Test   1

Certain words are italicized in the following sentences. In the space provided, identify whether the words are slang (*S*), clichés (*C*), or pretentious words (*PW*). Then replace them with more effective words.

_____   1. The sight of the car crash *sent chills down my spine.*

   _____

_____   2. That garbage *receptacle is at maximum capacity.*

   _____

_____   3. He thinks his apartment is *all that,* but it's in a *sketchy* part of town.

   _____

———— 4. The town *cheapskate* finally *kicked the bucket* and left all his money to charity.

_____

———— 5. I left work ten minutes early and made it home *in no time flat*.

_____

———— 6. Phyllis *lamented* her grandmother's *demise*.

_____

———— 7. The pitcher *hurled* the *sphere* toward the batter.

_____

———— 8. When she got her first paycheck, Kwan was *sitting on top of the world*.

_____

———— 9. After studying for three hours, we *packed it in* and *cruised over* to the pizza parlor.

_____

———— 10. Last year's popular television star turned out to be *a flash in the pan*.

_____

Review Test 2

Rewrite the following sentences, omitting needless words.

1. Before I woke up this morning, while I was still asleep, I had a dream about an airline disaster in which a plane crashed.

_____

_____

2. Tamika lifted up the empty suitcase, which had nothing in it, and tossed it onto the unmade bed covered with messy sheets and blankets.

_____

_____

3. While he glared at me with an unfriendly face, I just sat there silently, not saying a word.

    _____

    _____

4. Whereas some people feel that athletes are worth their salaries, I feel that the value of professional sports players in this country is vastly overrated moneywise.

    _____

    _____

5. I don't like reading the historical type of novel because this kind of book is much too long and, in addition, tends to be boring and uninteresting.

    _____

    _____

NAME: _____

DATE: _____

MASTERY TEST 1   Effective Word Choice

Certain words are italicized in the following sentences. In the spaces at the left, identify whether these words are slang (S), clichés (C), or pretentious words (PW). Then, in the spaces, below, replace the words with more effective diction.

_____   1. After she received an A, Barbara was *walking on air* for the rest of the day.

_____

_____   2. A *wheeler-dealer* salesman sold Jim a *lemon*.

_____   _____

_____   3. Robert's *rain garment was saturated.*

_____   _____

_____   4. He is inhumane to *members of the animal kingdom.*

_____

_____   5. I have a lot of studying to do, but *my brain is out to lunch.*

_____

_____   6. After moving the furniture, James lay down on the couch and *went out like a light.*

_____

_____   7. My parents *hit the roof* when they saw the dented car.

_____

_____   8. If I had known you were *broke*, I would have lent you the *dough*.

_____   _____

_____   9. I *extinguished my smoking material* before boarding the *aircraft*.

_____   _____

_____   10. Darlene gave the collection agency a *buzz* and asked to speak to the *head honcho*.

_____   _____

Effective Word Choice MASTERY TEST 2

Certain words are italicized in the following sentences. In the spaces at the left,
identify whether these words are slang (S), clichés (C), or pretentious words (PW).
Then, in the spaces below, replace the words with more effective diction.

_____ 1. The professor *perceived* that the students *had a negative response to the idea.*

_____   _____

_____ 2. The movie was *a total downer.*

_____

_____ 3. At nursery school, my child is learning to *interact in a positive manner* with her *peers.*

_____   _____

_____ 4. Carlos felt *like a fish out of water* at the party.

_____

_____ 5. I talked to my daughter until I was *blue in the face,* but my words *went in one ear and out the other.*

_____   _____

_____ 6. Leon *stuffed his face with* so many *munchies* that he felt sick.

_____   _____

_____ 7. Charlene *asserted* that her story was not a *fabrication.*

_____   _____

_____ 8. I tried to *sack out* for a while, but some *yo-yo* kept calling my number by mistake.

_____   _____

_____ 9. Teresa grabbed the rolls out of the oven *in the nick of time.*

_____

_____ 10. *Keep your mitts off* me or you'll get a *knuckle sandwich.*

_____   _____

NAME: _____

DATE: _____

MASTERY TEST 3 Effective Word Choice

The following sentences include examples of wordiness. Rewrite the sentences in the space provided, omitting needless words.

1. Because of the fact that a time span of only five seconds separates the lightning from the thunder, we may safely conclude that the storm is directly overhead.

   _____

   _____

2. After his long twelve-mile hike, Ruben was so exhausted that when he walked into his living room, he staggered.

   _____

   _____

3. My mouth dropped open in amazement when I heard the startling news that Tim had just had a nervous breakdown last month.

   _____

   _____

4. Julia was convinced in her heart that she was doing the very best thing for both of them when she returned Clark's ring.

   _____

   _____

5. A sad-eyed mournful-looking little dog, no bigger than a puppy, followed my son home and walked behind him into the house.

   _____

   _____

NAME: _____

DATE: _____

Effective Word Choice   **MASTERY TEST 4**

The following sentences include examples of wordiness. Rewrite the sentences in the space provided, omitting needless words.

1. My outgrown closet is filled to bursting with piles of useless junk that I no longer need.

   _____

   _____

2. The leaky faucet that wouldn't stop dripping annoyed and bothered me all night long.

   _____

   _____

3. If you are having difficulties with your schoolwork and are not keeping up with your assignments, you should budget your time so that you stick to a schedule.

   _____

   _____

4. The main idea that I am trying to get across in this essay is that no driver of a motor vehicle should be permitted to drive in excess of the speed limit of fifty-five miles per hour.

   _____

   _____

5. When we looked as if we didn't believe him, Frank got upset and indignant and insisted that his story was a true incident that had really happened.

   _____

   _____

PART 3

Reinforcement of the Skills

Introduction

To reinforce the sentence skills presented in Part Two, this part of the book—Part Three—provides combined mastery tests, editing and proofreading tests, and combined editing tests. The *combined mastery tests* will strengthen your understanding of important related skills. *Editing and proofreading tests* offer practice in finding and correcting one kind of error in a brief passage. *Combined editing tests* then offer similar practice—except that each contains a variety of mistakes. Five of these tests feature "real world" documents—résumés, cover letters, and a job application—so you can apply your skills to situations you are likely to encounter outside the classroom. The tests in Part Three ill help you become a skilled editor and proofreader. All too often, nts can correct mistakes in practice sentences but are unable in their own writing. You must learn to look carefully for ills errors and to make close checking a habit.

Write a paragraph in which you describe the advertisements shown here to someone who has never seen them. Don't forget to proofread your paragraph for sentence-skills mistakes. Use the Checklist for Sentence Skills on the inside back cover of your book.

Combined Mastery Tests

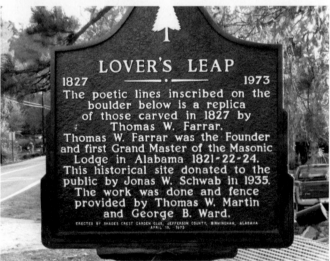

Can you find the sentence-skills errors in the two signs above? Rewrite the wording of each sign so that it is grammatically correct. Would you pay less attention to a sign that was confusing or grammatically incorrect? Why or why not?

Fragments and Run-Ons

COMBINED MASTERY TEST 1

Each of the word groups below is numbered. In the space provided, write C if a word group is a complete sentence, write F if it is a fragment, and write R-O if it is a run-on.

1. _____
2. _____
3. _____
4. _____
5. _____
6. _____
7. _____
8. _____
9. _____
10. _____
11. _____
12. _____
13. _____
14. _____
15. _____
16. _____
17. _____
18. _____
19. _____
20. _____

[1]A few years ago, an experiment was conducted in Germany. [2]To determine how dependent people are on their television sets. [3]The researchers chose 184 volunteers these people were paid to give up watching television for one year. [4]During the first months of the experiment. [5]Most of the subjects did not suffer any ill effects. [6]Or complain that they were missing anything important. [7]The volunteers said they had more free time, and they were grateful for the extra hours. [8]Spending them on reading, paying attention to their children, or visiting friends. [9]Another month went by, suddenly things took a turn for the worse. [10]The subjects became tense and restless. [11]In addition, quarreled frequently with other family members. [12]Their tension continued until the subjects were permitted to watch television again. [13]Nobody in the experiment survived an entire year without television, in fact, the longest anyone lasted was five months. [14]As soon as the television sets were turned on again. [15]The symptoms of anxiety disappeared. [16]This experiment suggests a conclusion. [17]Which would be dangerous to ignore. [18]Television is habit-forming it may be even more habit-forming than cigarettes or drugs. [19]Perhaps the little screen should carry a warning label. [20]Which says, "Caution—This Product May Be Hazardous to Your Health."

NAME: _____

DATE: _____

Fragments and Run-Ons

In the space provided, indicate whether each item below contains a fragment (F) or a run-on (R-O). Then correct the error.

_____ 1. With mounting horror, Eleni looked at the anxiously awaited snapshots. Which had just been developed. Not one picture had turned out.

_____ 2. Doug tried to grasp his new soft contact lens it was like trying to pick up a drop of water. The slippery little lens escaped from his fingers again and again.

_____ 3. Wearing huge, bright-blue sunglasses with gold wires. The new instructor strolled into class. One student whispered that she looked like a human dragonfly.

_____ 4. Because Sandy carried a large shoulder bag when she went shopping. Store security guards regarded her with suspicion. They had been trained to watch out for shoplifters with extra-large purses.

_____ 5. I watched my sister, a cleanliness fanatic, put away the produce. First she washed all the bananas and oranges, then she rubbed the onions with a towel.

_____ 6. The crowd became silent. Then, while the drums rolled. The acrobat attempted a triple somersault in midair.

_____ 7. Irene peeled off the itchy wool knee socks, she stared at the vertical red ridges the tight socks had left on the tender skin. With a sigh, she massaged her sore shins.

_____ 8. Although they sip nectar for energy. Butterflies never eat anything substantial. They have no need to because their bodies don't grow. Their only function is to mate.

_____ 9. When he smelled the acrid odor, Lee rushed to the kitchen. He popped up the smoking bread something was still aflame in the toaster's crumb tray.

_____ 10. Joanne painted her fingernails with pale-pink nail polish. And put a slightly deeper shade of pink on her toenails. Her fingertips and toes looked as if they were blushing.

Verbs

COMBINED MASTERY TEST 1

Each sentence contains a mistake involving (1) standard English or irregular verb forms, (2) subject-verb agreement, or (3) consistent verb tense. Cross out the incorrect verb and write the correct form in the space provided.

_____   1. The razor-sharp coral had tore a hole in the hull of the flimsy boat.

_____   2. The signs in the park warns that litterers will be fined.

_____   3. I cringe in embarrassment every time I started my car because its broken exhaust makes it sound like a hot rod.

_____   4. Somebody in the dorm keep the radio on all night long.

_____   5. Mike wants to overcome his shyness but hesitated to meet new people because he fears he won't have anything interesting to say.

_____   6. Each of my professors expect a term paper to be turned in before the holidays.

_____   7. The judge reminded the witness that she had swore to tell the truth.

_____   8. There were a heavy load of soggy clothes to be washed when Janet got home from camp.

_____   9. Thelma type the final word and fell back in her chair; her report was finished at last.

_____   10. Someone called Elaine at the office to tell her that her son had been bit by a stray dog.

NAME: _____

DATE: _____

COMBINED
MASTERY TEST 2

Verbs

Each sentence contains a mistake involving (1) standard English or irregular verb forms, (2) subject-verb agreement, or (3) consistent verb tense. Cross out the incorrect verb and write the correct form in the space provided.

_____ 1. Karen searched for the fifty-dollar bill she had hid in the thick book.

_____ 2. After I leave the dentist's office, my jaw and mouth feels numb.

_____ 3. After he stirred the thick paint for several minutes, Walt reels backward as the strong fumes made his head spin.

_____ 4. My nephew must have grew a foot since I last saw him.

_____ 5. Hovering overhead at the scene of the accident was several traffic helicopters.

_____ 6. When the nurse gave him the injection, Alfonso felt as if a huge bee had just stinged him.

_____ 7. When I caught my little boy pulling the dog's ears, I sat him down and talk to him about being kind to animals.

_____ 8. McDonald's has selled enough hamburgers to reach to the moon.

_____ 9. When he noticed Helen holding only a quart of milk, the man ahead of her in the checkout line motions for Helen to take his place.

_____ 10. Leaping out of the patrol car was two police officers with their guns drawn.

Pronouns   **COMBINED MASTERY TEST 1**

Choose the sentence in each pair that uses pronouns correctly. Then write the letter of that sentence in the space provided.

_____ 1. a. If someone wants to try out for the women's softball team, they should go to the practice field today after class.

b. If someone wants to try out for the women's softball team, she should go to the practice field today after class.

_____ 2. a. At the hardware store, they told me I would need specially treated lumber to build an outdoor deck.

b. At the hardware store, the clerks told me I would need specially treated lumber to build an outdoor deck.

_____ 3. a. Those greedy squirrels ate all the sunflower seeds in the bird feeder.

b. Them greedy squirrels ate all the sunflower seeds in the bird feeder.

_____ 4. a. Each of the student waiters had to write a report about their employment experience.

b. Each of the student waiters had to write a report about his employment experience.

_____ 5. a. We liked the price of the house, but you would have to do too much work to make it livable.

b. We liked the price of the house, but we would have to do too much work to make it livable.

NAME: _____

DATE: _____

Pronouns

In the spaces provided, write PE *for each of the nine sentences that contain pronoun errors. Write* C *for the sentence that uses pronouns correctly. Then cross out each pronoun error and write the correction above it.*

_____ 1. Bobby, Earl, and me are studying for the math test together.

_____ 2. Someone in the women's aerobics class complained that their back was sore.

_____ 3. If I fail the final exam, does that mean that you automatically fail the course?

_____ 4. Each of the twins had her name printed on her sweatshirt.

_____ 5. I enjoy my word-processing work, but you tend to have eyestrain by the end of the day.

_____ 6. When Juanita got her job as a waitress, they told her she would have to buy her own uniforms.

_____ 7. Tom read the paper while eating his lunch and then threw the rest of it away.

_____ 8. At the minicar racetrack, I proved that my reaction time was quicker than her's.

_____ 9. If anyone walks to the cafeteria, will they bring me a cup of coffee?

_____ 10. Since I've been up until two o'clock the last few nights and feel fine, I'm convinced that you need only six hours of sleep.

Faulty Modifiers and Parallelism

In the spaces provided, indicate whether each sentence contains a misplaced modifier (MM), a dangling modifier (DM), or faulty parallelism (FP). Then correct the error in the space under the sentence.

_____ 1. Before she went to bed, Sue brushed her teeth, took out her contact lenses, and was setting the alarm for six o'clock.

_____

_____ 2. After enjoying the fabulous meal, the bill dampened our spirits.

_____

_____ 3. Carmen read an article about exploring outer space in the dentist's office.

_____

_____ 4. While watching my favorite show, the smoke detector emitted a whistle.

_____

_____ 5. The wind blew over the card table, and the cups and plates were scattered.

_____

_____ 6. Backfiring and stalling, we realized that the car needed a tune-up.

_____

_____

_____ 7. Being left-handed, scissors seem upside down to me.

_____

_____ 8. A month ago, the Wallaces moved into the house next door from Ohio.

_____

_____ 9. I found an antique necklace in the old carton worn by my grandmother.

_____

_____ 10. The salesperson said we could pay for the furniture with cash, a credit card, or writing a check.

_____

NAME: _____

DATE: _____

Faulty Modifiers and Parallelism

In the spaces provided, indicate whether each sentence contains a misplaced modifier (MM), a dangling modifier (DM), or faulty parallelism (FP). Then correct the error in the space under the sentence.

_____ 1. Working in her vegetable garden, a bee stung Debbie on the shoulder.

_____

_____ 2. Our boss is smart and with plenty of dedication but coldhearted.

_____

_____ 3. Mr. Harris said he would be leaving the company during the meeting.

_____

_____ 4. The delivery boy placed the pizza on the couch with anchovies.

_____

_____ 5. Covered with wavy lines, the technician suggested that our computer monitor needed adjusting.

_____

_____

_____ 6. Twisted in several places, Karl straightened out the garden hose.

_____

_____ 7. As I waited, the secretary typed, filed, and was talking on the telephone.

_____

_____ 8. Jasmin saw a dress she was dying to wear in the department store window.

_____

_____

_____ 9. Weighing three tons, my neighbor pays an added registration fee for his truck.

_____

_____

_____ 10. While sitting in the traffic jam, I almost read the entire newspaper.

_____

SCORE
Number Correct

_____/10

_____%

Capital Letters and Punctuation

Each of the following sentences contains an error in capitalization or punctuation. Refer to the box below and write, in the space provided, the letter identifying the error. Then correct the error.

a. missing capital letter	c. missing quotation marks
b. missing apostrophe	d. missing comma

_____ 1. The elevator was stuck for more than an hour but all the passengers stayed calm.

_____ 2. "When I step onto dry land after weeks at sea, said the sailor, "I feel as if I'm standing on a sponge."

_____ 3. He doesn't talk about it much, but my uncle has been a member of alcoholics Anonymous for ten years.

_____ 4. My parents always ask me where Im going and when I'll be home.

_____ 5. Whenever Paul eats peanuts he leaves a pile of shells in the ashtray.

_____ 6. In the schools "food band," the children used pumpkins for drums and bags of pretzels for shakers.

_____ 7. "Stop making a fool of yourself," said Emily, and put that sword back on the wall."

_____ 8. The sweating straining horses neared the finish line.

_____ 9. The children a costumed horde of Halloween pirates and hoboes, fanned out through the neighborhood.

_____ 10. I decided to drink a glass of milk rather than order a pepsi.

NAME: _____

DATE: _____

Capital Letters and Punctuation

Each of the following sentences contains an error in capitalization or punctuation. Refer to the box below and write, in the space provided, the letter identifying the error. Then correct the error.

| a. missing capital letter | c. missing quotation marks |
| b. missing apostrophe | d. missing comma |

_____ 1. She had never seen anyone put mustard ketchup, and mayonnaise on French fries.

_____ 2. The schools janitor received nothing but a plaque for his loyal service.

_____ 3. "Using these chopsticks," said Wayne, "is like trying to eat soup with a fork.

_____ 4. Some people don't know that manhattan is an island.

_____ 5. Wanting to make a good impression Bill shaved twice before his date.

_____ 6. Crumpled sheets of paper and a spilled bottle of bayer aspirin littered Laurie's desk.

_____ 7. "German," said the history instructor, came within one vote of being named the official language of the United States."

_____ 8. My mothers checks are printed with pictures of endangered wild animals.

_____ 9. Feeling brave and silly at the same time Art volunteered to go onstage and help the magician.

_____ 10. My Uncle Tyrone fought in the Battle of the Bulge during World war II.

Word Use

Each of the following sentences contains a mistake identified in the left-hand margin. Underline the mistake and then correct it in the space provided.

Slang

1. At 50 percent off, this suit is a real steal.

_____

Wordiness

2. Although Yvette was on a reducing diet to lose weight, she splurged on some ice cream.

_____

Cliché

3. Ken knew his friends would be green with envy when they saw his new car.

_____

Pretentious language

4. We must complete the decision-making process.

_____

Adverb error

5. I tied the knot slow, making sure it wouldn't come loose again.

_____

Error in comparison

6. I felt more thirstier than I ever had in my life.

_____

Confused word

7. "Its the tallest building in the world," the guide said.

_____

Confused word

8. There parking the car in one of those enclosed garages.

_____

Confused word

9. He's the center who's teammates throw him the ball every time.

_____

Confused word

10. If you keep your wallet sticking out of a rear pocket, your bound to lose it to a pickpocket.

_____

NAME: _____

DATE: _____

Word Use

Each of the following sentences contains a mistake identified in the left-hand margin. Underline the mistake and then correct it in the space provided.

Slang

1. After his workout at the gym, Paul was too wiped out to cook dinner.

_____

Wordiness

2. I asked the attendant at the gas station to fill up my tank with gas as far as possible.

_____

Cliché

3. I try to turn the other cheek instead of getting angry.

_____

Pretentious language

4. Next fall, I plan to matriculate at a nearby college.

_____

Adverb error

5. Elizabeth hadn't been feeling good ever since the buffet lunch.

_____

Error in comparison

6. Sharon was more happier after she quit her job.

_____

Confused word

7. Charles knew he was all ready late for the interview, so he ran up the steps.

_____

Confused word

8. Michael's principle fault is his tendency to lose his temper.

_____

Confused word

9. The rabbi tried to advice the confused teenager.

_____

Confused word

10. Before the operation, the surgeon will carefully study you're x-rays.

_____

Editing and Proofreading Tests

holiday plans

hollygl_49@ccemail.com

To: sbecker@workemail.net

hi mom

i may have to work during the holidays. its real busy & they said they can't spare any of us so im not sure when ill be able to come down to visit. will talk to my manager tomorrow & see if i can get a 1/2 day. no promises. if i cant make it please save a piece of Dad's pecan pie for me. and some of your stuffing!!?!

love

H

re: holiday plans

sbecker@workemail.net

To: hollygl_49@ccemail.com

That's ok sweetie I understand. Try not to work to hard. I know you need the money but we're all worried your burning the candle at both ends :(Of course i'll save you some stuffing there should be plenty of leftovers. If you cant come Pop will send you a whole pie. :P

xoxo
Mom

How many sentence-skills errors can you locate in the e-mail correspondence shown above? Why do you think it is common for people to pay less attention to sentence skills when writing e-mails?

The passages in this section can be used in either of two ways: as editing tests or as guided composition activities.

As Editing Tests

Each passage contains a number of mistakes involving a single sentence skill. For example, the first passage (on page 472) contains five fragments. Your instructor may ask you to proofread the passage to locate the five fragments. Spaces are provided at the bottom of the passage for you to indicate which word groups are fragments. Your instructor may also have you correct the errors, either in the text itself or on separate paper. Depending on how well you do, you may also be asked to edit the second passage for fragments.

There are two passages for each skill area, and there are twelve skills covered in all. Here is a list of the skill areas:

Test 1	Fragments
Test 2	Fragments
Test 3	Run-Ons (Fused Sentences)
Test 4	Run-Ons (Comma Splices)
Test 5	Standard English Verbs
Test 6	Irregular Verbs
Test 7	Faulty Parallelism
Test 8	Capital Letters
Test 9	Apostrophes
Test 10	Quotation Marks
Test 11	Commas
Test 12	Commonly Confused Words

As Guided Composition Activities

To give practice in proofreading as well, your instructor may ask you to do more than correct the skill mistakes in each passage. You may be asked to rewrite the passage, correcting it for skill mistakes *and also* copying the rest of the passage perfectly. Should you miss one skill mistake or make even one copying mistake (for example, omitting a word, dropping a verb ending, misspelling a word, or misplacing an apostrophe), you may be asked to rewrite a different passage that deals with the same skill.

Here is how you would proceed. You would start with fragments, rewriting the first passage, proofreading your paper carefully, and then showing it to your instructor. He or she will check it quickly to see that all the fragments have been corrected and that no copying mistakes have been made. If the passage is error-free, you can proceed to run-ons.

If even a single mistake is made, the instructor may question you briefly to see if you recognize and understand it. (Perhaps he or she will put a check beside the line in which the mistake appears and then ask if you can correct it.) You may then be asked to write the second passage under a particular skill.

You will complete the program in guided composition when you successfully work through all twelve skills. Completing the twelve skills will strengthen your understanding of the skills, increase your ability to transfer the skills to actual writing situations, and markedly improve your proofreading.

In working on the passages, note the following points:

a. For each skill, you will be told how many mistakes appear in the passages. If you have trouble finding the mistakes, turn back and review the pages in this book that explain the skill in question.

b. Here is an effective way to go about correcting a passage. First, read it over quickly. Look for and mark off mistakes in the skill area involved. For example, in your first reading of a passage that has five fragments, you may locate and mark only three fragments. Next, reread the passage carefully so you can find the remaining errors in the skill in question. Finally, make notes in the margin about how to correct each mistake. Only at this point should you begin to rewrite the passage.

c. Be sure to proofread with care after you finish a passage. Go over your writing word for word, looking for careless errors. Remember that you may be asked to do another passage involving the same skill if you make even one mistake.

NAME: _____

DATE: _____

Fragments

Mistakes in each passage: 5

Passage A

¹During the year I spent cleaning pools for a living. ²I found that dogs could be either the joy or the terror of my workdays. ³I particularly enjoyed seeing Bugsy. ⁴A Jack Russell terrier who loved chasing water as it squirted from the garden hose. ⁵I also looked forward to seeing the twin chocolate Labrador retrievers, Butch and Sundance. ⁶Every week, they would take turns dropping tennis balls at my feet. ⁷Then bounding away, sometimes into the pool. ⁸Unfortunately, some of the pets on my route were not so welcoming. ⁹One day, while I was cleaning a filter. ¹⁰A German shepherd surprised me by stepping through a hole in the screened-in porch. ¹¹I turned to face the dog and spoke to it in low, soothing tones. ¹²Suddenly, the dog bared its huge, yellow teeth and lunged at me. ¹³Fueled by adrenaline. ¹⁴I managed to leap over the chain-link fence in a single bound. ¹⁵From then on, I asked to be formally introduced to family watchdogs before I set foot in their backyard.

Word groups with fragments: _____ _____ _____ _____ _____

Passage B

[1]Walter won't admit that he is out of a job. [2]Last month, Walter was laid off by the insurance company. [3]Where he had been working as a salesperson. [4]But Walter hasn't told anyone. [5]And continues to go downtown every morning. [6]Waiting at the bus stop with his newspaper folded under his arm and his briefcase on the sidewalk beside him. [7]He looks at his watch as if he were worried about being late. [8]When he gets downtown. [9]Walter goes to an arcade. [10]He plays video games for an hour or two. [11]Then he visits the public library. [12]To lose himself in the latest spy novel. [13]At five o'clock, Walter catches the bus for home. [14]His newspaper is still folded under his arm. [15]He has not opened the paper to look at the want ads. [16]I feel sorry for Walter, but I understand his desire to live in a fantasy world.

Word groups with fragments: _____ _____ _____ _____ _____

NAME: _____

DATE: _____

Fragments

Mistakes in each passage: 5

Passage A

¹Are you experiencing car trouble? ²Is your transmission acting up or your muffler rattling? ³By tuning in to your radio. ⁴You can find help. ⁵A weekly program mixing serious car advice and humor. ⁶Has become popular all over the country. ⁷The show began in Boston when a radio station invited a number of mechanics to take live calls on car problems. ⁸Although a large group of mechanics was expected. ⁹Only Tom and Ray showed up. ¹⁰Tom and Ray are brothers who liked fixing cars in their spare time. ¹¹And had opened a garage. ¹²The response to the show was so great that it became a weekly event. ¹³With no advance preparation, Tom and Ray take all car questions that the audience asks. ¹⁴They delight listeners with their wit, their down-to-earth philosophy, and their good car sense.

Word groups with fragments: _____ _____ _____ _____ _____

Passage B

[1]For thousands of years. [2]Humans have used certain animals to carry heavy loads. [3]The ox, the elephant, the donkey, and the mule are examples of these "beasts of burden." [4]Although they have a reputation for being stubborn at times. [5]These animals normally work very hard for long hours. [6]One beast of burden, however, refuses to be overworked. [7]The llama, a South American animal much like the camel, has very definite ideas of what it's willing to do. [8]Knowing just how much it can carry comfortably, the llama will sit down and refuse to budge. [9]If even an extra half pound is placed on its back. [10]In addition, the llama will carry a burden only a certain distance. [11]For example, nothing will persuade it to continue. [12]After it travels twenty miles. [13]Sometimes its owner tries to prod the llama with a stick once the animal has decided to quit. [14]When it is disturbed in this fashion. [15]The llama has an unusual way of striking back. [16]It puckers its lips and spits in its owner's face.

Word groups with fragments: _____ _____ _____ _____ _____

NAME: _____

DATE: _____

Run-Ons (Fused Sentences)

Mistakes in each passage: 5

Passage A

[1]How would you like to live in the most expensive part of New York City without paying any rent? [2]Recently, a fifty-five-year-old man did just that he set up residence on a thirty-five-foot-long traffic island in the middle of East River Drive. [3]His furniture was made from storage crates his stove was an oil drum. [4]His only protection from the weather was the elevated highway overhead. [5]People waved to him as they drove by some even donated food and beer. [6]Local television stations soon began to feature this unusual resident. [7]He was pictured relaxed and reading a book the traffic streamed by on both sides of him. [8]Social workers wanted to put him in a city shelter he refused, saying it was a pigpen. [9]Finally, the police took him away, but not before he had become a hero. [10]He had achieved the ultimate American dream; for a little while, he had beaten the system.

Sentences with run-ons: _____   _____   _____   _____   _____

Passage B

[1]Many common expressions have interesting origins one of these is the phrase "the real McCoy." [2]In fact, the real McCoy was not really named McCoy he was a farmer's son from Indiana named Norman Selby who got tired of farming and left home around 1890. [3]One year later, he began a boxing career, using the name Kid McCoy soon he was fighting every month. [4]He was willing to meet any opponent anywhere in the country. [5]He soon had a long string of victories most of them were knockouts. [6]A number of other fighters began calling themselves "Kid McCoy," thinking the name would get them more boxing matches and more money. [7]However, on March 24, 1899, the Kid defeated another great champion the fight lasted twenty rounds and cost the Kid three broken ribs. [8]In his report of the fight, the *San Francisco Examiner*'s sportswriter wrote, "Now you've seen the real McCoy!" [9]From them on, people have said "the real McCoy" whenever they have meant that something is not a fake.

Sentences with run-ons: _____ _____ _____ _____ _____

NAME: _____

DATE: _____

TEST 4 # Run-Ons (Comma Splices)

Mistakes in each passage: 5

Passage A

[1]One evening, a group of friends got together for a dinner party, after dinner they began telling stories. [2]As the evening wore on, the stories got wilder and wilder. [3]Some of the stories involved unusual scientific experiments, others were about strange creatures, such as werewolves and vampires. [4]The friends competed to see who could tell the most exciting story. [5]In the group was a young woman named Mary, who had recently been married. [6]When Mary went to bed that night, she had a frightening dream. [7]In her dream, a hideous monster came to life, she saw it bending over her. [8]The next morning, Mary told her dream to her new husband, Percy, he persuaded her to write it down. [9]After he read her account, Percy was so impressed that he urged her to expand it into a book. [10]The novel that Mary Shelley finally wrote, *Frankenstein,* is probably the most famous horror story of all time, hundreds of monster movies have been inspired by it.

Sentences with run-ons: _____   _____   _____   _____   _____

Passage B

[1]One of the coldest, snowiest, windiest places on earth is not in the Himalayas or the Arctic, it is on Mount Washington in the pleasant state of New Hampshire. [2]The top of this rather small mountain experiences hurricane-force winds, they slice through human beings like razors. [3]The world's highest wind speed was recorded on the mountain one April day in 1934, that speed was 231 miles per hour! [4]Snow is always possible, even in summer. [5]Supercooled fog, called *rime,* hugs the mountain, there is almost no visibility 55 percent of the time. [6]At least sixty people have lost their lives on Mount Washington in the last hundred years. [7]However, people continue to climb to the top, some take the auto route, open only in the summer. [8]The more foolish attempt to climb the mountain at other times of the year. [9]A warning sign on the mountain reads, "People don't die on this mountain. They perish."

Sentences with run-ons: _____   _____   _____   _____   _____

NAME: _____

DATE: _____

TEST 5 | Standard English Verbs

Mistakes in each passage: 5

Passage A

¹The scenes of flood damage on the network news tonight were horrible. ²Two weeks of steady, heavy rains had raise the waters of several Midwestern rivers past the levels of their banks, and they had overflow onto the surrounding houses and fields. ³Extensive damage had resulted, with some buildings actually torn from their foundations and suck helplessly into the swirling flood waters. ⁴Here and there a rooftop could be seen as it float by with one or two frightened survivors clinging to it. ⁵Many people's lives had been disrupted, and many millions of dollars' worth of damage had been cause. ⁶It would be several days yet until the waters receded. ⁷They say that "into every life some rain must fall," but no one could have predicted all this.

Sentences with nonstandard verbs (write the number of a sentence twice if it contains two nonstandard verbs):

_____ _____ _____ _____ _____

Passage B

[1]I read an odd item in the newspaper about a pet snail that nearly frighten its owner to death. [2]Actually, the owner did not even know that he had been keeping a pet. [3]The snail, which was very fancy, had been varnish and made into an ornament. [4]Its owner had bought the snail at a gift shop and place it on his desk. [5]Apparently the snail was not really dead but had been seal into hibernation by the varnish and was just asleep. [6]Three years later, when its owner accidentally knock the ornament off his desk, chipping the varnish, the snail woke up. [7]It began moving across the desk as the owner was writing a letter and startled him so much that he jumped out of his chair. [8]The owner is feeding his former ornament on cabbage before taking it back to the seashore where it belongs.

Sentences with nonstandard verbs: _____ _____ _____ _____ _____

NAME: _____

DATE: _____

TEST 6 Irregular Verbs

Mistakes in each passage: 10

Passage A

¹Vince choosed a job as a supermarket cashier because he liked people. ²After what happened yesterday, though, he isn't so sure. ³First, after he had rang up her entire order, a woman throwed a handful of coupons at him. ⁴Then she give him a hard time when he shown her that a few had expired. ⁵She begun making nasty comments about stupid supermarket help. ⁶The next person in line thought Vince had put the eggs on the bottom and would not leave until Vince had took everything out of the bag and repacked it. ⁷Later, two teenagers fighted with Vince over the price of a bag of M&M's, saying that it could never have rose so high in one week. ⁸Vince gone home in a terrible mood, wondering how he would ever force himself to go in the next day.

Sentences with irregular verbs (write the number of a sentence twice if it contains two irregular verbs):

_____ _____ _____ _____ _____

_____ _____ _____ _____ _____

Passage B

[1]A college professor has wrote a book about what he calls "urban legends." [2]These are folktales that have spreaded all over the country. [3]They usually have a moral to teach or touch on a basic fear holded by many Americans. [4]In one of the more gruesome legends, a young couple parked on a lovers' lane heared a report on the car radio about a one-armed killer stalking the area. [5]The couple leaved; after they gotten home, they seen a bloody hook hanging on the car's door handle. [6]The moral of this urban legend? [7]Don't park on lovers' lanes! [8]In another story, a man finded pieces of fried rat mixed in with his take-out fried chicken. [9]The professor has sayed that this story is related to the American consumer's fear of being contaminated with some dreadful substance. [10]No one can find a factual basis for any of these stories, although many tellers have swore they are true.

Sentences with irregular verbs (write the number of a sentence twice or more if it contains two or more irregular verbs):

_____ _____ _____ _____ _____

_____ _____ _____ _____ _____

NAME: _____

DATE: _____

TEST 7 Faulty Parallelism

Mistakes in each passage: 5

Passage A

[1]Some people today are "survivalists." [2]These people, because they fear some great disaster in the near future (like economic collapse or nuclear war), are preparing for a catastrophe. [3]Hoarding food, stockpiling weapons, and the achievement of self-sufficiency are some of the activities of survivalists. [4]In Arkansas, for example, one group has built a mountain fortress to defend its supplies and staying safe. [5]Arkansas, the group feels, is the best place to be for several reasons: it is an unlikely target for nuclear attack; it offers plentiful supplies of food and water; a good climate. [6]Some Americans feel that the attitude of survivalists is selfish and greed. [7]These people say that such a philosophy turns society into a "dog-eat-dog" race for life. [8]Other people believe that after a nuclear war, the world, with radiation and where there would be disease, wouldn't be worth living in.

Sentences with faulty parallelism: _____ _____ _____ _____ _____

Passage B

[1]Doing your own painting is easy, inexpensive, and you will enjoy it, if you know what you're doing. [2]First, you must properly prepare the surface you are going to paint. [3]This means removing dirt, rust, or mildew. [4]Also, you should get rid of loose paint and to fill any cracks with spackling compound. [5]Primers or sealers should be used on bare wood or over stains. [6]Another important rule to follow is to buy the right amount of paint. [7]Some painters guess how much paint they need and are failing to measure accurately. [8]Then they might buy too little or an excessive amount of paint for the job. [9]The result is making an extra trip to the hardware store or to have a lot of paint left over. [10]Finally, before you begin to paint, read the directions on the container. [11]These hints will save you time and money.

Sentences with faulty parallelism: _____ _____ _____ _____ _____

NAME: _____

DATE: _____

TEST 8 Capital Letters

Mistakes in each passage: 10

Passage A

¹Last november, joanne fisher put her turkey in the oven and drove into town to see the thanksgiving day parade. ²Parking downtown was almost impossible. ³Joanne saw the sign warning visitors not to park on the private lot at Tenth street, but she thought that since it was a holiday, nobody would mind. ⁴When she returned after the parade, her nissan was missing. ⁵It had been towed to a lot in a faraway section of the city. ⁶When Joanne finally got to the lot, the owner insisted on a cash payment and refused to accept a check for fifty dollars. ⁷Joanne lost her temper and screamed, "all right, go ahead and call the police, but I'm going to drive out of here!" ⁸A police car arrived immediately, and Joanne had visions of spending the next month in jail. ⁹But the officer, sgt. Roberts of the Sixteenth precinct, agreed to cash her check so she could pay the fine. ¹⁰Joanne was delighted until she got home and found that her turkey had burned to a crisp.

Sentences with missing capitals (write the number of a sentence as many times as it contains capitalization mistakes):

_____   _____   _____   _____   _____

_____   _____   _____   _____   _____

Passage B

[1]Liza never realized how expensive it was going to be to have a baby. [2]Before the birth, Liza visited dr. willis, her obstetrician, eleven times. [3]After her baby was born, a multiple-page bill from valley hospital arrived. [4]There were charges not only from Liza's own doctor, but also from a Dr. David, the anesthesiologist, and a Dr. Ripley, the hospital pediatrician. [5]After she had brought the baby home, Liza found herself visiting the supermarket more often. [6]She loaded her cart with boxes of expensive pampers, dozens of cans of enfamil formula, and lots of smaller items like johnson's baby powder and oil. [7]Liza realized that she would have to return to her job at richmond insurance company if she was going to make ends meet.

Sentences with missing capitals (write the number of a sentence as many times as it contains capitalization mistakes):

_____ _____ _____ _____ _____

_____ _____ _____ _____ _____

NAME: _____

DATE: _____

TEST 9 | Apostrophes

Mistakes in each passage: 10

Passage A

¹Two Minnesota brothers, Ed and Norman, are engaged in a war. ²It all started when Eds wife gave him a pair of pants that didnt fit. ³Ed wrapped up the pants and put them under Normans Christmas tree. ⁴When Norman opened the box, he recognized the unwanted pants. ⁵The next year, he gave them back to Ed, sealed in a heavy carton tied with knotted ropes. ⁶The War of the Pants was on. ⁷Each year, on one of the brothers birthdays, or on Christmas, the dreaded pants reappear. ⁸The war has escalated, however, with each brother trying to top the others pants delivery of the previous year. ⁹Two years ago, Norman bought an old safe, put the pants in it, welded it shut, and delivered it to Eds house. ¹⁰Somehow, Ed retrieved the pants (one of the wars rules is that the pants must not be damaged). ¹¹Last year, Ed went to an auto junkyard. ¹²The pants were placed in an ancient Fords backseat, and the car went through the huge auto crusher. ¹³On his birthday, Norman found a four-foot square of smashed metal on his doorstep; he knew it could only be Eds doing and the pants must be inside. ¹⁴Norman is still trying to get at the pants and prepare next years "topper."

Sentences with missing apostrophes (write the number of a sentence twice if it contains two missing apostrophes):

_____ _____ _____ _____ _____

_____ _____ _____ _____

Passage B

[1]Sometimes I wish the telephone hadnt been invented. [2]When I come home after class or work, all Im interested in is lying down for an hours nap. [3]Typically, five minutes after Ive closed my eyes, the phone rings. [4]Someone Ive never met is trying to sell me a subscription to *Newsweek*. [5]Or I may have just begun to mix up some hamburger when I hear the phones insistent ringing. [6]It wont stop, so I wipe the ground meat off my hands and run to answer it. [7]Yesterday, when this happened, it was my mothers best friend. [8]Shed found some clothes in her attic. [9]And she wanted to know if I could use an old evening gown. [10]Even if its someone I want to talk to, the phone call always seems to come at a bad time.

Sentences with missing apostrophes (write the number of a sentence twice if it contains two missing apostrophes):

_____ _____ _____ _____ _____

_____ _____ _____ _____ _____

NAME: _____

DATE: _____

Quotation Marks

Quotation marks needed in each passage: 10 pairs

Passage A

¹Tony and Lola were driving home from the movies when they saw a man staggering along the street. ²I wonder if he's all right, Tony said.

³Let's stop and find out, Lola suggested. ⁴They caught up to the man, who was leaning against a tree.

⁵Are you OK? Lola asked. ⁶Is there anything we can do?

⁷There's nothing the matter, the man answered. ⁸I guess I had a few too many after work. ⁹Now I can't seem to find my front door.

¹⁰Tony steadied the man and asked, Do you live anywhere near here?

¹¹He responded, Yes, if this is Forrest Avenue, I live at 3619.

¹²Tony and Lola walked the man to his door, where he fumbled in his pockets, took out a key, and began to stab wildly with it at the lock.

¹³Let me hold your key, and I'll let you in, Tony offered.

¹⁴The man refused, saying, Oh, no, I'll hold the key—you hold the house.

Sentences or sentence groups with missing quotation marks:

_____   _____   _____   _____   _____

_____   _____   _____   _____   _____

Passage B

[1]When Martin found a large dent in his new Nissan, he took it back to the agency. [2]We can fix that, the smiling mechanic said. [3]Just leave it for a few days.

[4]Martin waited three days and then called. [5]Is my car ready yet? he asked. [6]Not yet, the mechanic said. [7]Try the end of the week.

[8]The following Monday, Martin called again. [9]Is my car ready?

[10]The mechanic sounded apologetic. [11]Not yet. [12]We'll have it Friday for sure.

[13]On Friday, when Martin picked up his car, he noticed a new cigarette burn in the upholstery. [14]We'll fix that, but it takes a week to match the material, the manager said.

[15]Martin took the bus home, fuming. [16]A few minutes later, the phone rang. [17]It was the mechanic. [18]You left your owner's card here. [19]Want us to mail it?

[20]Martin said, You may as well keep it. [21]You're using the car more than I am.

Sentences or sentence groups with missing quotation marks:

_____   _____   _____   _____   _____

_____   _____   _____   _____   _____

NAME: _____

DATE: _____

TEST 11 # Commas

Mistakes in each passage: 10

Passage A

¹Frank has a hard time studying so he plays little games to get himself to finish his assignments. ²He will begin by saying to himself "Whenever I finish an assignment I'll give myself a prize." ³Frank has all kinds of prizes; his favorites are watching a detective show on television drinking a cold beer and spending an hour with his girlfriend. ⁴Of course too many of these rewards will mean that Frank won't get much else done. ⁵So Frank uses other strategies. ⁶He will for example set the stove timer for one hour. ⁷Then he will work at the kitchen table until the timer buzzes. ⁸Also he puts a paper clip on every tenth page of the book he is studying. ⁹As soon as he reaches the clip he can take a five-minute break.

Sentences with missing commas (write the number of a sentence as many times as it contains comma mistakes):

_____ _____ _____ _____ _____

_____ _____ _____ _____ _____

Passage B

[1]When Robert gets bored at his receptionist job he has a whole assortment of things to do to pass the time until five o'clock. [2]First he cleans out his desk. [3]Desk drawers he has found contain all sorts of hidden treasure. [4]Robert found an old CD belonging to the temp who had previously worked from his desk a faded Snoopy keychain and a couple of dog-eared Terry Pratchett novels the last time he "cleaned house." [5]The books kept him occupied during lunch break for a week. [6]He has also become a master at fixing paper jams in the company's ancient temperamental copy machine. [7]On particularly slow days Robert checks his e-mails or posts entries on his blog. [8]Lately however he has had to deactivate his IM account in order to actually get work done.

Sentences with missing commas (write the number of a sentence as many times as it contains comma mistakes):

_____ _____ _____ _____ _____

_____ _____ _____ _____ _____

NAME: _____

DATE: _____

TEST 12 Commonly Confused Words

Mistakes in each passage: 10

Passage A

¹Did you know that until May 5 of every year, your not really working for yourself? ²A group in Washington, D.C., has learned that it takes workers an average of four months and four days to earn enough to pay there taxes. ³The group found in it's study that taxes eat up 34 percent of all the income in the United States. ⁴So, if workers used their entire income for taxes, they would not be threw paying them until May. ⁵Being that May 5 is the first day people really work for themselves, the study group has some advise. ⁶It would like a bill past naming May 5 "Tax Freedom Day." ⁷On that day, you would give yourself a brake, irregardless of how hard you worked. ⁸For, from May 5 on, you would finally be your own boss.

Sentences with commonly confused words (write the number of a sentence twice if it contains two commonly confused words):

_____ _____ _____ _____ _____

_____ _____ _____ _____ _____

Passage B

[1]Did you ever daydream about writing you're life story? [2]Do you think that your life is to dull, or you can't right? [3]Everyone's life story is filled with fascinating events, and writing them down in the best way you know can give you a sense of accomplishment and, perhaps, leave a valuable inheritance to your family. [4]The first thing to do is to buy a lose-leaf notebook. [5]Each page of the book should be titled with a significant milestone in your life—from your first dog to your proudest moment. [6]You should than jot down a few key words in the book whenever a memory comes back to you. [7]The idea is *not* to begin with "I was born . . ." and try to write a chronological history of your hole life. [8]Just delve into your passed at random; one memory will trigger another. [9]Writing will become quiet easy after a while. [10]Its also important to write in your own language. [11]Plane, honest writing is the goal.

Sentences with commonly confused words (write the number of a sentence twice if it contains two commonly confused words):

_____ _____ _____ _____ _____

_____ _____ _____ _____ _____

Combined Editing Tests

Did you grow up in a rural, suburban, or urban area? Write down some of the advantages and disadvantages of living in that environment and then use the most interesting or important ideas to develop a paragraph about your home town or city.

Editing for Sentence-Skills Mistakes

The seventeen editing tests in this section will give you practice in finding a variety of sentence-skills mistakes. People often find it hard to edit a paper carefully. They have put so much work, or so little work, into their writing that it's almost painful for them to look at the paper one more time. You may simply have to *force* yourself to edit. Remember that eliminating sentence-skills mistakes will improve an average paper and help ensure a high grade on a good paper. Further, as you get into the habit of editing your papers, you will get into the habit of using the sentence skills consistently. They are a basic part of clear, effective writing.

NAME: _____

DATE: _____

COMBINED EDITING TEST 1

Identify the five mistakes in paper format in the student paper that follows. From the box below, choose the letter that describes each mistake and write it in the space provided.

a. The title should not be underlined.
b. The title should not be set off in quotation marks.
c. There should not be a period at the end of a title.
d. All the major words in a title should be capitalized.
e. The title should just be several words and not a complete sentence.
f. The first sentence of a paper should stand independent of the title.
g. A line should be skipped between the title and the first line of the paper.
h. The first line of a paper should be indented.
i. The right-hand margin should not be crowded.
j. Hyphenation should occur only between syllables.

	"Noise in quiet places"
	The quietest places make the most noise. A library is one exam-
	ple. If you crinkle a bag of potato chips in a quiet library, people
	will stare at you as if you had lit a firecracker under their feet.
	But you could drop a food tray in a noisy cafeteria and nobody
	would pay much attention to you. Then, there's the cough in church.
	A muffled cough bounces off the stained glass windows like a sonic
	boom. But you could cough up a storm at a rock concert and not
	one head would turn. Finally, elevators are hushed places. If you
	ask someone for the time in an elevator, everyone will look at his
	or her watch. Ask the same question on a busy city street, and
	chances are that no one will hear you. It takes a quiet place for
	sound to be really heard.

1. _____ 2. _____ 3. _____ 4. _____ 5. _____

NAME: _____

DATE: _____

Identify the five mistakes in paper format in the student paper that follows. From the box below, choose the letter that describes each mistake and write it in the space provided.

---

a. The title should not be underlined.
b. The title should not be set off in quotation marks.
c. There should not be a period at the end of a title.
d. All the major words in a title should be capitalized.
e. The title should just be several words and not a complete sentence.
f. The first sentence of a paper should stand independent of the title.
g. A line should be skipped between the title and the first line of the paper.
h. The first line of a paper should be indented.
i. The right-hand margin should not be crowded.
j. Hyphenation should occur only between syllables.

	"Bus Travel"
	It is the worst way to get to work or school in the mo-
	rning. First, the weather is unpredictable. Many bus stops are
	not sheltered, and the rider must wait in rain, cold, and heat.
	Another unpleasant thing about bus riding is the wait. It
	seems that buses are on time only when you're running late.
	Next, there is the matter of having exact change. If you try to
	enter without the right change, the driver looks at you as if
	your hair is on fire. Last, there's the problem of finding a seat.
	The elderly folks are saving seats for their friends, and most
	people look as if they will bite your nose if you sit next to
	them. Chances are that the only seat open will be next to a
	strange-smelling person with a wild look in his eye.

1. _____   2. _____   3. _____   4. _____   5. _____

NAME: _____

DATE: _____

COMBINED EDITING TEST 3

Identify the sentence-skills mistakes at the underlined spots in the selection that follows. From the box below, choose the letter that describes each mistake and write it in the space provided. (The same mistake may appear more than once.) Then, in the spaces provided between the lines, correct each mistake.

> a. fragment
> b. run-on
> c. dropped verb ending
> d. misplaced modifier
> e. incorrect end mark
> f. missing apostrophe
> g. missing comma

When I was little, I really hate visiting Aunt Martha. She was my fathers sister and
                                    1   2
had never married. Since she had no children of her own, she didnt know what to
                                                                                              3
do with me. I remember the sofa in her living room, which was dark brown. And
                                                                                      4
filled with horsehair. Every time I sat on it, I got stabbed by the stuffing. I had
         5
to plump up the cushion when I got up otherwise, she would frown at me. She
                                                       6
would sit opposite me with a stiff smile on her face and ask me what I was learn
                                                                                                7
in school or if I had been good? Things that I didn't want to talk about. I couldn't
                                        8   9
wait to say good-bye plump up the cushion, and escape.
                            10

1. _____   3. _____   5. _____   7. _____   9. _____

2. _____   4. _____   6. _____   8. _____   10. _____

Identify the sentence-skills mistakes at the underlined spots in the selection that follows. From the box below, choose the letter that describes each mistake and write it in the space provided. The same mistake may appear more than once. Then, in the space provided between the lines, correct each mistake. In one case, there is no mistake.

a. fragment	f. missing capital letter
b. run-on	g. missing quotation marks
c. dropped verb ending	h. missing comma
d. irregular verb mistake	i. no mistake
e. dangling modifier	

In the unending war of people versus machines, a blow was <u>striked</u> by a man in
₁
<u>pennsylvania</u> who had a run-in with an automatic banking machine. At about ten
₂
o'clock one night, he approached the machine to make a withdrawal. After he
inserted his <u>card the machine</u> spat it back at him. The same thing then <u>happen a</u>
₃   ₄
second time. He put his card in <u>again, this</u> time the machine kept the card. <u>And</u>
₅
<u>did not give him the money he had requested.</u> By now the customer was totally
₆
disgusted. <u>Hitting the machine with all his strength,</u> the card still did not come
₇
back. This was the last <u>straw he</u> grabbed a metal trash <u>can and</u> proceeded to beat
₈   ₉
up the machine. Unfortunately, the machine still had his card, and the man was
later arrested and charged with causing $2,500 worth of damage. He didn't mind.
"I've been ripped off so <u>often, he</u> said, "that it was time for me to get even."
₁₀

1. _____   3. _____   5. _____   7. _____   9. _____

2. _____   4. _____   6. _____   8. _____   10. _____

NAME: _____

DATE: _____

COMBINED EDITING TEST 5

Identify the sentence-skills mistakes at the underlined spots in the selection that follows. From the box below, choose the letter that describes each mistake and write it in the space provided. The same mistake may appear more than once. Then, in the space provided between the lines, correct each mistake. In one case, there is no mistake.

a. fragment	e. missing capital letter
b. run-on	f. mistake in subject-verb agreement
c. omitted word	g. irregular verb mistake
d. misplaced modifier	h. no mistake

If you were <u>asked name</u> our most dangerous insects or animals, which ones would you list? You might jot down black widow spiders, rattlesnakes, and scorpions. <u>Just to list a few.</u> However, our Public Enemy Number One is the <u>bee, more</u> people die from bee and wasp stings every year than are killed by animals. Not too long ago in Camden, <u>new</u> Jersey, over twenty-seven people were <u>took</u> to hospitals <u>who had been stung</u> by a runaway swarm of bees. The bees, which had escaped from a hive that <u>had</u> fallen off a truck, <u>was maddened</u> by what they thought was an attack on their hive and would <u>have</u> destroyed anyone who <u>came</u> near them. <u>If there is no threat to their hive.</u> Bees will usually not sting, for once they lose their stingers, they die. Wasps and yellow jackets, however, <u>is</u> able to sting repeatedly with no danger to themselves. For that 1 percent of the population allergic to insect stings, such attacks can be fatal.

1. _____   3. _____   5. _____   7. _____   9. _____

2. _____   4. _____   6. _____   8. _____   10. _____

NAME: _____

DATE: _____

Identify the sentence-skills mistakes at the underlined spots in the selection that follows. From the box below, choose the letter that describes each mistake and write it in the space provided. The same mistake may appear more than once. Then, in the space provided between the lines, correct each mistake. In one case, there is no mistake.

a. fragment	e. mistake in parallelism
b. run-on	f. apostrophe mistake
c. irregular verb mistake	g. missing comma
d. inconsistent verb tense	h. no mistake

As she walked into the dimly lit room. Julie was more nervous than usual. This was the first time she had ever went to a singles bar, and she wasn't sure how she should behave. She stood near the back wall and waited for her eyes' to adjust to the darkness. In a minute or so, she could see what was going on. Several women were sipping drinks at the bar, nearby, unattached men were whispering and glancing at the women. Seated at small tables pairs of men and women were talking animatedly and smiled at each other. They looked as if they were having a good time. Julie watches for a few minutes and then went to find the ladies room. Joining the singles scene, she thought could wait just a little longer.

1. _____   3. _____   5. _____   7. _____   9. _____

2. _____   4. _____   6. _____   8. _____   10. _____

NAME: _____

DATE: _____

COMBINED EDITING TEST 7

Identify the sentence-skills mistakes at the underlined spots in the selection that follows. From the box below, choose the letter that describes each mistake and write it in the space provided. The same mistake may appear more than once. Then, in the space provided between the lines, correct each mistake. In one case, there is no mistake.

a. fragment	f. mistake in parallelism
b. run-on	g. missing comma
c. mistake in pronoun reference	h. missing quotation marks
d. mistake in subject-verb agreement	i. no mistake
e. dangling modifier	

Recently a friend of mine has been on a crusade to reinvent the modern office. "Every day," she <u>says</u> "I feel as though my soul has been sucked out through a
₁
straw. One of her pet peeves <u>are</u> fluorescent <u>lighting.Fluttering and faintly blue,</u>
₂   ₃   ₄
<u>she</u> complains that the lighting in her office leaves her <u>drained and</u> practically
₅
hypnotized. She also rails against her cubicle workspace. <u>Which is so cramped</u>
₆
<u>that she feels claustrophobic after only an hour or two at work.</u> At the same time,
it <u>don't</u> provide any meaningful <u>privacy, she</u> can still hear every conversation within
₇   ₈
a twenty-foot radius. Worst of all, <u>they</u> have no intention of remodeling the office,
₉
even though workers in more modern, ergonomic, and ecologically <u>friendlier</u> work-
₁₀
places tend to be more productive.

1. _____	3. _____	5. _____	7. _____	9. _____
2. _____	4. _____	6. _____	8. _____	10. _____

NAME: _____

DATE: _____

Identify the sentence-skills mistakes at the underlined spots in the selection that follows. From the box below, choose the letter that describes each mistake and write it in the space provided. The same mistake may appear more than once. Then, in the space provided between the lines, correct each mistake. In one case, there is no mistake.

a. fragment	e. apostrophe mistake
b. run-on	f. missing comma
c. mistake in parallelism	g. dropped *-ly* ending (adverb mistake)
d. missing capital letter	h. no mistake

What would you do if you were driving to work during the morning rush hour and you saw a family of geese blocking the road? The adult <u>canada</u> goose

¹

and her goslings had been standing on the west side of River Drive, looking at the water on the other side. When a slight break in traffic <u>occurred the</u>

²

mother started across. Traffic <u>slowed brakes</u> squealed, and all the babies

³

except one made it to the other side. That one stood right in the middle of the highway. <u>Blocking one of the lanes.</u> Meanwhile, the mother goose honked <u>helpless</u>

⁴ ⁵

from the safety of the riverbank. Not a single car moved as all the <u>driver's</u> waited

⁶

for the gosling to cross. <u>Then, just</u> as one driver opened his door to get out

⁷

and rescue the little <u>one the</u> mother gave a deafening <u>honk, the</u> gosling quickly

⁸ ⁹

hurried over to join her. The drivers restarted their motors and <u>were continuing</u>

¹⁰

on their way, proud that they had helped save a life.

1. _____ 3. _____ 5. _____ 7. _____ 9. _____

2. _____ 4. _____ 6. _____ 8. _____ 10. _____

NAME: _____

DATE: _____

**COMBINED
EDITING TEST 9**

Locate and correct the ten sentence-skills mistakes in the following passage. The mistakes are listed in the box below. As you locate each mistake, write the number of the word group containing it in the space provided. Then, in the spaces between the lines, correct each mistake.

> 2 fragments _____ _____
> 2 run-ons _____ _____
> 1 irregular verb mistake _____
> 1 dangling modifier _____
> 1 missing comma after a quotation _____
> 2 missing apostrophes _____ _____
> 1 missing quotation mark _____

¹Our daughter was a happy, pleasant child until she reached the age of two. ²Then, she begun having tantrums—and not just any tantrums. ³No, Tasha would thrash on the floor, knock her head against the wall, and let out a bloodcurdling scream that pierced our eardrums like an ice pick. ⁴Consulting our child care books, the decision was made to ignore the screams, Tasha's attempts to capture our attention might then stop. ⁵Have you ever tried to ignore a toddler whose howls and moans make the walls shake? ⁶We had to think of something before Tasha drove us to a pair of padded cells, it was then that I came up with a notion of a "screaming place." ⁷The next time that Tasha started the low, sirenlike wail that preceded a full-fledged scream. ⁸I carried her to the bathroom. ⁹I said, "Tasha, this is your screaming place. ¹⁰It's small, so youll hear your screams nice and loud. ¹¹You can roll around on the soft carpet. ¹²You can even get a drink if your throat feels dry. ¹³Tasha came barreling out of the bathroom in about ten seconds—screaming—and I gently pushed her back in. ¹⁴When she came out the next time, she had stopped screaming. ¹⁵After a few more episodes like this. ¹⁶Tasha's tantrums started to subside. ¹⁷Apparently, the private screaming

place wasnt as much fun as the more public parts of the house. [18]I knew my system had triumphed when, one day, I passed Tasha's room and heard some muffled moans. [19]I poked my head in the door and asked her why she was crying. [20]"I'm not crying, Daddy," she said. [21]"Brownie's crying." [22]Brownie is the name of Tasha's teddy bear. [23]"But where is Brownie?" I asked. [24] Tasha walked over to the closet and opened it, revealing a rather lonely stuffed bear. [25]"He's in his screaming place" she replied.

NAME: _____

DATE: _____

COMBINED EDITING TEST 10

Locate and correct the ten sentence-skills mistakes in the following passage. The mistakes are listed in the box below. As you locate each mistake, write the number of the word group containing it in the space provided. Then, in the spaces between the lines, correct each mistake.

2 fragments _____ _____
2 run-ons _____ _____
1 dropped verb ending _____
1 irregular verb mistake _____
1 dangling modifier _____
1 apostrophe mistake _____
1 mistake in parallelism _____
1 missing capital letter _____

¹In 1940, an unusual young man was buried in a custom-built ten-foot-long casket. ²The young man needed such a gigantic casket because he himself was a giant. ³He was just a shade under nine feet tall. ⁴And weighed almost five hundred pounds. ⁵Robert Wadlow, an american born in 1918, lived a tragic, pain-filled life. ⁶Weighing eight pounds at birth, Robert's mother had given birth to a normal infant. ⁷But by the age of five, Robert stood over five feet tall. ⁸His exceptional growth never stopped he grew three inches every year until he died. ⁹Because a human's internal organs can't support an excessively large body. ¹⁰Robert was doomed to an early death. ¹¹Just before he died, he was fitted with ankle braces to help support his enormous weight. ¹²One of the braces cut into an ankle, triggering an infection that overload his already strained immune system.

¹³The Wadlow family's reaction to Robert's plight was an intelligent and loving one. ¹⁴They refused to let him be exploited, turning down offers from freak shows and greedy promoters. ¹⁵Robert's parents attempted to give him a normal life they encouraged him to read, to join the Boy Scouts, and playing sports.

^{16}When the company that made Robert's shoes offered to employ him as a traveling representative, Mr. Wadlow drove his son more than 300,000 miles—all over the United States—on behalf of the shoe company. ^{17}The Wadlows helped Robert to stay cheerful and avoid the depression and gloom he could so easily have sinked into. ^{18}Robert's life is an example of tremendous courage and persistence in the face of incredible handicap's.

NAME: _____

DATE: _____

COMBINED EDITING TEST 11

Locate and correct the ten sentence-skills mistakes in the following passage. The mistakes are listed in the box below. As you locate each mistake, write the number of the word group containing it in the space provided. Then, in the spaces between the lines, correct each mistake.

> 1 fragments _____
>
> 1 run-on _____
>
> 1 mistake in subject-verb agreement _____
>
> 2 missing commas around an interrupter _____ _____
>
> 1 missing comma after introductory words _____
>
> 2 clichés _____ _____
>
> 1 mistake in parallelism _____
>
> 1 irregular verb mistake _____

¹Everyone suffer from an occasional bad mood, but I get down in the dumps more often than other people. ²As a result, I've developed a list of helpful hints for dealing with depression, one thing I've learned to do is to keep a mood diary. ³About four times a day, I jot down a one-word description of my mood at that moment—sad, tired, frustrated, happy, and so on. ⁴Then I ask myself questions like "What event preceded this mood? ⁵Have I just eaten a lot of junk food or drank a lot of coffee? ⁶Have I felt this way before?" ⁷After keeping this diary for a while, I've begun to see patterns in my moods. ⁸I've found for example that consuming a lot of salty foods like chips or pretzels makes me feel tense. ⁹Another way I've found to control my moods is to exercise every day. ¹⁰Exercise seems to prevent depression; it also helps me to sleep better. ¹¹Any type of exercise works, including jogging, dancing, and even just to walk around the block. ¹²I can also overcome depression by giving myself a small treat at those times

when my spirits are under the weather. [13]For instance, I might go to a movie, listen to a CD, or buy a new shirt. [14]Finally, I try not to go to sleep in a bad mood. [15]I find that I will probably wake up in the same mood that I fell asleep in. [16]Before getting into bed I'll do some relaxation techniques like deep breathing or stretching exercises. [17]Sometimes, I'll try soaking in a hot tub. [18]Which seems to ease the tension in my muscles. [19]If I still feel miserable, I try to remain hopeful, for no bad mood lasts forever.

NAME: _____

DATE: _____

COMBINED EDITING TEST 12

Locate and correct the ten sentence-skills mistakes in the following passage. The mistakes are listed in the box below. As you locate each mistake, write the number of the word group containing it in the space provided. Then, in the spaces between the lines, correct each mistake.

2 fragments _____ _____
1 run-on _____
1 dropped verb ending _____
1 mistake in subject-verb agreement _____
1 mistake in pronoun agreement _____
1 missing capital letter _____
2 missing commas around an interrupter _____ _____
1 apostrophe mistake _____

¹A former advertising copywriter named Paul Stevens explain in a book called *I Can Sell You Anything* how advertisers use "weasel words" to persuade people to buy. ²Weasel words are slippery, sneaky words that may not really mean what they imply. ³Some of them make you believe things that have never been stated. ⁴For example, the weasel words *help* and *like*. ⁵How many ads can you think of that include the phrases *helps stop, helps prevent,* or *helps fight?* ⁶A toothpaste company couldn't possibly say that their product will "stop cavities forever," so that weasel word *helps* is put in front of the claim. ⁷Now the ad sounds impressive. ⁸But doesn't actually guarantee anything. ⁹The same is true of *like*. ¹⁰if a household cleanser claims that it cleans "like a white tornado," are you impressed? ¹¹The image of a powerful, dirt-sucking whirlwind may have gripped your mind. ¹²However if you think about it a tornado springing out of a bottle is clearly impossible. ¹³Then there is the weasel words that don't have

any particular meaning. [14]Words like *taste, flavor,* and *good looks* are all based on subjective standards that vary with each individual. [15]The truth is that every cigarette in the world can "taste best" every car manufacturer can claim the "most advanced design." [16]There's just no scientific way to measure qualities like these. [17]Advertisers, using weasel words, manipulate language to win the trust (and the cash) of consumer's.

NAME: _____

DATE: _____

Each numbered box in the application below contains a sentence-skills mistake. Identify each of the ten mistakes. Write the type of mistake you found followed by the corrected entry, in the space provided. The first one has been done for you.

1. *missing comma: August 15, 2008* _____   6. _____

_____   _____

2. _____   7. _____

_____   _____

3. _____   8. _____

_____   _____

4. _____   9. _____

_____   _____

5. _____   10. _____

_____   _____

DT Food Services Ltd. • Employment Application			1. Date of Application *August 15 2008*

Social Security # 123-45-6789		Last Name *Lee-Thomas*	First Name *Leona*	Middle Initial *F.*

Address (Street number and name) *550 Tenth Avenue*		2. City, State, and Zip Code *carson city, NV 89706*	

3. Desired Position *"Food Server"*	4. Date Available to Start *Tommorrow*	Home Phone	Business Phone

EDUCATION

Schools	Name and Location	Dates Attended (mo/yr) From: To:	Grad?	Major/Minor Course Work	Type of Degree
High School	5. *Kennedy High school*	9/80 to 6/84	YES NO		
College or University	*Washoe Community College*	9/84 to 6/85	YES NO X		
Other Training or Education	6. *Coarse in keyboarding*		YES X NO		

WORK HISTORY (include volunteer experience. Use additional sheets if necessary.)

7. Current or Last Employer: *Grocery outlet*	8. Address: *120 South Carson Street Carson City NV 89706*

9. Job Title: *Sales' Clerk*	Supervisor's Name and Title *Julie Leroy, Manager*	Telephone Number

Dates Employed (mo/yr–mo/yr) *10/05 to present*	Starting Salary *$ 6.00/hour*	Ending or Current Salary *$ 7.50/hour*	Reason for Leaving

10. List major duties in order of their importance in the job: *I operate the cash register. Also stock shelves.*

Each underlined area in the cover letter below contains a sentence-skills mistake. Identify the mistake and write its item number in the appropriate space in the box below. Then correct the mistake in the space above each error.

COMBINED EDITING TEST 14

Missing colon: _____   Homonym mistake: _____ _____

Missing apostrophe: _____   Dangling modifier: _____

Wrong verb tense: _____   Fragment: _____

Missing word: _____   Run-on: _____

Missing comma: _____

Karen Sanchez

Personnel Officer

Bay Adventures

Tampa, FL 33619

Dear Ms. <u>Sanchez</u>
            1

    I am replying to your ad in last <u>Sundays</u> newspaper that indicated an opening
                                                2
in Bay Adventures for a recreational activities coordinator. <u>Athletic and outgoing,</u>
                                                                        3
the position seems ideal for me.

    I <u>spend</u> the past two years working at an after-school program <u>wear</u> I developed
       4   5
fun activities for children in grades K–6. My job required me to think of creative
yet safe ways to promote physical fitness. <u>And encourage teamwork and cooperation</u>
<u>among the kids.</u>
            6
    Also, I took several physical education classes at <u>University of Tampa. I learned</u>
                                                        7
<u>about sports psychology, I even took a class on exercise techniques.</u> Right now, I
                                                        8
hope to apply what I have learned, which is why I am very interested in your job.

    Please feel free to call me for an interview. Thank you for <u>you're</u> consideration.
                                                                9
<u>Sincerely</u>
   10

Mark Rankins

NAME: _____

DATE: _____

**COMBINED
EDITING TEST 15**

Each underlined area in the cover letter below contains a sentence-skills mistake. Identify the mistake and write its item number in the appropriate space in the box below. Then correct the mistake in the space above each error.

> Missing period: _____
>
> Homonym mistake: _____
>
> Faulty parallelism: _____
>
> Run-on: _____
>
> Missing colon: _____
>
> Spelling error: _____
>
> Slang: _____
>
> Fragment: _____ _____
>
> Apostrophe mistake: _____

August 15, 2007

<u>Mr Gordon</u> Hebling
     1

Western Savings Bank

122 Mijo Way

Tucson, AZ 85706

Dear Mr. <u>Hebling</u>
          2

I attended a career fair last week at the Tucson Convention Center and discovered that <u>you're</u> company is hiring part-time and relief tellers. A <u>guy</u> I spoke to told me
          3   4
that I would be ideal for the position because of my experience working as a cashier.

I currently work as a cashier at an electronics <u>store. But would like to start a</u>
                                                                          5
<u>career in banking</u>. My job requires me to be responsible and accurate. I understand the importance of customer service and <u>am good at communicating.</u>
                                                                          6

In addition to my work experience. I am able to use the 10-key by touch, I have
                                    7   8
used several computer systems. If I am hired, I can work at various banks because
I have a valid drivers' lisense and my own car.
                        9   10
Please feel free to call me at (520) 222-2222. I hope that I will have an opportunity to talk with you in person.

Sincerely,

Monique Williamson

NAME: _____

DATE: _____

COMBINED EDITING TEST 16

Each underlined area in the resume excerpt below contains a sentence-skills mistake. Identify the mistake and write its item number in the appropriate space in the box below. Then correct the mistake in the space above each error.

> Missing capital letter: _____ _____
>
> Dangling modifier: _____
>
> Faulty parallelism: _____
>
> Fragment: _____ _____
>
> Inconsistent verb tense: _____
>
> Run-on: _____
>
> Apostrophe mistake: _____
>
> Missing comma: _____

Alyssa Leong

597 bagley Street
___1___

Torrance CA 90501
___2___

Phone: (310) 555-5555

OBJECTIVE: I hope to find a position as a certified nurse assistant at a nursing facility that will offer me rewarding work, <u>hours that are full time,</u> and medical
___3___
benefits.

QUALIFICATIONS: <u>Caring, competent, and hard working,</u> my experience
___4___
caring for people is present. <u>Having volunteered</u> at an adult residential care
home for two years. I am aware of the responsibilities for providing basic
___5___
care. <u>At the care home.</u> I helped staff members and sometimes fed, bathed,
___6___
and <u>dress</u> clients. My <u>supervisors'</u> encouraged me to enroll in a certified nurs-
___7___   ___8___
ing assistant program. <u>In 2007, I completed a six-month training, I also
received my CNA certification.</u>
___9___

EDUCATION:

2000–2004   Diploma, Roosevelt High School

2007   Certified Nursing Assistance Program, Los Angeles Adult
             Community School

WORK HISTORY:

Volunteer. South central adult residential Care Home, (9/2005 to 6/2007)

Assisted clients with personal hygiene and recreational activities.

Provided companionship.

NAME: _____

DATE: _____

Each numbered line in the resume below contains a sentence-skills mistake. Identify the mistake and write its item number in the appropriate space in the box below. Then correct the mistake in the space above each error.

> Missing capital letter: _____ _____
>
> Spelling error: _____
>
> Missing comma: _____
>
> Inconsistent verb tense: _____
>
> Homonym mistake: _____
>
> Missing -*s* ending: _____ _____
>
> Apostrophe error: _____ _____

Kalani Bowers

[1]203 Mahogany avenue

[2]St. Louis MO 63103

Phone: (314) 777-7777

[3]**Objective:** I wish to find a full-time sales position with an oportunity for advancement and personal growth.

Work History:

Inventory Clerk at Dave's TV & Appliance • St. Louis, MO • 2004 to present
Responsibilities:

4 • Used a computer system to catalog and monitor inventory (electronics and appliance)

5 • Conducted quarterly physical inventories'

Data Entry Clerk at CPK Trading Company • St. Louis, MO • 2001 to 2004

6 • Processed payments and invoice

7 • Maintain and audited numerous databases

8 • Entered daily sales receipts for too branch locations

9 • Generated reports' and memoranda

Education:

St. Anthony's High School • Columbia, MO

• Graduated June 2001

Special Skills:

• Experienced with Windows, Word, and Excel

10 • c.p.r. Certified

4

Readings for Writing

Introduction

Part Four provides a series of reading selections that should both capture your interest and enlarge your understanding. This part of the book begins by explaining the format of each selection, the four kinds of comprehension questions that accompany each reading, and four hints that can make for effective reading. After you read each selection, work through the reading comprehension, technique, and discussion questions that follow. They will help you understand, appreciate, and think about the selection. Then write a paragraph or essay on one of the three writing assignments provided.

As you work on a paper, refer as needed to the guidelines for effective writing in Part One and the rules of grammar, punctuation, and usage in Part Two. Doing so will help make these basic rules an everyday part of your writing.

What was your favorite thing to read when you were younger? What about now? (It doesn't have to be a book; it could also be a magazine, comic book, newspaper, or Web site.) Has it changed since you were younger? Why or why not?

Introduction to the Readings

This part of the book will help you become a better reader as well as a stronger writer. Reading and writing are closely connected skills—so practicing one skill helps develop the other. Included here are ten high-interest reading selections that provide inspiration for a wide range of paragraph and essay writing assignments.

The Format of Each Selection

To help you read the selections effectively—and write about them effectively—the following features are included.

Preview

A short preview introduces you to each reading selection and to its author. These previews will help you start thinking about a selection even before you start to read it.

"Words to Watch"

For each selection, there is a list of difficult words in the selection, with their paragraph numbers and their meanings as they are used in the reading. You may find it helpful to read through "Words to Watch" to remind yourself of meanings or to learn new ones. Within the reading itself, each listed word is marked with a small color bullet (°). When you're reading, if you are not sure of the definition of a word marked with this bullet, go back and look it up in "Words to Watch."

Reading Comprehension Questions

Following each selection, a series of questions gives you practice in four reading skills widely recognized as important to comprehension. These skills have to do with (1) vocabulary, (2) main and central ideas, (3) key details, and (4) inferences.

1 Understanding Vocabulary in Context   The *context* of a word is the words that surround it. We learn many words by guessing their meanings from their context. For example, look at the sentence below. Can you figure out the meaning of the italicized word? After reading the sentence, try to answer the multiple-choice item.

> Karen was *euphoric* when the college that was her first choice accepted her.
>
> The word *euphoric* in the above sentence means
>
> a. puzzled.
>
> b. angry.
>
> c. overjoyed.
>
> d. sad.

You can figure out the meaning of *euphoric* on the basis of its context. Since Karen was accepted by the college that was her first choice, we can assume that she was overjoyed (*c*) rather than puzzled, angry, or sad. Understanding vocabulary in context is a very useful skill to develop, since we often meet new words in our reading. If we pay attention to their context, we may not need a dictionary to figure out what they mean.

2 Determining Main Ideas and the Central Idea   As you learned in Part One of this book, a paragraph is about a point, or main idea, which is often expressed in a topic sentence; and in an essay, there is an overall main idea, often called the central idea. While the reading selections here are longer than the essays you write for your classes, they follow this same pattern. Sometimes the author of a selection states the central idea directly in one or more sentences; sometimes the reader must figure it out. In either case, to know what an author is really saying, readers must determine the central idea and the main ideas that support it.

3 Recognizing Key Supporting Details   Supporting details are reasons, examples, and other kinds of information that help explain or clarify main ideas and the central idea. Recognizing key supporting details is an important part of understanding an author's message.

4 Making Inferences   Often, an author does not state a point directly. Instead, he or she may only suggest the point, and the reader must *infer* it—in other words, figure it out. We make inferences every day, basing them on our understanding and experience. For example, suppose you take your seat in a lecture class in which the instructor always reads from notes in a boring tone of voice. A fellow student comments, "Well, this should be another thrilling lecture." You readily infer—you conclude from the circumstances—that your classmate is not saying what he or she means. The meaning is really the opposite of what was said.

Here is another example of inference. Consider the sentence below. What can you infer from it? Circle the letter of the most logical inference.

Two elderly men silently played chess on a park bench, ignoring both the hot July sun and a fortyish woman who held a red umbrella over her head while watching their game.

The sentence suggests that

a. the men disliked the woman.

b. the woman was related to one of the men.

c. it was raining heavily.

d. the woman wanted to protect herself from the sun.

If the men were concentrating on their game, they would be likely to ignore their surroundings, including the woman, so nothing in the sentence suggests that they disliked her, and *a* is therefore not a logical inference. Also, nothing in the sentence suggests that the men knew the woman, so *b* is not a logical inference either. And *c* is also incorrect, since the sentence mentions only the sun: if it were sunny and raining at the same time, the sentence would surely note such an unusual situation. That leaves only *d* as the correct inference—that the woman was using the umbrella to protect herself from the "hot July sun."

Making inferences like these is often necessary for a full understanding of an author's point.

Technique Questions

Questions about *technique* point to methods writers have used to present their material effectively. In particular, technique questions make you aware of directly stated central ideas, methods of organization, transition words, and vivid details that help writers make their ideas come alive for the reader. Focusing on such techniques will help you use them in your own writing.

Discussion Questions

The discussion questions help you think in detail about ideas raised by the selection and make connections between the selection and your own life. They will help you look closely at what you value, whom you respect, and how you react to people and situations.

Writing Assignments

The writing assignments following each selection are based specifically on that selection. Many assignments provide guidelines on how to proceed, including suggestions about prewriting, possible topic sentences and thesis statements, and methods of development.

Hints for Effective Reading

Effective reading, like effective writing, does not happen all at once. Rather, it is a process. Often you begin with a general impression of what something means, and then, by rereading, you move to a deeper level of understanding of the material.

Here are some hints for becoming a better reader.

1 **Read in the right place.**   Ideally, you should get settled in a quiet spot that encourages concentration. If you can focus your attention while lying on a bed or curled up in a chair, that's fine. But if you find that being very comfortable leads to daydreaming or dozing off rather than reading, then avoid getting too relaxed. You might find that sitting in an upright chair promotes concentration and keeps your mind alert.

2 **Preview the selection.**   Begin by reading the overview that precedes the selection. Then think for a minute about the title. A good title often hints at a selection's central idea, giving you insight into the piece even before you read it. For example, you can deduce from the title of Alice Walker's essay, "My Daughter Smokes," that Walker is likely going to offer a negative commentary about her daughter's habit.

3 **Read the selection right through for pleasure.**   Allow yourself to be drawn into the world that the author has created. Don't slow down or turn back. Instead, just read to understand as much as you can the first time through. After this reading, sit back for a moment and think about what you enjoyed in the piece.

4 **Deepen your sense of the selection.**   Go back and reread it, or at least reread the passages that may not have been clear the first time through. Look up any words that you cannot figure out from context, and write their meanings in the margin. Now ask yourself the following questions:

- What is the central idea of the piece?
- What are the main supporting points for the central idea?
- How does the author explain and illustrate these main supporting points?

Reread carefully the parts of the selection that seem most relevant to answering these questions. By asking yourself the questions and by rereading, you will gradually deepen your understanding of the material.

The Importance of Regular Reading

Chances are that you are not as good a reader as you should be to do well in college. If so, it's not surprising. You live in a culture where people watch an average of *over seven hours of television every day!* All that passive viewing does not allow much time for reading. Reading is a skill that must be actively practiced. The simple fact is that people who do not read very often are not likely to be strong readers.

Another reason for not reading much is that you may have a lot of responsibilities. You may be going to school and working at the same time, and you may have many family duties as well. Given a hectic schedule, you're not going to have much opportunity to read. When you have free time, you may be exhausted and find it easier to turn on the TV than to open a book.

A third reason for not reading is that our public school system may have soured you on it. One government study after another has said that our schools have not done a good job of turning people on to the rewards of reading. If you had to read a lot of uninteresting and irrelevant material in grade school and high school, you may have decided (mistakenly) that reading in general is not for you.

These reasons may help explain why you are not in the habit of regular reading. For people who are unpracticed readers, there is one overall key to becoming a better reader. That key, simple as it may sound, is to do a great deal of reading. The truth of the matter is that *reading is like any other skill. The more you practice, the better you get.*

Regular reading is a habit with many rewards. Research has shown that frequent reading improves vocabulary, spelling, reading speed, and comprehension, as well as grammar and writing style. All of these language and thinking skills develop in an almost painless way for the person who becomes a habitual reader.

The question to ask, then, is "What steps can I take to become a regular reader?" The first step is to develop the right attitude. Recognize that a person who can read well has more potential and more power than a person who cannot. Reading is a source of extraordinary power. Consider the experience of Ben Carson as told on pages 546–552 of this book. After he started reading two books a week, at his mother's insistence, his entire world changed. He moved from the bottom of his class to the head of his class, and he went on to become a world-famous surgeon. And Grant Berry, on pages 535–540, describes how a commitment to reading was the key to his hopes for the future. Increasingly in today's world, jobs involve processing information. More than ever, words are the tools of our trades. The better your command of words, the more success you are likely to have. And nothing else will give you a command of words like regular reading.

A second step toward becoming a regular reader is to subscribe to a daily newspaper and, every day, read the sections that interest you. Remember that it is not what you read that matters—for example, you should not feel obliged to read the editorial section if opinion columns are not your interest. Instead, what matters is *the very fact that you read.* Your favorite section may be the comics, or fashion, or sports, or movie reviews, or the front page. Feel perfectly free to read whatever you decide you want to read.

A third step is to subscribe to one or more magazines. On many college bulletin boards, you'll see displays offering a wide variety of magazines at discount rates for college students. You may want to consider a weekly newsmagazine, such as *Newsweek* or *Time,* or a weekly general-interest magazine such as *People.* You will also be able to choose from a wide variety of monthly magazines, some of which will suit your interests. You may also want to look over the magazine section at any newsstand or bookstore. Most magazines contain postage-paid subscriber cards inside that you can send in to start a subscription. Finally, you may want to visit the magazine section of your library on a regular basis to just sit and read for an hour or so.

A fourth step to regular reading is to create a half hour of reading in your daily schedule. That time might be during your lunch hour, or late afternoon before dinner, or the half hour or so before you turn off your light at night. Find a time that is possible for you and make reading then a habit. The result will be both recreation and personal growth.

A fifth step is to read aloud to your children, which will benefit both them and you. Alternatively, have a family reading time when you and your children take turns reading. There are many books on the market that can be enjoyed by both parents and children. One outstanding choice is *Charlotte's Web*, by E. B. White—a classic story available in any bookstore or library. The children's librarian at your local library may be a good source for books. There are also many choices in the children's section at almost any paperback bookstore. An excellent mail-order source of books for children is the Chinaberry Book Service, 2780 Via Orange Way, Suite B, Spring Valley, California 91978. In its catalog, recommended books are grouped in five levels, from titles suitable for the very young to titles for young adults. Many of the books are pictured, and each book is helpfully described. To get a catalog, you can call a toll-free number: 1-800-776-2242.

The most important step on the road to becoming a regular reader is to read books on your own. Reading is most valuable and most enjoyable when you get drawn into the special world created by a book. You can travel in that world for hours or days, unmindful for a while of everyday concerns. In that timeless zone you will come to experience the joy of reading. You will also add depth to your life and make more sense out of the world. Too many people are addicted to smoking or drugs or television; you should try, instead, to get hooked on books.

The books to read are simply any books that interest you. They might be comic books, science fiction, adventure stories, romances, suspense or detective stories, horror novels, autobiographies, or any other type of book. To select your books, browse in a paperback bookstore, a library, a reading center, or any other place with a large number of books. Or read the short descriptions of the widely popular books in the list that follows. Find something you like and begin your reading journey. If you stick to it and become a regular reader, you may find that you have done nothing less than change your life.

A List of Interesting Books
Autobiographies and Other Nonfiction

I Know Why the Caged Bird Sings, Maya Angelou

The author writes with love, humor, and honesty about her childhood and what it is like to grow up black and female.

Alicia: My Story, Alicia Appleman-Jurman

Alicia was a Jewish girl living with her family in Poland when the Germans invaded in 1941. Her utterly compelling and heartbreaking story shows some of the best and worst of which human beings are capable.

Growing Up, Russell Baker

Russell Baker's mother, a giant presence in his life, insisted that he make something of himself. In his autobiography, the prizewinning journalist shows that he did with an engrossing account of his own family and growing up.

In Cold Blood, Truman Capote

This book, a frightening true story about the murder of a family, is also an examination of what made their killers tick. Many books today tell gripping stories of real-life crimes. *In Cold Blood* was the first book of this type and may still be the best.

Gifted Hands, Ben Carson

This is the inspiring story of an inner-city kid with poor grades and little motivation who turned his life around. Dr. Carson is now a world-famous neurosurgeon at one of the best hospitals in the world; his book tells how he got there. In *Think Big* and *The Big Picture,* two related books, Dr. Carson tells more of his story and presents the philosophy that helped him make the most of his life.

Move On, Linda Ellerbee

A well-known television journalist writes about the ups and downs of her life, including her stay at the Betty Ford Center for treatment of her alcoholism.

The Diary of a Young Girl, Anne Frank

To escape the Nazi death camps, Anne Frank and her family hid for years in an attic. Her journal tells a story of love, fear, and courage.

Man's Search for Meaning, Viktor Frankl

How do people go on when they have been stripped of everything, including human dignity? In this short but moving book, the author describes his time in a concentration camp and what he learned there about survival.

The Story of My Life, Helen Keller

How Miss Keller, a blind and deaf girl who lived in isolation and frustration, discovered a path to learning and knowledge.

The Autobiography of Malcolm X, Malcolm X and Alex Haley

Malcolm X, the controversial black leader who was assassinated by one of his followers, writes about the experiences that drove him to a leadership role in the Black Muslims.

Makes Me Wanna Holler, Nathan McCall

A dramatic first-person account of how a bright young black man went terribly wrong and was lured into a life of crime. McCall, now a reporter for the *Washington Post,* eventually found a basis for self-respect different from that of his peers, who are murdered, commit suicide, become drug zombies, or wind up in prison.

Angela's Ashes, Frank McCourt

This widely popular autobiography tells the story of an Irish boy whose father was a drunkard and whose mother tried desperately to hold her family together. The poverty described is heartbreaking, and yet the book is wonderfully moving and often funny. You'll shake your head in disbelief at all the hardships, but at other times you'll laugh out loud at the comic touches.

A Hole in the World, Richard Rhodes

Little more than a year old when his mother killed herself, Rhodes has ever since been conscious of "a hole in the world" where his mother's love should have been. In this true and terrifying account of his boyhood, he describes how he managed to survive.

Down These Mean Streets, Piri Thomas

Life in a Puerto Rican ghetto is shown vividly and with understanding by one who experienced it.

Fiction

Watership Down, Richard Adams

A wonderfully entertaining adventure story about rabbits who act a great deal like people. The plot may sound unlikely, but it will keep you on the edge of your seat.

Patriot Games, Tom Clancy

In a story of thrills and suspense, a government agent helps stop an act of terrorism. The terrorists then plot revenge on the agent and his family.

The Cradle Will Fall, Mary Higgins Clark

A county prosecutor uncovers evidence that a famous doctor is killing women, not realizing that she herself is becoming his next target. One typical comment by a reviewer about Clark's books is that they are "a ticket to ride the roller coaster . . . once on the track, we're there until the ride is over."

Note: If you like novels with terror and suspense, many of Mary Higgins Clark's books are good choices.

And Justice for One, John Clarkson

In this adventure-thriller, a former Secret Service agent seeks revenge after his brother is almost killed and his girlfriend is kidnapped. Because of corruption in the police force, the agent must take the law into his own hands.

Deliverance, James Dickey

Several men go rafting down a wild river in Georgia and encounter beauty, violence, and self-knowledge.

Eye of the Needle, Ken Follett

A thriller about a Nazi spy—"The Needle"—and a woman who is the only person who can stop him.

Lord of the Flies, William Golding

Could a group of children, none older than twelve, survive by themselves on a tropical island in the midst of World War Three? In this modern classic, Golding shows us that the real danger is not the war outside but "the beast" within each of us.

Snow Falling on Cedars, David Guterson

This is a unique murder mystery. The story is set in the 1950s in an island community where a fisherman is found dead on his boat and another fisherman is quickly blamed for the death. The accused man is so proud that he refuses to defend himself for a crime he says he did not commit. Like all great stories, this one is about more than itself. It becomes a celebration of the mystery of the human heart.

The Silence of the Lambs, Thomas Harris

A psychotic killer is on the loose, and to find him, the FBI must rely on clues provided by an evil genius. Like some other works on this list, *The Silence of the Lambs* was made into a movie that is not as good as the book.

Flowers for Algernon, Daniel Keyes

A scientific experiment turns a retarded man into a genius. But the results are a mixture of joy and heartbreak.

The Shining, Stephen King

A haunted hotel, a little boy with extrasensory perception, and an insane father— they're all together in a horror tale of isolation and insanity. One review says, "Be prepared to be scared out of your mind. . . . Don't read this book when you are home alone. If you dare—once you get past a certain point, there's no stopping."

Note: If you like novels with terror and suspense, many of Stephen King's books are good choices.

Watchers, Dean Koontz

An incredibly suspenseful story about two dogs that undergo lab experiments. One dog becomes a monster programmed to kill, and it seeks to track down the couple who know its secret.

Note: If you like novels with a great deal of action and suspense, many of Dean Koontz's books are good choices.

To Kill a Mockingbird, Harper Lee

A controversial trial, involving a black man accused of raping a white woman, is the centerpiece of this story about adolescence, bigotry, and justice. One review described the book as "a novel of great sweetness, humor, compassion, and mystery carefully sustained."

The Natural, Bernard Malamud

An aging player makes a comeback that stuns the baseball world.

Waiting to Exhale, Terry McMillan

Four thirty-something black women all hope that Mr. Right will appear, but this doesn't stop them from living their lives. One reviewer wrote that McMillan "has such a wonderful ear for story and dialogue. She gives us four women with raw, honest emotions that breathe off the page."

Gone with the Wind, Margaret Mitchell

The characters and places in this book—Scarlett O'Hara, Rhett Butler, Tara— have become part of our culture because they are unforgettable.

A Day No Pigs Would Die, Robert Peck

A boy raises a pig that is intelligent and affectionate. Will the boy follow orders and send the animal off to be slaughtered? Read this short novel to find out.

Harry Potter and the Sorcerer's Stone, J. K. Rowling

The first in a series of award-winning stories that have captured the hearts of young and old alike, around the world. These funny, action-packed, touching books are about a likable boy who is mistreated by the relatives who take him in after his parents are killed. Then Harry discovers that he is a wizard, and his extraordinary adventures begin.

The Catcher in the Rye, J. D. Salinger

The frustrations and turmoil of being an adolescent have never been captured so well as in this book. The main character, Holden Caulfield, is honest, funny, affectionate, obnoxious, and tormented at the same time.

The Lord of the Rings, J. R. R. Tolkien

Enter an amazing world of little creatures known as Hobbits; you, like thousands of other readers, may never want to leave.

Charlotte's Web, E. B. White

This best-loved story, for children and adults, is about a little pig named Wilbur and his best friend, a spider named Charlotte. Wilbur is being fattened in order to be killed for a holiday meal; Charlotte must come up with a plan to save him.

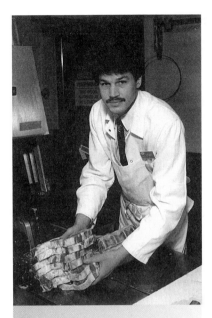

Grant continues to work as a butcher full time.

Working full time and raising a family leave me little free time. If I am not in class, I'm studying linking verbs or trying to figure out the difference between compound and complex sentences. 19

There are other obstacles and challenges staring me in the face. The tallest hurdle is a lack of time for meeting all my obligations. For instance, my wife works two nights a week, leaving me to care for my two daughters. A twelve-hour day at work can lead to an evening coma at home, so when Mom's punching little square buttons on a cash register, I hardly have the energy to pour cornflakes for my kids, let alone outline a research paper. 20

Going to college means making choices, some of which bring criticism. My neighbors, for example, hate my sickly, brown lawn sandwiched between their lush, green, spotless plots of earth, which would be the envy of any football field. Just walking to my mailbox can be an awful reminder of how pitiful my lawn looks when I receive an unforgiving scowl from one of the groundskeepers who live on either side of me. It is embarrassing to have such a colorless lawn, but it will have to wait because I want more out of life than a half-acre of green turf. Right now my time and money are tied up in college courses instead of fertilizer and weed killer. 21

But the toughest obstacle is having to take away time from those I love most. I am proud of the relationship I have with my wife and kids, so it tears 22

In the college computer lab, Grant works on a paper.

my guts out when I have to look into my daughter's sad face and explain that I can't go to the Christmas program she's been practicing for weeks because I have a final exam. It's not easy to tell my three-year-old that I can't push her on the swings because I have a cause-and-effect paper to write, or tell my seven-year-old that I can't build a snowman because I have an argument essay to polish. As I tell my family that I can't go sledding with them, my wife lets out a big sigh, and my kids yell, "Puleeze, Daddy, can't you come with us?" At these times I wonder if my dream of a college education can withstand such an emotional battering,* or if it is even worth it. But I keep on keeping on because I must set a good example for the four little eyes that are keeping watch over their daddy's every move. I must succeed and pass on to them the right attitude toward school. This time when I graduate, because of the hurdles I've overcome, there will be a celebration—a proper one.

■ Reading Comprehension Questions

1. The word *clique* in "In every high school there are cliques and classifications. I worked just hard enough to stay above the bottom, but I did not want to work hard enough to get into the clique with the honor roll students" (paragraph 5) means
   a. grade.
   b. school.
   c. group.
   d. sports.

2. The word *scowl* in "Just walking to my mailbox can be an awful reminder of how pitiful my lawn looks when I receive an unforgiving scowl from one of the groundskeepers who live on either side of me" (paragraph 21) means
   a. sincere smile.
   b. favor.
   c. angry look.
   d. surprise.

3. Which sentence best expresses the central idea of the selection?
   a. The author was never encouraged to attend college or to challenge himself mentally on the job.
   b. After years of not caring about education, Berry was led by some self-help books to love reading, gain self-esteem, and attend college.
   c. The author's wife and children often do not understand why he is unable to take part in many family activities.
   d. The author was given a high school diploma despite the fact that he did little work and rarely attended class.

4. Which sentence best expresses the main idea of paragraph 13?
   a. Influenced by self-help books, the author developed a hunger for reading.
   b. People who really care about improving themselves will find the time to do it, such as during the early morning, at breaks, and during the lunch hour.
   c. Self-help books send the message that everyone is full of potential and even greatness.
   d. There is no limit to the amount of information the brain can hold.

5. Which sentence best expresses the main idea of paragraph 22?
   a. The author's decision to attend college is hurting his long-term relationship with his wife and daughters.
   b. The author has two children, one age three and the other age seven.
   c. The author enjoys family activities such as attending his children's plays and building snowmen.
   d. Although he misses spending time with his family, the author feels that graduating from college will make him a better role model for his children.

6. The author's reading skills
   a. were strong even when he was a child.
   b. improved as he read more.
   c. were strengthened considerably in high school.
   d. were sharpened by jobs he held after high school graduation.

7. The author's father
   a. was rarely home while the author was growing up.
   b. often missed work and stayed out late at bars.
   c. was a college graduate.
   d. disliked school.

8. In stating that his graduation night "was quite a fitting closure for the end of high school," Berry implies that
   a. he was glad high school was finally over.
   b. car troubles were a common problem for him throughout high school.
   c. his behavior had ruined that night just as it had ruined his high school education.
   d. despite the problems, the evening gave him good memories, just as high school had given him good memories.

9. We can infer from paragraph 21 that the author
   a. does not tend his lawn because he enjoys annoying his neighbors.
   b. receives a lot of mail.
   c. is willing to make sacrifices for his college education.
   d. has neighbors who care little about the appearance of their property.

10. We can infer that the author believes children
    a. should be passed to the next grade when they reach a certain age, regardless of their test scores.
    b. should not require a great deal of time from their parents.
    c. fall into two categories: "born readers" and those who can never learn to read very well.
    d. benefit from having role models who care about education.

■ Technique Questions

1. In explaining that he followed his father's example, the author compares himself to "a man who double-crosses the mob [and] follows a cement block to the bottom of the river." In this comparison, Berry strikingly makes the point that his own actions led him to an undesirable situation. Find two other places where the author uses a richly revealing comparison. Write those images below, and explain what Berry means by each one.

   Image: _____

   _____

   Meaning: _____

   Image: _____

   _____

   Meaning: _____

2. In most of his essay, Berry uses time order, but in some places he uses listing order. For example, what does Berry list in paragraphs 20–22?

   _____

3. In closing his essay, Berry writes that at his college graduation, "there will be a celebration—a proper one." With what earlier event is he contrasting this graduation?

   _____

■ Discussion Questions

1. The author looks back at this period of reading self-help books as one in which his attitude improved, eventually leading to his enrollment in college. Has a particular occurrence ever sharply changed your outlook on life? Was it something that you read, observed, or directly experienced? How did it happen? How did it change your point of view?

2. Berry writes that his father did not encourage him to go on to college. Nevertheless, he sees many positive things about his father. In what ways was his father a positive role model for him? In other words, is Berry's positive behavior as an adult partly a result of his father's influence? What do you see in your own adult behavior that you can attribute to your parents' influence?

3. Berry discusses some of the difficulties he faces as a result of being in college—struggling to find time to meet his obligations, giving up lawn care, spending less time with his family. What difficulties do you face as a result

of fitting college into your life? What obligations must you struggle to fulfill? What activities remain undone?

■ Writing Assignments

1. Children are strongly influenced by the example of their parents (and other significant adults in their lives). For instance, the author of this essay followed his father's example of disliking school and getting a job that did not challenge him mentally.

   Think about your growing-up years and about adults who influenced you, both positively and negatively. Then write a paragraph that describes one of these people and his or her influence on you. Supply plenty of vivid examples to help the reader understand how and why this person affected you.

   The topic sentence of your paragraph should identify the person (either by name or by relationship to you) and briefly indicate the kind of influence he or she had on you. Here are some examples of topic sentences for this paper:

   > My aunt's courage in difficult situations helped me to become a stronger person.
   >
   > My father's frequent trouble with the law made it necessary for me to grow up in a hurry.
   >
   > The pastor of our church helped me realize that I was a worthwhile, talented person.

2. Write a paragraph about one way that reading has been important in your life, either positively or negatively. To discover the approach you wish to take, think for a moment about the influence of reading throughout your life. When you were a child, was being read to at bedtime a highlight of your day? Did reading out loud in elementary school cause you embarrassment? Do you adore mysteries or true-crime books? Do you avoid reading whenever possible? Find an idea about the role of reading in your life that you can write about in the space of a paragraph. Your topic sentence will be a clear statement of that idea, such as:

   > I first learned to read from watching *Sesame Street*.
   >
   > One key experience in second grade made me hate reading out loud in class.
   >
   > My parents' attitude toward reading rubbed off on me.
   >
   > Reading to my child at bedtime is an important time of day for both of us.
   >
   > Books have taught me some things I never would have learned from friends and family.
   >
   > There are several reasons why I am not a good reader.
   >
   > A wonderful self-help book has helped me build my self-esteem.

Develop your main idea with detailed explanations and descriptions. For example, if you decide to write about reading to your child at bedtime, you might describe the positions you and your child take (Is the child in bed? On the floor? On your lap?), one or two of the stories the child and you have loved, some of the child's reactions, and so on.

3. Berry's graduation-night celebration was a dramatic one and, he states, "a fitting closure for the end of high school." What was your high school graduation celebration like? Did you participate in any of the planning and preparation for the events? Were finding a date and shopping for clothing for the prom fun or nerve-racking experiences? Was the event itself wonderful or disappointing? Write an essay telling the story of your graduation celebration from start to finish. Use many sharp descriptive details to help your readers envision events, decorations, clothing, cars, the weather, and so on. In addition, add meaning to your story by telling what you were thinking and feeling throughout the event.

You might try making a list as a way of collecting details for this paper. At first, don't worry about organizing your details. Just keep adding to your list, which might at one point look like this:

decorations committee

considered asking my cousin to go with me, if necessary

shopping for prom dress with Mom (and arguing)

afraid I'd be asked first by someone I didn't want to go with

talk of being up all night

pressed orchid corsage afterward

florist busy that week

working on centerpieces

feet hurt

Eventually, you will have enough information to begin thinking about the organization of your essay. Here's what the scratch outline for one such essay looks like:

Central idea: My high school prom was a mixture of fun and disappointment.

(1) Before the dance
     Work on the decorations com. (theme: sky's the limit)
     Anxiety over getting a date, finally relief
     Worn out shopping for a dress
     Last-minute preparations (getting flowers, having hair done, decorating ballroom)

(2) Night of the dance
    Picture-taking at home
    Squeezing gown into car, hem gets stuck in car door and grease rubs on it
    Beautiful ballroom
    Rotten meal
    Great band (even teachers yelling requests)
    After two dances had to take off heels
    Date kept dancing with others
    Danced with my brother, who came with my girlfriend
    Early breakfast served at hotel

(3) After the dance
    Total exhaustion for two days
    Extensive phone analysis of dance with girlfriends
    Never went out with that date again
    Several years later, prom dress, wrapped in a garbage bag, went to Salvation Army

Perhaps you don't remember your graduation night celebration very well, or don't wish to. Feel free to write about another important social event instead, such as a high school reunion, a family reunion, or your own or someone else's wedding.

Do It Better!

Ben Carson, M.D., with Cecil Murphey

Preview

If you suspect that you are now as "smart" as you'll ever be, then read the following selection, taken from the book *Think Big*. It is about Dr. Ben Carson, who was sure he was "the dumbest kid in the class" in school. Carson tells how he turned his life around from what was a sure path to failure. Today he is a famous neurosurgeon at Johns Hopkins University Hospital in Baltimore, Maryland.

■ Words to Watch

inasmuch as (13): since

potential (18): capacity for development and progress

solely (20): alone

rebellious (46): resisting authority

indifferent (58): uninterested

startled (75): surprised

astonished (81): surprised

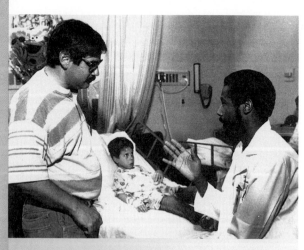

Dr. Carson speaks with a parent about his child's medical condition.

"Benjamin, is this your report card?" my mother asked as she picked up the folded white card from the table. 1

"Uh, yeah," I said, trying to sound casual. Too ashamed to hand it to her, I had dropped it on the table, hoping that she wouldn't notice until after I went to bed. 2

It was the first report card I had received from Higgins Elementary School since we had moved back from Boston to Detroit, only a few months earlier. 3

I had been in the fifth grade not even two weeks before everyone considered me the dumbest kid in the class and frequently made jokes about me. Before long I too began to feel as though I really was the most stupid kid in fifth grade. Despite Mother's frequently saying, "You're smart, Bennie. You can do anything you want to do," I did not believe her. 4

No one else in school thought I was smart, either.   5

Now, as Mother examined my report card, she asked, "What's this grade   6
in reading?" (Her tone of voice told me that I was in trouble.) Although I was
embarrassed, I did not think too much about it. Mother knew that I wasn't
doing well in math, but she did not know I was doing so poorly in every
subject.

While she slowly read my report card, reading everything one word at a   7
time, I hurried into my room and started to get ready for bed. A few minutes
later, Mother came into my bedroom.

"Benjamin," she said, "are these your grades?" She held the card in front   8
of me as if I hadn't seen it before.

"Oh, yeah, but you know, it doesn't mean much."   9

"No, that's not true, Bennie. It means a lot."   10

"Just a report card."   11

"But it's more than that."   12

Knowing I was in for it now, I prepared to listen, yet I was not all that   13
interested. I did not like school very much and there was no reason why I
should. Inasmuch as* I was the dumbest kid in the class, what did I have to look
forward to? The others laughed at me and made jokes about me every day.

"Education is the only way you're ever going to escape poverty," she said.   14
"It's the only way you're ever going to get ahead in life and be successful. Do
you understand that?"

"Yes, Mother," I mumbled.   15

"If you keep on getting these kinds of grades you're going to spend the   16
rest of your life on skid row, or at best sweeping floors in a factory. That's
not the kind of life that I want for you. That's not the kind of life that God
wants for you."

I hung my head, genuinely ashamed. My mother had been raising me   17
and my older brother, Curtis, by herself. Having only a third-grade education
herself, she knew the value of what she did not have. Daily she drummed into
Curtis and me that we had to do our best in school.

"You're just not living up to your potential*," she said. "I've got two   18
mighty smart boys and I know they can do better."

I had done my best—at least I had when I first started at Higgins   19
Elementary School. How could I do much when I did not understand anything
going on in our class?

In Boston we had attended a parochial school, but I hadn't learned much   20
because of a teacher who seemed more interested in talking to another
female teacher than in teaching us. Possibly, this teacher was not solely* to
blame—perhaps I wasn't emotionally able to learn much. My parents had
separated just before we went to Boston, when I was eight years old. I loved
both my mother and my father and went through considerable trauma over
their separating. For months afterward, I kept thinking that my parents
would get back together, that my daddy would come home again the way
he used to, and that we could be the same old family again—but he never
came back. Consequently, we moved to Boston and lived with Aunt Jean and

Uncle William Avery in a tenement building for two years until Mother had saved enough money to bring us back to Detroit.

Mother kept shaking the report card at me as she sat on the side of my 21 bed. "You have to work harder. You have to use that good brain that God gave you, Bennie. Do you understand that?"

"Yes, Mother." Each time she paused, I would dutifully say those words. 22

"I work among rich people, people who are educated," she said. "I watch 23 how they act, and I know they can do anything they want to do. And so can you." She put her arm on my shoulder. "Bennie, you can do anything they can do—only you can do it better!"

Mother had said those words before. Often. At the time, they did not 24 mean much to me. Why should they? I really believed that I was the dumbest kid in fifth grade, but of course, I never told her that.

"I just don't know what to do about you boys," she said. "I'm going to 25 talk to God about you and Curtis." She paused, stared into space, then said (more to herself than to me), "I need the Lord's guidance on what to do. You just can't bring in any more report cards like this."

As far as I was concerned, the report card matter was over. 26

The next day was like the previous ones—just another bad day in school, 27 another day of being laughed at because I did not get a single problem right in arithmetic and couldn't get any words right on the spelling test. As soon as I came home from school, I changed into play clothes and ran outside. Most of the boys my age played softball, or the game I liked best, "Tip the Top."

We played Tip the Top by placing a bottle cap on one of the sidewalk 28 cracks. Then taking a ball—any kind that bounced—we'd stand on a line and take turns throwing the ball at the bottle top, trying to flip it over. Whoever succeeded got two points. If anyone actually moved the cap more than a few inches, he won five points. Ten points came if he flipped it into the air and it landed on the other side.

When it grew dark or we got tired, Curtis and I would finally go inside 29 and watch TV. The set stayed on until we went to bed. Because Mother worked long hours, she was never home until just before we went to bed. Sometimes I would awaken when I heard her unlocking the door.

Two evenings after the incident with the report card, Mother came home 30 about an hour before our bedtime. Curtis and I were sprawled out, watching TV. She walked across the room, snapped off the set, and faced both of us. "Boys," she said, "you're wasting too much of your time in front of that television. You don't get an education from staring at television all the time."

Before either of us could make a protest, she told us that she had been 31 praying for wisdom. "The Lord's told me what to do," she said. "So from now on, you will not watch television, except for two preselected programs each week."

"Just *two* programs?" I could hardly believe she would say such a terrible 32 thing. "That's not—"

"And *only* after you've done your homework. Furthermore, you don't 33 play outside after school, either, until you've done all your homework."

write about, make a list of possible points of support. You may find it helpful to spend a few sessions in front of the TV with a notebook. Following, for instance, is part of a list of notes that can be used to support the point "TV advertising promotes poor nutrition."

<u>During kids' cartoon show:</u>

A sugary chocolate cereal in which marshmallow ghosts appear once milk is added. Children are pictured enjoying these ghosts' appearances and loving the cereal.

Chocolate-dipped cookies are included in boxes of another chocolate cereal. Appealing cartoon characters invite children to look for these boxes.

<u>During talk show:</u>

Ad for soda (empty calories) shows symbols of Christmas, making the soda seem like a healthy holiday drink.

An ad for corn chips (high fat) shows happy, healthy faces finishing up a huge bowl of the chips.

Lost Years, Found Dreams

Regina Ruiz

■ Preview

Divorced, far from home, with three children, not very fluent in English—Regina Ruiz could easily have become a sad statistic, a woman sunk in despair after a failed marriage. But Ruiz decided she had given up enough years of her life; she would reclaim the rest. Her story is hardly a fairy tale with a magical happy ending. But it is perhaps even better; it is the story of a courageous, life-loving commitment to a new and meaningful future.

■ Words to Watch

regal (2): royal

haze (3): confused state of mind

intervened (7): came in to change a situation

bleak (8): not hopeful

bleary-eyed (18): with blurry vision

preoccupation (18): extreme concern with something

Morpheus (20): the god of dreams in Greek mythology

I feel funny. So very funny, telling you about my life, my feelings, my secrets. I do not know how to welcome you into my heart and soul. You see, nobody ever asked me what I thought or how I felt about life's challenges. Or, maybe, nobody ever really cared about what I thought. 1

My journey to Burlington County College began many years ago in Caracas, Venezuela, where I was born and grew to be a young lady full of energy and life. My parents called me Regina because there was something regal° about the sound. They had high hopes of my marrying a local boy from a good, wealthy family. You know the kind—slick, black hair, long sideburns, driving a sports car. The kind who brings you flowers on every date and swears his undying love for you three days a week, and the other days he is sleeping with Maria, the local social worker. 2

To get even, or because I was in a romantic haze,° I met and married a U.S. Marine from Des Moines, Iowa, who was stationed at our local embassy, where I also worked. 3

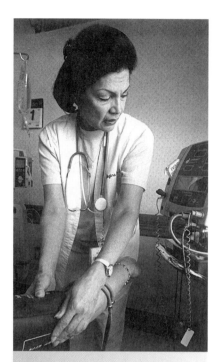

Regina Ruiz's nursing duties include taking a patient's blood pressure.

Marriage, a home in America, and three beautiful children occupied twenty-five years of my life. 4

Where did my life go? It went somewhere. But there is no lost-and-found department for lost years. 5

The marriage was bad. It was so bad that I cried every night for all those years. I would tell myself, "You are in a strange country—maybe the customs are different. The children need you, and you cannot admit failure to your parents back in Venezuela." 6

As luck would have it, fate intervened.° My ex-Marine husband found someone new and left me and the children with no money, very hurt and depressed. 7

I quickly took an inventory—foreign-born, with not a great command of the English language, no money, no job training, and two kids in college. The future looked bleak.° 8

But it did not stop. My father died. I loved him so much, and he was always my source of strength in need. Mother became ill. 9

I felt very hurt, lonely, angry, and very sorry for myself. 10

However, I remembered a saying my Dad would quote to me when things 11 were going wrong and the future looked black. He may have gotten this quotation from the Spanish edition of *Reader's Digest*. He would say, "My dear, it is always the darkest when you are fresh out of matches."

"Dad, I am out of matches." Or so I thought. 12

I decided to make my life something worthwhile by helping people. I 13 wanted to help and heal and maybe, at the same time, heal myself.

I appeared before the college doors with my knees shaking and full of 14 doubt. I wanted to be a nurse.

I enrolled in college. I was proud of myself for not falling into the garbage 15 pit waiting so close by.

Then the fun began—subjects which were very hard for me. 16

In order to survive, I managed to get two jobs to keep up with house pay- 17 ments and food. The kids found college money by working and by appealing to their father. I met my challenges on a daily basis.

Now, my days are very active and long. Before the sun makes its appear- 18 ance, I stumble bleary-eyed° to the shower and afterward select the day's outfit. After a quick check in the mirror, I make my way downstairs to prepare

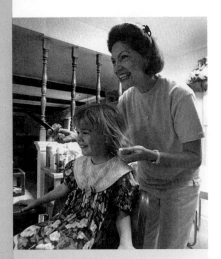

*Regina continues to cut hair of
her friends and family.*

a quick breakfast along with my lunch, feed the cat (who happens to be my alarm clock), and do what seem like a million other small chores. Then I drive for forty-five minutes to the Pemberton Campus, while studying my chemistry key notes on index cards before a test. I do this with tears in my eyes. You see, at the same time I am worrying about the situation with my water heater that slowly but surely is leaking and may not last until the new one can be installed. In addition, I am anxious to schedule my exterminator's visit to treat the termites discovered in my basement. My preoccupation* with such household woes is due to a canceled appointment to have my furnace cleaned, which resulted in a periodic spray of soot.

After a hectic morning of classes, I rush to my car for 19 a hurried thirty-minute ride to the office, where a desk piled high with import documents is waiting for me, along with innumerable phone calls from the brokers, customs officials, and suppliers. Meanwhile, an impatient boss wants to know the precise location of one of the fifty containers traveling between eastern Europe and Burlington, New Jersey.

As the clock winds toward 5 P.M., I get ready to travel back to the 20 Cinnaminson Campus for another round of classes. As I arrive on campus, I waste another thirty minutes searching for that nonexistent parking spot. My class continues until ten o'clock in the evening, and I praise the Lord it doesn't last longer. By that time, I am beginning to see double. I slowly make my way to the car and begin the long commute home, counting in my mind how many customers I will see as a result of my second job—hairdressing. On evenings when I have no classes scheduled, I take appointments to cut hair or give permanents. As I arrive home, I find a hungry son and starving cat, both waiting to be fed. I usually cook something simple for us, then proceed to do the few dishes because I hate the thought of adding one more chore to my early-morning schedule. By the time I finish getting ready for bed, it is midnight; I look up and see the stairway leading to the bedroom, which by then seems longer than the one outside the Philadelphia Museum of Art, and proceed to crawl in bed and into the arms of Morpheus.*

"I decided to make my life something worthwhile by helping people. I wanted to help and heal and maybe, at the same time, heal myself."

On many nights, I do not stay there long. At 3 A.M., maybe 4 A.M., my 21 eyes pop open. The thought, "Am I ready for the test? Do I understand the material?" makes me sit upright in a panic. Rather than toss and turn uneasily for the rest of the night, I get out of bed and open my textbooks for a couple of hours. If fatigue finally wins, I may fall back into bed before getting up for the day.

Without long luxurious stretches of time to study, I must constantly search 22 out such little windows of opportunity to prepare for class. When the laundry is washing, I study. While supper is simmering on the stove, I study. When a customer cancels her appointment for a haircut, I thank the Lord for a free hour, and I study. "Mom, if I studied half as hard as you, I'd be a straight-A student," says my son. But he understands that the life of a working mother is not designed to make going to college easy. If I do not budget my time carefully, I will fail.

People question the wisdom of my studying to be a nurse. It may take 23 four or five years.

"You will never last," they tell me. 24

"You will be too old to lift a bedpan," they mock. 25

But I am not discouraged. There are twenty more courses ahead of me 26 before I get into the nursing area. While all these things challenge me, the greatest of all is to be able to hold my head high.

Somehow, just somehow, I think it might be all worth it—if I can hold 27 the hand of someone dying all alone in a cold hospital ward and whisper in the patient's ear, "You are not alone, I am here, I am here, I will never leave you."

Maybe, just maybe, I will find that life that was lost. It is out there some- 28 where.

But I know one thing—I am in charge, and I will never let go again. 29 Never.

An Update

Regina Ruiz successfully completed her registered nurse degree and is 30 only a few credits away from earning her bachelor's degree at Jefferson University in Philadelphia. She is a nurse at Voorhees Pediatric Rehabilitation Hospital in New Jersey.

At the hospital, Regina's 31 patients range in age from newborns to eighteen-year-olds. As she grows attached to particular patients, she requests that they be assigned to her daily shift, giving "extra love" to children battling illness, fear, and loneliness. "To see tiny preemies and children who are so sick grow and get better and be released to their families—it is wonderful to be part of that. School was

Regina enjoys reading to her two grandchildren, Rachel and Nicole.

very difficult, and nursing is a demanding profession, but when I am at work I am in heaven."

When she is not working, she takes pride in keeping her home beauti- 32 ful. "After my divorce and through all those long difficult years, I worried so much about not being able to keep up with things," she said. "The roof leaked so badly at one point I had trash cans sitting in the living room. So I had to learn to budget my money as well as my time. When I had three jobs, one was for tuition and food, and the others were for repairs—a roof, siding, new windows, everything. Now I can look at the house and feel so good. A little neighbor boy told me the other day, 'Mrs. Ruiz, you have the nicest house on the street.'"

She still does hair for a handful of longtime clients. "They were my friends 33 for so many years," she said. "When I'd come home from a test crying because I was sure I'd failed, they'd be the ones to say, 'No, Regina! You're going to make it.' Now, maybe I don't have to cut hair anymore to earn a living," she says with a chuckle, "but how can I tell them to go jump in the lake?"

■ Reading Comprehension Questions

1. The words *took an inventory* in "I quickly took an inventory—foreign-born, with not a great command of the English language, no money, no job training, and two kids in college" (paragraph 8) mean
   a. fell asleep.
   b. made a detailed list.
   c. formed a plan of action.
   d. got a job.

2. The word *appealing* in "The kids found college money by working and by appealing to their father" (paragraph 17) means
   a. pretending.
   b. refusing.
   c. suggesting an alternative.
   d. making a request.

3. Which sentence best expresses the central idea of the selection?
   a. Ruiz could not tell her parents back in Venezuela that her marriage was unhappy.
   b. Ruiz should not have married the Marine and moved so far from home.
   c. After a bad marriage, Ruiz successfully took charge of her own life and future.
   d. Ruiz is often exhausted by her schedule of school and two jobs.

4. A main idea may cover more than one paragraph. Which sentence best expresses the main idea of paragraphs 11–13?
   a. Ruiz remembered a saying her father used to say.
   b. Ruiz at first saw no way out of a bad situation but then thought of a worthwhile path.

c. Ruiz's father may have gotten inspiration from the Spanish edition of *Reader's Digest*.
d. Ruiz thought helping people was a worthwhile goal.

5. Which sentence best expresses the main idea of paragraphs 21–22?
   a. Ruiz never has time to study, so she goes to class unprepared.
   b. Ruiz always chooses to sleep an extra hour or two rather than study for class.
   c. Ruiz values studying and uses every spare minute for schoolwork.
   d. Because of her excess leisure time, Ruiz always has enough opportunity for study.

6. Ruiz's marriage ended when
   a. she left her husband for another man.
   b. she enrolled in college and her husband divorced her.
   c. her husband left her for another woman.
   d. Ruiz's parents demanded that she come back to Venezuela.

7. According to the "Update," Ruiz now works as a(n)
   a. office worker and baby-sitter.
   b. nurse and occasional hairdresser.
   c. translator and cleaning woman.
   d. parking lot attendant and veterinarian's assistant.

8. We can infer that Ruiz
   a. wishes she had married "a local boy from a good, wealthy family."
   b. believes she married the U.S. Marine too quickly.
   c. regrets having three children.
   d. believes enrolling in the nursing program was not wise.

9. We can infer that in the passage below, the author uses the word *matches* to refer to
   a. heat.
   b. solutions.
   c. the love between a child and a parent.
   d. something that will light a cigarette.

   He would say, "My dear, it is always the darkest when you are fresh out of matches." "Dad, I am out of matches." Or so I thought. (Paragraphs 11–12)

10. We can conclude one reason Ruiz wanted to become a nurse was that
    a. she believed that helping other people would help her too.
    b. Venezuela needed more nurses.
    c. her father always wanted her to be a nurse.
    d. nursing was the easiest course offered by the college she attended.

■ Technique questions

1. In paragraph 5, Regina asks the question "Where did my life go?" Where in the essay does she return to the image of her "lost life"? Write here the number of the paragraph in which she returns to this image: _____ What is the difference between how she discusses her lost life in paragraph 5 and in the later paragraph?

   _____

2. Ruiz begins her essay by describing a series of disappointments and her resulting depression. Later, she describes her decision to make something good out of her life and what her life has been like since then. In what paragraph of her essay does she make the transition between those two sections, and what word marks that transition?

   _____

3. Who wrote paragraphs 1–29 of the reading? Was the update written by the same person? What evidence supports your answers to these questions?

   _____

   _____

   _____

■ Discussion questions

1. Ruiz stayed with an unhappy marriage for twenty-five years. During those years, she told herself, "You are in a strange country—maybe the customs are different. The children need you, and you cannot admit failure to your parents back in Venezuela." Judging from your own experience and observations of people around you, are these typical reasons for remaining in an unhappy relationship? Are these *good* reasons?

2. Like Ruiz, adults who return to college often have a difficult time balancing the demands of their work, family, and classes. What challenges do you face as a student? What ways have you found to deal with them?

3. Ruiz briefly explains her decision to become a nurse. Why have you chosen your own course of study? What about it interests you? What do you hope it will offer you after college?

■ Writing assignments

1. Ruiz and her parents had very different ideas about whom she should marry. How well have your plans for your life conformed to your parents' hopes for you? Write a paragraph about a decision in your life on which you and

positions she's held (buyer for cafeteria, assistant purchasing clerk for textile company), gives solid evidence that she performed her jobs well (saved the school $2,500, was promoted from mailroom), and explains what skills she has acquired (knows about controlling costs). Julia continues to be clear and concrete as she closes the letter. By saying, "I will telephone you next Tuesday morning," she leaves the reader with a helpful, specific piece of information. Chances are, her prospective employer will be glad to take her call. The chances are equally good that Bob will never hear from the company. His letter was so blandly° general that the employer will hardly remember receiving it.

> "Vague, general language is the written equivalent of baby food. It is adequate; it can sustain life. But it isn't very interesting."

Julia's letter demonstrates the power of specific detail—a power that we all appreciate intuitively.° Indeed, although we may not always be aware of it, our opinions and decisions are frequently swayed by concrete language. On a restaurant menu, are you more tempted by a "green salad" or "a colorful salad bowl filled with romaine and spinach leaves, red garden-fresh tomatoes, and crisp green pepper rings"? Would being told that a movie is "good" persuade you to see it as much as hearing that it is "a hilarious parody° of a rock documentary featuring a fictional heavy-metal band"? Does knowing that a classmate has "personal problems" help you understand her as well as hearing that "her parents are divorcing, her brother was just arrested for selling drugs, and she is scheduled for surgery to correct a back problem"?   8

When we read, all of us want—even crave°—this kind of specificity. Concrete language grabs our attention and allows us to witness the writer's world almost firsthand. Abstract language, on the other hand, forces us to try to fill in the blanks left by the writer's lack of specific imagery. Usually we tire of the effort. Our attention wanders. We begin to wonder what's for lunch and whether it's going to rain, as our eyes scan the page, searching for some concrete detail to focus on.   9

Once you understand the power of concrete details, you will gain considerable power as a writer. You will describe events so vividly that readers will feel they experienced them directly. You will sprinkle your essays with nuggets of detail that, like the salt on a pretzel, add interest and texture.   10

Consider the following examples and decide for yourself which came from a writer who has mastered the art of the specific detail.   11

Living at Home

Unlike many college students, I have chosen to live at home with my parents. Naturally, the arrangement has both good and bad points. The most difficult part is that, even though I am an adult, my parents sometimes still think of me as a child. Our worst disagreements occur when they expect me to report to them as though I were still twelve years old. Another drawback to living with my parents is that I don't feel free to have friends over to "my place." It's not that my parents don't welcome my friends in their home, but I can't tell my friends to drop in anytime as I would if I lived alone.

But in other ways, living at home works out well. The most obvious plus is that I am saving a lot of money. I pay room and board, but that doesn't compare to what renting an apartment would cost. There are less measurable advantages as well. Although we do sometimes fall into our old parent-child roles, my parents and I are getting to know each other in new ways. Generally, we relate as adults, and I think we're all gaining a lot of respect for one another.

The Pros and Cons of Living at Home

Most college students live in a dormitory or apartment. They spend their hours surrounded by their own stereos, blaring hip-hop or rock music; their own furnishings, be they leaking beanbag chairs or Salvation Army sofas; and their own choice of foods, from tofu-bean sprout casseroles to a basic diet of Cheetos. My life is different. I occupy the same room that has been mine since babyhood. My school pictures, from gap-toothed first-grader to cocky senior, adorn the walls. The music drifting through my door from the living room ranges from Lawrence Welk to . . . Lawrence Welk. The food runs heavily to Mid-American Traditional: meatloaf, mashed potatoes, frozen peas.

Yes, I live with my parents. And the arrangement is not always ideal. Although I am twenty-four years old, my parents sometimes slip into a time warp and mentally cut my age in half. "Where are you going, Lisa? Who will you be with?" my mother will occasionally ask. I'll answer patiently, "I'm going to have pizza with some people from my psych class." "But where?" she continues. "I'm not sure," I'll say, my voice rising just a hair. If the questioning continues, it will often lead to a blowup. "You don't need to know where I'm going, OK?" I'll say shrilly. "You don't have to yell at me," she'll answer in a hurt voice.

Living at home also makes it harder to entertain. I find myself envying classmates who can tell their friends, "Drop in anytime." If a friend of mine "drops in" unexpectedly, it throws everyone into a tizzy. Mom runs for the dustcloth while Dad ducks into the bedroom, embarrassed to be seen in his comfortable, ratty bathrobe.

On the other hand, I don't regret my decision to live at home for a few years. Naturally, I am saving money. The room and board I pay my parents wouldn't rent the tiniest, most roach-infested apartment in the city. And despite our occasional lapses, my parents and I generally enjoy each other's company. They are getting to know me as an adult, and I am learning to see them as people, not just my parents. I realized how true this was when I saw them getting dressed up to go out recently. Dad was putting on a tie, and Mom one of her best dresses. I opened my mouth to ask where they were going when it occurred to me that maybe they didn't care to be checked up on any more than I did. Swallowing my curiosity, I simply waved good-bye and said, "Have a good time!"

Both passages could have been written by the same person. Both   12 make the same basic points. But the second passage is far more interesting because it backs up the writer's points with concrete details. While the first passage merely *tells* that the writer's parents sometimes treat her like a child, the second passage follows this point up with an anecdote* that *shows* exactly what she means. Likewise with the point about inviting friends over: the first passage only states that there is a problem, but the second one describes in concrete terms what happens if a friend does drop in unexpectedly. The first writer simply says that her room and board costs wouldn't pay for an apartment, but the second is specific about just how inadequate the money would be. And while the first passage uses abstract language to say that the writer and her parents are "getting to know each other in new ways," the second shows what that means by describing a specific incident.

Every kind of writing can be improved by the addition of concrete detail. 13 Let's look at one final example: the love letter.

Dear April,

   I can't wait any longer to tell you how I feel. I am crazy about you. You are the most wonderful woman I've ever met. Every time I'm near you I'm overcome with feelings of love. I would do anything in the world for you and am hoping you feel the same way about me.

Love,

Paul

Paul has written a sincere note, but it lacks a certain something. That 14 something is specific detail. Although the letter expresses a lot of positive feelings, it could have been written by practically any love-struck man about any woman. For this letter to be really special to April, it should be unmistakably about her and Paul. And that requires concrete details.

Here is what Paul might write instead. 15

Dear April,

   Do you remember last Saturday, as we ate lunch in the park, when I spilled my soda in the grass? You quickly picked up a twig and made a tiny dam to keep the liquid from flooding a busy anthill. You probably didn't think I noticed, but I did. It was at that moment that I realized how totally I am in love with you and your passion for life. Before that I only thought you were the most beautiful woman in the world, with your eyes like sparkling pools of emerald water and your chestnut hair glinting in the sun. But now I recognize what it means when I hear your husky laugh and I feel a tight aching in my chest. It means I could stand on top of the Empire State Building and shout to the world, "I love April Snyder." Should I do it? I'll be waiting for your reply.

Paul

There's no guarantee that April is going to return Paul's feelings, but she 16 certainly has a better idea now just what it is about her that Paul finds so lovable, as well as what kind of guy Paul is. Concrete details have made this letter far more compelling.

Vague, general language is the written equivalent of baby food. It is 17 adequate; it can sustain* life. But it isn't very interesting. For writing to have satisfying crunch, sizzle, and color, it must be generously supplied with specifics. Whether the piece is a job application, a student essay, or a love letter, it is concrete details that make it interesting, persuasive, and memorable.

■ Reading Comprehension Questions

1. The word *swayed* in "our opinions and decisions are frequently swayed by concrete language" (paragraph 8) means
   a. hidden.
   b. repeated.
   c. influenced.
   d. shown to be wrong.

2. The word *compelling* in "she certainly has a better idea now just what it is about her that Paul finds so lovable . . . . Concrete details have made this letter far more compelling" (paragraph 16) means
   a. forceful and interesting.
   b. long and boring.
   c. empty and vague.
   d. silly but amusing.

3. Which sentence best expresses the central idea of the selection?
   a. Communication skills of all types are useful throughout life.
   b. Always be specific when applying for a job.
   c. Specific language will strengthen your writing.
   d. Most people need help with their writing skills.

4. Main ideas may cover more than one paragraph. Which sentence best expresses the main idea of paragraphs 6–7?
   a. In letters of application for a job, Bob and Julia have included their background and job goals.
   b. Bob and Julia have written letters of application for a job.
   c. While Bob says only that he's a college graduate, Julia goes into detail about where and what she studied and her grades.
   d. While Bob's job-application letter is probably too vague to be successful, Julia's very specific one is likely to get a positive response.

5. Which sentence best expresses the main idea of paragraph 8?
   a. Julia's letter is a good example of the power of specific details.
   b. Our opinions and decisions are often influenced by specific language.
   c. We want to hear exactly what's in a salad or movie before spending money on it.
   d. When we know just what someone's "personal problems" are, we understand him or her better.

6. Johnson states that abstract language
   a. is rare.
   b. lets us clearly see what the writer's world is like.
   c. tends to lose our attention.
   d. makes us want to read more of the writer's piece.

7. Johnson feels that concrete language
   a. is hard to follow.
   b. makes readers' eyes glaze over.
   c. helps readers picture what the author is writing about.
   d. is not appropriate for a menu or a parody.

8. In paragraphs 6–7, the author suggests that Bob Cole
   a. is not qualified to enter the business world.
   b. is lying about his education and work experience.
   c. should have written a less wordy letter.
   d. should have written a more detailed letter.

9. Which of the following sentences can we assume Beth Johnson would most approve of?
   a. Shore City is an amusing but expensive place.
   b. Shore City is an interesting place to spend a bit of time.
   c. Shore City has an amusement park and racetrack, but all the hotel rooms cost over $100 a day.
   d. There is a city near the shore which has some interesting attractions, but its hotels are quite expensive.

10. We can infer from the reading that specific details would be very important in
    a. a novel.
    b. a history textbook.
    c. a biography.
    d. all of the above.

■ Technique Questions

1. Essays often begin with an introduction that prepares readers for the author's central idea. How does Johnson begin her essay? Why do you think she chose this kind of introduction?

   _____

   _____

   _____

2. The authors of the papers on "living at home" are essentially using listing order. What are they listing?

   _____

3. Johnson takes her own advice and uses many concrete details in her essay. Locate two particularly strong examples of specific details in the reading that are not in the three pairs of samples, and write them below:

_____

_____

_____

■ Discussion Questions

1. At some earlier point in school, did you learn the importance of writing specifically? If so, do you remember when? If not, when do you think you should have been taught about the power of specific details in writing?

2. Johnson provides three pairs of examples: two job-application letters, two passages about living at home, and two love letters. Which pair most effectively makes her point for you about the value of writing specifically?

3. What kinds of writing will you be doing over the next few weeks, either in or out of school? Will it be papers for other classes, answers to essay questions, reports at work, letters of application for jobs, letters to friends, or other types of writing? Name one kind of writing you will be doing, and give an example of one way you could make that writing more specific.

■ Writing Assignments

1. Using the same level of detail as Julia's application letter in the reading, write a one-paragraph letter of application for a part-time or a full-time job. Like Julia Moore, be sure to include the following in your paragraph:

> What kind of job you are applying for
> Where you have worked previously
> What positions you have held
> Evidence that you performed your job well
> Which skills you have acquired

2. In this reading, "The Pros and Cons of Living at Home" is a strong example of a "pro and con" analysis—one that details the advantages and disadvantages of something. Think of a topic about which you have conflicting views. It could be a decision you are struggling with, such as changing jobs or moving to a larger (or smaller) house or apartment. Or it could be a situation in which you already find yourself, such as attending school while holding a job or having an elderly parent living with you. Write a paragraph in which you explain in detail what the pros and cons of the issue are.

Once you've chosen a topic, do some prewriting. A good strategy is to make two lists; one of the advantages, the other of the disadvantages. Here is a sample:

<u>Advantages of moving to a smaller apartment</u>

Save money on rent ($325 a month instead of $400 a month)

Save money on utilities (smaller heating bill)

Less space to clean (one bedroom instead of two)

<u>Disadvantages of moving to a smaller apartment</u>

Less space for all my furniture (big chest of drawers, sofa bed)

No spare bedroom (can't have friends sleep over)

Will get more cluttered (little space to display all my trophies, souvenirs, and sports equipment)

If you are not sure about which issue to write about, make lists for two or three topics. Then you'll have a better idea of which one will result in a better paper.

Use the lists of advantages and disadvantages as an outline for your paragraph, adding other ideas as they occur to you. Begin with a topic sentence such as "_____ has both advantages and disadvantages" or "I'm having a hard time deciding whether or not to _____." Next, write the supporting sentences, discussing first one side of the issue and then the other.

Be sure to include plenty of specific details. For inspiration, reread "The Pros and Cons of Living at Home" before writing your essay.

3. Johnson uses sharp, concrete details to make a point she feels strongly about—that specific language gives writing real power. Write an essay persuading readers of the importance of something you believe in strongly. Be sure to include at least one or two concrete, convincing examples for every point that you make. You might write about the value of something, such as:

Regular exercise

Volunteer work

Reading for pleasure

Gardening

Spending time with young (or grown) children

Periodic intense housecleaning

Alternatively, you can write about the negative aspects of something, such as:

Excessive television watching

Compulsive shopping

Tabloid journalism

Procrastinating

Smoking

Following is an example of an informal outline for this assignment. As the writer developed this outline into paragraphs, she added, subtracted, and rearranged some of her examples.

<u>Central idea:</u> Cleaning out closets every now and then can be rewarding.

(1) I get rid of things I no longer need, or never needed:
Pair of ten-year-old hiking boots, which I kept because they were expensive but that are thoroughly worn out
Portable TV that no longer works
Yogurt maker given to me by my first husband on our anniversary

(2) I make room for things I do need:
All my shoes and pocketbooks, which can be arranged in neat rows on the shelves instead of crammed into cartons
Christmas presents I buy for my family in July and want to hide

(3) I find things that I thought were lost forever or that I forgot I ever had:
Box of photographs from our first family vacation
My bowling trophy
Presents I bought for last Christmas and forgot about

8. In paragraph 3, the author implies
   a. a more experienced teacher would not have threatened Mark with tape.
   b. her decision to tape Mark's mouth shut was a good one.
   c. Mark was trying to annoy her by talking more often than usual.
   d. in order to correct Mark's behavior, she should have been more strict.

9. The author implies that
   a. she had known all along how important the lists were to her students.
   b. she did not support the war in Vietnam.
   c. the lists meant more to the students than she had ever realized.
   d. Mark's parents were jealous of her relationship with him.

10. It is reasonable to conclude that Mark
    a. cared as much for Sister Helen as she cared for him.
    b. never talked much about his past.
    c. planned to become a math teacher himself.
    d. had not stayed in touch with his classmates.

■ Technique Questions

1. Although Mark is described as someone who talks a lot, the author chooses to include Mark's spoken words just three times in her essay. Look at these three instances. What do they share? Why do you think Sister Helen chose to include these quotes?

   _____

   _____

   _____

   _____

2. How does Sister Helen present most of the information in her essay—in listing order or in time order? Find three examples from the essay which support your answer.

   _____

   _____

   _____

   _____

3. In paragraph 20, the author introduces a number of people who had not appeared elsewhere in the essay. What does Sister Helen accomplish by including these people at the end of her story?

   _____

   _____

_____

_____

_____

■ Discussion Questions

1. In this story, we read of two classroom incidents involving Sister Helen and her students. In one, she briefly taped a third-grader's mouth closed. In another, she encouraged junior-high students to think of things they liked about one another. In your opinion, what do these two incidents tell about Sister Helen? What kind of teacher was she? What kind of person?

2. At the end of the story, Sister Helen tells us that she "cried for Mark and for all his friends who would never see him again." Do you think she might have been crying for other reasons, too? Explain what they might be.

3. "All the Good Things" has literally traveled around the world. Not only has it been reprinted in numerous publications, but many readers have sent it out over the Internet for others to read. Why do you think so many people love this story? Why do they want to share it with others?

■ Writing Assignments

1. Do you have any souvenir that, like Sister Helen's lists, you have kept for years? Write a paragraph about that souvenir. Start your paragraph with a topic sentence such as "_____ is one of my oldest and proudest possessions." Then describe just what the item is, how you originally obtained it, and where you keep it now. Most importantly, explain why the souvenir is precious to you.

2. Although Sister Helen didn't want to do it, she felt she had to tape Mark's mouth shut after announcing that she would do so. When have you done something you didn't really want to do because others expected it? Write a paragraph about that incident. Explain why you didn't want to do it, why you felt pressure to do it, and how you felt about yourself afterward. Here are sample topic sentences for such a paragraph:

   > Even though I knew it was wrong, I told my friend's parents a lie to keep my friend out of trouble.

   > Last year, I pretended I didn't like a girl that I really did like because my friends convinced me she wasn't cool enough.

3. Mark Eklund obviously stood out in Sister Helen's memory. She paints a vivid "word portrait" of Mark as a third-grader. Write an essay about three fellow

students who, for positive or negative reasons, you have always remembered. The three may have been your classmates at any point in your life. Your essay should focus on your memories of those students in the classroom—not on the playground, in the cafeteria, or outside of school. As you describe your memories of those three classmates in that setting, include details that appeal to as many senses as possible—hearing, sight, touch, smell—to make your readers picture those individuals and that time and place in your history.

Alternatively, you may write an essay about three teachers whom you will always remember.

Responsibility

M. Scott Peck

■ Preview

The Road Less Traveled, a well-known book by psychiatrist and author M. Scott Peck, begins with this famous line: "Life is difficult." Peck encourages people to embrace the messy difficulties that make up life, stressing that growth and development are achieved only through hard work. The following excerpt from *The Road Less Traveled* emphasizes one of Peck's favorite themes: personal responsibility.

■ Words to Watch

self-evident (1): not requiring any explanation

ludicrous (2): laughable because of being obviously ridiculous

inquired (11): asked

clarified (19): made clear

amenable (23): agreeable

glared (37): stared angrily

We cannot solve life's problems except by solving them. This statement may seem idiotically self-evident*, yet it is seemingly beyond the comprehension of much of the human race. This is because we must accept responsibility for a problem before we can solve it. We cannot solve a problem by saying, "It's not my problem." We cannot solve a problem by hoping that someone else will solve it for us. I can solve a problem only when I say, "This is my problem and it's up to me to solve it." But many, so many, seek to avoid the pain of their problems by saying to themselves: "This problem was caused by other people, or by social circumstances beyond my control, and therefore it is up to other people or society to solve this problem for me. It is not really my personal problem."   1

The extent to which people will go psychologically to avoid assuming responsibility for personal problems, while always sad, is sometimes almost ludicrous*. A career sergeant in the army, stationed in Okinawa and in serious trouble because of his excessive drinking, was referred for psychiatric evaluation and, if possible, assistance. He denied that he was an alcoholic, or even that his use of alcohol was a personal problem, saying, "There's nothing else to do in the evenings in Okinawa except drink."   2

"Do you like to read?" I asked.   3

"Oh yes, I like to read, sure."   4

"Then why don't you read in the evening instead of drinking?"   5

blamed others or circumstances rather than accepted responsibility. Be sure to include, as Peck does, specific details, such as direct quotes or vivid descriptions, so readers can see the person and the situation you've chosen to write about.

2. Peck draws examples of irresponsible behavior from his practice as a military psychiatrist. But you can find examples of people dodging responsibility everywhere. What kinds of responsibility do students often avoid? Write a paragraph giving details about two or three ways students try to escape their responsibilities. In your paragraph, explain what kind of excuses they frequently make for their behavior. Using Peck's essay as a model, you may even choose to present a series of questions and answers between a student and an instructor to illustrate your main point.

3. Peck explains that the only way to solve a problem is to solve it—in other words, to take responsibility for the problem and find a solution. Write an essay about a time in your own life when you had to accept responsibility for a problem and figure out a solution for it. As you decide on a topic, you might list areas in which you have experienced problems. Here is one imaginary student's list:

- Getting along with parents
- Breaking off with friends who were a bad influence
- Managing money
- Holding a job
- Keeping up with schoolwork

Once you have decided on a topic to write about, you might begin with a statement like this:

> After blaming my teachers for my problems in school, I finally accepted responsibility for my own poor grades.

Alternatively, write about two or three problems you've had to face and solve.

The Most Hateful Words

Amy Tan

■ **Preview**

For years, a painful exchange with her mother lay like a heavy stone on Amy Tan's heart. In the following essay, Tan, author of best-selling novels including *The Joy Luck Club* and *The Kitchen God's Wife*, tells the story of how that weight was finally lifted. This essay is from her memoir, *The Opposite of Fate*.

■ **Words to Watch**

tormented (3): hurt or tortured

forbade (3): would not allow

impenetrable (3): impossible to get inside

frantically (9): excitedly, with great worry

1   The most hateful words I have ever said to another human being were to my mother. I was sixteen at the time. They rose from the storm in my chest and I let them fall in a fury of hailstones: "I hate you. I wish I were dead. . . ."

2   I waited for her to collapse, stricken by what I had just said. She was still standing upright, her chin tilted, her lips stretched in a crazy smile. "Okay, maybe I die too," she said between huffs. "Then I no longer be your mother!" We had many similar exchanges. Sometimes she actually tried to kill herself by running into the street, holding a knife to her throat. She too had storms in her chest. And what she aimed at me was as fast and deadly as a lightning bolt.

3   For days after our arguments, she would not speak to me. She tormented° me, acted as if she had no feelings for me whatsoever. I was lost to her. And because of that, I lost, battle after battle, all of them: the times she criticized me, humiliated me in front of others, forbade° me to do this or that without even listening to one good reason why it should be the other way. I swore to myself I would never forget these injustices. I would store them, harden my heart, make myself as impenetrable° as she was.

4   I remember this now, because I am also remembering another time, just a few years ago. I was forty-seven, had become a different person by then, had become a fiction writer, someone who uses memory and imagination. In fact, I was writing a story about a girl and her mother, when the phone rang.

5   It was my mother, and this surprised me. Had someone helped her make the call? For a few years now, she had been losing her mind through Alzheimer's disease. Early on, she forgot to lock her door. Then she forgot where she lived. She forgot who many people were and what they had meant to her. Lately, she could no longer remember many of her worries and sorrows.

"Amy-ah," she said, and she began to speak quickly in Chinese. "Some- 6 thing is wrong with my mind. I think I'm going crazy."

I caught my breath. Usually she could barely speak more than two words 7 at a time. "Don't worry," I started to say.

"It's true," she went on. "I feel like I can't remember many things. I can't 8 remember what I did yesterday. I can't remember what happened a long time ago, what I did to you. . . ." She spoke as a drowning person might if she had bobbed to the surface with the force of will to live, only to see how far she had already drifted, how impossibly far she was from the shore.

She spoke frantically*: "I know I did something to hurt you." 9

"You didn't," I said. "Don't worry." 10

"I did terrible things. But now I can't remember what. . . . And I just want 11 to tell you . . . I hope you can forget, just as I've forgotten."

I tried to laugh so she would not notice the cracks in my voice. "Really, 12 don't worry."

"Okay, I just wanted you to know." 13

After we hung up, I cried, both happy and sad. I was again that sixteen- 14 year-old, but the storm in my chest was gone.

My mother died six months later. By then she had bequeathed to me her 15 most healing words, as open and eternal as a clear blue sky. Together we knew in our hearts what we should remember, what we can forget.

■ Reading Comprehension Questions

1. The word *stricken* in "I waited for her to collapse, stricken by what I had just said" (paragraph 2) means
   a. wounded.
   b. amused.
   c. annoyed.
   d. bored.

2. The word *bequeathed* in "By then she had bequeathed to me her most healing words, as open and eternal as a clear blue sky" (paragraph 15) means
   a. denied.
   b. sold.
   c. given.
   d. cursed.

3. Which sentence best expresses the central idea of the selection?
   a. Because of Alzheimer's disease, the author's mother forgot harsh words the two of them had said to one another.
   b. Amy Tan had a difficult relationship with her mother that worsened over the years.
   c. Years after a painful childhood with her mother, Amy Tan was able to realize peace and forgiveness.
   d. Despite her Alzheimer's disease, Amy Tan's mother was able to apologize to her daughter for hurting her.

4. Which sentence best expresses the main idea of paragraphs 1–2?
   a. Amy Tan's mother was sometimes suicidal.
   b. Amy Tan wanted to use words to hurt her mother.
   c. It is not unusual for teenagers and their parents to argue.
   d. Amy Tan and her mother had a very hurtful relationship.

5. Which sentence best expresses the main idea of paragraphs 8–9?
   a. The author's mother was deeply disturbed by the thought that she had hurt her daughter.
   b. Alzheimer's disease causes people to become confused and unable to remember things clearly.
   c. The author's mother could not even remember what she had done the day before.
   d. The author's mother had changed very little from what she was like when Tan was a child.

6. After arguing with her daughter, the author's mother would
   a. say nice things about her to others.
   b. immediately forget they had argued.
   c. refuse to speak to her.
   d. apologize.

7. When she was a young girl, the author swore that she would
   a. never forget her mother's harsh words.
   b. never be like her mother.
   c. publicly embarrass her mother by writing about her.
   d. never have children.

8. The first sign that the author's mother had Alzheimer's disease was
   a. she forgot where she lived.
   b. she could speak only two or three words at a time.
   c. she forgot people's identities.
   d. she forgot to lock her door.

9. We can infer from paragraph 2 that
   a. the author wished her mother was dead.
   b. the author immediately felt guilty for the way she spoke to her mother.
   c. the author's mother was emotionally unstable.
   d. the author's mother was physically abusive.

10. The author implies, in paragraphs 9–15, that
   a. she was pleased her mother realized how badly she had hurt her.
   b. her love and pity for her mother was stronger than her anger.
   c. she did not recall what her mother was talking about.
   d. she was annoyed by her mother's confusion.

■ Technique Questions

1. Tan begins her essay from the perspective of a sixteen-year-old girl, but finishes it from the perspective of a woman in her late forties. Where in the essay does Tan make the transition between those two perspectives? What words does she use to signal the change?

_____

_____

_____

2. In paragraph 2, the author quotes her mother speaking in English, her second language. What features stand out in her mother's speech? Why do you think Tan chose to include her mother's actual words rather than rewrite them into "standard" English?

_____

_____

_____

_____

3. Tan uses weather images throughout her essay. Find three instances in which Tan mentions weather and list them below. What does she accomplish with this technique?

_____

_____

_____

_____

_____

_____

_____

■ Discussion Questions

1. At age sixteen, Tan recalls "the times [my mother] criticized me, humiliated me in front of others, forbade me to do this or that without even listening to one good reason why it should be the other way." Did you have a difficult relationship with one or both of your parents? Were problems the result of your teenage behavior or of their behavior?

2. This essay brings to mind the phrase, "Forgive and forget." But is this advice always fair or realistic? Are there times when it is better to hold someone accountable than to forgive and forget? Explain.

3. In their discussion at the end of the essay, Tan chooses to keep her emotions hidden from her mother. Why do you think she does this?

■ Writing Assignments

1. Despite being an adult, Tan recalls feeling like "the same sixteen-year-old" girl when she speaks to her mother. Think about something in your life that has the power to reconnect you to a vivid memory. Write a paragraph in which you describe your memory and the trigger that "takes you back" to it. Begin your paragraph with a topic sentence that makes it clear to readers what you are going to discuss. Then provide specific details so readers can understand your memory. Here are sample topic sentences.

> Whenever I see swings, I remember the day in second grade when I got into my first fist fight.
>
> The smell of cotton candy takes me back to the day my grandfather brought me to my first baseball game.
>
> I can't pass St. Joseph's Hospital without remembering the day, ten years ago, when my brother was shot.

2. In this essay, we see that Tan's relationship with her mother was very complicated. Who is a person with whom you have a complex relationship—maybe one you'd describe as "love/hate" or "difficult"? Write a paragraph about that relationship. Be sure to give examples or details that show readers why you have such difficulties with that person.

   Your topic sentence should introduce who you plan to discuss, such as:

> My mother-in-law and I have contrasting points of view on several issues.
>
> While I respect my boss, he is simply a very difficult person.
>
> Even though I love my sister, I can't stand to be around her.

   Whoever you choose, be sure to provide specific examples or details to help your reader understand why the relationship is so difficult for you. For example, if you decided to write about your boss, you will want to describe things he does that show just why you consider him so "difficult."

3. Like Tan's mother, most of us have done something in our lives we wish we could undo. If you could have a chance to revisit your past and change one of your actions, what would it be? Write an essay in which you describe something you would like to undo.

In your first paragraph, introduce exactly what you did. Here are three thesis statements that students might have written:

> I wish I could undo the night I decided to drive my car while I was drunk.

> If I could undo any moment in my life, it would be the day I decided to drop out of high school.

> One moment from my life I would like to change is the time I picked on an unpopular kid in sixth grade.

Be sure to provide details and, if appropriate, actual words that were spoken, so that your readers can "see and hear" what happened. Once you've described the moment that you wish to take back, write three reasons why you feel the way you do. Below is a scratch outline for the first topic.

> I wish I could undo the night I decided to drive my car while I was drunk.
>
> 1. Caused an accident that hurt others.
> 2. Lost my license, my car, and my job.
> 3. Affected the way others treat me.

In order to write an effective essay, you will need to provide specific details to explain each of the reasons you identify. For instance, to support the third reason above, you might detail possible new feelings of guilt and anger you have about yourself as well as provide examples of how individual people now treat you differently. To end your essay, you might describe what you would do today if you could replay what happened.

My Daughter Smokes

Alice Walker

■ Preview

Alice Walker is a famous writer, probably best known for her novel *The Color Purple*. In "My Daughter Smokes," her daughter's habit is a stepping stone to a broader discussion of smoking than the title suggests. She goes on to also tell of her father's experience with tobacco and from there slips into a discussion of tobacco that moves through the centuries and across continents.

■ Words to Watch

consort (2): spouse

pungent (3): having a sharp, bitter taste

dapper (4): stylishly dressed

perennially (6): continually

ritual (12): activity done regularly

emaciated (13): thin

futility (16): uselessness

empathy (17): understanding

denatured (17): changed from its natural state

mono-cropping (17): growing of single crops apart from other crops

suppressed (18): kept down

redeem (18): restore the honor of

cajole (20): gently urge

My daughter smokes. While she is doing her homework, her feet on the bench in front of her and her calculator clicking out answers to her algebra problems, I am looking at the half-empty package of Camels tossed carelessly close at hand. Camels. I pick them up, take them into the kitchen, where the light is better, and study them—they're filtered, for which I am grateful. My heart feels terrible. I want to weep. In fact, I do weep a little, standing there by the stove holding one of the instruments, so white, so precisely rolled, that could cause my daughter's death. When she smoked Marlboros and Players I hardened myself against feeling so bad; nobody I knew ever smoked these brands.

She doesn't know this, but it was Camels that my father, her grandfather, 2 smoked. But before he smoked "ready-mades"—when he was very young and very poor, with eyes like lanterns—he smoked Prince Albert tobacco in cigarettes he rolled himself. I remember the bright-red tobacco tin, with a picture of Queen Victoria's consort,* Prince Albert, dressed in a black frock coat and carrying a cane.

The tobacco was dark brown, pungent,* slightly bitter. I tasted it more 3 than once as a child, and the discarded tins could be used for a number of things: to keep buttons and shoelaces in, to store seeds, and best of all, to hold worms for the rare times my father took us fishing.

By the late forties and early fifties no one rolled his own anymore (and few 4 women smoked) in my hometown, Eatonton, Georgia. The tobacco industry, coupled with Hollywood movies in which both hero and heroine smoked like chimneys, won over completely people like my father, who were hopelessly addicted to cigarettes. He never looked as dapper* as Prince Albert, though; he continued to look like a poor, overweight, overworked colored man with too large a family; black, with a very white cigarette stuck in his mouth.

I do not remember when he started to cough. Perhaps it was unnoticeable 5 at first. A little hacking in the morning as he lit his first cigarette upon getting out of bed. By the time I was my daughter's age, his breath was a wheeze, embarrassing to hear; he could not climb stairs without resting every third or fourth step. It was not unusual for him to cough for an hour.

It is hard to believe there was a time when people did not understand 6 that cigarette smoking is an addiction. I wondered aloud once to my sister— who is perennially* trying to quit—whether our father realized this. I wonder how she, a smoker since high school, viewed her own habit.

It was our father who gave her her first cigarette, one day when she had 7 taken water to him in the fields.

"I always wondered why he did that," she said, puzzled, and with some 8 bitterness.

"What did he say?" I asked. 9

"That he didn't want me to go to anyone else for them," she said, "which 10 never really crossed my mind."

So he was aware it was addictive, I thought, though as annoyed as she 11 that he assumed she would be interested.

I began smoking in eleventh grade, also the year I drank numerous bottles 12 of terrible sweet, very cheap wine. My friends and I, all boys for this venture, bought our supplies from a man who ran a segregated bar and liquor store on the outskirts of town. Over the entrance there was a large sign that said COLORED. We were not permitted to drink here, only to buy. I smoked Kools, because my sister did. By then I thought her toxic darkened lips and gums glamorous. However, my body simply would not tolerate smoke. After six months I had a chronic sore throat. I gave up smoking, gladly. Because it was a ritual* with my buddies—Murl, Leon, and "Dog" Farley—I continued to drink wine.

My father died from "the poor man's friend," pneumonia, one hard 13 winter when his bronchitis and emphysema had left him low. I doubt he had much lung left at all, after coughing for so many years. He had so little breath that, during his last years, he was always leaning on something. I remembered once, at a family reunion, when my daughter was two, that my father picked her up for a minute—long enough for me to photograph them—but the effort was obvious. Near the very end of his life, and largely because he had no more lungs, he quit smoking. He gained a couple of pounds, but by then he was so emaciated° no one noticed.

When I travel to Third World countries I see many people like my   14
father and daughter. There are large billboards directed at them both: the tough, "take-charge," or dapper older man, the glamorous, "worldly" young woman, both puffing away. In these poor countries, as in American ghettos and on reservations, money that should be spent for food goes instead to the tobacco companies; over time, people starve themselves of both food and air, effectively weakening and addicting their children, eventually eradicating themselves. I read in the newspaper and in my gardening magazine that cigarette butts are so toxic that if a baby swallows one, it is likely to die, and that the boiled water from a bunch of them makes an effective insecticide.

> "It is hard to believe there was a time when people did not understand that cigarette smoking is an addiction."

My daughter would like to quit, she says. We both know the statistics are   15
against her; most people who try to quit smoking do not succeed.*

There is a deep hurt that I feel as a mother. Some days it is a feeling of   16
futility.° I remember how carefully I ate when I was pregnant, how patiently I taught my daughter how to cross a street safely. For what, I sometimes wonder; so that she can wheeze through most of her life feeling half her strength, and then die of self-poisoning, as her grandfather did?

But, finally, one must feel empathy° for the tobacco plant itself. For thou-   17
sands of years, it has been venerated by Native Americans as a sacred medicine. They have used it extensively—its juices, its leaves, its roots, its (holy) smoke—to heal wounds and cure diseases, and in ceremonies of prayer and peace. And though the plant as most of us know it has been poisoned by chemicals and denatured° by intensive mono-cropping° and is therefore hardly the plant it was, still, to some modern Indians it remains a plant of positive power. I learned this when my Native American friends, Bill Wahpepah and his family, visited with me for a few days and the first thing he did was sow a few tobacco seeds in my garden.

Perhaps we can liberate tobacco from those who have captured and   18
abused it, enslaving the plant on large plantations, keeping it from freedom and its kin, and forcing it to enslave the world. Its true nature suppressed,° no wonder it has become deadly. Maybe by sowing a few seeds of tobacco in our gardens and treating the plant with the reverence it deserves, we can redeem° tobacco's soul and restore its self-respect.

°Three months after reading this essay, my daughter stopped smoking.

Besides, how grim, if one is a smoker, to realize one is smoking a slave.   19

There is a slogan from a battered women's shelter that I especially like: 20
"Peace on earth begins at home." I believe everything does. I think of a slogan for people trying to stop smoking: "Every home a smoke-free zone." Smoking is a form of self-battering that also batters those who must sit by, occasionally cajole° or complain, and helplessly watch. I realize now that as a child I sat by, through the years, and literally watched my father kill himself; surely one such victory in my family, for the rich white men who own the tobacco companies, is enough.

■ Reading Comprehension Questions

1. The word *eradicating* in "over time, people starve themselves of both food and air, effectively weakening and addicting their children, eventually eradicating themselves" (paragraph 14) means
   a. curing.
   b. feeding.
   c. destroying.
   d. controlling.

2. The word *venerated* in "For thousands of years, it has been venerated by Native Americans as a sacred medicine. They have used it extensively" (paragraph 17) means
   a. honored.
   b. ignored.
   c. ridiculed.
   d. forgotten.

3. Which of the following sentences best expresses the central idea of the essay?
   a. Most people who try to quit smoking are not successful.
   b. Pained by her daughter's cigarette addiction and the misdeeds of the tobacco companies, Walker urges people to stop smoking.
   c. Native Americans have used the tobacco plant for thousands of years as a sacred medicine and in ceremonies of prayer and peace.
   d. Tobacco advertisements that show healthy, attractive people are misleading.

4. Which sentence best expresses the main idea of paragraph 4?
   a. For Walker's father and others, the reality of smoking was very different from the images shown in ads and movies.
   b. Walker's father smoked because he wanted to be as stylish as Prince Albert.
   c. No one rolled his or her own cigarettes by the 1950s.
   d. Walker's father was poor, overweight, and overworked.

5. Which sentence best expresses the main idea of paragraph 5?
   a. Walker does not know when her father began to cough.
   b. When Walker was her daughter's age, she was embarrassed to hear her father wheezing.
   c. Walker's father's cough began quietly but grew to become a major problem.
   d. Walker's father had great difficulty climbing stairs.

6. Walker is especially upset that her daughter smokes Camel cigarettes because
   a. she believes Camels to be especially bad for people's health.
   b. Camels are the brand that Walker herself smoked as a teenager.
   c. Walker's father, who died as a result of smoking, smoked Camels.
   d. Camels' advertisements are glamorous and misleading.

7. When Walker's father picked up his granddaughter at a family reunion, he
   a. burned the child with his cigarette.
   b. put her down quickly so he could have another cigarette.
   c. warned her against smoking.
   d. was too weak to hold her for long.

8. We can infer that Walker
   a. believes people who are poor, uneducated, and nonwhite have been especially victimized by the tobacco industry.
   b. believes that tobacco should be made illegal.
   c. blames her father for her daughter's decision to smoke.
   d. believes Native Americans were wrong to honor the tobacco plant.

9. We can infer that, for Walker, smoking as a teenager
   a. was strictly forbidden by her parents.
   b. was an exciting experiment.
   c. was quickly habit-forming.
   d. was the end of her friendship with Murl, Leon, and "Dog" Farley.

10. We can infer that Walker's daughter
    a. did not care that her mother was concerned about her smoking.
    b. may have been helped to quit smoking by her mother's essay.
    c. remembered her grandfather well.
    d. did not believe that smoking was harmful to people's health.

■ Technique Questions

1. In which parts of her essay does Walker use time order? _____

_____

2. Write down what you think are two of the most vivid images in Walker's essay. Then explain how each helps to further her central idea.

_____

_____

_____

3. How does Walker enlarge the significance of her essay so that it becomes more than the story of her daughter's smoking?

_____

_____

_____

_____

_____

_____

■ Discussion Questions

1. How would you deal with a friend who engages in self-destructive behavior, such as smoking, excessive drinking, or taking drugs? Would you ignore the behavior or try to educate the friend about its dangers? Is letting a friend know you are concerned worth risking the friendship?

2. The dangers of smoking are well documented. Study after study shows that smoking leads to a variety of illnesses, including cancer, emphysema, and heart disease. Newer studies are proving that secondhand smoke—smoke that nonsmokers breathe when they are around smokers—is dangerous as well. If you had the power to do so, would you make smoking illegal? Or do you believe that smoking should continue to be an individual's right?

3. Imagine learning that your sixteen-year-old child has begun smoking or drinking, or has become sexually active. Which discovery would worry you most? Would it make a difference if the child were a girl or a boy? What fears would each of these discoveries raise in you? How would you respond to your child?

■ Writing Assignments

1. Write a paragraph in which you try to persuade a friend to quit smoking. Explain in detail three reasons you think he or she should quit. Use transitions such as *first of all, second, another,* and *finally* as you list the three reasons.

2. In her essay, Walker is critical of the glamorous, healthy image presented by cigarette advertisements. Write a paragraph in which you describe what you think an honest cigarette advertisement would look like. Who would appear

in the ad? What would they be doing? What would they be saying? Use the following as a topic sentence, or write one of your own.

> The elements of an honest cigarette "advertisement" would tempt people not to smoke.

In preparation for this assignment, you might study two or three cigarette ads, using them as inspiration for this assignment. Use the name of a real cigarette or make up a name.

3. What bad habits do *you* have? Write an essay explaining how you believe you acquired one of those habits, how you think it harms you, and how you could rid yourself of it. You might begin by making a list or questioning to help you find a bad habit you wish to write about. (We all have plenty of bad habits, such as smoking, drinking too much, spending money impulsively, biting our nails, eating too much food, and so on.)

Remember to write an informal outline to guide you in your writing. Here, for example, is one possible outline for this assignment:

> Central idea: A bad habit I intend to change is studying for tests at the last minute.
>
> (1) I acquired the habit in high school, where studying at the last minute was often good enough.
> For example, I studied for spelling tests in the hallway on the way to class.
> Even history tests were easy to study for because our teacher demanded so little.
>
> (2) I've learned the hard way that last-minute studying doesn't work well in college.
> During my first quarter, I got the first D I've ever gotten.
> I thought memorizing a few names would get me through my first business class, but was I ever wrong.
>
> (3) I took a study skills course, and what I learned is helping me get on the right track.
> I learned the benefits of taking class notes, and I'm trying to get better at getting down a written record of each lecture.
> I also learned that keeping up with readings and taking notes on a regular basis are needed for some classes.

The writer of the above outline still has to come up with many more details to expand each of her points. For instance, why did she get the D, and how did that help motivate her to improve her study habits? Also, what techniques is she experimenting with in her effort to improve her note-taking? She could add such details to her outline, or she could begin working them into her essay when she starts writing.

Wonder in the Air

Jeff Gammage

■ **Preview**

Here is a chance to apply your understanding of addition and time relationships to a full-length reading. The following story tells about a loving father who decides never to lie to his child—and then has to deal with Santa Claus. Read it and then answer the relationships questions that follow. There are also questions on understanding vocabulary in context, finding main ideas, and identifying supporting details.

■ **Words to Watch**

innumerable (3): too many to count

leprechauns (5): Irish elves

by osmosis (7): like a sponge

allegedly and purportedly (7): supposedly

deceived (8): misled

literal (9): factual

weasel words (9): deliberately misleading language

prevalent (14): widely held

stark (17): plain

ponder (23): think over

subtleties (24): less obvious details

When my wife and I had our first child, we established one firm parental 1
rule:
No lies. 2
Our daughter, Jin Yu, spent her first two years in an orphanage in China, 3
and we knew that as she grew, she would ask innumerable° questions about her life there. We wanted to be able to answer from an established position of truth-telling.
For me, the "All the truth, all the time" policy extended onto the symbols 4
and myths of the holidays.
Every April, I gladly helped fill a basket with candy rabbits and colored 5
eggs for our daughter, and then for her new sister, but skipped the story of the Easter bunny. I avoided any mention of leprechauns°, tried to ignore the tooth fairy.

Most of all, I was adamant about not telling Jin Yu tales about a certain   6
red-suited fat man who spends every December 24 breaking into people's
homes.

Of course, like the Grinch, I couldn't stop Christmas—or Santa Claus—   7
from coming. Jin Yu absorbed a belief in Santa as if by osmosis°. By age 4 she
knew who he (allegedly°) was, how he (purportedly°) looked, and what he
(supposedly) did.

I didn't want to ruin her fun, but also didn't want her to feel deceived°   8
later on.

So, I responded to her questions about the big man with what I liked to   9
think of as precise and technically accurate versions of the literal° truth—and
what she would no doubt characterize as weasel words°.

At the mall, we'd walk past a jolly Santa sitting upon a velvet throne.   10

"Is that really Santa?" my daughter would ask.   11

I'd reply with a lawyerly, "The people in line must think so."   12

The worst was when she wondered if Santa truly kept lists of children who   13
behaved and misbehaved.

"That's the prevalent° belief," I said.   14

By last Christmas Eve, I had done such an expert job of parenting, made   15
such a successful effort to be truthful, that as I tucked my daughter into bed,
she was confused and near tears.

"Daddy, will Santa"—here her voice almost broke—"bring me any pres-   16
ents?"

This was it, the question squarely placed, a moment that offered a stark°   17
choice between fable and fact, that demanded a reasoned response from a
father grounded in principle. I looked at my adored child, her dark brown eyes
threatening to overflow, knowing there was but one choice, and I made it:

I lied.   18

On Christmas Eve, the holy of holy nights, I lied to my 5-year-old daughter   19
so fully, so deliberately, and in such compelling detail that I nearly believed
it myself.

"Darling, of course Santa is going to bring you presents. He would never   20
overlook you. You're such a good girl [that part was true] that I know Santa
will stop here. Listen, do you hear that sound outside? I think it's jingle bells!
It must be his sleigh!"

Jin Yu turned to the window, hoping to glimpse a team of reindeer in   21
flight, then lay back and drifted off, content, or at least relieved.

The next morning, she awoke to find that, sure enough, Santa had visited   22
her home, proving his existence by magically delivering a wardrobe of princess gowns and dress-up shoes in exactly her size.

I think he left something for me as well: The power of a child's belief. A   23
reminder that the best things in life cannot be seen with the naked eye. And
that while there will be plenty of time for my daughter to ponder° cold and
painful truths, her time of wonder should be savored.

This year, fully 6, Jin Yu is happily preparing for Santa by drawing crayon 24
snowscapes and discussing his impending arrival with friends. She counsels
her 3-year-old sister, Zhao Gu, on the subtleties° of naughty and nice.

Last week Jin Yu came to me with a very specific Christmas question, the 25
sort that once again required a father's sure guidance: What kind of cookies
should she leave for Santa on Christmas Eve?

I was firm in my response: Chocolate chip. Definitely, I told her, Santa likes 26
chocolate chip.

■ Reading Comprehension Questions

1. The word *adamant* in "Most of all, I was adamant about not telling Jin Yu tales
   about a certain red-suited fat man who spends every December 24 breaking
   into people's homes" (paragraph 6) means
   a. hysterical.
   b. glad.
   c. unwavering.
   d. dishonest.

2. The phrase *drifted off* in "Jin Yu turned to the window, hoping to glimpse a
   team of reindeer in flight, then lay back and drifted off, content, or at least
   relieved" (paragraph 21) means
   a. fell asleep.
   b. floated.
   c. daydreamed.
   d. sighed.

3. The word *impending* in "This year, fully 6, Jin Yu is happily preparing for
   Santa by drawing crayon snowscapes and discussing his impending arrival
   with friends" (paragraph 24) means
   a. late.
   b. soon to take place.
   c. surprising.
   d. possible.

4. Which sentence best expresses the central point of the selection?
   a. Holiday myths are so common in our culture that it is impossible to always
      tell the truth to children.
   b. If a child wants to believe in Santa Claus, there is little a parent can do to
      stop her.
   c. The author reluctantly goes along with his daughter's belief in Santa Claus.
   d. When he sees how important a belief in Santa Claus is to his daughter, the
      author comes to understand that all children should be permitted their time
      of wonder.

5. The main idea of paragraphs 1–5 is that
   a. the author's daughter was adopted from an orphanage in China as a two-year-old.
   b. the author knew that his adopted daughter would ask questions about her first two years in China.
   c. the author and his wife vowed never to lie to their adopted daughter, even about holiday symbols and myths.
   d. the author allowed his daughter to celebrate holidays, but skipped telling her holiday myths.

6. The author breaks his vow never to lie to his daughter
   a. when they see a Santa at the shopping mall.
   b. a few days before Easter.
   c. on Christmas Eve.
   d. when she asks him what kind of cookies she should leave for Santa on Christmas Eve.

7. For Jin Yu, Santa's existence is proven when
   a. she sees him at the shopping mall.
   b. she finds that he has eaten all the chocolate chip cookies she left him on Christmas Eve.
   c. she finds that he has magically delivered princess gowns and dress-up shoes in exactly her size.
   d. all her friends tell her that he exists.

8. Paragraph 23 suggests that the author
   a. regrets Jin Yu's belief in Santa Claus.
   b. appreciates children's sense of wonder.
   c. intends to tell Jin Yu that Santa isn't real.
   d. thinks Jin Yu suspects the truth.

9. *True or false?* _____ Paragraph 24 suggests that Jin Yu is passing her belief in Santa Claus on to her sister.

10. Gammage implies that
   a. encouraging children to believe in stories is a harmless form of lying.
   b. he continues to feel guilty about his deception.
   c. Jin Yu will be heartbroken when he tells her the truth.
   d. he never believed in Santa Claus.

■ Discussion Questions

1. Was the author right to lie to his daughter? Why or why not?

2. When or if you have children, will you encourage them to believe in Santa, the Easter Bunny, and the tooth fairy? Why or why not?

3. The author and his wife decided that "no lies" would be their "one firm parental rule." What do you think are some other good parental rules?

■ Writing Assignments

1. In explaining why he refused at first to encourage his daughter's belief in Santa Claus, Gammage states that he wanted to be able to answer his daughter's questions about China "from an established position of truth-telling." Do you think Jin Yu will later doubt her father because he "lied" to her about Santa Claus? Or will it make a difference? Write a paragraph which explains your thinking, drawing on an incident in your own life in which a parent or authority figure either lied or told you a half-truth.

2. Write a paragraph that supports one of the following main ideas: "I believe that parents should encourage their children to believe in Santa Claus, the Easter Bunny, and the tooth fairy" or "I believe that it is important for parents to discourage their children's belief in Santa Claus, the Easter Bunny, and the tooth fairy." Explain your thinking, giving specific examples from your life experiences and comparing or contrasting them with Gammage's observations in the article.

3. Although Gammage and his wife decided that "no lies" would be their one firm parental rule, they eventually come to realize that the rule is not realistic. What do you think are two or three good (and realistic) parental rules? Write an essay in which you state and then discuss each rule.

    Your topic sentence should name the three rules you will write about. Here is such a topic sentence:

    > Kindness, fairness, and patience should be the guiding principles of any loving parent.

    The first sentence of your main paragraphs should then specify what makes each of these "rules" or guidelines important. For example:

    > Kindness demands patience and understanding from the parent and sets an example for the child of how to treat others.

    Such a main idea sentence would then be followed by a description of your own parent's kindness (or unkindness) in a specific incident in your life, as well as an explanation of what you learned from the experience. Repeat this process for each of the three rules you are writing about.

The Warrior Within

Dawn Cogliser

■ Preview

For Dawn, being abused was a way of life. It took a terrifying experience, one that she barely survived, to convince her that she could leave the horrors of her past behind.

■ Words to Watch

petitioned (5): formally requested

whacked (8): crazy (slang)

fundamental (19): basic

Sometimes life can be a punch in the face. I don't just mean the hard   1
blows that we receive from life. I also mean actual punches that your mother
lands on your chin. Trust me—life has thrown me a lot of punches, and so
did my mom.

I grew up in a really violent world. When I was one year old, my parents split   2
up. To get a clean start with their lives, they decided to get rid of me. Luckily my
grandparents stepped in and took me. I stayed with them until I was about six.
Then good old Mom stepped back into the picture, deciding that she wanted
to have a family again. The court granted her custody, and suddenly I was back
with her. She got her wish of a family, including me and a new husband.

The dream family didn't work out so well for me. My stepfather was the   3
most evil man I've ever met. Like Mom, he liked to throw punches. But his
evil didn't end there. He decided to sexually molest me as well. So there I was,
not yet eight years old, back with Mom and her new man, being beaten and
molested. Nice family life, right?

I guess in that situation, some kids would have just shut down and   4
become passive and withdrawn. But that was never my style, and that's probably something that helped save me. I was a fighter from the start. When my
parents got rid of me, it made me tough. I had to be. To actually let myself
feel the pain of what was happening would have been too much. So instead
I grew tough and angry and took it out on anyone around me.

Although my mother had custody of me, the courts had given my grand-   5
parents weekends with me. So each weekend I was packed up and shipped
off to their home. At the end of the weekend, I was shipped back to Mom's.
And each time I arrived at the new home, I was grilled for at least a day
about what went on in the other place. When my grandparents learned that
I was being abused, they petitioned˚ the court to give custody to them. The
back-and-forth court battle went on longer than I can tell you. I remember

being dragged into court over and over to tell the judge who I wanted to live with and why. And before each court date it was the same routine—my family members would drill me about what to say to make the others look bad. It was while all this was going on that I started to run away. Somebody would always find me and ship me back to my mother. Around this same time I discovered alcohol, and soon after that, drugs. Drugs and alcohol never solved my problems, but they helped me briefly escape the pain I was in. And escaping the pain was the only real motivation in life I had.

As I got closer to my teens, a new issue came up: my grandfather. He was   6 my grandmother's third husband, so he wasn't actually a blood relative, but he was the only grandfather I'd ever known on my father's side. It was he and my grandmother who had taken me in when my parents gave me up. Like my stepfather, he was an alcoholic. Also like my stepfather, he was a molester. My stepfather did far more to me sexually than my grandfather, but just the fact that my grandfather tried to go down that road made me insanely angry and violent. From that point on I would lash out at anyone for any reason. If you looked at me wrong, I'd punch you in the face. Even if you were bigger than me and could beat my ass, when we were done you'd know I'd been there!

By the time I was in my teens, I was living on the streets more than in   7 any home. I became a warrior, one who was ready for battle at all times. My "family" was the rough kids I hung out with. They were what I lived for. We had each other's backs, and as twisted as it seems now, they helped me go on with life. In order to keep them as friends, I had to be at least as tough as they were. The sense of safety I had when I was around them motivated me, simply because I was afraid that if I didn't keep up with them, I would lose them. This made me fight harder, drink longer, and always be the last one standing at the end of the night. No one knew that I was a crushed, scared kid inside.

I stayed in school, even though I never attended the same one for more   8 than a year. I bounced up and down the East Coast, from family to family and friend to friend. Each time I got settled somewhere, I got into a fight and got thrown out, or ran away before I could get thrown out. But I stayed in school. Other kids skip school to hang out at home, but not me. School was my escape from home. It was the only place I could simply hang with my friends, get some lunch, take a shower, and be at peace. Sounds whacked*, but I was motivated to go to school to get away from things. My grades were horrible, and I didn't understand much of what I was being taught, but I went every day.

I actually graduated. The same night, I left town. I caught a bus and went   9 to some friends who lived in the projects in another city. I lived in the shadows there, never on anybody's lease, just couch-surfing from place to place, sleeping all day and partying all night. The fact is that I didn't expect to live past the age of 21. I was drinking and using drugs more heavily than ever, and fighting to the point that I was causing real damage to people. Secretly, I wished that someone would kill me during a fight. I was in that much pain from life. But I didn't show that pain. I couldn't. And the truth of it all is that there was something way down in my core that wanted to keep alive. Maybe, somehow, my inner warrior knew there was a worthwhile life out there for me.

I had just turned 19 when I met a guy at a party. I thought I was in love, 10
and soon we were living together. For the first few years, everything was fine.
We bought a house—the first house I'd ever lived in that no one could kick
me out of. I felt like I had arrived. I had someone to share my life with, and
a shot at a family of my own. We partied together.

Then his mother died, and something inside him snapped. He turned 11
violent. His yelling at me and putting me down turned into pushing me and
then punching me. My warrior, which had dozed off at that point, woke up
with a vengeance. For the next four years we battled nonstop.

My friends couldn't understand why someone with my history of abuse 12
would stay with a jerk who was beating the crap out of me. At first, I stayed
with him because I thought I loved him. I believed the lies he fed me about
how sorry he was he'd hit me and how he would never do it again. Furthermore, I thought it was normal for a man to beat his woman. That was all I had
ever experienced. But there was a deeper reason I stayed. I battled that man
because this was MY HOUSE, and I swore when I moved in that no one would
ever take it away from me. I hated the fighting, but that wasn't anything new
to me. In my mind I was warrior woman, and this man would not win. But at
the end of it all, we had the mother of all battles. When it was over I was left
lying in the woods, bloody and beaten and left for dead. But I did not die.

When I woke up in those woods, I realized that things had to change. I 13
climbed into my car and drove away and never looked back. I had no idea where
I was going; I just drove. And as I drove, I cried. I cried the kind of hard, sobbing
tears that made my whole body shake. I tasted the blood and tears streaming
into my mouth, and it was like tasting my life leaking away. That taste shocked
me. I realized I had been willing to lose my precious life for a house. That feeling
I had way down in my core, the one that wanted me to stay alive, was strong
now. It told me that it was time to move forward. It was time to see what else
life had to offer. It told me life wasn't about getting high or drunk or getting
my ass beat or keeping someone else from winning. I knew there was something
else, something for me, and I wanted to find it. I have never let myself forget the
taste of that blood and those tears. The memory motivates me to keep moving
forward towards all the great things that life has to offer me.

With the help of friends, I moved to a new area and began a new life. 14
Another friend took me to visit his college campus, and I was blown away by the
experience. I had never known anything about college, never given it a thought,
but from that first moment I realized this was something I wanted. There was
a sense of importance in the air, and I liked it. These people were doing something; they were working on their futures. I had never thought about my future,
because I didn't believe I would have one. It would be years before I found the
courage to start college myself, but just that glimpse inspired me.

I took a job in the corporate world that allowed me chances for advance- 15
ment. Before I knew it, I was the assistant vice president of a high-powered
firm. I got married and found myself living in a real home—not just a house,
but a home filled with love. At age 35 I had my first child. I left my job to
stay home and care for him. This was my dream life—I had a home, a great
husband, and now I was a stay-at-home mom.

Still, this wonderful new life had its issues. For instance, when I was the vice 16 president of a company, people treated me a certain way. And now, even though mommies are the hardest-working people in the world, people treated me differently. I didn't know how to deal with this change in my identity. The great thing was that instead of turning to my old friends alcohol or drugs, I chose a new direction. I decided to take a college class. It was a basic English class, and the instructor was a young guy who had just started teaching. He seemed pretty cool, so I told him I didn't have any real education and might need some extra help along the way. And I did have problems—lots of them—and he did help me. I passed the class with a decent grade and really enjoyed the experience. It helped me realize that not only was I motivated, but that I was smart!

Feeling encouraged, I took a few more college classes, and then met with 17 a school counselor to see if there was a field I wanted to get a degree in. The idea of being a nurse really appealed to me, but I just knew there was no way I could do that. I obviously wasn't smart enough, or at least that's what I thought, and I was horrible at math.

But I really wanted to be a nurse.   18

So I waited until I had two choices: Drop out of college, or tackle the 19 fundamental° math class I was required to pass.

I took the class. I took it three times. But I finally passed it. And my inner war- 20 rior said, "It's time to take on nursing school." I applied to two schools and was accepted at both. Me—the "stupid" chick who partied and fought all the time. The schools could see my worth, even if I sometimes struggled to do that.

As I write this, I have just completed my first semester in nursing school with 21 all B's and one A, and I am looking forward to next semester. Succeeding here has not only taught me about school stuff: it has taught me about myself. What I have learned is that despite all the mess and mistakes in my past, I matter in this world. I plan on making a big difference before I am done. My inner warrior is still fighting big time—but now it is for my future, not against my past. I have learned that I am not about what I came from. I am about where I am going.

■ Reading Comprehension Questions

1. The word *grilled* in "And each time I arrived at the new home, I was grilled for at least a day about what went on in the other place" (paragraph 5) means
   a. burned
   b. abused
   c. told
   d. interrogated

2. The word *drill* in "And before each court date it was the same routine—my family members would drill me about what to say to make the others look bad" (paragraph 5) means
   a. rehearse
   b. force
   c. insult
   d. demand

3. Which sentence best expresses the central idea of the selection?
   a. Dawn's violent background made it difficult for her to hold a job.
   b. People like Dawn who have been victims of abuse tend to abuse others.
   c. Dawn has learned to channel her fighting spirit into reaching her goals, not battling others.
   d. The horrors of her past life will continue to haunt Dawn.

4. The main idea of paragraph 5 is that
   a. Dawn lived part of the time with her mom and part of the time with her grandparents.
   b. Dawn was physically abused while she lived at her mom's place.
   c. Dawn's family members constantly demand that she say things in court to make each other look bad.
   d. the custody battle between Dawn's mom and grandparents caused her to run away, and eventually led Dawn to seek relief in alcohol and drugs.

5. Which sentence best expresses the main idea of paragraph 13?
   a. Dawn had gotten used to being beaten by her husband.
   b. Her "inner warrior" had helped her to defend herself.
   c. She is still haunted by the taste of blood in her mouth.
   d. Dawn decided she wanted a better life for herself.

6. *True or False?* _____ Though Dawn was interested in college, her fears prevented her from continuing her education for several years.

7. Shortly after leaving her first husband, Dawn
   a. took a job in the corporate world.
   b. remarried and became a stay-at-home mom.
   c. decided to take a college class.
   d. enrolled in nursing school.

8. Based on paragraph 15, we can infer that
   a. Dawn was tempted to drink and take drugs after she became a stay-at-home mom.
   b. Dawn didn't get the same respect as a stay-at-home mom that she got as a corporate vice-president.
   c. Dawn liked to brag about how intelligent she was.
   d. Dawn's new husband did not support her decision to take a college class.

9. We can infer from this selection that Dawn
   a. intends to keep setting new goals for herself.
   b. knows that her troubled background has limited her options in life.
   c. feels that she has accomplished enough in life.
   d. will continue to battle others as she makes her way through life.

■ Discussion Questions

1. From early on, Dawn developed an image of herself as a "warrior woman." What were the hazards of thinking of herself in such a way? What were the benefits?

2. In this selection, Dawn mentions that when she became a stay-at-home mom, people treated her differently than they had when she was the vice president of a company. Why do you think this was so? In your experience, how do people tend to view stay-at-home moms? Do you believe these attitudes are reasonable or unreasonable? Explain.

3. In the course of "The Warrior Within," Dawn Cogliser refers to the different roles she has played in the course of her life—from "warrior" teen to battered wife, from corporate vice president to stay-at-home mom and later, successful college student. What are some of the roles you've played in the course of your life? What are some of the rewards and challenges of each?

Writing Assignments

1. After leaving an abusive marriage, a glimpse of college life inspired Dawn to eventually take college courses herself. Write a paragraph about an experience you had that inspired you to "work on your future." In your paragraph, describe what you were doing at the time and what the experience inspired you to do. Your topic sentence could be something like "I was inspired to work on my future when . . ." In completing your paragraph, be sure to describe what effect this inspirational moment had on your life.

2. As Dawn admits in "The Warrior Within," she did not succeed at her first attempt at passing the basic math class she needed to enroll in nursing school. Write a paragraph about a time when you had to exert extra effort to achieve a goal. What was your goal? What obstacles did you overcome to achieve it? What did you learn from the experience?

3. Shakespeare famously wrote that "All the world's a stage, / and all the men and women [are] merely players." In "The Warrior Within," Dawn Cogliser plays the roles of "warrior" teen, battered (and battling) wife, corporate vice president, stay-at-home mom, and successful college student and future nurse. Write an essay in which you discuss three roles that you have played or are continuing to play. Your thesis statement could be something like the following:

   Thesis: In the course of my life, I've played the roles of _____, of _____, and of _____.

   You'll need to develop three supporting paragraphs to provide details about each role you play or have played. What were/are the challenges and rewards of each role? Were you satisfied with this role, or did you seek a new role? After you develop your supporting paragraphs, add a concluding paragraph in which you round off your paper by providing a final thought or two.

Appendixes

Introduction

Six appendixes follow. Appendix A contains tips on how a computer can help in the writing process. Appendix B consists of further practice in using parts of speech, and Appendix C is a series of ESL pointers. Appendixes D and E consist of a diagnostic test and an achievement test that measure many of the skills in this book. The diagnostic test can be taken at the outset of your work; the achievement test can be used to measure your progress at the end of your work. Finally, Appendix F supplies answers to the introductory activities and the practice exercises in Part Two. The answers, which you should refer to only after you have worked carefully through each exercise, give you responsibility for testing yourself. (To ensure that the answer key is used as a learning tool only, answers are *not* given for the review and mastery tests in Part Two or for the reinforcement tests in Part Three. These answers appear only in the Instructor's Manual; they can be copied and handed out at the discretion of your instructor.)

Write a paragraph about your proudest moment. Retell the experience with as many vivid details as you can so that it is brought to life for your readers.

How a Computer Can Help

A computer is a powerful writing tool. Equipped with word-processing software, a computer can aid each phase of the writing process.

With a computer, for example, you can correct, move, or delete text with a mouse click. You can also change fonts, set margins, space lines, or number pages with ease. A computer can even help you check spelling, grammar, and style in your writing.

Learning to use a computer is easy. Just as you don't need to know how a car works to drive one, you don't need to understand how a computer functions to use it. Once you have learned a few simple keystrokes, you can begin. You do not even need to own your own computer. Nearly every college has a computer center. There you will find computers with word-processing software and staff who can help you get started.

Tips on Using a Computer

- If you are using your school's computer center, allow enough time. You may have to wait for a computer or printer to be free. In addition, you may need several sessions at the computer and printer to complete your paper.

- Word-processing programs allow you to save your work with a mouse click. *Save your work frequently as you write your draft.* A saved file is stored safely on the computer or on an external disk, flash drive, or server. A file that is not saved may be lost if the program quits, the computer crashes, or if the power is turned off.

- If you are using your own computer, keep your work in two places—the hard drive you are working on and a backup device such as a flash drive, disk, or recordable CD. Otherwise, save the file to a backup device and to your files on the school server or another server, or e-mail a copy to yourself (ask the staff in your computer center for help if needed). At the end of each session with the computer, copy your work onto the backup device. Then if the hard drive becomes damaged, you'll have the backup copy.

Insert any appropriate noun into each of the following blanks.

1. The shoplifter stole a(n) _____ from the department store.

2. _____ threw the football to me.

3. Tiny messages were scrawled on the _____.

4. A _____ crashed through the window.

5. Give the _____ to Keiko.

Singular and Plural Nouns

A *singular noun* names one person, place, object, or idea. A *plural noun* refers to two or more persons, places, objects, or ideas. Most singular nouns can be made plural with the addition of *s*.

Some nouns, like *box,* have irregular plurals. You can check the plural of nouns you think may be irregular by looking up the singular form in a dictionary.

Singular and Plural Nouns

Singular	Plural
goat	goats
alley	alleys
friend	friends
truth	truths
box	boxes

For more information on nouns, see "Subjects and Verbs," pages 68–81.

Underline the three nouns in the following sentences. Some are singular, and some are plural.

1. Two bats swooped over the heads of the frightened children.

2. The artist has purple paint on her sleeve.

3. The lost dog has fleas and a broken leg.

4. Tiffany does her homework in green ink.

5. Some farmers plant seeds by moonlight.

Pronouns

A *pronoun* is a word that stands for a noun. Pronouns eliminate the need for constant repetition. Look at the following sentences:

> The phone rang, and Malik answered the phone.

> Lisa met Lisa's friends in the music store at the mall. Lisa meets Lisa's friends there every Saturday.

> The waiter rushed over to the new customers. The new customers asked the waiter for menus and coffee.

Now look at how much clearer and smoother these sentences sound with pronouns.

> The phone rang, and Malik answered *it*.
> (The pronoun *it* is used to replace the word *phone*.)

> Lisa met *her* friends in the music store at the mall. *She* meets *them* there every Saturday.
> (The pronoun *her* is used to replace the word *Lisa's*. The pronoun *she* replaces *Lisa*. The pronoun *them* replaces the words *Lisa's friends*.)

> The waiter rushed over to the new customers. *They* asked *him* for menus and coffee.
> (The pronoun *they* is used to replace the words *the new customers*. The pronoun *him* replaces the words *the waiter*.)

Following is a list of commonly used pronouns known as personal pronouns:

Personal Pronouns

I	you	he	she	it	we	they
me	your	him	her	its	us	them
my	yours	his	hers		our	their

Fill in each blank with the appropriate personal pronoun.

1. André feeds his pet lizard every day before school. _____ also gives _____ flies in the afternoon.

2. The reporter interviewed the striking workers. _____ told _____ about their demand for higher wages and longer breaks.

3. Students should save all returned tests. _____ should also keep _____ review sheets.

4. The pilot announced that we would fly through some air pockets. _____ said that we should be past _____ soon.

5. Adolfo returned the calculator to Sheila last Friday. But Sheila insists that _____ never got _____ back.

There are several types of pronouns. For convenient reference, they are described briefly in the box below.

Types of Pronouns

Personal pronouns can act in a sentence as subjects, objects, or possessives.

> *Singular:* **I, me, my, mine, you, your, yours, he, him, his, she, her, hers, it, its**

> *Plural:* **we, us, our, ours, you, your, yours, they, them, their, theirs**

Relative pronouns refer to someone or something already mentioned in the sentence.

> **who, whose, whom, which, that**

Interrogative pronouns are used to ask questions.

> **who, whose, whom, which, what**

Demonstrative pronouns are used to point out particular persons or things.

> **this, that, these, those**

Note: Do not use *them* (as in *them* shoes), *this here, that there, these here,* or *those there* to point out.

continued

Types of Pronouns, *continued*

Reflexive pronouns end in *-self* or *-selves*. A reflexive pronoun is used as the object of a verb (as in *Cary cut **herself***) or the object of a preposition (as in *Jack sent a birthday card to **himself***) when the subject of the verb is the same as the object.

Singular: **myself, yourself, himself, herself, itself**

Plural: **ourselves, yourselves, themselves**

Intensive pronouns have exactly the same forms as reflexive pronouns. The difference is in how they are used. Intensive pronouns are used to add emphasis. (*I **myself** will need to read the contract before I sign it.*)

Indefinite pronouns do not refer to a particular person or thing.

each, either, everyone, nothing, both, several, all, any, most, none

Reciprocal pronouns express shared actions or feelings.

each other, one another

For more information on pronouns, see "Pronoun Types," pages 221–235.

Verbs

Every complete sentence must contain at least one verb. There are two types of verbs: action verbs and linking verbs.

Action Verbs

An *action verb* tells what is being done in a sentence. For example, look at the following sentences:

Mr. Jensen *swatted* at the bee with his hand.

Rainwater *poured* into the storm sewer.

The children *chanted* the words to the song.

In these sentences, the verbs are *swatted, poured,* and *chanted.* These words are all action verbs; they tell what is happening in each sentence.

For more about action verbs, see "Subjects and Verbs," pages 68–81.

Insert an appropriate word in each blank. That word will be an action verb; it will tell what is happening in the sentence.

1. The surgeon _____ through the first layer of skin.

2. The animals in the cage _____ all day.

3. An elderly woman on the street _____ me for directions.

4. The boy next door _____ our lawn every other week.

5. Our instructor _____ our papers over the weekend.

Linking Verbs

Some verbs are *linking verbs.* These verbs link (or join) a noun to something that is said about it. For example, look at the following sentence:

> The clouds *are* steel-gray.

In this sentence, *are* is a linking verb. It joins the noun *clouds* to words that describe it: *steel-gray.*

Other common linking verbs include *am, is, was, were, look, feel, sound, appear, seem,* and *become.* For more about linking verbs, see "Subjects and Verbs," pages 68–81.

In each blank, insert one of the following linking verbs: *am, feel, is, look, were.* Use each linking verb once.

1. The important papers _____ in a desk drawer.

2. I _____ anxious to get my test back.

3. The bananas _____ ripe.

4. The grocery store _____ open until 11 P.M.

5. Whenever I _____ angry, I go off by myself to calm down.

Helping Verbs

Sometimes the verb of a sentence consists of more than one word. In these cases, the main verb will be joined by one or more *helping verbs*. Look at the following sentence:

> The basketball team *will be leaving* for the game at six o'clock.

In this sentence, the main verb is *leaving*. The helping verbs are *will* and *be*.

Other helping verbs include *do, has, have, may, would, can, must, could,* and *should.* For more information about helping verbs, see "Subjects and Verbs," pages 68–81, and "Irregular Verbs," pages 159–173.

Practice

6

In each blank, insert one of the following helping verbs: *does, must, should, could, has been.* Use each helping verb once.

1. You _____ start writing your paper this weekend.

2. The victim _____ describe her attacker in great detail.

3. You _____ rinse the dishes before putting them into the dishwasher.

4. My neighbor _____ arrested for drunk driving.

5. The bus driver _____ not make any extra stops.

Prepositions

A *preposition* is a word that connects a noun or a pronoun to another word in the sentence. For example, look at the following sentence:

A man *in* the bus was snoring loudly.

In is a preposition. It connects the noun *bus* to *man.* Here is a list of common prepositions:

Prepositions

about	before	down	like	to
above	behind	during	of	toward
across	below	except	off	under
after	beneath	for	on	up
among	beside	from	over	with
around	between	in	since	without
at	by	into	through	

The noun or pronoun that a preposition connects to another word in the sentence is called the *object* of the preposition. A group of words beginning with a preposition and ending with its object is called a *prepositional phrase.* The words *in the bus,* for example, are a prepositional phrase.

Now read the following sentences and explanations.

An ant was crawling *up the teacher's leg*.

The noun *leg* is the object of the preposition *up. Up* connects *leg* with the word *crawling*. The prepositional phrase *up the teacher's leg* describes *crawling*. It tells just where the ant was crawling.

The man *with the black mustache* left the restaurant quickly.

The noun *mustache* is the object of the preposition *with*. The prepositional phrase *with the black mustache* describes the word *man*. It tells us exactly which man left the restaurant quickly.

The plant *on the windowsill* was a present *from my mother*.

The noun *windowsill* is the object of the preposition *on*. The prepositional phrase *on the windowsill* describes the word *plant*. It describes exactly which plant was a present.

There is a second prepositional phrase in this sentence. The preposition is *from,* and its object is *mother*. The prepositional phrase *from my mother* explains *present*. It tells who gave the present. For more about prepositions, see "Subjects and Verbs," pages 68–81, and "Sentence Variety II," pages 272–287.

In each blank, insert one of the following prepositions: *of, by, with, in, without.* Use each preposition once.

Practice

7

1. The letter from his girlfriend had been sprayed _____ perfume.

2. The weed killer quickly killed the dandelions _____ our lawn.

3. _____ giving any notice, the tenant moved out of the apartment.

4. Donald hungrily ate three scoops _____ ice cream and an order of french fries.

5. The crates _____ the back door contain glass bottles and old newspapers.

Adjectives

An *adjective* is a word that describes a noun (the name of a person, place, or thing). Look at the following sentence.

The dog lay down on a mat in front of the fireplace.

Now look at this sentence when adjectives have been inserted.

The *shaggy* dog lay down on a *worn* mat in front of the fireplace.

The adjective *shaggy* describes the noun *dog;* the adjective *worn* describes the noun *mat*. Adjectives add spice to our writing. They also help us to identify particular people, places, or things.

Adjectives can be found in two places:

1. An adjective may come before the word it describes (a *damp* night, the *moldy* bread, a *striped* umbrella).

2. An adjective that describes the subject of a sentence may come after a linking verb. The linking verb may be a form of the verb *be* (he *is* **furious,** I *am* **exhausted,** they *are* **hungry**). Other linking verbs include *feel, look, sound, smell, taste, appear, seem,* and *become* (the soup *tastes* **salty,** your hands *feel* **dry,** the dog *seems* **lost**).

> **TIP** The words *a, an,* and *the* (called *articles*) are generally classified as adjectives.

For more information on adjectives, see "Adjectives and Adverbs," pages 236–245.

Practice

8

Write any appropriate adjective in each blank.

1. The _____ pizza was eaten greedily by the _____ teenagers.

2. Melissa gave away the sofa because it was _____ and _____.

3. Although the alley is _____ and _____, Jian often takes it as a shortcut home.

4. The restaurant throws away lettuce that is _____ and tomatoes that are _____.

5. When I woke up in the morning, I had a(n) _____ fever and a(n) _____ throat.

Adverbs

An *adverb* is a word that describes a verb, an adjective, or another adverb. Many adverbs end in the letters *-ly*. Look at the following sentence:

The canary sang in the pet store window as the shoppers greeted each other.

Now look at this sentence after adverbs have been inserted.

The canary sang *softly* in the pet store window as the shoppers *loudly* greeted each other.

The adverbs add details to the sentence. They also allow the reader to contrast the singing of the canary and the noise the shoppers are making.

Look at the following sentences and the explanations of how adverbs are used in each case.

The chef yelled **angrily** at the young waiter.

(The adverb *angrily* describes the verb *yelled*.)

My mother has an **extremely** busy schedule on Tuesdays.

(The adverb *extremely* describes the adjective *busy*.)

The sick man spoke **very** faintly to his loyal nurse.

(The adverb *very* describes the adverb *faintly*.)

Some adverbs do not end in *-ly*. Examples include *very, often, never, always,* and *well*.

For more information on adverbs, see "Adjectives and Adverbs," pages 236–245.

Fill in each blank with any appropriate adverb.

1. The water in the pot boiled _____.

2. Carla _____ drove the car through _____ moving traffic.

3. The telephone operator spoke _____ to the young child.

4. The game show contestant waved _____ to his family in the audience.

5. Wes _____ studies, so it's no surprise that he did _____ poorly on his finals.

Practice

9

Conjunctions

A *conjunction* is a word that connects. There are two types of conjunctions: coordinating and subordinating.

Coordinating Conjunctions

Coordinating conjunctions join two equal ideas. Look at the following sentence:

Kevin *and* Steve interviewed for the job, *but* their friend Anne got it.

In this sentence, the coordinating conjunction *and* connects the proper nouns *Kevin* and *Steve*. The coordinating conjunction *but* connects the first part of the sentence, *Kevin and Steve interviewed for the job,* to the second part, *their friend Anne got it.*

Following is a list of all the coordinating conjunctions. In this book, they are simply called *joining words.*

Coordinating Conjunctions (Joining Words)			
and	so	nor	yet
but	or	for	

For more on coordinating conjunctions, see information on joining words in "Run-Ons," pages 106–126, and "Sentence Variety I," pages 127–144.

Practice

10

Write a coordinating conjunction in each blank. Choose from the following: *and, but, so, or, nor.* Use each conjunction once.

1. Either Jerome _____ Alex scored the winning touchdown.

2. I expected roses for my birthday, _____ I received a vase of plastic tulips from the discount store.

3. The cafeteria was serving liver and onions for lunch, _____ I bought a sandwich at the corner deli.

4. Marian brought a pack of playing cards _____ a pan of brownies to the company picnic.

5. Neither my sofa _____ my armchair matches the rug in my living room.

Subordinating Conjunctions

When a *subordinating conjunction* is added to a word group, the words can no longer stand alone as an independent sentence. They are no longer a complete thought. For example, look at the following sentence:

Karen fainted in class.

The word group *Karen fainted in class* is a complete thought. It can stand alone as a sentence. See what happens when a subordinating conjunction is added to a complete thought:

When Karen fainted in class

Now the words cannot stand alone as a sentence. They are dependent on other words to complete the thought:

When Karen fainted in class, we put her feet up on some books.

In this book, a word that begins a dependent word group is called a *dependent word*. Subordinating conjunctions are common dependent words. Below are some subordinating conjunctions.

Subordinating Conjunctions				
after	before	since	when	wherever
although	even if	though	whenever	whether
as	even though	unless	where	while
because	if	until		

Following are some more sentences with subordinating conjunctions:

After she finished her last exam, Irina said, "Now I can relax."

(*After she finished her last exam* is not a complete thought. It is dependent on the rest of the words to make up a complete sentence.)

Lamont listens to books on tape **while** he drives to work.

(*While he drives to work* cannot stand by itself as a sentence. It depends on the rest of the sentence to make up a complete thought.)

Since apples were on sale, we decided to make an apple pie for dessert.

(*Since apples were on sale* is not a complete sentence. It depends on *we decided to make an apple pie for dessert* to complete the thought.)

For more information on subordinating conjunctions, see information on dependent words in "Fragments," pages 82–105; "Run-Ons," pages 106–126; "Sentence Variety I," pages 127–144; and "Sentence Variety II," pages 272–287.

| **Practice** | Write a logical subordinating conjunction in each blank. Choose from the following: *even though, because, until, when, before.* Use each conjunction once. |
| **11** | |

1. The bank was closed down by federal regulators _____ it lost more money than it earned.

2. _____ Paula wants to look mysterious, she wears dark sunglasses and a scarf.

3. _____ the restaurant was closing in fifteen minutes, customers sipped their coffee slowly and continued to talk.

4. _____ anyone else could answer it, Leon rushed to the phone and whispered, "Is that you?"

5. The waiter was instructed not to serve any food _____ the guest of honor arrived.

Interjections

An *interjection* is a word that can stand independently and is used to express emotion. Examples are *oh, wow, ouch,* and *oops.* These words are usually not found in formal writing.

> "*Hey!*" yelled Maggie. "That's my bike."
> *Oh,* we're late for class.

A Final Note

A word may function as more than one part of speech. For example, the word *dust* can be a verb or a noun, depending on its role in the sentence.

> I *dust* my bedroom once a month. (verb)
> The top of my refrigerator is covered with an inch of *dust.* (noun)

APPENDIX C
ESL Pointers

This section covers rules that most native speakers of English take for granted but that are useful for speakers of English as a second language (ESL).

Articles

Types of Articles

An *article* is a noun marker—it signals that a noun will follow. There are two kinds of articles: indefinite and definite. The indefinite articles are *a* and *an*. Use *a* before a word that begins with a consonant sound:

> **a d**esk, **a p**hotograph, **a u**nicycle
> (*A* is used before *unicycle* because the *u* in that word sounds like the consonant *y* plus *u,* not a vowel sound.)

Use *an* before a word beginning with a vowel sound:

> **an e**rror, **an o**bject, **an h**onest woman
> (*Honest* begins with a vowel sound because the *h* is silent.)

The definite article is *the:*

> **the** sofa, **the** cup

An article may come right before a noun:

> **a** magazine, **the** candle

Or an article may be separated from the noun by words that describe the noun:

> **a** popular magazine, **the** fat red candle

TIP There are various other noun markers, including quantity words (*a few, many, a lot of*), numerals (*one, thirteen, 710*), demonstrative adjectives (*this, these*), possessive adjectives (*my, your, our*), and possessive nouns (*Raoul's, the school's*).

Articles with Count and Noncount Nouns

To know whether to use an article with a noun and which article to use, you must recognize count and noncount nouns. (A *noun* is a word used to name something—a person, place, thing, or idea.)

Count nouns name people, places, things, or ideas that can be counted and made into plurals, such as *pillow, heater,* and *mail carrier* (*one pillow, two heaters, three mail carriers*).

Noncount nouns refer to things or ideas that cannot be counted and therefore cannot be made into plurals, such as *sunshine, gold,* and *toast.* The box below lists and illustrates common types of noncount nouns.

Common Types of Noncount Nouns

Abstractions and emotions: **justice, tenderness, courage, knowledge, embarrassment**

Activities: **jogging, thinking, wondering, golf, hoping, sleep**

Foods: **oil, rice, pie, butter, spaghetti, broccoli**

Gases and vapors: **carbon dioxide, oxygen, smoke, steam, air**

Languages and areas of study: **Korean, Italian, geology, arithmetic, history**

Liquids: **coffee, kerosene, lemonade, tea, water, bleach**

Materials that come in bulk or mass form: **straw, firewood, sawdust, cat litter, cement**

Natural occurrences: **gravity, sleet, rain, lightning**

Other things that cannot be counted: **clothing, experience, trash, luggage, room, furniture, homework, machinery, cash, news, transportation, work**

The quantity of a noncount noun can be expressed with a word or words called *qualifiers,* such as *some, more,* or *a unit of.* In the following two examples, the qualifiers are shown in *italic* type, and the noncount nouns are shown in **boldface** type.

How *much* **experience** have you had as a salesclerk?

Our tiny kitchen doesn't have *enough* **room** for a table and chairs.

Some words can be either count or noncount nouns depending on whether they refer to one or more individual items or to something in general:

Three **chickens** are running around our neighbor's yard.
(This sentence refers to particular chickens; *chicken* in this case is a count noun.)

Would you like some more **chicken**?
(This sentence refers to chicken in general; in this case, *chicken* is a noncount noun.)

Using a *or* an *with Nonspecific Singular Count Nouns*

Use *a* or *an* with singular nouns that are nonspecific. A noun is nonspecific when the reader doesn't know its specific identity.

A photograph can be almost magical. It saves a moment's image for many years.
(The sentence refers to any photograph, not a specific one.)

An article in the newspaper today made me laugh.
(The reader isn't familiar with the article. This is the first time it is mentioned.)

Using the *with Specific Nouns*

In general, use *the* with all specific nouns—specific singular, plural, and non-count nouns. A noun is specific—and therefore requires the article *the*—in the following cases:

• When it has already been mentioned once:

An article in the newspaper today made me laugh. **The** article was about a talking parrot who frightened away a thief.
(*The* is used with the second mention of *article*.)

• When it is identified by a word or phrase in the sentence:

The CD that is playing now is a favorite of mine.
(*CD* is identified by the words *that is playing now*.)

• When its identity is suggested by the general context:

The service at Joe's Bar and Grill is never fast.
(*Service* is identified by the words *at Joe's Bar and Grill*.)

• When it is unique:

Some people see a man's face in **the** moon, while others see a rabbit.
(Earth has only one moon.)

- When it comes after a superlative adjective (for example, *best, biggest,* or *wisest*):

  The funniest movie I've seen is *Young Frankenstein.*

Omitting Articles

Omit articles with nonspecific plurals and nonspecific noncount nouns. Plurals and noncount nouns are nonspecific when they refer to something in general.

Stories are popular with most children.

Service is almost as important as food to a restaurant's success.

Movies can be rented from many supermarkets as well as video stores.

Using *the* with Proper Nouns

Proper nouns name particular people, places, things, or ideas and are always capitalized. Most proper nouns do not require articles; those that do, however, require *the.* Following are general guidelines about when not to use *the* and when to use *the.*

Do not use *the* for most singular proper nouns, including names of the following:

- *People and animals* (Katie Couric, Fluffy)
- *Continents, states, cities, streets, and parks* (South America, Utah, Boston, Baker Street, People's Park)
- *Most countries* (Cuba, Indonesia, Ireland)
- *Individual bodies of water, islands, and mountains* (Lake Michigan, Captiva Island, Mount McKinley)

Use *the* for the following types of proper nouns:

- *Plural proper nouns* (the Harlem Globetrotters, the Marshall Islands, the Netherlands, the Atlas Mountains)
- *Names of large geographic areas, deserts, oceans, seas, and rivers* (the Midwest, the Kalahari Desert, the Pacific Ocean, the Sargasso Sea, the Nile River)
- *Names with the format* "the _____ of _____" (the Strait of Gibraltar, the University of Illinois)

Practice

1

Underline the correct word or words in parentheses.

1. (Indiana, The Indiana) is a state where basketball is extremely popular.

2. (Dictionaries, The dictionaries) provide both the spelling and the definition of words.

3. On Friday, I'll be going to (a birthday party, the birthday party).

4. (A birthday party, The birthday party) will be held at an Italian restaurant.

5. Theo spends all his spare time playing (soccer, the soccer).

6. Rice, coconuts, and pineapples are some important products of (Philippines, the Philippines).

7. (Amazon River, The Amazon River) carries more water than any other river in the world.

8. (Lucky man, The lucky man) won a two-week trip to Paris.

9. The name of (the National Organization for Women, National Organization for Women) is often abbreviated as NOW.

10. (Cereal, The cereal) my sister likes has tiny blue and pink marshmallows in it.

Subjects and Verbs

Avoiding Repeated Subjects

In English, a particular subject can be used only once in a word group with a subject and a verb (that is, a clause). Don't repeat a subject in the same word group by following a noun with a pronoun.

> Incorrect: My *parents they* live in Miami.
>
> Correct: My **parents** live in Miami.
>
> Correct: **They** live in Miami.

Even when the subject and verb are separated by several words, the subject cannot be repeated in the same word group.

> Incorrect: The *windstorm* that happened last night *it* damaged our roof.
>
> Correct: The **windstorm** that happened last night **damaged** our roof.

Including Pronoun Subjects and Linking Verbs

Some languages omit a subject that is a pronoun, but in English, every sentence other than a command must have a subject. In a command, the subject *you* is understood: (You) Hand in your papers now.

> Incorrect: The soup tastes terrible. *Is* much too salty.
>
> Correct: The soup tastes terrible. **It is** much too salty.

Every English sentence must also have a verb, even when the meaning of the sentence is clear without the verb.

Incorrect: The table covered with old newspapers.

Correct: The table **is** covered with old newspapers.

Including *There* and *Here* at the Beginning of Sentences

Some English sentences begin with *there* or *here* plus a linking verb (usually a form of *to be: is, are,* and so on). In such sentences, the verb comes before the subject.

There are ants all over the kitchen counter.
(The subject is the plural noun *ants,* so the plural verb *are* is used.)

Here is the bug spray.
(The subject is the singular noun *spray,* so the singular verb *is* is used.)

In sentences like those above, remember not to omit *there* or *here*.

Incorrect: *Are* several tests scheduled for Friday.

Correct: **There are** several tests scheduled for Friday.

Not Using the Progressive Tense of Certain Verbs

The progressive tenses are made up of forms of *be* plus the *-ing* form of the main verb. They express actions or conditions still in progress at a particular time.

The garden **will be blooming** when you visit me in June.

However, verbs for mental states, the senses, possession, and inclusion are normally not used in the progressive tense.

Incorrect: I **am knowing** a lot about auto mechanics.

Correct: I **know** a lot about auto mechanics.

Incorrect: Gerald **is having** a job as a supermarket cashier.

Correct: Gerald **has** a job as a supermarket cashier.

The following box lists the common verbs not generally used in the progressive tense.

> ## Common Verbs Not Generally Used in the Progressive
>
> *Verbs relating to thoughts, attitudes, and desires:* **agree, believe, imagine, know, like, love, prefer, think, understand, want, wish**
>
> *Verbs showing sense perceptions:* **hear, see, smell, taste**
>
> *Verbs relating to appearances:* **appear, seem, look**
>
> *Verbs showing possession:* **belong, have, own, possess**
>
> *Verbs showing inclusion:* **contain, include**

Using Gerunds and Infinitives after Verbs

Before learning the rules about gerunds and infinitives, you must understand what they are. A *gerund* is the *-ing* form of a verb that is used as a noun:

Reading is a good way to improve one's vocabulary.
(*Reading* is the subject of the sentence.)

An *infinitive* is *to* plus the basic form of the verb (the form in which the verb is listed in the dictionary), as in **to eat.** The infinitive can function as an adverb, an adjective, or a noun.

On weekends, Betsy works at a convenience store **to make** some extra money.
(*To make some extra money* functions as an adverb that describes the verb *works.*)

I need a pencil **to write down** your telephone number.
(*To write down your telephone number* functions as an adjective describing the noun *pencil.*)

To forgive can be a relief.
(*To forgive* functions as a noun—it is the subject of the verb *can be.*)

Some verbs can be followed by only a gerund or only an infinitive; other verbs can be followed by either. Examples are given in the following lists. There are many others; watch for them in your reading.

Verb + gerund (*enjoy + skiing*)
Verb + preposition + gerund (*think + about + coming*)

Some verbs can be followed by a gerund but not by an infinitive. In many cases, there is a preposition (such as *for, in,* or *of*) between the verb and the gerund. Some verbs and verb-preposition combinations that can be followed by gerunds but not by infinitives are listed below:

admit	believe in	feel like	practice
apologize for	deny	finish	suspect of
appreciate	discuss	insist on	talk about
approve of	dislike	look forward to	thank for
avoid	enjoy	postpone	think about
be used to			

Incorrect: The governor *avoids to make* enemies.

Correct: The governor **avoids making** enemies.

Incorrect: I *enjoy to go* to movies alone.

Correct: I **enjoy going** to movies alone.

Verb + infinitive (*agree + to leave*)

Common verbs that can be followed by an infinitive but not by a gerund are:

agree	decide	manage
arrange	expect	refuse
claim	have	wait

Incorrect: I *arranged paying* my uncle's bills while he was ill.

Correct: I **arranged to pay** my uncle's bills while he was ill.

Verb + noun or pronoun + infinitive (*cause + them + to flee*)

Common verbs that are followed first by a noun or pronoun and then by an infinitive, not a gerund are:

cause	force	remind
command	persuade	warn

Incorrect: The flood *forced them leaving their home.*

Correct: The flood **forced them to leave their home.**

Following are common verbs that can be followed either by an infinitive alone or by a noun or pronoun and an infinitive:

ask	need	want
expect	promise	would like

Rita **expects to go** to college.

Rita's parents **expect her to go** to college.

Verb + gerund or infinitive (*begin* + *packing* or *begin* + *to pack*)

Following are verbs that can be followed by either a gerund or an infinitive:

begin	hate	prefer
continue	love	start

The meaning of each of the verbs above remains the same or almost the same whether a gerund or an infinitive is used.

I love **to sleep** late.

I love **sleeping** late.

With the verbs below, the gerunds and the infinitives have very different meanings.

forget	remember	stop

Yuri **forgot putting money** in the parking meter.
(He put money in the parking meter, but then he forgot that he had done so.)

Yuri **forgot to put money** in the parking meter.
(He neglected to put money in the parking meter.)

Underline the correct word or words in parentheses.

1. The waitress (she looks, looks) grumpy, but she is really quite pleasant.

2. Our picnic will have to be put off until another day. (Is raining, It is raining) too hard to go.

3. (Are, There are) some good articles in this magazine.

4. A very famous writer (coming, is coming) to talk to our class on Friday.

5. I (have, am having) a few questions to ask you.

6. Lila's mother (prefers, is preferring) that we call her by her first name.

7. If your boss is so unpleasant, you should think about (getting, to get) another job.

8. Standing in front of the mirror, Omar practiced (to give, giving) his speech for hours.

9. Because she was angry at her boyfriend, Delores refused (going, to go) to the movies with him.

10. Now that he's done it for several weeks, Sergei is used to (ride, riding) the city buses.

Adjectives

Following the Order of Adjectives in English

Adjectives describe nouns and pronouns. In English, an adjective usually comes directly before the word it describes or after a linking verb (a form of *be* or a "sense" verb such as *look, seem,* or *taste*), in which case it modifies the subject of the sentence. In each of the following two sentences, the adjective is **boldfaced** and the noun it describes is *italicized*.

Marta has **beautiful** *eyes*.

Marta's *eyes* are **beautiful**.

When more than one adjective modifies the same noun, the adjectives are usually stated in a certain order, though there are often exceptions. The box at the top of the next page lists the typical order of English adjectives.

Typical Order of Adjectives in a Series

1. Article or other noun marker: a, an, the, Helen's, this, seven, your

2. Opinion adjective: rude, enjoyable, surprising, easy

3. Size: tall, huge, small, compact

4. Shape: triangular, oval, round, square

5. Age: ancient, new, old, young

6. Color: gray, blue, pink, green

7. Nationality: Greek, Thai, Korean, Ethiopian

8. Religion: Hindu, Methodist, Jewish, Muslim

9. Material: fur, copper, stone, velvet

10. Noun used as an adjective: book (as in *book report*), picture (as in *picture frame*), tea (as in *tea bag*)

Here are some examples of the order of adjectives:

an exciting new movie

the petite young Irish woman

my favorite Chinese restaurant

Greta's long brown leather coat

In general, use no more than two or three adjectives after the article or other noun marker. Numerous adjectives in a series can be awkward: **that comfortable big old green velvet** couch.

Using the Present and Past Participles as Adjectives

The present participle ends in *-ing*. Past participles of regular verbs end in *-ed* or *-d;* a list of the past participles of many common irregular verbs appears on pages 160–162. Both types of participles may be used as adjectives. A participle used as an adjective may come before the word it describes:

There was a **frowning** *security guard.*

A participle used as an adjective may also follow a linking verb and describe the subject of the sentence:

The *security guard* was **frowning.**

While both present and past participles of a particular verb may be used as adjectives, their meanings differ. Use the present participle to describe whoever or whatever causes a feeling:

a **disappointing** *date*

(The date *caused* the disappointment.)

Use the past participle to describe whoever or whatever experiences the feeling:

the **disappointed** *neighbor*

(The neighbor *is* disappointed.)

Here are two more sentences that illustrate the differing meanings of present and past participles.

The waiter was **irritating.**

The diners were **irritated.**

(The waiter caused the irritation; the diners experienced the irritation.)

Following are pairs of present and past participles with similar distinctions.

annoying, annoyed	exhausting, exhausted
boring, bored	fascinating, fascinated
confusing, confused	surprising, surprised
depressing, depressed	tiring, tired
exciting, excited	

Practice 3

Underline the correct word or wording in parentheses.

1. We were glad to find such a (young helpful, helpful young) guide to show us the new city.

2. The children spent hours stacking the (little square yellow, yellow little square) blocks into different arrangements.

3. Our family attends the (old Orthodox Greek, old Greek Orthodox) church on Maple Avenue.

4. After his long workday, Ezra is often very (tired, tiring).

5. The (tired, tiring) journey lasted for almost five days.

Prepositions Used for Time and Place

The use of a preposition in English is often not based on the preposition's common meaning, and there are many exceptions to general rules. As a result, the correct use of prepositions must be learned gradually through experience. Following is a chart showing how three of the most common prepositions are used in some customary references to time and place:

Use of *On*, *In*, and *At* to Refer to Time and Place

Time

On a specific day: on Wednesday, on January 11, on Halloween

In a part of a day: in the morning, in the daytime (but *at* night)

In a month or a year: in October, in 1776

In a period of time: in a second, in a few days, in a little while

At a specific time: at 11 P.M., at midnight, at sunset, at lunchtime

Place

On a surface: on the shelf, on the sidewalk, on the roof

In a place that is enclosed: in the bathroom, in the closet, in the drawer

At a specific location: at the restaurant, at the zoo, at the school

---

Underline the correct preposition in parentheses.

1. Kids like to play tricks (on, at) April Fool's Day.

2. The baby usually takes a nap (on, in) the afternoon.

3. (In, At) a few minutes, the show will begin.

4. You'll find paper clips (on, in) the cup on my desk.

5. I didn't see anyone I knew (on, at) the party.

Practice

4

Review Test

Underline the correct word or words in parentheses.

1. At the beach, the children enjoyed playing in the (sand, sands).

2. (Are, There are) more stars in the sky tonight than I have ever seen.

3. Doesn't watching such a sad movie make you feel (depressed, depressing)?

4. On my way to the restaurant I had a (depressed, depressing) thought: I had no money.

5. I'll never throw away my (favorite old denim, old favorite denim) jacket.

6. The girl's parents suspect her of (to use, using) drugs.

7. The old woman carefully hung the picture of her grandchildren (in, on) the wall.

8. That umbrella by the door (belongs, is belonging) to my uncle.

9. (Happiness, The happiness) is something everyone hopes to find in life.

10. Many people dislike (to wait, waiting) in a long line.

APPENDIX D
Sentence-Skills Diagnostic Test

Part 1

This diagnostic test will help check your knowledge of a number of sentence skills. In each item below, certain words are underlined. Write *X* in the answer space if you think a mistake appears at the underlined part. Write *C* in the answer space if you think the underlined part is correct.

The headings within the test ("Fragments," "Run-Ons," and so on) will give you clues to the mistakes to look for. However, you do not have to understand the heading to find a mistake. What you are checking is your own sense of effective written English.

Fragments

_____ 1. Because I didn't want to get wet. I waited for a break in the downpour. Then I ran for the car like an Olympic sprinter.

_____ 2. The baby birds chirped loudly, especially when their mother brought food to them. Their mouths gaped open hungrily.

_____ 3. Trying to avoid running into anyone. Cal wheeled his baby son around the crowded market. He wished that strollers came equipped with flashing hazard lights.

_____ 4. The old woman combed out her long, gray hair. She twisted it into two thick braids. And wrapped them around her head like a crown.

Run-Ons

_____ 5. Irene fixed fruits and healthy sandwiches for her son's lunch, he traded them for cupcakes, cookies, and chips.

_____ 6. Angie's dark eyes were the color of mink they matched her glowing complexion.

_____ 7. My mother keeps sending me bottles of <u>vitamins</u>, but I keep forgetting to take them.

_____ 8. The little boy watched the line of ants march across the <u>ground, he</u> made a wall of Popsicle sticks to halt the ants' advance.

Standard English Verbs

_____ 9. When she's upset, Mary <u>tells</u> her troubles to her houseplants.

_____ 10. The street musician counted the coins in his donations basket and <u>pack</u> his trumpet in its case.

_____ 11. I tried to pull off my rings, but they <u>was</u> stuck on my swollen fingers.

_____ 12. Bella's car <u>have</u> a horn that plays six different tunes.

Irregular Verbs

_____ 13. I've <u>swam</u> in this lake for years, and I've never seen it so shallow.

_____ 14. The phone <u>rung</u> once and then stopped.

_____ 15. Five different people had <u>brought</u> huge bowls of potato salad to the barbecue.

_____ 16. The metal ice cube trays <u>froze</u> to the bottom of the freezer.

Subject-Verb Agreement

_____ 17. The DVDs in my collection <u>is</u> arranged in alphabetical order.

_____ 18. There <u>was</u> only one burner working on the old gas stove.

_____ 19. My aunt and uncle <u>gives</u> a party every Groundhog Day.

_____ 20. One of my sweaters <u>have</u> moth holes in the sleeves.

Consistent Verb Tense

_____ 21. After I turned off the ignition, the engine <u>continued</u> to sputter for several minutes.

_____ 22. Before cleaning the oven, I lined the kitchen floor with newspapers, <u>open</u> the windows, and shook the can of aerosol foam.

Pronoun Reference, Agreement, and Point of View

_____ 23. All visitors should stay in <u>their</u> cars while driving through the wild animal park.

_____ 24. At the library, <u>they</u> showed me how to use the microfilm machines.

_____ 25. As I slowed down at the scene of the accident, <u>you</u> could see long black skid marks on the highway.

Pronoun Types

_____ 26. My husband is more sentimental than <u>me</u>.

_____ 27. Andy and <u>I</u> made ice cream in an old-fashioned wooden machine.

Adjectives and Adverbs

_____ 28. Brian drives so <u>reckless</u> that no one will join his car pool.

_____ 29. Miriam pulled <u>impatiently</u> at the rusty zipper.

_____ 30. I am <u>more happier</u> with myself now that I earn my own money.

_____ 31. The last screw on the license plate was the <u>most worn</u> one of all.

Misplaced Modifiers

_____ 32. I stretched out on the lounge chair <u>wearing my bikini</u>.

_____ 33. I replaced the shingle on the roof <u>that was loose</u>.

Dangling Modifiers

_____ 34. <u>While doing the dishes</u>, a glass shattered in the soapy water.

_____ 35. <u>Pedaling as fast as possible</u>, Todd tried to outrace the snapping dog.

Faulty Parallelism

_____   36. Before I could take a bath, I had to pick up the damp towels on the floor, gather up the loose toys in the room, and the tub had to be scrubbed out.

_____   37. I've tried several cures for my headaches, including drugs, meditation, exercise, and massaging my head.

Capital Letters

_____   38. This fall we plan to visit Cape Cod.

_____   39. Vern ordered a set of tools from the spiegel catalog.

_____   40. When my aunt visits us, she insists on doing all the cooking.

_____   41. Maureen asked, "will you split a piece of cheesecake with me?"

Numbers and Abbreviations

_____   42. Before I could stop myself, I had eaten 6 glazed doughnuts.

_____   43. At 10:45 A.M., a partial eclipse of the sun will begin.

_____   44. Derrick, who is now over six ft. tall, can no longer sleep comfortably in a twin bed.

End Marks

_____   45. Jane wondered if her husband was telling the truth.

_____   46. Does that stew need some salt?

Apostrophe

_____   47. Elizabeths thick, curly hair is her best feature.

_____   48. I tried to see through the interesting envelope sent to my sister but couldnt.

_____   49. Pam's heart almost stopped beating when Roger jumped out of the closet.

_____   50. The logs' in the fireplace crumbled in a shower of sparks.

Quotation Marks

_____ 51. Someone once said, "A lie has no legs and cannot stand."

_____ 52. "This repair job could be expensive, the mechanic warned."

_____ 53. "My greatest childhood fear," said Sheila, "was being sucked down the bathtub drain."

_____ 54. "I was always afraid of everybody's father, said Midori, except my own."

Comma

_____ 55. The restaurant's "sundae bar" featured bowls of whipped cream chopped nuts and chocolate sprinkles.

_____ 56. My sister, who studies karate, installed large practice mirrors in our basement.

_____ 57. When I remove my thick eyeglasses the world turns into an out-of-focus movie.

_____ 58. Gloria wrapped her son's presents in pages from the comics section, and she glued a small toy car atop each gift.

Spelling

_____ 59. When Terry practises scales on the piano, her whole family wears earplugs.

_____ 60. I wondered if it was alright to wear sneakers with my three-piece suit.

_____ 61. The essay test question asked us to describe two different theorys of evolution.

_____ 62. A theif stole several large hanging plants from Marlo's porch.

Omitted Words and Letters

_____ 63. After dark, I'm afraid to look in the closets or under the bed.

_____ 64. I turned on the television, but baseball game had been rained out.

_____ 65. Polar bear cubs stay with their mother for two year.

Commonly Confused Words

_____ 66. Before <u>your</u> about to start the car, press the gas pedal to the floor once.

_____ 67. The frog flicked <u>it's</u> tongue out and caught the fly.

_____ 68. I was <u>to</u> lonely to enjoy the party.

_____ 69. The bats folded <u>their</u> wings around them like leather overcoats.

Effective Word Choice

_____ 70. If the professor <u>gives me a break</u>, I might pass the final exam.

_____ 71. Harry <u>worked like a dog</u> all summer to save money for his tuition.

_____ 72. Because Monday is a holiday, <u>sanitation engineers</u> will pick up your trash on Tuesday.

_____ 73. Our family's softball game <u>ended in an argument</u>, as usual.

_____ 74. <u>As for my own opinion</u>, I feel that nuclear weapons should be banned.

_____ 75. This law is, <u>for all intents and purposes</u>, a failure.

Part 2 (Optional)

Do the following at your instructor's request. This second part of the test will provide more detailed information about skills you need to know. On separate paper, number and correct all the items you have marked with an *X*. For example, suppose you had marked the word groups below with an *X*. (Note that these examples were not taken from the actual test.)

4. <u>When I picked up the tire.</u> Something in my back snapped. I could not stand up straight as a result.

7. The phone started <u>ringing, then</u> the doorbell sounded as well.

15. <u>Marks</u> goal is to save enough money to get married next year.

29. Without checking the rearview <u>mirror the</u> driver pulled out into the passing lane.

Here is how you should write your corrections on a separate sheet of paper:

4. When I picked up the tire, something in my back snapped.

7. The phone started ringing, and then the doorbell sounded as well.

15. Mark's

29. mirror, the

There are over forty corrections to make in all.

Sentence-Skills Achievement Test

Part 1

This achievement test will help you check your mastery of a number of sentence skills. In each item below, certain words are underlined. Write *X* in the answer space if you think a mistake appears at the underlined part. Write *C* in the answer space if you think the underlined part is correct.

The headings within the test ("Fragments," "Run-Ons," and so on) will give you clues to the mistakes to look for.

Fragments

_____ 1. When the town bully died. Hundreds of people came to his funeral. They wanted to make sure he was dead.

_____ 2. Suzanne adores junk foods, especially onion-flavored potato chips. She can eat an entire bag at one sitting.

_____ 3. My brother stayed up all night. Studying the rules in his driver's manual. He wanted to get his license on the first try.

_____ 4. Hector decided to take a study break. He turned on the TV. And scrolled through the onscreen guide to find that night's listings.

Run-Ons

_____ 5. Ronnie leaned forward in his seat, he could not hear what the instructor was saying.

_____ 6. Our television obviously needs repairs the color keeps fading from the picture.

_____ 7. Nick and Fran enjoyed their trip to Chicago, but they couldn't wait to get home.

_____ 8. I tuned in the weather forecast on the radio, I had to decide what to wear.

Standard English Verbs

_____ 9. My sister Louise <u>walks</u> a mile to the bus stop every day.

_____ 10. The play was ruined when the quarterback <u>fumble</u> the handoff.

_____ 11. When the last guests left our party, we <u>was</u> exhausted but happy.

_____ 12. I don't think my mother <u>have</u> gone out to a movie in years.

Irregular Verbs

_____ 13. My roommate and I <u>seen</u> a double feature this weekend.

_____ 14. My nephew must have <u>growed</u> six inches since last summer.

_____ 15. I should have <u>brought</u> a gift to the office Christmas party.

_____ 16. After playing touch football all afternoon, Al <u>drank</u> a quart of Gatorade.

Subject-Verb Agreement

_____ 17. The cost of those new tires <u>are</u> more than I can afford.

_____ 18. Nick and Fran <u>give</u> a New Year's Eve party every year.

_____ 19. There <u>was</u> only two slices of cake left on the plate.

_____ 20. Each of the fast-food restaurants <u>have</u> a breakfast special.

Consistent Verb Tense

_____ 21. After I folded the towels in the basket, I <u>remembered</u> that I hadn't washed them yet.

_____ 22. Before she decided to buy the wall calendar, Joanne <u>turns</u> its pages and looked at all the pictures.

Pronoun Reference, Agreement, and Point of View

_____ 23. All drivers should try <u>their</u> best to be courteous during rush hour.

_____ 24. When Bob went to the bank for a home improvement loan, <u>they</u> asked him for three credit references.

_____ 25. I like to shop at factory outlets because <u>you</u> can always get brand names at a discount.

Pronoun Types

_____   26. My brother writes much more neatly than <u>me</u>.

_____   27. Vonnie and <u>I</u> are both taking Introduction to Business this semester.

Adjectives and Adverbs

_____   28. When the elevator doors closed <u>sudden</u>, three people were trapped inside.

_____   29. The homeless woman glared <u>angrily</u> at me when I offered her a dollar bill.

_____   30. Frank couldn't decide which vacation he liked <u>best</u>, a bicycle trip or a week at the beach.

_____   31. I find proofreading a paper much <u>more difficult</u> than writing one.

Misplaced Modifiers

_____   32. The car was parked along the side of the road <u>with a flat tire</u>.

_____   33. We bought a television set at our neighborhood video store <u>that has stereo sound</u>.

Dangling Modifiers

_____   34. <u>While looking for bargains at Sears</u>, an exercise bike caught my eye.

_____   35. <u>Hurrying to catch the bus</u>, Donna fell and twisted her ankle.

Faulty Parallelism

_____   36. Before she leaves for work, Ana makes her lunch, does fifteen minutes of calisthenics, and <u>her two cats have to be fed</u>.

_____   37. Three remedies for insomnia are warm milk, <u>taking a hot bath</u>, and sleeping pills.

Capital Letters

_____   38. Every <u>Saturday</u> I get up early, even though I have the choice of sleeping late.

_____   39. We stopped at the drugstore for some <u>crest</u> toothpaste.

_____   40. Rows of crocuses appear in my front yard every <u>spring</u>.

_____   41. The cashier said, "<u>sorry</u>, but children under three are not allowed in this theater."

Numbers and Abbreviations

_____ 42. Our train finally arrived—<u>2</u> hours late.

_____ 43. Answers to the chapter questions start on page <u>293</u>.

_____ 44. Three <u>yrs.</u> from now, my new car will finally be paid off.

End Marks

_____ 45. I had no idea who was inside the gorilla suit at the Halloween party<u>.</u>

_____ 46. Are you taking the make-up exam<u>.</u>

Apostrophe

_____ 47. My <u>fathers</u> favorite old television program is *Star Trek*.

_____ 48. I <u>couldnt</u> understand a word of that lecture.

_____ 49. My <u>dentist's</u> recommendation was that I floss after brushing my teeth.

_____ 50. Three <u>house's</u> on our street are up for sale.

Quotation Marks

_____ 51. <u>Garfield the cat is fond of saying, "I never met a carbohydrate I didn't like."</u>

_____ 52. <u>"This restaurant does not accept credit cards, the waiter said."</u>

_____ 53. <u>Two foods that may prevent cancer," said the scientist, "are those old standbys spinach and carrots."</u>

_____ 54. <u>"I can't get anything done," Dad complained, if you two insist on making all that noise."</u>

Comma

_____ 55. The snack bar offered <u>overdone hamburgers rubbery hot dogs and soggy pizza</u>.

_____ 56. My sister, <u>who regards every living creature as a holy thing,</u> cannot even swat a housefly.

_____ 57. When I smelled something <u>burning</u> I realized I hadn't turned off the oven.

_____ 58. Marge plays the xylophone at <u>parties, and her</u> husband does Dracula imitations.

Spelling

_____ 59. No one will be <u>admited</u> without a valid student identification card.

_____ 60. Trisha <u>carrys</u> a full course load in addition to working as the night manager at a supermarket.

_____ 61. Did you feel <u>alright</u> after eating Rodolfo's special chili?

_____ 62. My parents were disappointed when I didn't enter the family <u>busines</u>.

Omitted Words and Letters

_____ 63. <u>Both high schools in my hometown offer evening classes for adults.</u>

_____ 64. <u>I opened new bottle of ketchup and then couldn't find the cap.</u>

_____ 65. <u>Visiting hour for patients at this hospital are from noon to eight.</u>

Commonly Confused Words

_____ 66. Shelley has always been <u>to</u> self-conscious to speak up in class.

_____ 67. <u>Its</u> not easy to return to college after raising a family.

_____ 68. "Thank you for <u>you're</u> generous contribution," the letter began.

_____ 69. Nobody knew <u>whose</u> body had been found floating in the swimming pool.

Effective Word Choice

_____ 70. My roommate keeps <u>getting on my case</u> about leaving clothing on the floor.

_____ 71. Karla decided to <u>take the bull by the horns</u> and ask her boss for a raise.

_____ 72. Although Lamont <u>accelerated his vehicle</u>, he was unable to pass the truck.

_____ 73. When the movie <u>ended suddenly</u>, I felt I had been cheated.

_____ 74. <u>In light of the fact that</u> I am on a diet, I have stopped eating between meals.

_____ 75. <u>Personally, I do not think</u> that everyone should be allowed to vote.

Part 2 (Optional)

Do the following at your instructor's request. This second part of the test will provide more detailed information about which skills you need to know. On separate paper, number and correct all the items you have marked with an *X*. For example, suppose you had marked the word groups below with an *X*. (Note that these examples were not taken from the actual test.)

4. <u>When I picked up the tire.</u> Something in my back snapped. I could not stand up straight as a result.

7. The phone started <u>ringing, then</u> the doorbell sounded as well.

15. <u>Marks</u> goal is to save enough money to get married next year.

29. Without checking the rearview <u>mirror the</u> driver pulled out into the passing lane.

Here is how you should write your corrections on a separate sheet of paper:

4. When I picked up the tire, something in my back snapped.

7. The phone started ringing, and then the doorbell sounded as well.

15. Mark's

29. mirror, the driver

There are more than forty corrections to make in all.

APPENDIX F

Answers to Introductory Activities and Practice Exercises in Part Two

This answer key can help you teach yourself. Use it to find out why you got some answers wrong—to uncover any weak spot in your understanding of a skill. By using the answer key in an honest and thoughtful way, you will master each skill and prepare yourself for many tests in this book that have no answer key.

SUBJECTS AND VERBS

Introductory Activity (68)

Answers will vary.

Practice 1 (70)

1. Rachel poured
2. company offered
3. host introduced
4. Taryn adjusted
5. butt burned
6. bathroom is
7. Royden tripped
8. drink quenched
9. trimmer tossed
10. Volunteers collected

Practice 2 (71)

1. shows . . . were
2. burp is
3. sunglasses . . . look
4. voice sounds
5. Tamika became
6. lotion smells
7. Visitors . . . appear
8. vibrations are
9. cold feels
10. change . . . seems

Practice 3 (72)

1. light glowed
2. kite soared
3. Manuel caught
4. skaters shadowed
5. lights emphasized
6. Tracy reads
7. glasses slipped
8. Jane gave
9. squirrel jumped
10. Carpenters constructed

Practice 4 (73)

1. Stripes ~~of sunlight~~ glowed ~~on the kitchen floor~~.
2. The black panther draped its powerful body ~~along the thick tree branch~~.
3. A line ~~of impatient people~~ snaked ~~from the box office to the street~~.
4. ~~At noon,~~ every siren ~~in town~~ wails ~~for fifteen minutes~~.
5. The tops ~~of my Bic pens~~ always disappear ~~after a day or two~~.
6. Joanne removed the lint ~~from her black socks with Scotch tape~~.
7. The mirrored walls ~~of the skyscraper~~ reflected the passing clouds.
8. Debris ~~from the accident~~ littered the intersection.
9. ~~Above the heads of the crowd,~~ a woman swayed ~~on a narrow ledge~~.
10. The squashed grapes ~~in the bottom of the vegetable bin~~ oozed sticky purple juice.

Practice 5 (75)

1. Einstein could have passed
2. She could have been killed
3. children did not recognize
4. strikers have been fasting
5. I could not see
6. People may be wearing

7. He should have studied
8. Rosa has been soaking
9. lines . . . were flying
10. brother can ask

Practice 6 (75)

1. trees creaked and shuddered
2. girl fell . . . and landed
3. I will vacuum . . . and change
4. sun shone . . . and turned
5. Sam and Billy greased
6. man and . . . friend rode
7. sister and I . . . race
8. Nia breathed and . . . began
9. Phil draped . . . and pretended
10. wrestler and opponent strutted . . . and pounded

FRAGMENTS

Introductory Activity (82)

1. verb
2. subject
3. subject . . . verb
4. express a complete thought

Practice 1 (86)

Answers will vary.

Practice 2 (87)

NOTE: The underlined part shows the fragment (or that part of the original fragment not changed during correction).

1. Since she was afraid of muggers, Barbara carried a small can of pepper spray on her key ring.
2. When I began watching the TV mystery movie, I remembered that I had seen it before.
3. Tulips had only begun to bloom when a freakish spring snowstorm blanketed the garden.
4. Whenever I'm in the basement and the phone rings, I don't run up to answer it. If the message is important, the person will call back.
5. Since she is a new student, Carla feels shy and insecure. She thinks she is the only person who doesn't know anyone else.

Practice 3 (89)

1. Julie spent an hour at her desk, staring at a blank piece of paper.
2. Rummaging around in the kitchen drawer, Tyrone found the key he had misplaced a year ago.
3. As a result, I lost my place in the checkout line.

Practice 4 (90)

Rewritten versions may vary.

1. I tossed and turned for hours. *Or:* Tossing and turning for hours, I felt like a blanket being tumbled dry.
2. It fluffed its feathers to keep itself warm. *Or:* A sparrow landed on the icy windowsill, fluffing its feathers to keep itself warm.
3. The reason was that she had to work the next day. *Or:* Alma left the party early, the reason being that she had to work the next day.
4. Grasping the balance beam with her powdered hands, the gymnast executed a handstand.
5. To cover his bald spot, Walt combed long strands of hair over the top of his head.

Practice 5 (92)

1. For instance, he folds a strip of paper into the shape of an accordion.
2. Marco stuffed the large green peppers with hamburger meat, cooked rice, and chopped parsley.
3. For example, he craves Bugles and Doritos.

Practice 6 (92)

Rewritten versions may vary.

1. For instance, he has his faded sweatshirt from high school.
2. For example, she borrows my sweaters.
3. To improve her singing, Amber practiced some odd exercises, such as flapping her tongue and fluttering her lips.
4. For example, she had put on forty pounds.
5. Stanley wanted a big birthday cake with candles spelling out STAN.

Practice 7 (94)

Rewritten answers may vary.

1. Then she quickly folded her raggedy towels and faded sheets.
2. Wally took his wool sweaters out of storage and found them full of moth holes.

3. Also, she is learning two computer languages.
4. Then he hides under the bed.
5. A tiny bug crawled across my paper and sat down in the middle of a sentence.

RUN-ONS

Introductory Activity (106)

1. period
2. but
3. semicolon
4. although

Practice 1 (109)

1. coffee. His
2. way. She
3. coughing. A
4. me. It
5. time. The
6. machine. We
7. closely. They
8. Lauren. She
9. victims. They
10. late. The

Practice 2 (110)

1. cockroaches. Both
2. blood. The
3. counselor. She's
4. death. He
5. seen. One
6. beautiful. Now
7. penalty. The
8. down. It
9. Germany. In
10. request. He

Practice 3 (111)

Answers will vary.

Practice 4 (112)

1. drawer, but
2. paper, for
3. therapy, so
4. drive, and
5. on, and
6. summer, so
7. truck, so
8. break, but
9. faded, and
10. fit, so

Practice 5 (113)

Answers will vary.

Practice 6 (114)

1. backward; his
2. indestructible; it
3. cards; she
4. moth; it
5. book; it

Practice 7 (115)

Answers may vary.

1. month; on the other hand, they (*or* however)
2. sick; therefore, she (*or* consequently *or* as a result *or* thus)

3. hydrant; however, she
4. guests; furthermore, he (*or* also *or* moreover *or* in addition)
5. money; consequently, she (*or* therefore *or* as a result *or* thus)

Practice 8 (115)

1. wait; however, she
2. computers; as a result, she
3. abused; moreover, many
4. smoking; otherwise, I
5. carefully; nevertheless, the

Practice 9 (116)

Answers may vary.

1. After
2. before
3. When
4. If
5. until

Practice 10 (117)

1. Even though I had a campus map, I still could not find my classroom building.
2. When a cat food commercial came on, Marie started to sing along with the jingle.
3. Since the phone in the next apartment rings all the time, I'm beginning to get used to the sound.
4. After Michael gulped two cups of coffee, his heart began to flutter.
5. As a car sped around the corner, it sprayed slush all over the pedestrians.

SENTENCE VARIETY I

The Simple Sentence
Practice 1 (128)

Answers will vary.

The Compound Sentence
Practice 2 (129)

Answers may vary.

1. I am majoring in digital media arts, for I hope to find a job doing video-game animation.
2. My children were spending too much time in front of the TV and computer, so I signed up my entire family for a one-year gym membership.
3. Nicole's skin was blemished and sun damaged, so she consulted with a plastic surgeon about a chemical face peel.

4. Riley insists on buying certified-organic fruits and vegetables, but I cannot distinguish organic from conventionally grown produce.
5. I was recently promoted to shift manager at work, so I need to drop down to part-time status at school next semester.

Practice 3 (130)
Answers will vary.

The Complex Sentence
Practice 4 (131)
Answers may vary.

1. Because the movie disgusted Dena, she walked out after twenty minutes.
2. After the house had been burglarized, Dave couldn't sleep soundly for several months.
3. When my vision begins to fade, I know I'd better get some sleep.
4. Since the family would need a place to sleep, Fred told the movers to unload the mattresses first.
5. When the hurricane hit the coast, we crisscrossed our windows with strong tape.

Practice 5 (132)
Answers may vary.

1. Although the muffler shop advertised same-day service, my car wasn't ready for three days.
2. Because the hypertension medication produced dangerous side effects, the government banned it.
3. While Phil lopped dead branches off the tree, Michelle stacked them into piles on the ground below.
4. Anne wedged her handbag tightly under her arm because she was afraid of muggers.
5. Although Ellen counted the cash three times, the total still didn't tally with the amount on the register tape.

Practice 6 (133)
Answers may vary.

1. The boy who limps was in a motorcycle accident.
2. Raquel, who is my neighbor, is a champion weight lifter.
3. The two screws that held the bicycle frame together were missing from the assembly kit.
4. The letter that arrived today is from my ex-wife.
5. The tall hedge that surrounded the house muffled the highway noise.

Practice 7 (134)
Answers will vary.

The Compound-Complex Sentence
Practice 8 (135)
Answers will vary.

1. Since . . . for
2. When . . . and
3. until . . . so
4. When . . . or
5. but . . . because

Practice 9 (135)
Answers will vary.

Review of Coordination and Subordination
Practice 10 (136)
Answers will vary.

1. I needed butter to make the cookie batter, but I couldn't find any, so I used vegetable oil instead.
2. Although Tess had worn glasses for fifteen years, she decided to get contact lenses. She would be able to see better, and she would look more glamorous.
3. When the children at the day care center took their naps, they unrolled their sleeping mats, and they piled their shoes and sneakers in a corner.
4. When Jerry dialed the police emergency number, he received a busy signal. He dropped the phone and ran because he didn't have time to call back.
5. Louise disliked walking home from the bus stop because the street had no overhead lights, and it was lined with abandoned buildings.
6. When the rain hit the hot pavement, plumes of steam rose from the blacktop. Cars slowed to a crawl, for the fog obscured the drivers' vision.
7. While his car went through the automated car wash, Harry watched from the sidelines. Floppy brushes slapped the car's doors, and sprays of water squirted onto the roof.
8. Since the pipes had frozen and the heat had gone off, we phoned the plumber. He couldn't come for days because he had been swamped with emergency calls.
9. When my car developed an annoying rattle, I took it to the service station. The mechanic looked under the hood, but he couldn't find what was wrong.
10. The childproof cap on the aspirin bottle would not budge even though the arrows on the bottleneck and cap were lined up. When I pried the cap with my fingernails, one nail snapped off, and the cap still adhered tightly to the bottle.

STANDARD ENGLISH VERBS

Introductory Activity (145)

played . . . plays
hoped . . . hopes
juggled . . . juggles

1. past time . . . . *-ed* or *-d*
2. present time . . . *-s*

Practice 1 (147)

1. wears
2. says
3. subscribes
4. believes
5. sees
6. distributes
7. C
8. feeds
9. overcooks
10. polishes

Practice 2 (148)

Lou works for a company that delivers singing telegrams. Sometimes he puts on a sequined tuxedo or wears a Cupid costume. He composes his own songs for birthdays, anniversaries, bachelor parties, and other occasions. Then he shows up at a certain place and surprises the victim. He sings a song that includes personal details, which he gets in advance, about the recipient of the telegram. Lou loves the astonished looks on other people's faces; he also enjoys earning money by making people happy on special days.

Practice 3 (149)

1. turned
2. bounced
3. paged
4. crushed
5. C
6. washed
7. cracked
8. collected
9. pulled
10. lacked

Practice 4 (149)

Brad hated working long hours, but he needed money to support his growing family and to pay for school. He started working at the auto body shop when he graduated from high school because he liked cars, but the job bored him. He wished that he could spend more time at home with his wife and new baby girl. He also wanted to dedicate more time to his homework. Brad knew that he had made his own choices, so he decided to appreciate his job, his family, and his chance to move ahead in life.

Practice 5 (152)

1. is
2. has
3. is
4. does
5. did
6. was
7. had
8. was
9. did
10. was

Practice 6 (152)

1. is
2. has
3. has
4. are
5. are
6. do
7. do
8. has
9. does
10. are

Practice 7 (153)

My friend Tyrell is a real bargain-hunter. If a store has a sale, he runs right over and buys two or three things, whether or not they are things he needs. Tyrell does his best, also, to get something for nothing. Last week, he was reading the paper and saw that the First National Bank's new downtown offices were offering gifts for new accounts. "Those freebies sure do look good," Tyrell said. So he went downtown, opened an account, and had the manager give him a Big Ben alarm clock. When he got back with the clock, he was smiling. "I am a very busy man," he told me, "and I really need the free time."

IRREGULAR VERBS

Introductory Activity (159)

1. R . . . screamed . . . screamed
2. I . . . wrote . . . written
3. I . . . stole . . . stolen
4. R . . . asked . . . asked
5. R . . . kissed . . . kissed
6. I . . . chose . . . chosen
7. I . . . rode . . . ridden
8. R . . . chewed . . . chewed
9. I . . . thought . . . thought
10. R . . . danced . . . danced

Practice 1 (162)

1. took
2. chosen
3. caught
4. stolen
5. saw
6. gone
7. fallen
8. sworn
9. shrunk
10. spoken

Practice 2 (163)

1. (a) loses
   (b) lost
   (c) lost
2. (a) brings
   (b) brought
   (c) brought
3. (a) swim
   (b) swam
   (c) swum
4. (a) goes
   (b) went
   (c) gone
5. (a) begins
   (b) began
   (c) begun
6. (a) hides
   (b) hid
   (c) hidden
7. (a) choose
   (b) chose
   (c) chosen
8. (a) speak
   (b) spoke
   (c) spoken
9. (a) takes
   (b) took
   (c) taken
10. (a) wake
    (b) woke
    (c) woken

Practice 3 (166)

1. laid
2. lay
3. laid
4. lying
5. lay

Practice 4 (167)

1. set
2. set
3. sit
4. set
5. setting

Practice 5 (168)

1. rise
2. raised
3. raised
4. rose
5. raised

SUBJECT–VERB AGREEMENT

Introductory Activity (174)

Correct: There were many applicants for the position.
Correct: The pictures in that magazine are very
   controversial.
Correct: Everybody usually watches the lighted numbers
   in an elevator.

1. applicants . . . pictures
2. singular . . . singular

Practice 1 (176)

1. leaders of the union have
2. One of Omar's pencil sketches hangs
3. days of anxious waiting finally end

4. members of the car pool chip
5. woman with the teased, sprayed hairdo looks
6. addition of heavy shades to my sunny windows
   allows
7. houses in the old whaling village have
8. stack of baseball cards in my little brother's
   bedroom is
9. puddles of egg white spread
10. box of Raisinets sells

Practice 2 (177)

1. were . . . trucks
2. are . . . coyotes
3. are rows
4. are . . . boots
5. was . . . boy
6. was . . . animal
7. is . . . shampooer
8. was . . . stream
9. is . . . box
10. is . . . sign

Practice 3 (178)

1. is
2. remembers
3. fit
4. has
5. wanders
6. needs
7. keeps
8. sneaks
9. is
10. eats

Practice 4 (179)

1. seem
2. is
3. are
4. help
5. impresses

Practice 5 (179)

1. roam
2. begins
3. thunder
4. fear
5. tastes

CONSISTENT VERB TENSE

Introductory Activity *(189)*

Mistakes in verb tense: Alex discovers . . . calls a . . . present . . . past

Practice 1 *(190)*

1. prepares
2. filled
3. found
4. began
5. are
6. separated
7. send
8. sells
9. said
10. likes

ADDITIONAL INFORMATION ABOUT VERBS

Practice 1 *(198)*

1. had watched
2. has written
3. am taking
4. had lifted
5. has improved
6. are protesting
7. have dreaded
8. has vowed *or* is vowing
9. were peeking
10. are getting *or* have gotten

Practice 2 *(200)*

1. P
2. G
3. I
4. G
5. I
6. P
7. P
8. P
9. G
10. I

Practice 3 *(202)*

Answers may vary.

1. The beautician snipped off Carla's long hair.
2. The parents protested the teachers' strike.
3. The alert bank teller tripped the silent alarm.
4. Relentless bloodhounds tracked the escaped convicts.
5. A famous entertainer donated the new PET scanner to the hospital.
6. A stock clerk dropped a gallon glass jar of pickles in the supermarket aisle.

7. A car struck the deer as it crossed the highway.
8. My doctor referred me to a specialist in hearing problems.
9. Family photographs cover one wall of my living room.
10. Fear gripped the town during the accident at the nuclear power plant.

PRONOUN REFERENCE, AGREEMENT, AND POINT OF VIEW

Introductory Activity *(206)*

1. b
2. b
3. b

Practice 1 *(208)*

Answers will vary. Rewritten sentences may have meanings different from the answers provided.

1. When we pulled into the gas station, the attendant told us one of our tires looked soft.
2. Nora broke the heavy ashtray when she dropped it on her foot.
3. Vicky asked for a grade transcript at the registrar's office, and the clerk told her it would cost three dollars.
4. Don't touch the freshly painted walls with your hands unless the walls are dry.
5. Maurice's habit of staying up half the night watching *Chiller Theater* really annoys his wife.
6. Robin went to the store's personnel office to be interviewed for a sales position.
7. Leon told his brother, "You need to lose some weight."
8. I wrote to the insurance company but haven't received an answer.
9. I went to the doctor to see what he could do about my itchy, bloodshot eyes.
10. I took the loose pillows off the chairs and sat on the pillows.
   Or: I sat on the loose pillows, which I had taken off the chairs.

Practice 2 *(210)*

1. them
2. their
3. they
4. them
5. it

Practice 3 (212)

1. her	6. its
2. he	7. her
3. her	8. his
4. his	9. their
5. she	10. his

Practice 4 (214)

1. we see	6. I get depressed
2. I can buy	7. I save
3. we were given	8. he or she could make
4. we relax	9. she can buy
5. they serve	10. I can stop

PRONOUN TYPES

Introductory Activity (221)

Correct sentences:

Ali and I enrolled in a computer course.

The police officer pointed to my sister and me.

Lola prefers men who take pride in their bodies.

The players are confident that the league championship is theirs.

Those concert tickets are too expensive.

Our parents should spend some money on themselves for a change.

Practice 1 (224)

2. I (*S*)
3. her (*O*)
4. me (*O*)
5. her and him (*O*)
6. I (*can* is understood) (*S*)
7. We (*S*)
8. she (*S*)
9. me (*O*)
10. he (*S*)

Practice 2 (225)

Answers will vary.

2. me *or* her *or* him *or* them
3. I *or* she *or* he
4. I *or* she *or* he *or* they
5. me *or* him *or* her *or* them
6. I *or* he *or* she *or* they
7. them
8. him *or* her *or* them

9. I *or* he *or* she
10. she *or* he

Practice 3 (227)

1. who	4. who
2. which	5. who
3. whom	

Practice 4 (227)

Answers will vary.

Practice 5 (228)

1. hers	4. its
2. mine	5. their
3. ours	

Practice 6 (230)

1. This	4. Those
2. Those	5. that
3. These	

Practice 7 (230)

Answers will vary.

Practice 8 (232)

1. ourselves	4. yourself
2. himself	5. ourselves
3. themselves	

ADJECTIVE AND ADVERBS

Introductory Activity (236)

Answers will vary for 1–4.

adjective . . . adverb . . . *ly* . . . *er* . . . *est*

Practice 1 (239)

1. kinder . . . kindest
2. more ambitious . . . most ambitious
3. more generous . . . most generous
4. finer . . . finest
5. more likable . . . most likable

Practice 2 (239)

1. thickest	6. best
2. lazier	7. less
3. harshest	8. less vulnerable
4. more flexible	9. most wasteful
5. worse	10. shinier

Practice 3 (240)

1.	hesitantly	6.	regretfully
2.	easily	7.	quickly
3.	sharply	8.	messily
4.	abruptly	9.	envious
5.	aggressive	10.	terribly

Practice 4 (241)

1. good
2. good
3. well
4. well
5. well

MISPLACED MODIFIERS

Introductory Activity (246)

1. Intended: The farmers were wearing masks.
   Unintended: The apple trees were wearing masks.
2. Intended: The woman had a terminal disease.
   Unintended: The faith healer had a terminal disease.

Practice 1 (247)

NOTE: In the corrections below, the underlined part shows what had been a misplaced modifier. In some cases, other corrections are possible.

1. Driving along the wooded road, we noticed several dead animals.
2. In her mind, Maya envisioned the flowers that would bloom.
3. In my tuxedo, I watched my closest friends being married.
4. Zoe carried her new coat, which was trimmed with fur, on her arm.
5. We just heard on the radio that all major highways were flooded.
6. Fresh-picked blueberries covered almost the entire kitchen counter.
7. Making sounds of contentment, Betty licked the homemade peach ice cream.
   Or: Betty, making sounds of contentment, licked the homemade peach ice cream.
8. With a grin, the salesman confidently demonstrated the vacuum cleaner.
9. Dressed in a top hat and tails, Natasha is delivering singing telegrams.
10. The local drama group badly needs people to build scenery.

Practice 2 (248)

1. Using caution, I rolled down my car window only a few inches for the police officer.
2. Tabloids all over the world publish unflattering photos of celebrities who are arrested for drunk driving or for possession of illicit drugs.
3. The mongoose, which resembles the ferret, was brought to Hawaii to kill rats but has since destroyed much of the native plant life.
4. Led Zeppelin's fourth album has sold almost 22 million copies.
5. Elisa decided to undergo laser eye surgery at the university medical center to correct her astigmatism.

DANGLING MODIFIERS

Introductory Activity (254)

1. Intended: The giraffe was munching leaves.
   Unintended: The children were munching leaves.
2. Intended: Michael was arriving home. . . .
   Unintended: The neighbors were arriving home. . . .

Practice 1 (256)

1. The dog warden had the stray, which was foaming at the mouth, put to sleep.
2. Marian finally found her slippers, which had been kicked carelessly under the bed.
3. I tried out the old swing set, which was rusty with disuse.
4. The manager decided to replace his starting pitcher, who had given up four straight hits.
5. The farmers lost their entire tomato crop, which had frozen on the vines.
6. *C*
7. The audience cheered wildly as the elephants, which were dancing on their hind legs, paraded by.
8. Marta took the overdone meat loaf, which was burned beyond all recognition, from the oven.
9. We decided to replace the dining room wallpaper, which was tattered, faded, and hanging in shreds.
10. A person can keep membership cards clean by sealing them in plastic.
    Or: When sealed in plastic, membership cards can be kept clean.

Practice 2 (257)
Answers will vary.

FAULTY PARALLELISM

Introductory Activity (262)
Correct sentences:

I use my computer to write papers, to search the Internet, and to play video games.

One option the employees had was to take a cut in pay; the other was to work longer hours.

Dad's favorite chair has a torn cushion, a stained armrest, and a musty odor.

Practice 1 (263)
1. waved pennants
2. to stay indoors
3. make a cream sauce
4. turn down the heat
5. overdone hamburgers
6. coughed
7. demanding
8. drinking two milk shakes
9. puts a frozen waffle into the toaster
10. to leave the company

Practice 2 (265)
Answers will vary.

SENTENCE VARIETY II

-ing Word Groups
Practice 1 (272)
Answers may vary.
1. Fluffing out its feathers, the sparrow tried to keep warm.
2. Squeezing the tube as hard as I could, I managed to get enough toothpaste on my brush.
3. Checking the glass-faced gauges, the janitor started up the enormous boiler.
4. Staring straight ahead, the runner set his feet into the starting blocks.
5. The produce clerk, chatting with each customer, cheerfully weighed bags of fruit and vegetables.

Practice 2 (273)
Answers will vary.

-ed Word Groups
Practice 3 (274)
Answers may vary.
1. Bored with the talk show, I dozed off.
2. Crinkled with age, the old dollar bill felt like tissue paper.
3. Crowded into a tiny, windowless room, the students acted nervous and edgy.
4. Loaded down with heavy bags of groceries, I waited for someone to open the door.
5. Tired of his conservative wardrobe, Ron bought a green-striped suit.

Practice 4 (274)
Answers will vary.

-ly Openers
Practice 5 (275)
1. Abruptly, Clarissa hung up on the telemarketer.
2. Casually, the thief slipped one of the watches into her coat sleeve.
3. Swiftly, I tugged on my shoes and pants as the doorbell rang.
4. Gruffly, the defense lawyer cross-examined the witnesses.
5. Carefully, Estelle poked the corner of a handkerchief into her eye.

Practice 6 (276)
Answers will vary.

To Openers
Practice 7 (277)
1. To anchor the flapping tablecloth, we set bricks on the ends of the picnic table.
2. To break up the coating of ice, Darryl scraped the windshield with a credit card.
3. To make the basketball game more even, we gave our opponents a ten-point advantage.
4. To give my wife a rest, I offered to drive the next five hundred miles.
5. To feed the unexpected guests, Fran added Hamburger Helper to the ground beef.

Practice 8 *(277)*
Answers will vary.

Prepositional Phrase Openers
Practice 9 *(278)*
Answers may vary.

1. On the bus, the old man wrote down my address with a stubby pencil.
2. During the day, special bulletins about the election returns interrupted regular programs.
3. At 6:00 A.M., my clock radio turned itself on with a loud blast of rock music.
4. At the concert, the security guard looked in Sue's pocketbook for concealed bottles.
5. On the highway, a plodding turtle crawled toward the grassy shoulder of the road.

Practice 10 *(279)*
Answers will vary.

Series of Items: Adjectives
Practice 11 *(280)*

1. Impatient and excited, the child gazed at the large, mysterious gift box.
2. Sticky juice squirted out of the fuzzy crushed caterpillar.
3. The battered car dangled from the gigantic yellow crane.
4. Patty squeezed her swollen, tender, sunburned feet into the tight shoes.
5. The tall white-aproned cook flipped the thick, juicy hamburgers on the grooved metal grill.

Practice 12 *(281)*
Answers will vary.

Series of Items: Verbs
Practice 13 *(281)*

1. In the sports bar, Tanner placed a bet on his favorite basketball team, took a swig from his bottle of Budweiser, and sat back to watch the NBA playoff semifinals.
2. The robber scanned the liquor store for a surveillance camera, fidgeted with his dark sunglasses and baseball cap, and signaled to the clerk behind the counter that he had a handgun.
3. The phlebotomist pressed down on Logan's forearm, slid the needle into his arm, and let out a heavy sign as the needle missed his vein.

4. The comedy hypnotist invited a volunteer to the stage, quickly brought her into a trance, and offered her a clove of garlic, which she thought was a cashew nut.
5. The paparazzo stalked the Hollywood actor on vacation, adjusted his telephoto lens, and snapped hundreds of candid photos.

Practice 14 *(283)*
Answers will vary.

PAPER FORMAT

Introductory Activity *(288)*
In "A," the title is capitalized and centered and has no quotation marks around it; there is a blank line between the title and the body of the paper; the first line is indented; there are left and right margins around the body of the paper; no words are incorrectly hyphenated.

Practice 1 *(290)*
1. Do not use quotation marks around the title.
2. Capitalize the major words in the title (Too Small to Fight Back).
3. Skip a line between the title and the first line of the paper.
4. Indent the first line of the paper.
5. Keep margins on both sides of the paper.

Practice 2 *(290)*
Answers will vary.

1. My First-Grade Teacher
2. My Hardest Year
3. My Father's Sense of Humor
4. Ways to Conserve Energy
5. Violence in the Movies

Practice 3 *(291)*
1. Effective communication is often the key to a healthy relationship.
2. Reality TV shows are popular for several reasons.
3. Correct
4. The best vacation I ever had began when my friends from high school booked a one-week trip to Cancun, Mexico.
5. Most professional athletes say that they don't use steroids to enhance athletic performance.

CAPITAL LETTERS

Introductory Activity (295)

1–13: Answers will vary, but all should be capitalized.
14–16: On . . . Let's . . . I

Practice 1 (298)

1. Fourth . . . July . . . Veterans' Day
2. When . . . I
3. Toyota . . . Long Island Expressway
4. *Entertainment Weekly . . . Sixty Minutes*
5. National Bank . . . Samsung
6. Melrose Diner . . . Business Institute
7. A Sound . . . Thunder
8. Pacific School . . . Cosmetology
9. Sears . . . Ninth Street
10. Slim–Fast . . . Boca

Practice 2 (302)

1. Uncle David
2. Motorola Razr . . . Bluetooth
3. United States President Jimmy Carter . . . Nobel Peace Prize
4. Pacific Islander . . . Samoa . . . East Coast
5. Principles . . . Marketing

Practice 3 (302)

1. high school . . . principal . . . discipline
2. father . . . creature . . . wing
3. skull . . . hair . . . bones
4. monument . . . settlers' . . . plague . . . locusts
5. motorcycle . . . tractor-trailer . . . motel

NUMBERS AND ABBREVIATIONS

Introductory Activity (311)

Correct choices:
First sentence: 8:55 . . . 65 percent
Second sentence: Nine . . . forty-five
Second sentence: brothers . . . mountain
Second sentence: hours . . . English

Practice 1 (313)

1. five
2. eleven . . . seventy-seven
3. five . . . five
4. 2:30

5. 15
6. 206
7. 15
8. two hundred
9. July 7, 2007,
10. *The Seven Samurai*

Practice 2 (314)

1. department . . . purchase
2. Route . . . Florida
3. America . . . pounds
4. pair . . . inch
5. appointment . . . doctor . . . month
6. library . . . minutes . . . magazine
7. teaspoon . . . French
8. license . . . driving . . . road
9. finish . . . assignment . . . point
10. limit . . . senator . . . representative

END MARKS

Introductory Activity (318)

1. depressed.
2. paper?
3. parked.
4. control!

Practice 1 (313)

1. door?
2. massage.
3. jerk!"
4. shocked.
5. psychology.
6. Gotcha!"
7. ads.
8. storm.
9. think?"
10. officer.

APOSTROPHE

Introductory Activity (323)

1. To show ownership or possession
2. To indicate missing letters and shortened spellings
3. Because *families* signals a plural noun, while *family's* indicates ownership or possession

Apostrophe in Contractions
Practice 1 (325)

shouldn't	can't
doesn't	who's
isn't	wouldn't
won't	aren't
they're	

Practice 2 *(325)*

1. you'll . . . it's
2. hadn't . . . couldn't
3. isn't . . . doesn't
4. I'm . . . I'm
5. Where's . . . who's

Practice 3 *(325)*

Answers will vary.

Practice 4 *(326)*

1. It's . . . it's
2. they're . . . their
3. You're . . . your
4. whose . . . who's
5. it's . . . your . . . who's

Apostrophe to Show Ownership or Possession
Practice 5 *(327)*

1. The assassin's rifle
2. his mother's inheritance
3. Ali's throat
4. Sam's parking space
5. The chef's hat
6. the president's wife
7. The mugger's hand
8. Harry's briefcase
9. Sandy's shoulder bag
10. The dog's leash

Practice 6 *(328)*

2. instructor's
3. astrologer's
4. Ellen's
5. lemonade's
6. sister's
7. Brian's
8. Nita's
9. Ted's
10. hypnotist's

Practice 7 *(329)*

Sentences will vary.

2. bus's
3. computer's
4. Ross's
5. pizza's

Apostrophe versus Simple Plurals
Practice 8 *(330)*

1. restaurant: restaurant's meaning "the hamburgers of the restaurant"
   hamburgers: simple plural meaning more than one hamburger
   steaks: simple plural meaning more than one steak
2. San Franciscos: San Francisco's, meaning "the cable cars of San Francisco"
   cars: simple plural meaning more than one car
   hills: simple plural meaning more than one hill
3. brothers: brother's, meaning "the collection of my brother"
   cards: simple plural meaning more than one card
   boxes: simple plural meaning more than one box

4. toothpicks: simple plural meaning more than one toothpick
   years: year's, meaning "the fashions of this year"
   fashions: simple plural meaning more than one fashion
5. Pedros: Pedro's, meaning "the blood pressure of Pedro"
   minutes: simple plural meaning more than one minute
   spaces: simple plural meaning more than one space
6. write-ups: simple plural meaning more than one write-up
   Rubys: Ruby's, meaning "the promotion of Ruby"
   co-workers: simple plural meaning more than one co-worker
7. sons: son's, meaning "the fort of my son"
   pieces: simple plural meaning more than one piece
   nails: simple plural meaning more than one nail
   shingles: simple plural meaning more than one shingle
8. mayors: mayor's, meaning "the double-talk of the mayor"
   reporters: simple plural meaning more than one reporter
   heads: simple plural meaning more than one head
   notebooks: simple plural meaning more than one notebook
9. cuts: simple plural meaning more than one cut
   boxers: boxer's, meaning "the left eye of the boxer"
   rounds: simple plural meaning more than one round
10. cafeterias: cafeteria's, meaning "the loudspeakers of the cafeteria"
    loudspeakers: simple plural meaning more than one loudspeaker
    exams: simple plural meaning more than one exam

Apostrophe with Plural Words Ending in *-s*
Practice 9 *(332)*

1. stores'
2. friends'
3. Cowboys'
4. students'
5. voters'

QUOTATION MARKS

Introductory Activity *(340)*

1. Quotation marks set off the exact words of a speaker.
2. They go inside the quotation marks.

Practice 1 (342)

1. "This is the tenth commercial in a row," complained Niko.
2. The police officer said sleepily, "I could really use a cup of coffee."
3. My boss asked me to step into his office and said, "Joanne, how would you like a raise?"
4. "I'm out of work again," Miriam sighed.
5. "I didn't know this movie was R-rated!" Lorraine gasped.
6. "Why does my dog always wait until it rains before he wants to go out?" Donovon asked.
7. A sign over the box office read, "Please form a single line and be patient."
8. "Unless I run three miles a day," Marty said, "my legs feel like lumpy oatmeal."
9. "I had an uncle who knew when he was going to die," claimed Dan. "He saw the date in a dream."
10. The unusual notice in the newspaper read, "Young farmer would be pleased to hear from young lady with tractor. Send photograph of tractor."

Practice 2 (343)

1. The firefighter asked the neighbors, "Is there anyone else still in the building?"
2. "You'll have to remove your sunglasses," the security guard reminded the customers at the bank.
3. Upon eating a few drops of Horacio's homemade habanero sauce, Trudy yelped, "That's hot!"
4. "Good things come to those who wait," Zhao told himself as he waited in line for hours to buy an iPhone.
5. "If at first you don't succeed," my wife joked, "you should read the directions."

Practice 3 (343)

Answers will vary.

Practice 4 (345)

2. Marian said, "It was the worst day of my life."
3. Luis said, "Tell me all about it."

4. Marian insisted, "You wouldn't understand my job problems."
5. Luis said, "I will certainly try."

Practice 5 (345)

1. He said that he needed a vacation.
2. Gretchen said that purple was her favorite color.
3. She asked the handsome stranger if she could buy him a drink.
4. My brother asked if anyone had seen his frog.
5. Françoise complained that she married a man who falls asleep during horror movies.

Practice 6 (346)

1. My recently divorced sister refused to be in the talent show when she was told she'd have to sing "Love Is a Many-Splendored Thing."
2. Disgusted by the constant dripping noise, Brian opened his copy of Handy Home Repairs to the chapter titled "Everything about the Kitchen Sink."
3. My little brother has seen Star Wars at least eight times.
4. Before they bought new car tires, Nick and Fran studied the article "Testing Tires" in the February, 2007 issue of Consumer Reports.
5. Many people mistakenly think that Huckleberry Finn and The Adventures of Tom Sawyer are children's books only.
6. I just found out that the musical My Fair Lady is based on a play by George Bernard Shaw called Pygmalion.
7. The ending of Shirley Jackson's story "The Lottery" really surprised me.
8. I sang the song "Mack the Knife" in our high school production of The Threepenny Opera.
9. Unless he's studied the TV Guide listings thoroughly, my father won't turn on his television.
10. Stanley dreamed that both Time and Newsweek had decided to use him in their feature article "Person of the Year."

COMMA

Introductory Activity (355)

1. a.
2. b.
3. c.
4. d.
5. e.
6. f.

Practice 1 (357)

1. sunglasses, a bottle of water, and a recent issue
2. check e-mail, play games, surf the Internet, download music, and send instant messages,
3. igloo-shaped doghouse, several plastic toys, trampled flowers, and a cracked ceramic gnome.

Practice 2 (357)

1. A metal tape measure, a pencil, a ruler, and a hammer dangled from the carpenter's pockets.
2. The fortune-teller uncovered the crystal ball, peered into it, and began to predict my future.
3. That hairdresser is well-known for her frizzy perms, butchered haircuts, and brassy hair colorings.

Practice 3 (358)

1. hands,
2. storm,
3. help,

Practice 4 (358)

1. In order to work at that fast-food restaurant, you have to wear a cowboy hat and six-shooters. In addition, you have to shout "Yippee!" every time someone orders the special Western-style double burger.
2. Barely awake, the woman slowly rocked her crying infant. While the baby softly cooed, the woman fell asleep.
3. When I painted the kitchen, I remembered to cover the floor with newspapers. Therefore, I was able to save the floor from looking as if someone had thrown confetti on it.

Practice 5 (360)

1. gadget, ladies and gentlemen,
2. Tigers, because they eat people,
3. dummy, its straw-filled "hands" tied with rope,

Practice 6 (360)

1. My brother, who likes only natural foods, would rather eat a soybean patty than a cheeseburger.
2. That room, with its filthy rug and broken dishwasher, is the nicest one in the building.
3. My aunt, who claims she is an artist, painted her living room ceiling to look like the sky at midnight.

Practice 7 (361)

1. hour, or
2. fine, but
3. releases, and
4. one, but
5. *C*
6. *C*
7. housecleaning, and
8. melted, and
9. telephone, but
10. *C*

Practice 8 (362)

1. asked, "Do
2. wrote, "2
3. of," said Richie, "is

Practice 9 (362)

1. "Could you spare a quarter," the boy asked passersby in the mall, "for a video game?"
2. "Man does not live by words alone," wrote Adlai Stevenson, "despite the fact that sometimes he has to eat them."
3. "That actress," said Velma, "has promoted everything from denture cleaner to shoelaces."

Practice 10 (363)

1. sorry, sir, but
2. May 6, 1954, Roger
3. June 30, 2010, will
4. Seven Seas, P.O. Box 760, El Paso, TX
5. Leo, turn

Practice 11 (364)

1. A new bulletproof material has been developed that is very lightweight.
2. The vet's bill included charges for a distemper shot.
3. Since the firehouse is directly behind Ken's home, the sound of its siren pierces his walls.
4. Hard sausages and net-covered hams hung above the delicatessen counter.
5. The students in the dance class were dressed in a variety of bright tights, baggy sweatshirts, and woolly leg warmers.

6. A woman in the ladies' room asked me if she could borrow a safety pin.
7. Telephone books, broken pencils, and scraps of paper littered the reporter's desk.
8. The frenzied crowd at the game cheered and whistled.
9. Splitting along the seams, the old mattress spilled its stuffing on the ground.
10. To satisfy his hunger, Enrique chewed on a piece of dry rye bread.

OTHER PUNCTUATION MARKS

Introductory Activity (374)

1. list:
2. life-size
3. (1856–1939)
4. track;
5. breathing—but alive.

Practice 1 (375)

1. follows:
2. things:
3. life:

Practice 2 (376)

1. outlets; otherwise,
2. spider; he
3. 9 A.M.; . . . 10:00;

Practice 3 (377)

1. well—
2. see—
3. hoped—no, I prayed—

Practice 4 (378)

1. hole-in-the-wall . . . hoity-toity
2. rabbit-ear . . . high-definition
3. hard-working . . . out-of-towners

Practice 5 (378)

1. prices (fifty to ninety dollars) made
2. election (the April primary), only
3. you (1) two sharpened pencils and (2) an eraser.

DICTIONARY USE

Introductory Activity (382)

1. fortituous (fortuitous)
2. hi/er/o/glyph/ics
3. be

4. oc/to/ge/nar′/i/an
5. (1) an identifying mark on the ear of a domestic animal
   (2) an identifying feature or characteristic

Answers to the activities are in your dictionary. Check with your instructor if you have any problems.

SPELLING IMPROVEMENT

Introductory Activity (394)

Misspellings:
akward . . . exercize . . . buisness . . . worryed . . . shamful . . . begining . . . partys . . . sandwichs . . . heros

Practice 1 (397)

1. carried
2. revising
3. studies
4. wrapping
5. horrified
6. permitted
7. gliding
8. angrily
9. rebelling
10. grudges

Practice 2 (398)

1. buses
2. patches
3. therapies
4. batches
5. reefs
6. avocados
7. fifties
8. knives
9. daughters-in-law
10. theses

OMITTED WORDS AND LETTERS

Introductory Activity (405)

bottles . . . in the supermarket . . . like a windup toy . . . his arms . . . an alert shopper . . . with the crying

Practice 1 (406)

1. In the rest room, Jeff impatiently rubbed his hands under the mechanical dryer, which blew out feeble puffs of cool air.
2. On February 10, 1935, the *New York Times* reported that an eight-foot alligator had been dragged out of a city sewer by three teenage boys.
3. Dave dressed up as a stuffed olive for Halloween by wearing a green plastic garbage bag and a red knitted cap.
4. Mrs. Chan nearly fainted when she opened the health insurance bill and saw an enormous rate increase.

5. At 4 A.M., the all-night supermarket where I work hosts an assortment of strange shoppers.
6. With a loud hiss, the inflated beach ball suddenly shrank to the size of an orange.
7. The boiling milk bubbled over the sides of the pot, leaving a gluey white film on the stove top.
8. Susan turned to the answer page of the crossword book, pretended to herself that she hadn't, and turned back to her puzzle.
9. In order to avoid stepping on the hot blacktop of the parking lot, the barefoot boy tiptoed along the cooler white lines.
10. The messy roommates used hubcaps for ashtrays and scribbled graffiti on their own bathroom walls.

Practice 2 (407)

1. shaves . . . blades
2. legs . . . hurdles
3. fads . . . ants
4. owners . . . monkeys
5. photographers . . . sharks
6. spores . . . leaves
7. cages . . . plants
8. pounds . . . grapes . . . cents
9. soles . . . shoes
10. cheeseburgers . . . shakes

Practice 3 (408)
Answers will vary.

COMMONLY CONFUSED WORDS

Introductory Activity (412)

1. Incorrect: your   Correct: you're
2. Incorrect: who's   Correct: whose
3. Incorrect: there   Correct: their
4. Incorrect: to   Correct: too
5. Incorrect: Its   Correct: It's

Homonyms (413)
Answers will vary for sentences only.

already . . . all ready
brake . . . break
course . . . coarse
hear . . . here
whole . . . hole
It's . . . its

knew . . . new
know . . . no
pair . . . pear
passed . . . past
peace . . . piece
plane . . . plain
principal . . . principle
right . . . write
then . . . than
There . . . their . . . they're
through . . . threw
two . . . to . . . too
where . . . wear
weather . . . whether
whose . . . Who's
your . . . you're

Other Words Frequently Confused (424)
Answers will vary for sentences only.

an . . . a
accept . . . except
advise . . . advice
effect . . . affect
Among . . . between
Besides . . . beside
can . . . may
cloths . . . clothes
desert . . . dessert
dose . . . does
fewer . . . less
former . . . latter
learn . . . teach
loose . . . lose
quiet . . . quite
Though . . . thought

Incorrect Word Forms (432)
being that (432)

1. Because the boss heard my remark,
2. because my diet
3. since his dad

can't hardly, couldn't hardly (433)

1. I could hardly
2. I can hardly
3. everyone can hardly

could of, must of, should of, would of *(433)*

1. Thelma must have
2. You should have
3. I would have
4. No one could have

irregardless *(434)*

1. Regardless of what anybody else does,
2. Regardless of the weather,
3. Regardless of what my parents say,

EFFECTIVE WORD CHOICE

Introductory Activity *(440)*

Correct sentences:
1. After a disappointing movie, we devoured a pizza.
2. Mourning the death of his best friend, Tennyson wrote the moving poem "In Memoriam."
3. Psychological tests will be given on Wednesday.
4. I think the referee made the right decision.

 1 . . . 2 . . . 3 . . . 4

NOTE: The answers may vary for all of the following word-choice practices.

Practice 1 *(442)*

EXAMPLE

1. When I confronted my ex-boyfriend about cheating on me, he simply shrugged and said, "It was my fault."
2. My friend thinks that Chantel is attractive, but I think she's too emotional.
3. Rayna is on her cell phone all the time, but that's fine.
4. Joe wanted to quickly leave the family dinner so that he could meet his friends.
5. They were excited about the party, but they knew they'd have to leave early.

Practice 2 *(443)*

1. Substitute <u>make me very angry</u> for <u>make my blood boil</u>.
2. Substitute <u>depressed</u> for <u>down in the dumps</u>.
3. Substitute <u>extraordinary</u> for <u>one in a million</u>.
4. Substitute <u>have a celebration</u> for <u>roll out the red carpet</u>.
5. Substitute <u>free</u> for <u>free as a bird</u>.

NOTE: The above answers are examples of how the clichés could be corrected. Other answers are possible.

Practice 3 *(444)*

Answers will vary.

Practice 4 *(445)*

Answers may vary.

1. I do not understand that person's behavior.
2. He erased all the mistakes in his notes.
3. She thought about what he said.
4. The police officer stopped the car.
5. Inez told the counselor about her career hopes.

Practice 5 *(447)*

Answers will vary.

1. I am a vegetarian.
2. Last Tuesday, I started going to college full-time.
3. Since I'm broke, I can't go to the movies.
4. I repeated that I wouldn't go.
5. Everything I say and do annoys my father.

Credits

Index